The Style of a Law Firm

To John W. Riely

1917–1986

The Style of a Law Firm

Eight Gentlemen from Virginia

by Anne Hobson Freeman

Algonquin Books of Chapel Hill

1992

Published by
Algonquin Books of Chapel Hill
Post Office Box 2225
Chapel Hill, North Carolina 27515-2225

a division of
Workman Publishing Company, Inc.
708 Broadway
New York, New York 10003

Published in association with
Hunton & Williams, Richmond, Virginia.

Photographs not otherwise credited were lent
by Margaret Robertson Christian, B. Warwick
Davenport, Pamela Gibson Farrar, Miriam
Riggs Gay, Thomas B. Gay, Jr., Pearson
Grymes Gibson, H. Brice Graves, Eppa
Hunton, Carolyn Moore McCue, Margaret
Williams McElroy, John L. McElroy, Jr.,
T. Justin Moore, Jr., Beverley B.
Munford III, H. Merrill Pasco, Lewis F.
Powell, Jr., Jean Roy Riely, and Frances
Richardson Shield.

Library of Congress Cataloging-in-Publication Data
Freeman, Anne Hobson, 1934–
The style of a law firm : eight gentlemen from
Virginia / by Anne Hobson Freeman.
        p.   cm.
Includes bibliographical references.
ISBN 0-945575-25-4
1. Hunton & Williams—History.   2. Law firms
—Virginia—Richmond—History.
3. Lawyers—Virginia—Richmond—Biography.
        I. Title.
KF355.R5F74   1989
340′.06′0755451—dc 20   89-17782

3 5 7 9 10 8 6 4

Contents

Introduction

by Justice Lewis F. Powell, Jr.

It is fortunate that Hunton & Williams invited Anne Hobson Freeman to write this book. A native of Richmond, she attended St.
Catherine's School and Bryn Mawr College and did graduate work
in English at London University on a Fulbright scholarship. In
1958 she married George Clemon Freeman, Jr., then a young associate lawyer at Hunton & Williams, and since then she has had a
special interest in the firm.

Anne has published numerous short stories, poems, and essays.
She successfully combined her writing career with raising three
children, earning an M.A. degree in English at the University of
Virginia, and teaching a creative writing course there for some fifteen years. Her preparation for writing this book extended over
several years during which, in addition to numerous interviews,
she did painstaking research with the result that is so evident.
At her invitation, I am happy to have the opportunity to write
this introduction to *The Style of a Law Firm: Eight Gentlemen from
Virginia.*

On December 31, 1971, when I left the firm that today bears
the abbreviated name of Hunton & Williams, it was styled Hunton, Williams, Gay, Powell & Gibson. I approve of the abbreviated
name. When I joined the firm in 1935 as its youngest associate,
it bore the name of Hunton, Williams, Anderson, Gay & Moore.
Four of them were living: E. Randolph Williams, Henry W. Anderson, Thomas B. Gay, and T. Justin Moore, all lawyers with reputa-

tions well beyond the state of Virginia. George Gibson and Eppa Hunton IV—as I recall—had just become junior partners.

I was privileged to know all of these partners, * and to work personally at various times with all except Randolph Williams. Anne Freeman, with commendable accuracy and insight, has written chapters that are portraits in words of each of them. At the risk of some duplication, I add my own "remembrances" of these lawyers whom I greatly admired.

E. Randolph Williams—a lineal descendant of Edmund Randolph—had partially retired from active practice by 1935. He remained general counsel of the Richmond, Fredericksburg and Potomac Railroad and also did some work for First & Merchants National Bank of which he was a director. Randolph Williams was respected and beloved by partners and associates alike. The firm did not have a written partnership agreement until after the deaths of Williams and Anderson. The four name partners, with little or no consultation with other partners, made all firm decisions, including participation in firm earnings. The respect for Randolph Williams was so general that when he made or reported a decision it was accepted without question by younger partners and, of course, by associate lawyers. The door to his office was always open, and he welcomed younger lawyers to share their legal and other concerns with him. I had a genuine affection for him.

Henry W. Anderson, with quite a different personality, was nationally known as a specialist in railroad reorganization law. When I returned to the firm after service in World War II, Colonel Anderson—as he preferred to be called—was co-receiver and later chairman of the board of the Seaboard Railroad. He also represented bondholders' committees in the reorganization of several other railroads. He and George Gibson wrote a special statute for

---

*I do not include Beverley Munford or Eppa Hunton, Jr., in this introduction as, of course, I did not know either. Their names were revered. Nor do I include Eppa Hunton IV in this introduction, as the name "Hunton" in the firm was that of his father. Eppa, with a warm and generous personality, was a prominent citizen, influential in the firm, and popular with lawyers all over the state. He was a friend I will always miss.

the reorganization of the Baltimore & Ohio Railroad. My only opportunity to work directly with Colonel Anderson was on his representation of a bondholders' committee in the ill-fated first reorganization of the New Haven Railroad. This also was my only opportunity to appear before Judge Learned Hand. Matters in the New Haven reorganization were being argued before the Second Circuit Court of Appeals, with Hand the presiding judge. When Colonel Anderson exceeded the time allotted to him, without a request from Anderson, Judge Hand, calling him "Colonel," permitted him to continue. At that time the Colonel was about seventy-five years of age and in poor health.

As Anne Freeman makes clear in her chapter on Anderson, he lived elegantly in his Richmond home. When he traveled any distance he used his private railroad car as chairman of the Seaboard, and he maintained a suite at the old Ritz-Carlton in New York. I accompanied him to New York on occasion and was fascinated by his status at this European-style hotel. Upon arrival he did not check in. He was recognized by room clerks and bellmen alike, maids unpacked his luggage, and when he left the dining room he signed no check and left no gratuities. Responding to my question about this, he said that signing checks and giving cash gratuities were unnecessary, as everyone knew who he was. At Christmas he would send, from his farm in Dinwiddie County, a large shipment of hams and food products to be distributed to the staff and service people at the Ritz-Carlton.

Thomas B. Gay, with whom I worked closely for a number of years, emulated the life-style of Colonel Anderson. In some ways I thought "Mr. Gay," as he preferred to be called, was more formal than Henry Anderson. The specialization that now prevails in law firms did not exist. Gay was a successful trial lawyer despite the fact that sometimes, in addressing a jury, he spoke with a broad "A"—but only part of the time. He had a substantial corporate practice, and was the statutory agent for a number of foreign corporations. When the Securities Acts of 1933 and 1934 were under consideration, Gay was retained by the New York Stock Exchange to represent its interests before congressional committees.

Mr. Gay was the first partner in the firm to become a leader in the American Bar Association. He participated in rewriting its constitution in 1937 to create a House of Delegates that enabled each state, through delegates elected by its lawyers, to have a voice in its decisions. He became chairman of the House of Delegates of the ABA, but never chose to seek the presidency.

Gay also was a sportsman with a variety of interests. He owned and rode horses until he was thrown, while riding on his farm in Goochland County when he was in his late eighties. Of course he was a member of the Deep Run Hunt Club. Surprisingly for a horseman, he also enjoyed quail hunting, owned bird dogs, and leased land for hunting in southside Virginia. I shot with him there on several occasions. He was proud of being an excellent marksman, but even in the field with dogs he was formal.

The third named partner when I became associated with the firm was T. Justin Moore. He had been general counsel to Virginia Electric and Power Company, and retained this position after he joined the firm in the early 1930s. He was a powerful lawyer, and by the time of his early death was the best-known utility lawyer in the United States. He worked long hours, and expected younger lawyers to do the same. He produced more revenue for the firm than any other partner, served as President of the Virginia State Bar Association, and he also was a widely respected citizen, active in religious and community affairs. He and Mrs. Moore gave an elegant party for the firm each year.

I add a word about George D. Gibson, my closest friend among the named partners, and a dear friend until his death in 1988. As Anne Freeman knew George personally, her chapter on him is an accurate portrayal of the intellect and personality of one of the most gifted people I have ever known. He worked closely with Colonel Anderson in the representation of bondholders' committees in railroad reorganizations, and it was his genius that enhanced Anderson's reputation.

George had no superior in general corporate law. He chaired the Corporation, Banking and Business Law Section of the ABA, and was one of the principal authors of the Model Corporate Law

Code. He rewrote the corporation laws of the state of Virginia, and ranked with the best corporate lawyers in the great New York law firms. Quite apart from his brilliance as a lawyer, George was a thoughtful and profound scholar, widely read in the classics, well-traveled, and fluent in French. The residence he and his wife, Pearson, shared on River Road is charmingly furnished and decorated. George's death was a grievous personal loss to me, as I have never had a closer friend.

These are brief personal vignettes of five superb lawyers, each different in personality and style, who would have been prominent at the bar of any state and leaders in any community. They had a perception of the practice of law that I admired. Law was one of the ancient professions. The primary purpose of practicing was not to make money. Indeed, the partnership agreement George Gibson and I drafted in the mid-1950s expressly recognized that lawyers have professional responsibilities. Partners and associates alike were encouraged to engage in *pro bono* activities and to take part in community affairs. Of course the firm also emphasized the duty to render quality service to clients, whether rich or poor. I was proud to be a lawyer and to be a member of what is now known as Hunton & Williams. Lawyers share with judges the privilege and responsibility of preserving the rule of law in our country. This includes the liberties and rights guaranteed by our constitution. I know of no other calling with a greater opportunity to serve the public good.

As the only surviving name partner, I am grateful to Anne Freeman for this book. It will preserve for future generations memories of partners of this nationally known firm who were prominent citizens as well as lawyers of the highest quality.

Foreword

by W. Taylor Reveley III

Whether universities, regiments, or law firms, some institutions move powerfully from one generation to the next. Others find themselves becalmed, or they founder. Reasons for success or failure are legion. But those institutions that prevail usually take strength from their past. They remember their heroes, their times of peril and triumph, and their basic beliefs. The importance of the past as a source of confidence and poise grows with the turmoil of the present.

In recent years, the legal profession has been in turmoil. Radical change has buffeted law firms and lawyers alike. Change has come in many forms. There has been an enormous growth in the number of lawyers belonging to a single firm. Firms have created far-flung empires, linking together many geographically separate offices. The legal generalist has died, and been replaced by swarms of legal specialists who respond to the growing complexity and instability of the law itself. There is new ambition, and the sheer physical capacity, to ply one's specialty wherever on earth it can be sold, no matter how far from home. Women have become a major force in the profession, bringing with them different perspectives and needs. Confusion exists over whether the profession remains a profession at all, or whether it has turned simply into a business. There is growing mechanization, growing bureaucracy, growing resort to administrators who are not also lawyers, and growing use of advertising and other tools of open, aggressive competition. Lawyers' comings and goings, their deeds and misdeeds, their pay here versus their pay there, are now printed in prurient detail in a new, glossy trade press focused exclusively on the bar. Lawyers have come into heightened power and wealth as the country proves increasingly unable to operate its Byzantine regulatory and commercial constructs without legal pathfinders. There is simultaneously a concern that this new power and wealth has curdled the traditional impulse for at least some public service without regard for influence or money. There is a new, brisk trade in lawyers moving from one firm to another, much like the trade in ballplayers and bulls. And the din is constant as one law firm after another hits the rocks after misjudging the winds and tides of revolutionary change.

As never before, law firms need the direction and dignity that come from knowing their roots. When firms reorganize their structure to adapt to current realities, if their basic character is to endure, it becomes all the more crucial that they know what *not* to change. The best of their past usually provides a guide.

The struggles and mistakes of the past are also a useful guide. They reassure and comfort. Disputes over promotion and pay are nothing new. Nor is the introduction into the firm, sometimes with wrenching impact, of seasoned lawyers who began their careers elsewhere. Ways of governing the firm come and go, not always happily. People get angry. But, if successful, the firm goes forward, tempered by the passage through its fires. And at places like Hunton & Williams, the fires are always damped by the respect and affection traditional among the partners.

To learn from the past, you first have to remember it. Hunton & Williams began almost ninety years ago, at the turn of this century. By 1982, memories about even the firm's second generation of lawyers, much less its first, were dimming perilously. This book began as a race to record oral histories before the historians, some already in their nineties, went the way of all flesh. The race has been won. Since June 1982, more than fifty-five oral histories have been compiled. Typed, edited, and footnoted, these encounters approach 2,000 pages about Hunton & Williams and its milieu. This information alone has enduring value.

From it, Anne Freeman has spun biographies of the most engaging sort. The men she sketches come vibrantly to life in her prose. Anne grasps their essence, and it is an essence worth savoring.

Her subjects are the eight lawyers whose names have appeared in the firm's name—in its style: four of them came from the first generation of Hunton & Williams, Messrs. Munford, Hunton, Williams, and Anderson, and four from the second generation, Messrs. Gay, Moore, Powell, and Gibson. Since 1976 the firm's name has been fixed simply as "Hunton & Williams." It no longer changes whenever mighty partners rise and fall. There will be no more names in the style of the law firm. But what about the exploits of the third and fourth generations? They must first be finished and then allowed to cool a while. They await another day and another book.

This book deals with men whose like will not be seen again at Hunton & Williams or elsewhere. They were lawyers of sweeping scope, both because they had the ability and drive to be generalists and because the law was sufficiently uncluttered and sufficiently stately in its evolution to permit a Renaissance approach. They were people of enormous grace and culture. Thoroughly Virginian in a courtly manner now rare, they were also citizens of the nation. Entrepreneurs splendidly rewarded for their efforts, they also understood the imperative of public service. Those who could serve were expected to, and they did, even at severe cost to themselves. These founding fathers were an extraordinary assembly. Their legacy is compelling.

Though less inspiring, the story of their times is also engrossing. Anne Freeman captures Virginia and Richmond emerging from the shock and destitution of military defeat and entering an era rich with privilege for men like the fathers of Hunton & Williams. This was not an era fair to women or blacks. But it was a time that fascinates those interested in the aftermath of the War Between the States and the nascent efforts of the new South to redress old wrongs.

Few cities have touched American history more vigorously than Richmond. It, however, has not been a major American city since 1865. Indeed, it is by far the smallest city in the United States to have spawned a great law firm of national and international reach. The explanation for this seeming anomaly lies with the eight Virginians who gave their names to the style of the firm.

From their firm have come a justice of the United States Supreme Court and the first black justice of the Virginia Supreme Court, who was the first black partner of Hunton & Williams. Within the firm have been a former governor and future senator of Virginia and a former minority leader of Congress. The firm has nurtured other public servants, including a federal district judge, as well as leaders of the bar and of civic and ecclesiastical organizations, trustees of colleges and universities: in short, a host of lawyers schooled in service. And, of course, there has been service to clients who pay, service of relentless quality and integrity, given without regard to personal convenience. From the beginning, the Calvinist ethic has ruled. By any measure, it is an august tradition, rooted in the lives of the eight men celebrated here.

Author's Note

For the past six years I have been cornering people at weddings, cocktail parties, political rallies, and bar conventions; in airplanes, taxis, limousines, and chartered buses, asking them to dig into their memories for stories about the Hunton & Williams firm and its lawyers, particularly the "great eight" whose names were in the firm's style. For the patience and generosity with which they have responded to my probing, I want to thank them all collectively.

To those who gave literally hours of their time to the more formal interviews, I am particularly grateful. Among them were: William W. Archer, Jr., Lawrence E. Blanchard, Jr., Lewis Booker, Evelyn Brown, Amanda Bryan Kane, David Tennant Bryan, Robert Pegram Buford, Joseph C. Carter, Jr., Leslie Cheek, Jr., Mary Tyler Cheek, Virginius Dabney, Pamela Gibson Farrar, George Clemon Freeman, Jr., Miriam Riggs Gay, Thomas B. Gay, Thomas B. Gay, Jr., Sarah Geer Dale Gayle, George D. Gibson, Pearson Gibson, Dorothy Grady, H. Brice Graves, Oliver W. Hill, Helen Pettway Craig Jefferson, John Calvin Jeffries, Jr., Elizabeth Taylor Little, Carolyn Moore McCue, Margaret Williams McElroy, George Modlin, T. Justin Moore, Jr., H. Merrill Pasco, Justice Lewis F. Powell, Jr., John W. Riely, Archibald G. Robertson, Frances Richardson Shield, J. Harvie Wilkinson, Jr., John Page Williams, and Langbourne Meade Williams.

To the families and friends of the firm's lawyers who searched through their papers and photographs and trusted me with what they found, I am also indebted. Among them were Barbara Catlett, Margaret Robertson Christian, Mate Branch Converse, Jean Bowie Evans, Pamela Gibson Farrar, Martha Davenport, Lenore Gay, Miriam Riggs Gay, Thomas B. Gay, Jr., Pearson Gibson, Eppa Hunton, Mary Hunton, Carolyn Moore McCue, Margaret Williams McElroy, Sorrell McElroy, John Lee McElroy, Jr., T. Justin Moore, Jr., Beverley B. Munford III, John D. Munford, H. Merrill Pasco, Josephine Rucker Powell, Justice Lewis F. Powell, Jr., Jean Roy Riely, and Frances Richardson Shield.

For gathering facts as well as photographs, I am grateful to members of the staff of Dementi-Foster Studios, the Richmond Public Library, the Virginia Historical Society, the Virginia Historic Landmarks Board, the Virginia State Library, the University of Richmond, the College of William and Mary, Washington and Lee University, the Law Library of the University of Virginia, and the Curator's Office of the U.S. Supreme Court. I am especially grateful to Brian Shaw of the News Office at Washington and Lee University, Linda Leazer of the Virginia Historical Society, Lacy Dick of the Valentine Museum, Mark H. Rainer and Mark Scala of the Virginia State Library, and Gail Galloway and Sally Smith at the U.S. Supreme Court.

Though they are not responsible for any errors or shortcomings of this book, I want to thank Edward Ayers, Staige Blackford, and Alexander Gilliam of Charlottesville, Virginia; Langbourne Meade Williams, of Rapidan, Virginia; and Susan T. Burtch and Seymour Rennolds of Richmond, Virginia, for reading early drafts and offering suggestions.

In Richmond, also, Sarah Bearss prepared the index, Rozanne Epps, Maria Tabb, and David Zivan did proofreading, Jean Underwood helped transcribe the tapes, and Margo Peters Millure and Elizabeth Herbener cheerfully and tirelessly pursued elusive facts in libraries all over the city. I am grateful to them all.

At the firm of Hunton & Williams, there were many people, particularly Frances Minner, Jane Ketron, and Karen Molzhon, who put in extra hours proofreading and retyping portions of the manuscript and preparing lists for the appendixes.

To Taylor Reveley, the firm's managing partner and an author, himself, I am grateful for continuing support, advice, and sympathy, especially during the dark days halfway through the project when I faced the task of trying to distill thousands of pages of interviews into a readable text. I also want to thank another partner, Robert Dean Pope, a scholar of American history and a graceful writer, for his generosity with his time, his skills, and his knowledge during the editing process.

So many of the firm's lawyers welcomed me into their offices and shared their memories with me that it is impossible to single them out here. Yet I must acknowledge the four senior partners who were deeply involved in the genesis of this book.

First, Thomas Benjamin Gay, who fired my imagination in the 1960s when I was working as his research assistant, gathering facts on the founding partners for his history, *The Hunton Williams Firm*. Standing at his window on the tenth floor of the old Electric Building, looking down the slope of Seventh Street toward Main, he would ask me, "What year are we talking about now?" If I answered, "1901" he would transform the streets below us into the ones that he had worked as a runner for John L. Williams & Sons, pointing where there had been a barber shop, a tobacconist, Rueger's hotel, and off we'd go. After his book was published in 1971, Mr. Gay (as he will always be for me, despite the editorial decision to drop the "Mr." in the main text of this book) and Eppa Hunton IV continued to fill file folders with memos, notes, and photographs, looking forward to the day a second book would be written. Miriam Gay has told me that as her husband lay dying at the age of ninety-eight, she told him that the firm had asked me to write that book and that he had seemed to be pleased.

Four interviews with the firm's other septuagenarian, Archibald Robertson, made firmer the foundations that Mr. Gay had given me. With a crooked smile and a mischievous twinkle in his eye, Archie Robertson would take me back to lunches in the 1930s when he, Randolph Williams, and Eppa IV used to meet in the Pan Tree Restaurant for Brunswick stew, and Williams would talk to them about the early days.

Then there was George Gibson, a source of endlessly surprising insights and a loyal friend, although he did not soften for me, much less for himself, the bright light of his inquiry or the sharp bite of his wit. Even in the last months of his illness, he made his judgment, his fine mind, and his memory instantly available to me.

His close friend, Justice Lewis F. Powell, Jr., was still active on the Supreme Court when I conducted seven of my eight interviews with him. Yet he would push aside a pile of "cert" petitions two feet tall to make room for my notepad and my tape recorder, then lean back in his chair and talk to me about the firm that he had loved so much, as if there were nothing else that afternoon he'd rather do. Unknowingly, he changed the form this book would take with his answer to the question: What would you like to see in a book about the firm? It was: "Fuller portraits of the founders." Eventually I expanded those portraits to include not only the four founders but all eight of the lawyers whose names were in the firm's style. I am therefore doubly grateful to Justice Powell for writing the introduction to this book.

Louis Rubin, my editor at Algonquin Books of Chapel Hill, has been a faithful friend since the day five years ago when he and his assistant at the time, Garrett Epps, first took it on. For his constancy, his judgment, and his faith in me as a writer, I would like to thank him now. I also want to thank Marjorie Hudson, for her steady, careful work as copy editor.

My husband, George Freeman, has lived with this project for the past six years. His contribution to it is as immeasurable as it has been consistent and consoling.

Most of all I want to thank my assistant, Kathleen Murat Williams, who has been a perfect partner in this project from the transcribing and annotating of the first interview through the final, nerve-wrenching push to get the final proof to the typesetter. I could not have written this book without her help.

John Riely was the originator of the Hunton & Williams oral history project and therefore of the book that came from it. As the project inevitably widened, he gave me fair and frequent warning that if I didn't hurry up and finish interviewing people and start writing the book, he wasn't going to live to see it published. His ferocious allegiance to the unvarnished truth was a source of his immense vitality. I hope that I have preserved some of that vitality in this book that is dedicated to his memory.

ONE

Main Street, 1901

In the fall of 1901, the Richmond, Virginia, *News* announced: "The papers have just been signed for the formation of a big new law firm in the City, the style of which will be Munford, Hunton, Williams & Anderson."[1]

Big is a relative word. The total number of lawyers in that new law firm was four. If you count the part-time stenographer, the number swells to five. Yet it was still the biggest law firm in Richmond. More important, the idea behind it was big: to establish in Virginia a firm "patterned after the larger New York firms and equipped to handle all kinds of legal business"—in short, a full-service law firm to compete with the best firms in the country.[2]

Considering the impoverished state of Richmond, Virginia, and the entire South, still struggling to recover from the Civil War and its long aftermath, it seemed to be a daring idea. But the timing of it was just right.

The whole country was emerging from the financial crises of the 1890s. An entrepreneurial spirit was abroad. In Virginia, a convention had been called to draft a new state constitution—to purge the state of graft and fraud in its elections and regulate the railroads and modernize the courts.[3] Its progressive leaders aimed to make Virginia safe for business. And that meant stable enough to attract the Northern capital it would have to attract before it could get back into the mainstream of the Northeast.

As a later partner in the law firm put it, "Richmond was still paying tribute to New York in just about every way you can think of." If a business on Main Street wanted to borrow a few hundred thousand dollars, it had to go north for its financing. If it got involved in a complex corporate matter it had to go north for its legal advice. Randolph Williams and Henry Anderson thought that they could at least change the second situation; so "they conceived the idea of organizing a law firm that could do first-class work, as good . . . as any work in the country."[4]

They were ambitious young men—barely thirty years old. Practicing law on the same block of East Main Street, they had become good friends. The previous December, Randolph Williams's senior partner had died. Now Henry Anderson's was gravely ill. Meanwhile the Williams family's banking firm, John L. Williams & Sons, was at the peak of its success, developing railroads, street railways, and power companies all over the South. It needed sophisticated lawyers to represent it. Why, asked Williams and Anderson, should those lawyers have to come from Wall Street? If the two of them joined forces with the right senior lawyers, why couldn't they establish a law firm in Richmond that could meet all of its clients' needs?

They took their idea first to Beverley Munford, the senior partner in Anderson's two-man firm, who had just been forced into virtual retirement by tuberculosis. Munford agreed to give his name and all that his name stood for—and as much of his time as his health would permit—to the new law firm.

Still, they would need an active senior partner. So they took their idea up the hill to the state capitol, where some of the best lawyers in the state had gathered to draft the new state constitution.[5] A few prospects turned them down, most notably A. Caperton Braxton, who would emerge as the leader of that constitutional convention. But Eppa Hunton, Jr., chairman of the Courts of Justice Committee and member of Braxton's Corporation Committee, was interested in their idea.[6]

In late September the four partners-to-be met in Washington, and on November 1 the firm was officially founded.[7]

Munford was not even in Richmond that day. Still gravely ill and trying to recuperate in Lakewood, New Jersey, he was not expected to return to active practice until the following spring.[8]

In the meantime, the Richmond *News* announced that Eppa Hunton, Jr., the only member of the new firm who was not already a resident of Richmond, would take up his "permanent residence here at once."[9] With the two junior partners, he immediately set to work representing Munford's clients, helping John L. Williams & Sons with its multiplying legal problems, and generally developing a high profile for the new law firm.

On November 1, the first day of the firm's official existence, Henry Anderson continued to keep a careful record of time spent on legal matters. On a fresh page of an old Munford & Anderson ledger, he recorded that he had had a conference in the morning with a Mr. Todd, who decided to take an appeal in the case of *Ruffin v. Todd*, and that he had also filed a motion for dismissal in the case of the *Washington, Alexandria and Mount Vernon Railway v. the Southern Railway*. And then he added: "Mr. Hunton busy on the brief for *Rowe v. Dresgill*, Court of Appeals," a case the firm had inherited from Munford & Anderson.[10]

While the partners looked for larger quarters, they continued to use the old offices of Munford & Anderson. And so the new style of "Munford, Hunton, Williams & Anderson" first appeared on the door of room 16 of the Merchants National Bank at Eleventh and Main.

Main Street 1901 was very different from Main Street of the 1980s. No automobiles, only horse-drawn carriages and carts, were parked at the curb or clattering across the cobblestones. Down the gleaming steel rails in the middle of the street, rattling and clanging, came the electric streetcars that had become a symbol of the city's pride since 1888, when the first commercially successful electric streetcar system in the world was developed in Richmond.[11] The electric utility system spawned by those street railways would soon become the new firm's major client.

As the twentieth century dawned, the effects of the Civil War were still evident on Main Street, not only architecturally—in the rows of fireproof ironfronts that had risen from the ruins of the 1865 Evacuation Fire—but also financially, and even more important, psychologically. The older generation of leaders still struggled with the memory of their society's defeat, the crippling poverty that followed it, and an almost morbid preoccupation with the past.

But a younger generation, which had not experienced the war, was now coming into power. Randolph Williams and Henry Anderson would be among its leaders. Both men had been born in the early 1870s, when Virginia ceased to be "Military District Number One" and was accepted back into the Union.

On November 1, 1901, Williams must have been feeling fairly optimistic as he walked up Main Street, from what had been the offices of Henry & Williams in the State Bank Building, to his new firm, four doors to the west, above the Merchants Bank.

Down the hill behind him rose the Spanish-tiled tower of the Main Street Station, which would open later that same month to receive passengers from two of the six major railroads serving Richmond: The Chesapeake & Ohio and the Seaboard Air Line, which his older brother, John Skelton Williams, had just put together, linking Richmond with Tampa, Florida, the Gulf of Mexico, and a future canal to the Pacific.[12]

If his own brother Johnny could organize a national railroad, it did not seem unreasonable to Williams to hope that he and Henry Anderson could establish a national law firm.

Across the street from him, at the far end of Eleventh, he could see the sloping, leaf-strewn lawn of Capitol Square and the walkways leading to the pillared Capitol itself, now brilliant in the sunlight. The sight of Jefferson's building, where Aaron Burr had been brought to trial before John Marshall, where Robert E. Lee had accepted command of Virginia's troops, called to mind the history that was attached to this particular state, this particular city, and this patch of cobblestone called Main Street where he and his partners had just launched their new law firm.

As Main Street rises westward from the railroad station—deep in Shockoe Valley where the town of Richmond started, where Captains Christopher Newport and John Smith met Chief Powhatan's son back in 1607—it climbs a very steep slope, then levels off at Twelfth Street to a plateau of four blocks that is the heart of Richmond's business district. Most of the city's major banks, brokerage houses, insurance firms, and law firms were clustered there in 1901, as they are today.

Down the flattened crest from Eleventh west to Eighth (where the street begins to rise again) was the familiar awning of John L. Williams & Sons on the northeast corner, at Tenth Street. There Williams's father and his brothers were working frantically on railroad ventures further south, the power plant at Twelfth Street, and the streetcar companies that had been mired in litigation for the last two months. What a relief it would be to have Henry Anderson and Eppa Hunton to help represent them.

Next door to John L. Williams & Sons was the old Customs House, the only building on the north side of Main Street, between Thirteenth and Ninth, that had survived the flames of the Evacuation Fire.[13] The facade of the First National Bank, directly across the street from him now, had also survived the flames, but the building behind it and the contents of its vaults had been destroyed. Williams's father had once showed him an old newspaper etching of a lonely figure sitting on the steps, below those two granite pillars, surrounded by the ruins of the business district.

How had his father felt when he came downtown that morning of April 3, 1865, and saw that almost all of what the businessmen called "Main Street" had been destroyed?

All his life Randolph Williams had heard stories about the war and the fire and the Fall of Richmond, the awful poverty that had followed it, military rule and political chaos, carpetbaggers, scalawags, and the Underwood Constitution that Virginians had to ratify in order to get back into the Union. But he had not *experienced* those events, nor had Henry Anderson, the way that Beverley Munford and Eppa Hunton had.

The older partners differed from the younger ones in this notable respect. They knew what war and its aftermath were like.

Beverley Bland Munford

1856–1910

Beverley Munford's association with lawyers began with his birth. On September 10, 1856, he was born in a house built by his grandfather, William Munford, the compiler of *Munford's Reports* on decisions of the Virginia Supreme Court of Appeals. It was a handsome brick house on an elevated lot at the corner of Fifth and Canal streets in Richmond. A few months later, Beverley's father, John D. Munford, moved his family to Tazewell Hall, a barnlike but comfortable house on the outskirts of Williamsburg. It had once belonged to Edmund Randolph, the nation's first attorney general.

At Tazewell Hall Beverley Munford spent the first, and probably the last, truly carefree and comfortable years of his life. Before he was five years old, the Civil War broke out and his father went off to war. Within a year, the sleepy little town of Williamsburg became the scene of a battle. In his autobiography, *Random Recollections*, written in 1905, Munford describes the sounds of that battle and then the sight of McClellan's army streaming "for days" through the main street of Williamsburg on its way to the battles around Richmond.[1]

From May 1862 until the end of the war, Williamsburg would remain within the Federal lines. "Because of her unprotected situation and her desire to be where she might sometimes see or hear from my father," Munford wrote, his mother, Margaret Copland Munford, secured "the necessary passport" into Confederate territory, left Tazewell Hall to the Federal troops—who were already camped in the front yard and the orchard—and became a war refugee. With Beverley and his baby brother, William, she traveled first to their grandmother Munford's house in Richmond, then to her brother Peter Copland's farm in Botetourt County in the mountains of Virginia.

As they were traveling up the Kanawha Canal, six-year-old Beverley stepped ashore at one of the locks to stretch his legs. To his horror, a few minutes later, he saw the packet boat "proceeding upstream with . . . wild celerity." His terror at being abandoned, the sound of his own voice wailing, and "the frantic efforts of men ashore and people aboard to get [him] back upon the boat" left an indelible "impress" on his mind.

Once he had arrived at his Uncle Peter Copland's farm, at the upper end of the Great Valley of Virginia, he settled down to a normal boy's life, roaming happily through woods and fields with "the little negro boys who were [his] boon companions" every day but Sunday, when his strict Presbyterian uncle would not allow him beyond the paling fence that surrounded the house.

At the end of July 1863, Beverley's mother died of tuberculosis. Soon afterwards he and his brother were brought back to Richmond, where his father, who had been released from the army and given a position with the Confederate government, "sought to establish a home and gather around him all his children," including three daughters by an earlier marriage.

By that time the blockade, the almost-incessant fighting during the previous two years, and the enormous consumption, as well as destruction, of food supplies had left the South, and especially Virginia and Richmond, almost destitute. "The most distinct impression left upon my mind of this period—the last eighteen months of the war—is that of cold and hunger," wrote Munford:

Some relief was found in the many makeshifts and substitutes adopted by the people. Thus coffee was made from rye, corn or potatoes; sorghum took the place of sugar, and gravies figured as a substitute for butter. Even the staples of life—bread

7

and meat—were very scarce, or so advanced in price that they were most difficult to obtain. Nearly every patriotic citizen—my father included—had sold everything salable and loaned the proceeds to the Confederate government. . . . And so to the scarcity of provisions was added that of money. Corn bread furnished, as it did to our forefathers, the principal stay of life. Equally dear and difficult to obtain were coal and wood, so in our home one fire was the rallying point around which the whole family assembled.

Another characteristic of the times which I recall was the clothing worn by the people. Nearly all the women were in mourning, as death had entered almost every home. Old clothes long out of fashion, ancient coats, dresses made out of curtains were brought into requisition. I cannot recall any particular article of my make-up, except a pair of shoes made at the penitentiary and a cavalry soldier's cap—the latter many sizes too large. . . . I presented—a small boy of eight—a most grotesque figure, arrayed in this great cap, which turned over when I walked, but stood up like a beaver when I ran. I learned afterwards that my appearance was a source of great mortification to my sisters, when on Sundays, [they were] walking home from St. Paul's Church with their soldier beaux, [and] I would appear upon the scene and run up and down along the sidewalk arrayed in my wonderful cap, penitentiary shoes and much-worn clothes.[2]

He also remembered the almost constant military funerals:

These occasions, especially when some general or popular hero was buried, were notable to me because of the brass bands, the marching legions, and the large concourse of people. I would follow as best I could the processions, seeming never to tire so long as I could hear the measured tramp of the soldiers and the strains of martial music.

I cannot now recall that I had at the time any impression that the existing order of things was unusual, or that my lot was peculiarly hard. Just such conditions had existed from the dawn of my memory, and my lot seemed to be only that of other little boys of my age and station.

I realized, however, on the fateful Sunday of April, 1865, that some extraordinary event was about to happen. What it meant or why it should occur, I could not, of course, understand. Its direful import, however, became more manifest when, on the following day, I witnessed the scenes incident to the evacuation of Richmond. The great fire enveloping the whole business portion of the city in its folds, the many explosions which resulted from the flames, the sight of squads of convicts from the penitentiary . . . the incoming of thousands of blue-coated federal troops, the crowds of bewildered people hurrying through the streets—all combined to form a picture which I shall never forget, and which gradually made known to me the momentous fact that the war was over.[3]

In May of 1865 Beverley Munford found himself on a steamboat traveling down the James River toward Williamsburg and Tazewell Hall. Although a large body of troops had occupied the orchard in the back of Tazewell Hall, the old frame house was unharmed.

"I cannot attempt," he wrote in 1905, "any description of the changes in Williamsburg wrought by the war, the poverty of the people, nor the political and industrial confusion which existed. Of civil government there was none. The military authorities held sway, and, indeed, continued their rule until Virginia was formally readmitted into the Union in 1870."[4]

Instead, he described his education, which had suffered during the war, but was now resumed under a "superabundance of teachers"—his three older sisters and his father. The latter,

> after listening with rather ill-concealed impatience while I read with many halts and failures my appointed lesson, . . . would take the book himself, read off the lesson, and then to impress me with the necessity for facility and expression would read copious extracts from his favorite poets. . . .

9

I recall, too, that as a part of my daily exercise I was required to learn the Church Catechism. . . . The great hall at home will always be associated in my mind with my efforts to master "The Desire" and "My Duty to my Neighbor" while rolling back and forth on the floor between the doors, ofttimes suffused in a flood of tears.[5]

Understandably, he "did not make much headway under those methods of pedagogics" and was eventually sent to the grammar school connected with William and Mary College. There his "trials and triumphs were those of the ordinary boy," with one terrifying exception. The president of the college, Benjamin Stoddert Ewell, would appear on alternate Fridays to hear the young scholars declaim or read original compositions. He was always accompanied by a fierce bullterrier, named John Brown, and "the presence of those two was sufficient," Munford recalled, "to drive almost every idea from a boy's head." Munford, who would become one of the foremost orators in the state, attributed his "comparative freedom from stage-fright in after years . . . in no small degree to [his] experience on those occasions."[6]

When he was not at school, he was fishing and swimming in the summer, skating in the winter, or playing the games of his time, including "marbles, tops, bandy, baseball, football, cat, high anthony, foot and a half, leap-frog and hop-scotch."

He was also devising schemes for making money, which was scarce, to say the least, in those days of Reconstruction. At one point he took to selling old bones, supplemented occasionally with old iron, brass and rags, which he and two black playmates gathered from the slaughterhouses and camps of the Federal troops stationed on his and adjoining farms.

One of the greatest joys of Beverley Munford's boyhood was music, wherever he might hear it—in "the soft lullabies of some old colored mammy, the stirring chorus of a group of schoolboys, [or] the solemn roll of the grand *Te Deum*."

His love of music dominates his description of the wheat harvests on his father's farm:

the field waving in its wealth of golden grain; the cradlers, bind-
ers and shockers with their glowing black faces, crowned here
and there with white turbans or red bandannas; the measured
cadence of the swinging cradlers, as strong arms bore them
through the falling grain; the eager boys following on in search
of partridge nests or to catch young rabbits; the cheery call of
the workers for "More water!" and above all the rich mellow
notes of the negro voices as they sang the harvest songs.[7]

He also remembered the music of the corn-shucking, which was
very different from that of the harvest. "The workers at the corn-
shucking sang under the soft light of the moon in the cool crisp
air of October nights, seated in groups around the great corn pile.
The music of the wheat harvest was martial and inspiring; that of
the corn-shucking religious and sympathetic."[8]

In the town of Williamsburg the custom of serenading was still
practiced.

Coteries of musicians, usually with violins or banjos, would set
out after midnight. . . . I would hear the music of these strolling
minstrels, and quickly leaving my bed, hie away and become a
most appreciative, if not bidden member of the band. I kept so
quiet, and showed such an appreciation both of the music and
the spirit of the expeditions, that I was at first tolerated and then
welcomed into quasi-membership, [and eventually] appointed
to play the triangle.[9]

At Bruton Parish Church he often lingered after the morning
service to hear the choir practicing. One day when the organ-
blower was away, he volunteered to work the bellows and eventually worked his way into the choir.

Naturally gregarious, Munford was always delighted to receive
an invitation to a party, though he suffered over the fact that
even his best or "company" clothes were generally homemade and
always out of style:

My doleful suggestions that my appearance was not . . . con-
ducive to my success as a beau [were] always met with the re-

mark, doubtless designed to be comforting: "Run along; nobody will notice you. It's all right if you are clean." Nobody would notice me! Small comfort, indeed! To be noticed was the one great ambition nearest my heart. Then the suggestion, "If I was clean!" My hands in summer partook of the shade of russet brown which comes from cider-making, a pastime in which I often indulged. In the fall they acquired a dark mahogany color—stains from the hulls of new walnuts—while in winter the contents of my trouser pockets—tops, marbles, nails and lead bullets, especially the latter—gave them a gloss very much resembling stove-polish.[10]

At the age of fifteen, he entered William and Mary College, ill prepared for the freedom it offered from "the careful oversight and discipline of the school-room," but stimulated by "the very atmosphere which invests the old college," the oldest in America, next to Harvard. The thought that George Washington had received his first commission, as surveyor of public lands, from the college and served as its chancellor and that Thomas Jefferson, James Monroe, and John Marshall had been students there nourished a profound, if slightly romantic, interest in American history that would enrich his political and legal careers, strengthen his commitment to progressive reforms at the turn of the century, and sustain him through the last ten years of debilitating illness.

What engaged Beverley Munford's interest was not "the history of events, recorded in their bare chronological order, but the causations and sequence; the evolution of principles, the establishment of institutions as results of conflicts in council, forum and field—often far remote in time and place from the hour of fruition—and the evident forward movement, despite set-backs and failures, of the condition, thought and conscience of mankind."[11]

His professors at William and Mary

early indoctrinated [him] with the theory that the government which governs least governs best; that only so much of the citizen's liberty as is absolutely essential to the public good should be restrained; that the community should retain the discharge of all the functions which it can exercise, only delegating to the general government the control of matters evidently beyond its province; that any interference with the freedom of contracts and commerce is to be deplored; that all exemptions from the burdens common to the mass of the citizenship are wrong; that the bestowal of special privileges and advantages by the government are a perversion of its powers, and that in the last analysis its proper function is simply to keep clear the great highway along which each citizen without help or hindrance must work out for himself the problem of his future and destiny.[12]

"Among the hindrances which kept me from my books, I must reckon my fondness for society," he confessed in 1905, and there is no record of his receiving an undergraduate degree from William and Mary. Nevertheless, in the college's debating society he won a gold medal and, more important,

a victory over myself, in that I at least attempted to speak without a manuscript. The ability to think upon one's feet, as it is termed, can only be acquired by such practice; while the power to impress and move an audience is largely dependent upon the magnetic influence which flows from the speaker. His eyes should join with his voice in bearing his message, which should come from a soul so stirred as not to need the aid of manuscript to remind him of its purport. . . .

I had long cherished an ambition to become a lawyer, and so, my college days over, I returned to my father's home in Botetourt, to which he had removed, intent if possible upon carrying this aspiration into effect. . . . Between me and the attainment of my desire, however, loomed a great barrier—the want of money. . . . My father fully sympathized with me, and with characteristic generosity set about making arrangements to enable me to enter the law school of the University of Virginia. My hopes were high, and the future seemed assured, when suddenly the prospect was completely changed by my father's death.[13]

In several paragraphs of "affectionate remembrance," he described his father as

> a high type of the Virginia gentleman—the best product of the ante-bellum days. Chivalrous, honorable, refined—a great lover of books, and with no small degree of literary taste and attainment. To write poetry or pore over the pages of some favorite author possessed for him far more attraction than the status of his bank-account or the condition of his larder. He was generous and courteous, something of a dreamer, with a touch of knightly impulsiveness. He had little of the controversialist or skeptic in his make-up. He walked in the old paths, accepting the faiths and standards which he learned at his mother's knee.[14]

As his son Beverley walked in the new paths toward an increasingly urban and business-oriented Virginia at the turn of the century, his thoughts and actions were always tempered by the example of his father's "gentle and unselfish life."

In the fall of 1876 Beverley Munford's brother-in-law, Judge James Doddridge Coles, "saved his ambition" to become a lawyer by inviting him to come live with him in Chatham, the county seat of Pittsylvania, near Danville, and read law in his office.

"From the day of my arrival until the following summer," he wrote, "I devoted myself with great assiduity to the study of the law" under the sympathetic direction of Judge Coles. Then in 1877 he entered the Summer Law School at the University of Virginia and studied briefly under the venerable Professor John B. Minor.[15]

In the fall of 1877 he returned to Chatham and to Judge Coles's office, explaining later that "my financial straits prevented me from returning to the University, [though] I had then, as I have now, the liveliest appreciation of the loss thus occasioned me."[16]

The following February, he was examined by two judges and awarded a license, though he claimed that this "was no sign of great erudition . . . as the examinations then in vogue were far from difficult."[17]

He continued:

So it was that early in the year 1878 the long-looked-for hour arrived. Just twenty-one years of age, with a very modest sum in bank, twelve law-books in hand and a moderate knowledge of their contents, I stepped into the arena, where so many try and so many fail, and offered my services as Counselor and Attorney to a confiding public. Whatever my shortcomings, or the slender store of this world's goods with which my craft was freighted, I was young—hope and enthusiasm beat high—and with the poet I felt that "In the glorious lexicon of Youth there was no such word as 'fail.'"[18]

Beverley Munford was always grateful that he began the practice of law in the country. He firmly believed that the "cordiality of the lawyers, the neighborliness of the people, and above all, the opportunities . . . for studying human nature in its many forms and phases" that a country practice offered more than compensated for any lack of diversity in its legal problems:

No where [*sic*] can the art of getting on with one's fellow-man, or measuring his character, sentiments, and prejudices, be more thoroughly acquired than amid the experiences of a county Courtroom, or on the Court green in Old Virginia. Not only does the lawyer appear before a cloud of witnesses, but he must appreciate the stupidity, integrity, craftiness, patriotism and all other characteristics of that curious aggregation denominated "the people." Unless the lawyer or man of affairs understands and reckons with these varying peculiarities, he is destined to slow success.[19]

Munford learned enough about those varying peculiarities to build up a solid practice in Pittsylvania County and to be elected by those same people in 1881, when he was barely twenty-five years old, to represent them in the General Assembly in Richmond. He never regretted the many hours he spent in political campaigns:

From . . . my first experience as a political worker [carrying an old man with rheumatism to the polls] . . . [and] many forms

of service subsequently rendered, I am convinced that no one
can feel the warmest sense of loyalty and devotion for his Party
who has not sturdily borne his share in the labor necessary to
achieve its victories, . . . suffered the pangs of fatigue, . . . [had]
his face . . . burned by explosions from powder in celebrating
its victories, or his back drenched with coal-oil as he bore aloft
in some parade his torch.[20]

Munford's views are reflected in his own description of the times:

[D]uring the period immediately following the Civil War there
were, strictly speaking, no organized political parties in Virginia.
From 1865 to 1870 the whole population—white and black—
was disfranchised, and the State [was] governed from Washington as Military District No. 1. When under the provisions of
the Federal Legislation, so curiously styled "Reconstruction," the
State was readmitted into the Union, the shibboleths and sentiments which usually divided thoughtful men as Whigs, Democrats or Republicans were subordinated in the supreme desire to
save the political, economic and social life of the Commonwealth
from the disasters which would follow the rule of ignorance and
venality.[21]

A new organization, composed of Whigs, Democrats, Union
men, Secessionists, and Republicans and called "The Conservative
Party" nominated and eventually elected a moderate Republican,
Gilbert C. Walker of Binghamton, New York, over the radical
Republican, Henry H. Wells. Virginia was thus saved, Munford
explained, from "the humiliations and excesses which afflicted so
many of the Southern States" and came out of Reconstruction six
years earlier.

Munford's first major political effort was a passionate speech
in 1876 urging Virginia voters to elect the Democrat, Samuel J.
Tilden, over the Republican, Rutherford B. Hayes, for president.
Five years later, in 1881, Munford was elected as a Conservative from Pittsylvania County and the city of Danville to the Virginia General Assembly. This particular legislature was dominated
by the ex-Confederate general and railroad speculator William

Mahone and his Readjuster Party—so-called because they advo-
cated partial repudiation or "re-adjustment" of the huge public
debt left from prewar improvements. This state debt was the most
complex and financially devastating problem that faced the Virginia legislature between 1870 and 1893, when it was finally resolved, with help from Beverley Munford. The almost paranoid
fear of acquiring new state debt that would bind so many Virginia
politicians to a "pay-as-you-go" policy in the twentieth century may
be traced back to that epic struggle.[22]

In 1883 the former Conservatives, who had recently reorganized and changed their name to Democrats, regained control of
the legislature, and Beverley Munford led the ticket from Pittsylvania County. He was promptly appointed to the Asylums and
Prisons, Courts of Justice, Federal Relations, and Resolutions committees. The following year he celebrated the election of Grover
Cleveland with a triumphant speech in Richmond, hailing the
Democrat as a truly "national" president and his victory as a sign
that sectional passions aroused by the Civil War were finally abat-
ing.[23]

By his third term, Munford had emerged as one of the strong-
est leaders in the House. In December 1885 he gave an eloquent
speech nominating John W. Daniel, "the lame lion of Lynchburg,"
for the seat in the U.S. Senate formerly occupied by General
Mahone.[24]

As chairman of the Courts of Justice Committee and the joint
House-Senate Committee on the Revision of the Virginia Code,
Munford worked very closely with Waller Staples, one of the three
lawyers who drafted the Code of 1887. After the work was finished, Judge Staples invited Beverley Munford to form a partnership with him in Richmond.[25]

And so, late in 1887, after ten years of practice as a country
lawyer in Pittsylvania County, Beverley Munford moved back to
the city of his birth and entered the firm of Staples & Munford at
1113 East Main Street.

As a result of this move, the nature of his practice and his alle-
giances changed. In 1886, on behalf of his rural constituents who

feared the increasing power of the railroads, he had led the fight in the House for a stronger Railroad Commissioners' bill. But soon after his move to Richmond, he was appointed trial counsel for the Richmond & Danville Railroad (which would come out of receivership in 1894 as the Southern Railway), in charge of "all suits instituted against the Company in some fifteen counties, cities and towns." Through this work, he managed to keep in close contact with the country people who then represented eighty percent of Virginia's population and came regularly to their county court houses for diversion as well as justice.[26]

Some of the tallest tales Munford included in his *Random Recollections* were drawn from railroad damage suits in which the plaintiffs or their lawyers displayed remarkable ingenuity in establishing the value of a hog or cow that had been killed by a Richmond & Danville locomotive, or in establishing the train's excessive speed.

Perhaps the most colorful argument was made by a lawyer whose client's arm had been injured when it was sticking out of a train window and was struck by the side of a bridge. The railroad was clearly at fault, the plaintiff's lawyer argued, because its cars were so wide and its bridge was so narrow that "every train which leaves the City of Richmond bound for Danville has to be greased from cow-catcher to back platform in order to squeeze it through that miserable bridge." He then went on to speculate on the number of people that had been killed by that same bridge and secretly buried by the railroad. Playing on the fears that most Virginians must have felt in the 1890s as they watched huge out-of-state corporations buy up local railroads, textile mills, and tobacco companies, he said:

> And this reflection leads me, Gentlemen of the Jury, to inquire who is the directing spirit—who the master hand that manages the affairs of this great corporation? The time was when men to the manor born—bone of our bone and flesh of our flesh—were the officers of the Richmond & Danville Railroad. Into their sympathetic ears our people were accustomed to pour their complaints, which always received the kindest con-

sideration. But those days have, unfortunately for you and me, long since passed. A new type of men now control the affairs of this railroad company. Who are they? I repeat, Where is the home and what the name of the master spirit? Way up yonder somewhere in the frigid regions of the North he lives. What is his name? I am frank to say I never saw the man. I venture to say that not a member of this intelligent jury ever saw the man. I go further and affirm that his Honor—the learned Judge of this Court—never saw the man. But though we have never seen him, the evidence in this case convinces me that he is one of your white-livered, unfeeling specimens, so cold-blooded that were you to cut him open on the fifteenth of July you would find icicles hanging from his heart as long as my walking cane.[27]

Early in his practice with Judge Staples, Munford became involved in the financial institutions of Main Street, serving as director of the Virginia Trust Company, the Richmond Trust and Safe Deposit Company, and the Merchants National Bank. He also organized the South Atlantic Insurance Company, which later became the Atlantic Life Insurance Company, and served as its president until illness forced him to resign in the early 1900s.

As he was building a large and lucrative practice on Main Street, Munford lamented the loss of informality and intimacy that had been so much a part of his country practice. And he hoped that the increasing emphasis on corporation, banking, and business law, and modern office methods would not destroy what was best about the traditional Virginia lawyer:

> His high estimate of the profession; his pride in the intellectual achievements of his confreres, past and present; the mingled humor and seriousness with which he meets its responsibilities,—all serve to render him a most attractive personality, and to lift his avocation far above the prosaic plane of a mere bread-winning occupation. . . . The advent of the stenographer, type-writer, telephone and file-case will contribute to the despatch of business and the more orderly conduct of affairs committed to his charge, but with respect to many weightier

matters we may hope that the old order will survive. Thus, he may forbear to write with his own hand in unintelligible characters his legal documents, and to find a more suitable file-case for his papers than his silk hat or coat pocket; and yet we trust his simplicity and genuineness of character will remain unchanged. More and more he must bear a part in the strictly business life of his day, but let us hope that his idealism will not be destroyed amid this new environment. The magnitude of the financial interests which he guards, and the exacting demands of corporations, may tend to limit his time and specialize his sympathies, yet may he continue to recognize the obligations, literary, political and social, which have heretofore adorned his life and enriched his country. Among the legal digests hot from the press, which crowd his library shelves, we would find as of yore copies of Addison, Macaulay and Horace; and his standards of authority for all the great emergencies of life, whether individual or social, remain the Virginia Bill of Rights, the Federal Constitution, and the Bible.[28]

However demanding his clients might be, Beverley Munford believed that a lawyer has a higher obligation to his community, his state, and his country. Despite the demands of the burgeoning practice of Staples & Munford, he continued to be actively involved in politics. In the gubernatorial race of 1889, in which the Democrat Philip W. McKinney defeated the Republican Mahone, Beverley Munford contributed a pamphlet describing some of the more excessive measures proposed by the Mahone majority in the 1881–82 legislature.[29]

Two years later, in 1891, Beverley Munford was elected to the House of Delegates from the city of Richmond. In that session he served as chairman of the House Committee on Finance and was also chairman of the committee in charge of preparing a House bill to put into effect the "Olcutt Settlement" of the Virginia state debt. The Richmond *Dispatch* reported that "his speech in presenting that bill was regarded as one of the clearest and most exhaustive presentations ever made of that much-vexed subject."[30]

During the severe national depression that began in 1893 and continued until the end of the 1890s, rural Virginians, who still outnumbered the urbanites four to one, threw their support behind William Jennings Bryan and his inflationary "free silver" platform. This fact initiated a violent "family quarrel" among Virginia Democrats, threatening the alliance between the agricultural interests and financial interests which had supported the party for the past ten years.[31]

Munford, a leader of the Cleveland Democrats, as well as a recently converted urbanite and corporation lawyer, was a "goldbug," while his future partner, Eppa Hunton, Jr., who represented Fauquier and Loudoun counties in the Virginia House of Delegates in 1892–93, and his father, General Hunton, a former U.S. congressman (1872–79) and senator (1892–95), were avid "silverites."[32]

In June of 1896, at the State Democratic Convention in Staunton, Munford delivered the minority report, pleading for a sound money policy, saying that he had come to the convention "to show to the world that the people of Virginia had not all gone crazy" over the silver question. Though his report was rejected by a majority of almost four to one, the Richmond *Times, Dispatch*, and *State* all commented on his tact and good humor in presenting the goldbugs' arguments to a potentially hostile audience.[33]

In 1897 Munford was elected by the voters of Richmond to a four-year term in the state senate. During this period, from 1897 until 1901, when tuberculosis forced him to retire from politics, he reached the peak of his career as an orator as well as a lawyer. On numerous public occasions, particularly dedications of Confederate monuments, he delivered eloquent orations praising the South's most recent heroes and the cause for which they fought. But he also recalled the role that earlier Virginians had played in the founding of the nation. And he insisted that the time had come to look to the future, as well as the past, to forget old animosities and join the rest of the country in its progress toward renewed prosperity, industrialization, better education, and more enlightened social programs.[34]

Though his conservatism on the currency question and ties to the Democratic "organization" separated him from the "Independents," who are usually identified with the Progressive movement in Virginia, Beverley Munford, by the end of the 1890s, had emerged as one of the most effective advocates for reforms in public education, labor relations, and race relations. Part of his leadership may be attributed to a profound historical sense that kept him from ever being trapped by party slogans, and to his deep, though by modern standards paternalistic, concern for the blacks with whom he had spent so much of his boyhood. Part of it must also be attributed to his wife.[35]

One evening in the early 1880s, he went to the house of a friend in Richmond and noticed a young girl standing at the edge of the party, regarding it with "rather unapproving eyes. There was about her an air of mingled diffidence and audacity. A lithe figure, earnest brown eyes, clean-cut features. . . . This much I took in at a glance, and with it came the startled thought that no more should I stand alone upon the threshold of my individual life."[36]

A few years later, when that same young girl, Mary Cooke Branch, was presented to society at an "open house" on New Year's Day, as was the custom at that time, Munford searched the newspapers to find out where and when she would be receiving and then took advantage of that chance to meet her.[37]

"It was, however, no instance of veni, vidi, vici; years followed in which the hope of success alternated with the fear of failure." His sister worried about his being "too much in love" and a favorite aunt offered him little consolation when she said, "I have watched her for many years. She was a scholar at my son-in-law's school. She is as lovely in mind as she is in person, and is a sensible girl— not crazy about men."[38]

"Not crazy about men! In the years which followed," wrote Beverley Munford, "there seemed a grim irony in the fact that she had been commended to my favor because of her little concern for men."[39]

What she was concerned with, once she gave up the idea of defying her mother and going to college, was getting a child-labor law through the General Assembly, establishing a club for working girls, and founding a Woman's Club to educate the women of her own class for fuller participation in the modern world. Already, Mary Cooke Branch was well on her way to becoming one of the most effective leaders, male or female, that Virginia would produce in the first two decades of the twentieth century.[40]

Claude Swanson, Beverley Munford's friend from Pittsylvania County, later best man at his wedding, governor of Virginia, U.S. congressman, senator, and Franklin Roosevelt's secretary of the navy, wrote him during the courtship: "How is your lady friend? I have not yet recovered from the defeat I received at her hand in our discussion. Give her my kindest regards and inform her that I am rapidly being convinced of her way of thinking."[41]

Eventually Beverley Munford must have converted her to his way of thinking, on the subject of marriage at least, because the wedding finally took place on November 11, 1893, when she was twenty-eight and he was thirty-seven.

After a wedding trip to Asheville, North Carolina, and New York City, by private railroad car, they settled down on Laurel Street opposite Monroe Park in Richmond. The following year their twelve-year-old nephew, Walter Russell Bowie, came to live with them.[42]

"Hardly a couple more gifted or more beautiful ever lived in Richmond," wrote the architectural historian Mary Wingfield Scott. She described the house the Munfords moved into in 1899 as a handsome Greek Revival mansion on Shockoe Hill near Fifth and Grace streets. It was on the lot where George Wythe's house had stood, and Beverley Munford's grandfather had studied. Before the city's boundaries were expanded, it was the highest point in Richmond.[43]

With Mary Munford as his partner, and with a young daughter and infant son, a seat in the Virginia senate, and a thriving law practice, Beverley Munford now stood at the highest point of his life.[44] In his mid-forties he was already one of the most widely respected lawyers in Virginia. The Richmond Bar Association had, in fact, just selected him to preside at the centennial celebration of John Marshall's appointment to the Supreme Court.

Then a shadow fell over his life. During the winter of 1900, he began to show signs of a serious illness. His wife took him to New York to consult a specialist, and he was told that he had tuberculosis and was given only a year to live.[45]

In January 1901 he was still well enough to attend the extra session of the General Assembly called to make arrangements for the proposed Constitutional Convention in May. And in February he presided over the centennial celebration of John Marshall's appointment as chief justice. But by summertime it was clear that he would not be able to return to his law practice the following winter. His doctors had advised him to seek the only cure they knew of then: a long rest in the clear, dry climate of the West.

It was at this point that his junior partner, Henry Anderson, and another young lawyer, Randolph Williams, came to him with the idea of establishing a law firm that would combine Munford's reputation and his clients with the energy and good health of the two younger men—and that of another senior lawyer yet to be selected.

Henry Anderson stayed with him for several days in August, in Lakewood, New Jersey, discussing these plans as well as matters pertaining to their major client, the South Atlantic Life Insurance Company. Afterwards, Munford wrote to a fellow lawyer informing him that "negotiations are underway to the formation of a law firm of which my junior partner and myself will be the senior and junior members respectively, in association with two other lawyers" and asking his friend's advice on how they should divide the profits. The other lawyer replied that in his judgment, "a legal partnership cannot be formed as between merchants or men who deal in money. There is obliged to be a community of interest and brainpower which money does not exactly measure," deftly avoiding the delicate question of compensation.[46]

Back in Richmond Henry Anderson continued to carry the full work load of Munford & Anderson through October, by himself, as he had been doing all summer, taking depositions for the Southern Railway, presenting a case for the Chatham National Bank, and spending a full week on his argument in *Ginter's Executors v. the Farmville & Powhatan Railway.*

By the end of October, only half of the ledger book had been used. At that point, Henry Anderson—who could hardly be accused of frugality later in his life—decided against investing in a brand-new ledger for the new law firm.

Instead, he gave up just one page, number 173, to indicate the change to new bookkeeping records for:

Munford, Hunton, Williams & Anderson
November 1, 1901

Then on page 174 he began to add brief notations on the activities and disbursements of Eppa Hunton, Jr., and Randolph Williams, as well as himself.

During the first two years of the new law firm's existence, Beverley Munford was a partner in name only. On his doctors' advice, he and his family spent the last month of 1901, all of 1902, and the first three months of 1903 in Colorado, hoping that the dry climate and clean air would clear his lungs.

During this involuntary exile from Virginia, he kept his mind busy with reading and correspondence, preparing talks, like the one on "Lawlessness in Our Land" that he gave to the Winter Nights Society of Colorado Springs in January 1903, and making notes for the autobiography *Random Recollections*, which he would publish in 1905.[47]

He also spent a great deal of time with his children. Blessed with a playful nature and an irrepressible sense of humor, he moved easily into the children's world, and they loved to be with him. Their mother, by comparison, seemed to them aloof and preoccupied with her crusade for improving public education in Virginia. She was also burdened with the financial worries that increased steadily with her husband's illness. Though she was devoted to her children, Mary Munford was apparently never able to enjoy them as simply and completely as her husband did.[48]

On November 1, 1902, the original partnership agreement was amended to elevate Henry Anderson to equality with Eppa Hunton, Jr., and Randolph Williams in the division of the profits and to exclude Munford from participating in any further profits until his health allowed him to participate in the work.[49]

Though such treatment may seem harsh today, it was not so for those days when the idea of a law firm as an institution was still very new, and the principle of laissez-faire prevailed in almost every aspect of life. A lawyer practicing then "took all the risks of life," as one of the founding partners put it, and stood or fell on the strength of the fees that he brought in.[50]

The wonder is that Munford was paid his full share of the first year's profits, when he did not even come into the office. But then, of course, it was his name and his statewide reputation that had set the style for the law firm.

By the time the second winter in Colorado ended, Beverley Munford's health had improved so much that he and his family were able to come back east in the spring of 1903 in time to attend the sixth annual Southern Education Conference, which Governor Andrew Montague had encouraged to meet in Richmond, late in April.[51]

In 1899 the Munfords had attended their first Southern Education Conference, in Athens, Georgia, riding to it on the special train the Northern philanthropist Robert Ogden had chartered for seventy-five guests. As a result, they had become deeply involved in the "Ogden Movement," an almost evangelical crusade for better education for both whites and blacks throughout the South.[52]

On April 28, 1903, immediately after the sixth conference in Richmond, Beverley Munford was named to the Board of Trustees of the Hampton Normal and Agricultural Institute, the famous school for blacks and American Indians, of which Robert Ogden was chairman.[53] The following summer, at "The Priory," the home of Mary R. Sanford in Bennington, Vermont, Munford worked on the manuscript of his autobiography. Then he returned to the beautiful old house at 503 East Grace Street and to his law practice.[54]

On October 1, 1903, a third partnership agreement was signed, allowing Munford longer vacations and shorter work days and setting his share of the profits at a little more than half that of a full-time partner.

At this point the firm converted to a fiscal year ending December 31, and for the next two years Munford's share remained at roughly one-seventh. The records show him doing work for the Southern Railway, as of old, and helping Henry Anderson with a new client, Frank Jay Gould, who would soon gain control of the electric utility industry that was emerging in Virginia.

The winter of 1904–5 took a heavy toll on Munford's health, and by March of 1905, he was seriously ill again, according to his nephew Walter Russell Bowie. After a summer vacation, again in Bennington, Vermont, he was "a little better" and back at work by mid-October 1905.

During the previous spring, Mrs. Munford had been deeply involved in the "May Campaign" for better education in Virginia. By the fall of 1905, the movement had gained so much momentum that all major candidates for election that year—the retiring Independent governor, Andrew Jackson Montague, now running for the Democratic nomination for the U.S. Senate seat; his opponent, the "organization" chief and incumbent senator, Tom Martin; and the Democratic candidate for governor, Claude Swanson—pledged their support for the creation of high schools all over the state, compulsory attendance laws, better pay for teachers, and better roads.[55]

By the end of 1905, at the same time that his best man, Swanson, was preparing to move into the Governor's Mansion, Munford had become so weakened by tuberculosis that he could no longer practice law. On January 1, 1906, he retired from the firm and spent the rest of that winter in the milder climate of Camden, South Carolina, the following summer in Vermont, and the winter of 1906–7 in Tucson, Arizona.

By the summer of 1907, the Munford family had returned to Richmond. By this time he was an invalid and it was clear that he could never return to the active practice of the law. Instead, he focused his attention on a second book, a scholarly examination of Virginia's attitude toward slavery and secession from 1619 until 1861, corresponding with historians and archivists all over the country and dictating a large proportion of the manuscript from his sickbed.[56]

In the fall of 1908, Munford published a series of articles in the *Times-Dispatch* urging local businessmen not to desert the Democratic party to vote for the Republican candidate for president, William Howard Taft, as his former partner Henry Anderson was urging them to do.[57] At the same time he was putting the final touches on *Virginia's Attitude toward Slavery and Secession*, which was published in October 1909 and received favorable reviews not only in the South, but also in Boston, New York, and London.

The *New York Times*, on November 27, 1909, called it "a candid and temperate examination of all the events and currents of sentiment and opinion leading up to the war, resulting in the conclusion that the secession of the State was in reality due to the decision of the Federal Government to coerce the already seceded states."

Most interesting of all was a letter to Munford from the historian Charles Francis Adams:

> Of course a large part of your argument is already familiar to students of American history. Everyone who has any knowledge at all of the record of Virginia knows of the anti-slavery sentiment which there existed prior to 1830 and the Nat Turner insurrection [and] the very memorable utterances of the great Virginians on this head, more especially those of Jefferson and the Randolphs. . . . The portion of your work . . . which to me seems to have a real present value is that wherein you develop the record of Virginia during the critical period of 1861. You speak within correct historical bounds when you say . . . had Virginia, when its vote was taken in February, 1861, "declared

for a policy of immediate secession, it is almost certain that the remaining Southern States would have followed her example. In such event President Lincoln would on the day of his inauguration have found the capital of the Union encompassed by the States of Virginia and Maryland, both members of the new confederation." Largely overlooked in the glaring light of immediately subsequent events, this statement is literally true; nor have the historians of that period given due weight to the vital importance of the vote then cast in Virginia; but remembering vividly almost every detail in the course of events of that period, I can bear personal evidence of the truth of what you assert. Had the strong hereditary Union sentiment then existing in Virginia not made itself felt and had Virginia on February 4, 1861, thrown her voice and influence as decisively in favor of immediate secession as the six cotton States had already thrown theirs, I entertain no doubt that, when the fourth of March dawned, the Confederacy would have been in full possession of the national capital, and consequently have demanded recognition from foreign Powers as the de facto government. It would also, in accordance with international usage, have been recognized as such. . . . It was the voice of Virginia which then called a halt, temporary, but all-important, in the headlong course of events. That halt at the critical moment in the crisis of affairs was decisive of ultimate results. . . . As a not uninformed participant in the course of events, my own guess . . . is that decisive, though precipitate, action then taken by Virginia would have been conclusive as to the result of the impending struggle. . . . Maryland would have followed the lead given by Virginia in the February preceding, and, with the Confederacy in possession of the national capital, foreign recognition could hardly have been prevented. The result of the subsequent struggle would, I believe, have in that case been wholly different from what the historian has now to record. . . . I cannot therefore but believe that to the whole history of this continent there was never a more momentous election utterance than that indecisive protest of Virginia's expiring Unionism. In bringing this fact to the front and emphasizing it, you make a veritable contribution to history.[58]

The following year Munford's book was adopted as a text for the first year of Virginia's high schools and went into a second edition.

Today's reader is likely to find the book hard going. In presenting Virginia's varying attitudes toward the "peculiar institution" of slavery, Beverley Munford "briefed" each aspect of it, destroying at the outset any possibility of narrative momentum. Nevertheless, it is a solid, scholarly work, rich with examples and surprising contradictions. And it succeeds in its aim to "vindicate Virginia from the unworthy motives so often imputed to her . . . by an adequate presentation of the facts of history."[59]

Why did Munford choose to spend his last energies on this particular book? Could he have sensed that in the century to come, as in the one that had just ended, the race problem would be the most difficult one facing his state, his region, and, indeed, perhaps his country? Though he was a man of his time in that he thought of blacks as "a childlike race" not yet capable of voting wisely, he saw education, rather than legislation, as the most humane and constructive way to solve the race problem in the South. After his death, the newspaper of the Hampton Institute stated that: "He and his brilliant wife realized, as few Southerners have done, the absolute necessity of training the youth of the Negro race and gave to the Hampton School the advantage of their commanding social position and broad sympathies. They are largely responsible for the cordial relation which the State of Virginia and its people have sustained to the institution."[60]

"The long years of illness never dimmed his glowing interest in the problems of our day," said the writer of a memorial essay in a small New York publication called *The Survey.* One of his chief interests was the promotion of popular education for both whites and blacks. From its formation, Munford had been a member of the National Child Labor Committee, and during the 1910 session, "when the Virginia ten-hour law for women and children was assailed both before the courts and in the Legislature, it was in part the sagacious counsel of Mr. Munford which in the end enabled its friends to keep it intact."[61]

One of the last things Munford did before his death was to draft, in his large generous handwriting, the resolution that was "the means of saving the John Marshall House" from demolition. The Richmond School Board had decided to pull the house down on the theory that it "disfigured" the front of the new John Marshall High School building. In a note scrawled on the back of the resolution, Mrs. Munford explained that she learned of the demolition plans purely by chance, "through a passing conversation with a member of the Board." When she told her husband about it, he immediately drafted a resolution, on behalf of the Richmond Education Association of which Mrs. Munford was then president, urging the city council to pass the necessary ordinance for repairs to the John Marshall House and for its preservation in the years to come:

> Every consideration affecting the reputation of our city, in the estimation of the world, requires this action. The educational influence of this building, so long the home of Richmond's most illustrious citizen, upon the minds of the young is of the highest value. Marshall was not only a great man in the realm of statecraft and jurisprudence, but he exemplified, in the most striking manner, the sterling virtues of character, which must forever constitute the basis of individual and national worth.[62]

As a historian, Munford had struggled to reconcile Virginia's tragic role in the 1860s with its creative one in the days of the Revolution and the Early Republic. The warm reception of his book *Virginia's Attitude toward Slavery and Secession* by historians in the North as well as by his colleagues in the senate of Virginia was a source of comfort as he grew steadily weaker in the spring of 1910 and the specialists could do nothing to save him.

On Monday afternoon, May 30, as his wife wheeled him in from the porch of their rented house on Hermitage Road, and helped him into bed for the last time, he insisted that she raise the window

shade to give "more light," he said. "It may have been a consequence of his illness," she wrote to her nephew and adopted son,
Russell Bowie. "But it made me think of Goethe's 'Mehr licht,
mehr licht.'"[63]

On the morning of May 31, 1910, Beverley Munford died. For
the next three days the newspapers extolled his "brilliant career
cut short by fatal illness," his deep interest in history, and his quiet
but effective work for social reform—which his wife would continue for the next two decades. And a few of them mentioned "the
sweetness of his character," which was probably his single most
outstanding trait.[64]

Years later, after Russell Bowie had become rector of Grace
Episcopal Church in New York City, he paid tribute to his uncle's
courage in his losing battle with tuberculosis in a sermon:

> There was a man—I knew him and loved him—who was bro-
> ken by illness in the prime of his strength. He was a lawyer
> of brilliant ability, widely beloved. . . . He could have climbed
> to almost any place of public authority in the gift of his state.
> But the illness which came to him cut all that short. Every un-
> folding of the future which he might have looked forward to
> was blighted as completely as fruit buds are blighted when the
> killing frost comes. . . . [And yet he] permitted round himself no
> atmosphere of brooding wistfulness, but filled it instead with a
> gallant gayety. . . . Within the prison of his limitation his spirit
> shone so grandly that men who looked toward its windows saw
> it as a place where a king kept festival. And when the doors
> opened, and his spirit went on the eternal highways, all the word
> and thought and spirit of him floated back to those who listened,
> like a song.[65]

Eppa Hunton, Jr.

1855–1932

On the day that Beverley Munford was buried, June 2, 1910, the offices of Munford, Hunton, Williams & Anderson, and the Virginia Historical Society, were closed, and the door of the Merchants Bank was draped with crepe.

An enormous crowd had turned out for the funeral. Governor Mann and ex-Governor Montague were there, and, of course, Senator Swanson, who was an honorary pallbearer along with Eppa Hunton, Jr.[1] Munford's junior partners, Randolph Williams and Henry Anderson, were active pallbearers, and the firm's new associate—in fact its only associate at the time—Thomas B. Gay, probably stood quietly at the back of the church.

Eppa Hunton was now the only senior partner, though he had been carrying most of that responsibility since the firm was founded nine years earlier. His father used to worry that the work would break his health. Yet Hunton thrived on the work and was in good form today, though saddened as the whole city was. He held his handsome head high and his frame erect as he walked behind the casket, first at St. Paul's Church and then at Hollywood Cemetery.[2]

He was burying the only law partner who really understood him. Though they had had their differences—in politics especially— they were contemporaries. Randolph Williams and Henry Anderson were fifteen years younger, another generation altogether. They had not grown up as refugees in a bloody and destructive war. Nor had they lived through the civil and economic chaos that followed that war. In a way, they would always seem a little immature to Eppa Hunton, Jr. Or maybe the right word was "innocent."

It was the war that separated him from his younger partners, far more than the fifteen years' difference in their ages. After all, Hunton and his father were thirty years apart in age, yet of all the men in his life, the one who had been closest to him was his father. To him he could say whatever came into his mind, exactly as it came.

The life of Eppa Hunton, Jr., was, in fact, almost inseparable from the life of General Eppa Hunton. As an only child, he had participated in his father's life to an extraordinary degree, living in camp with him the winter after Gettysburg, watching him lose every stick of property he owned and then build up again from scratch a successful law practice and later a career in Congress. As a young adult, Eppa Jr. had shared his father's law practice, and except for the war years and a few years during his first marriage, he had lived with his father all his life.

By the late 1890s, when the two Eppas, both widowers, were living together in Warrenton, Virginia, their relationship had clearly passed from that of father and son to best friends.[3]

So it is not surprising that when Randolph Williams and Henry Anderson came to Eppa Jr. in the summer of 1901 with their proposal for a law firm in Richmond, he said that he could not give them an answer until he had talked the matter over with his father.

In his *Autobiography*, written in 1904, General Hunton recalled that Eppa Jr. "came home" during a break in the Constitutional Convention in Richmond and "laid the matter before me." They discussed the pros and cons, the opportunities that a large city practice in association with a man of Beverley Munford's stature would open up; the fact that the "practice in Fauquier and the surrounding country was very small, very few large cases, and although Eppa made a right large income every year, it was by going some distance from home into the surrounding country."[4]

On balance, the general concluded that the advantages of the move outweighed the disadvantages.

Then Eppa Jr. said, "Will you go with me to Richmond?"

"That's another matter," General Hunton said.

"Well unless you go with me to Richmond, I will not consider the proposition."

"It was a right sore thing to me," wrote the old man who had been born and raised in Fauquier County, "to give up my home in Warrenton, . . . [but it] was still harder for me to break up what I considered a brilliant partnership for my son."[5]

General Hunton sold his property in Warrenton for ten thousand dollars and turned the money over to his son to help him buy a house in Richmond. Thus it happened that these two men —with Eppa Jr.'s new wife, the former Virginia ("Jincy") Payne, put down their roots in Richmond.[6]

Though Eppa Hunton, Jr., had lived in Warrenton, the county seat of Fauquier, since he was ten years old, he was actually born (on April 14, 1855) in Prince William County, at "Brentsville," a farm his father had bought in 1849 and made into a very comfortable home. There, as a little boy, he lived in peace and plenty until the Civil War turned his life upside down.

The first sign of the impending change came in February 1861, when the Huntons moved into rooms at the Exchange and Ballard Hotel on East Main Street in Richmond while Eppa Sr. attended the Secession Convention up the street.[7] The debates over whether Virginia should stay with the Union, which she had worked so hard to put together some seventy years earlier, or secede with the "Cotton States" were passionate and sometimes bitter, and they dragged on for two months. Finally, on April 17, three days after Eppa Jr. celebrated his sixth birthday, and two days after Lincoln called for volunteers to force the seceding states back into the Union, "[t]he old, able and patriotic Whigs, who had so violently opposed secession, now became earnest advocates of it and the Ordinance of Secession was passed by a good majority, 88 to 55."[8]

Eppa Hunton, Sr., had been a secessionist from the start. As a candidate for the convention back in January, he had stood for "immediate secession for the sake of the Union," arguing "that if Virginia would go out of the Union, at once, followed by some of the border states, the movement would be so formidable that the United States Government would not make war upon the Confederate States, but that the doctrine which was held by a great many Northern people, to 'Let the erring sisters go in peace,' would be adopted even by the Lincoln Administration." [9]

"Of course my theory was but a theory," he wrote in 1904, "but I have always thought that if war could have been avoided by an early secession of all the Southern States, reconstruction would have taken place [on terms] satisfactory to both sides and permanent." [10]

His young son, Eppa, seems to have been equally convinced. At the Exchange and Ballard Hotel that winter there were "some Massachusetts ladies," the senior Eppa recalled, "and they had a little boy a little older and larger than my son Eppa. This little Massachusetts boy was a violent Unionist, and my son a violent Secessionist. They used to fight every day. Eppa most always got the advantage in the fight, but one day I was crossing the bridge which spanned the street between the Exchange and Ballard House and found them in a fight; Eppa had kicked at the little Yankee, and the Yankee caught his foot and had Eppa hopping up and down in a pretty bad way. I passed on and did not release him, but he finally released himself and got the better of the boy." [11]

By the time the secession ordinance was ratified in May 1861, Eppa Hunton, now a colonel in the Confederate army, was in Leesburg forming a regiment to guard the fords and ferries of the Potomac River in Loudoun County.

Six-year-old Eppa and his mother had returned to their farm at Brentsville, just five miles from Manassas Junction. All day long on July 21, 1861, they listened to the booming of cannon and the rattle of muskets from the First Battle of Manassas, knowing that Colonel Hunton was in it. In fact, Mrs. Hunton, who was suffering from a liver ailment, spent most of that day in bed, with a feather pillow over her ears. The next day she and Eppa were immensely relieved to see Colonel Hunton arrive on his war horse, Morgan, for a two-hour visit. [12]

The following spring, the Confederate army evacuated the country around Manassas, forcing young Eppa Hunton, like his future partner Beverley Munford, to become a war refugee. He and his mother, who was still ill and had to be moved on a bed in a wagon, were put "on the last train that went out," abandoning to the Federal army not only their house, their slaves, and all of their household and kitchen furniture, but also a crop of wheat that had just been threshed.[13]

At first they boarded with a Mrs. Brown in Lynchburg; later, with some friends named Lipscombe in Amherst County. Then, in the fall of 1863, life suddenly brightened with an invitation to spend the winter at the newly commissioned General Hunton's headquarters in the overseer's house at Chaffin's Farm, eight miles below Richmond.[14]

At the Battle of Gettysburg, Pickett's division—to which Hunton's brigade belonged—had sustained so many losses that, according to Douglas Southall Freeman, it "could not move with the rest of the First Corps to Georgia, and because of its glorious record it was given a post of temporary ease at Chafin's [sic] Bluff on the Richmond defenses."[15]

For the Hunton family, the winter of 1863–64 was "an extremely pleasant winter, notwithstanding the war. I appointed Eppa on my Staff," General Hunton recalled:

He believed the appointment was a legal one, and it was very interesting to see how he carried my commands around. I had brigade drills every few days, and on one occasion I sent an order by Eppa to Colonel Edmund Berkeley of the 8th Regiment. He started off, riding the horse that my body-servant used, in full uniform, and provided with spurs on his bare feet. He delivered the order and as soon as the soldiers saw the spurs on his bare feet they began to yell at him, "Come out of them spurs, I see your ears sticking out. . . ." Soon his horse became very excited and restless and Eppa's legs were too short to keep the spurs out of his sides and the horse ran away, and the whole line of the brigade cheered him. I was in agony for the safety of my son, who was only eight years old; but I did not budge from my position. Eppa sat and managed his horse admirably, but he could not stop him until he ran into the stable some distance from the parade grounds.[16]

It was here, in camp, that young Eppa's schooling began in earnest. His mother struggled to teach him reading and writing and spelling during the day, while his father taught him arithmetic at night. "All that I had before the war was gone," his father wrote,

> and I was afraid that if I was killed, my boy would have no education, and one night I put him in long division. His mind was so thoroughly taken up with the brigade that I could not get him to think about his arithmetic, and I whipped him, and before bedtime he could do any sum in long division. But I felt very unhappy about it, and determined then and there that I never would give him another "lick" during the war.[17]

It was not until young Eppa tried unsuccessfully to draw pay that he learned that his appointment as "Captain" on his father's staff was purely honorary. By that time he knew more men in the brigade by name than his father did, and he continued to serve them loyally, though unofficially, until the spring of 1864 when the Union General Benjamin F. Butler began moving up the James River toward Richmond. Hunton's brigade was ordered to join Lee's forces at Hanover Junction, and Eppa Jr. and his mother returned to Lynchburg.

The last year of the war was the hardest. Confederate money had depreciated to such an extent that even a general's pay would not support the family. General Hunton had to draw rations partly in the army and partly in Lynchburg, and his wife and child lived on those rations. "On one occasion they were reduced to a single beef bone," General Hunton recalled. "My wife put it on to boil for a pot of soup for dinner, and going out to visit a neighbor left Eppa in the house to mind the soup, with strict injunctions not to touch the pot; but boylike he thought he must stir the soup, and in doing so turned it over and spilled every drop. Their last chance for dinner was gone, and my wife did not have a mouthful, but she was able to give Eppa some bread and molasses."[18]

The new firm's opening shared the front page of the Richmond *News* of October 7, 1901, with the Goddess Electra announcing the opening of Carnival Week festivities.

Original partnership agreement, November 1, 1901.—*A. R. Dementi*

Munford, Hunton, Williams & Anderson's first offices were on the second floor of the Merchants Bank Building (left) at Eleventh and Main streets.—*Valentine Museum*

Early in 1902, Munford, Hunton, Williams & Anderson moved into the Hanewinckel Building, also called the *Dispatch* Building and later the *News-Leader* Building, at Ninth and Main streets.—*Valentine Museum*

JNO. SKELTON WILLIAMS
President S. A. L.

GEO. W. STEVENS
President C & O

HEADS OF THE GREAT SYSTEMS CONTROLLING THE NEW STATION.
Mr. George W. Stevens, President of the C. & O., and President Williams, of the S. A. L., are Responsible for the Great Station.

The Renaissance-style Main Street Station, built to serve John Skelton Williams's Seaboard Air Line Railway and the Chesapeake & Ohio Railway, opened three weeks after the law firm did, in November 1901. The activities of John L. Williams & Sons, particularly Randolph's oldest brother, John Skelton, were the principal source of business for the firm in its first years.—*Virginia Historical Society*

All three railroads in this famous photograph of the three-level crossing on South Dock Street were represented by Hunton & Williams attorneys at one time or another: the Chesapeake & Ohio (top) by George Gibson and John Riely; the Seaboard Air Line (middle) by all four founders and by Eppa Hunton IV; and the Southern by Munford, Hunton, Gay, H. Merrill Pasco and Robert Buford.—*Valentine Museum*

Main Street, April 1865, looking east from Ninth Street. The only complete building still standing was the Customs House (now the U.S. Court House Building and Post Office).—*Valentine Museum*

By 1910 Main Street was teeming with activity, although automobiles were still rare.—*Virginia State Library*

Beverley Munford's birthplace, the William Munford house, was built on the corner of Fifth and Canal streets in 1810 and torn down in 1871. — *from Robert Munford,* Richmond Homes and Memories

Tazewell Hall, boyhood home of Beverley Munford in Williamsburg, was built in the mid-eighteenth century near the present Williamsburg Lodge. It was moved in 1908 and dismantled around 1945. In 1965, the interior paneling was used in a new Tazewell Hall built in Newport News.—*Virginia State Library*

As a young man, Beverley Munford had a gift for the dramatic that brought him quick success as a politician in Pittsylvania County. On December 15, 1885, his speech in the General Assembly nominating John W. Daniel for the U.S. Senate established his reputation as one of Virginia's foremost orators.—*Valentine Museum*

Staples & Munford were not shy about advertising in the Richmond City Directories of the 1890s.—*Virginia State Library*

Beverley Munford
served three terms in
the Virginia House of
Delegates, from 1881 to
1887, representing
Pittsylvania County.
In 1891, when this
photograph was taken,
he had just been elected
to the Virginia House of
Delegates to represent
the City of Richmond.
—*Virginia State Library*

Mary Cooke Branch,
before her marriage,
November 22, 1893. Her
cool, clear-eyed idealism,
combined with a capacity
for hard work and a very
fine mind, made her a
strong force for change
in her later years as wife,
then widow, of Beverley
Munford.—*Valentine
Museum*

Claude Swanson (1862–1939), best man in Munford's wedding, served as congressman from the Fifth District of Virginia (1893–1905), governor of Virginia (1906–1910), U.S. senator (1910–1933), and Secretary of the Navy in Franklin D. Roosevelt's administration. —*Virginia State Library*

After his defeat in a discussion with Munford's strong-willed bride-to-be, Claude Swanson, future governor of Virginia, starts to write "ladies" then remembers his lesson.—*Virginia Historical Society*

Mary Munford, Beverley Munford, and their children Beverley and Mary Safford on vacation during the summer of 1899. In the upper left is Mrs. Munford's nephew, Walter Russell Bowie, who lived with the Munfords.

The Munfords' house at 503 East Grace Street, on the site of George Wythe's house, was demolished in 1934.—*Valentine Museum*

November 15th, 1909.

My dear Mr. Munford:-

At last I have been able to give myself the pleasure of reading your book. I am afraid I am very tardy in expressing my appreciation of it, but that appreciation is very genuine and very deep. I think you have done not only Virginia, but the whole country, a real service in writing it. It ought to remove many misapprehensions and throw a new light upon a very difficult and perplexing period of our history. The book is so thoroughly done, is so judicially written, and is so illuminating, that I hope it will have the widest circulation.

Cordially and sincerely yours,

Woodrow Wilson

Mr. Beverly B. Munford.

P.S. I am returning the advance sheets you were kind enough to let me see to the publishers in New York.

Future United States president Woodrow Wilson wrote to congratulate Munford on *Virginia's Attitude toward Slavery and Secession*, which had been published the month before.—*Virginia Historical Society*

The signs of the illness that ended Beverley Munford's life prematurely, in May 1910, are apparent in this photograph taken several years earlier in Bennington, Vermont.

On April 6, three days before Appomattox, at Sayler's Creek, General Hunton surrendered his brigade to General George Armstrong Custer. It was a very cold night for April and Hunton was so ill from chronic diarrhea and the fistula that had plagued him since the beginning of the war that "when I was captured, I took it for granted, if sent to prison, I would die." General Custer, hearing that he was sick, "sent his physician to me with a bottle of imported French brandy, and furnished me with a hair mattress to sleep on." [19]

It was snowing on April 7, when General Hunton and seven other Confederate generals were conducted to a log fire at General Grant's headquarters and given hot whiskey punch. From there they were taken by ambulance to City Point, where the Appomattox River meets the James, then by boat to Washington, and by train and ferries from Washington to Boston. On the ferry crossing from New Jersey to New York, Hunton saw General Benjamin F. Butler reading a newspaper and noticed that he was wearing mourning. He then learned that Lincoln had been shot the night before.[20]

Anti-Confederate feeling was running high that week, and at every depot on the last lap of their trip from New York to Boston, "an effort was made to raise a mob to hang us." One man jumped on the train, and rode sixty miles, just to jump out at each station and cry "Hang them! Hang the Rebel Generals!"

As they were approaching Boston, the officer in charge, "a first-rate man," according to General Hunton, was so apprehensive about his prisoners' safety that he telegraphed ahead to have hacks waiting to meet them. They were then "rushed into these hacks and driven at full speed to the wharf," put in a boat and whisked across the harbor to Fort Warren.[21]

The next three months General Hunton spent in prison at Fort Warren. The change of climate and particularly the change in diet from Confederate officer's rations to U.S. Army prison fare "acted very beneficially" upon his constitution. For the first time in four years, his health improved substantially, and he gained weight.

The view from the ramparts of the whole of Boston Harbor

curving around him was "the most beautiful [he had] seen in his life," General Hunton wrote to his family. Military prisoners like himself were being treated well, he assured them, and allowed to walk on the ramparts as much as they liked. Political prisoners, like former Confederate Vice-President Alexander Stephens, who was also at Fort Warren, did not fare so well, Hunton wrote. They were frequently kept in isolation, given meager rations and allowed on the ramparts only one hour a day.[22]

For almost twenty years before the war, General Hunton had practiced law, and he hoped to do so again. In preparation, he used to lie on his bed at Fort Warren and "study law without any books." Through this discipline, he managed to bring his professional knowledge back into his mind and refine it to the point that he left the prison "a better lawyer than when the war began."[23]

Meanwhile ten-year-old Eppa and his mother were in Lynchburg in "very destitute circumstances," trying to make fifty dollars they had borrowed last them until young Eppa's uncle, Silas Hunton, could come to get them and take them to an aunt's house in Culpeper County.

Years later Eppa Hunton, Jr., wrote a brief description of their three-day train trip from Lynchburg to Culpeper, Virginia, a distance of about a hundred miles. Since they were "the first after the war to attempt the trip north from Lynchburg," he hoped that his account would "show the conditions of the time, and its hardships."[24]

Silas Hunton, Eppa, and his mother, accompanied by two ex-slaves, one with infant in arms, took a train from Lynchburg as far as the Tye River, where the bridge had been destroyed. They were ferried across the river to a waiting handcar, which was partitioned across the middle to form a stall for a mule. The passengers rode in front of the stall; the baggage was loaded behind it.

A mule pulled the car on the upgrades. "When we reached a downgrade, we stopped and the mule was put into the stall in the car and we proceeded by gravity, making much better time than when the mule was pulling us."

By nightfall they reached North Garden, where the tracks became impassable again. After spending the night at a farmhouse there, they hired a farm wagon to take them into Charlottesville to a hotel.

A day later they resumed their journey in the farm wagon, fording the Rivanna River where, again, the bridge had been destroyed. On the other side was a train to take them to Culpeper Court House. The train moved slowly, stopping frequently so grass could be dug out of the tracks, until finally it could go no further. Once more they were transferred to a handcar. When it began to rain, there was no covering to protect them. They and all of their possessions were soaking wet when they finally reached Culpeper that night.

By the fall of 1865, General Hunton was back from prison, trying to start a law practice in Fauquier County. "Toward the close of the year," he wrote, "I brought my wife and son to Warrenton. I was not able to go to housekeeping, but went to room-keeping, which was then quite fashionable with the poor Confederates."

When a man from Bedford County offered him five hundred dollars in greenbacks for his faithful horse Morgan, he confessed that it was "a great temptation. . . . I told him I would give him an answer in an hour. I went to our rooms, called a council of war consisting of my wife, my son and myself. I laid the matter before them, and we voted unanimously to stand by old 'Morgan' if we starved."[25]

Soon afterwards he got a chance to defend "a very rich old man" in Loudoun, in "one of the hardest fights I ever had at the bar." John Randolph Tucker of Middleburg was the lawyer on the other side, and he and General Hunton "stood up and fought each other over every inch of the ground." In the end, Hunton won the verdict and, in Randolph Tucker, a "beloved friend" for the rest of his life.[26]

The fact that after that case he and Tucker were "on the opposite side of every important case in the county" only brought them closer together. Since neither had an office in Leesburg, when they attended court, they used to stay in the same room in a boarding-house. Eppa Jr. recalled that: "Once, when I, as a boy, rode on horseback from Warrenton to Leesburg with Father, I was put in the same room with these distinguished gentlemen. When a client desired to confer with either, the other one was asked to leave the room. Mr. Tucker was subsequently made professor of law at Washington and Lee, and was then elected to Congress, and he and my father served together, and always lived at the same boarding house in Washington."[27]

General Hunton's fee for the case that brought him and Tucker together was "a good retainer and a large contingent one." More important, his client "paid . . . every dollar," and from then on he had "all of the business he could attend to" in Fauquier, Prince William and Loudoun counties.[28]

By 1867 he was able to buy a house on Rappahannock Street in Warrenton. Young Eppa was sent first to schools in Warrenton, then to Bellevue Academy in Bedford County, and finally, in 1873, to the University of Virginia, where he studied under John B. Minor, "the George Wythe of his time."[29]

In 1877, after Eppa Jr. received his law degree from Virginia, he came back to Warrenton to practice in the firm of Hunton & Son at a salary of fifty dollars a month. By that time his father's service in Congress had virtually "ruined [his] fine practice." Young Hunton managed to keep together "a portion of it, and soon became a good and popular lawyer."[30]

From the beginning he found himself practicing alone most of the time, dealing with the wide variety of legal problems that came up in a practice that extended through three counties and included the work of trial counsel for the Richmond & Danville Railway Company.

From 1880 to 1900 the firm Hunton & Son appeared in the Virginia Supreme Court of Appeals in thirty-nine cases. Eppa Hunton, Jr., appeared alone in twenty-seven of those cases involving equity pleading and practice, common law pleading, creditors' rights, wills and the administration of trusts and estates, vendors' liens on real estate, fraud in the procurement and performance of contracts, fire insurance, partnership agreements, contracts, suretyships, domestic relations, guardian and ward, limitations of actions, taxation and eminent domain, but strangely, no criminal proceedings.[31]

In 1881, when General Hunton finished his fourth term in Congress and returned to the practice of law full-time, "there was not business enough for my son and myself in Warrenton, and [after] careful deliberation and consultation with my wife and son, I decided that he was to be the lawyer in Virginia and I would open a law office in Washington."[32]

The general still maintained his principal residence in Warrenton in the large stucco house on Main Street that he had bought from Colonel John S. Mosby, the famous "Gray Ghost" of the Confederacy, in 1877. His son was also living there with him.[33]

By 1884 Eppa Jr. felt that he was doing well enough to support a wife. In November he married Erva Winston Payne, the oldest daughter of General William H. Payne, a leader of the Warrenton bar and intimate friend of the Huntons. "This was an exceedingly agreeable marriage on both sides," General Hunton wrote. "They lived with me almost all of their married life." He then went on to describe his daughter-in-law as "one of the most brilliant women of her day . . . splendidly educated . . . [and] a talented musician." Unfortunately her health was poor, and "she scarcely saw a well month from the time she was married."[34]

Over the next thirteen years, young Hunton tried "anything that could be suggested" to restore his wife's health, taking her to all of the springs in Virginia, to a hospital in Baltimore, and to Narragansett Pier in Rhode Island, according to General Hunton:

> They went to housekeeping after living with us for ten or twelve years, and fitted up a beautiful little establishment next to General Payne's; but Erva's health became worse . . . and [she] died on October 9, 1897.[35]
>
> The largest concourse attended her funeral that had been seen in Warrenton since the war. . . . Eppa was almost heartbroken by her death, and for months could hardly be aroused. I was afraid at one time that he could not be gotten back to his professional work.[36]

At that point, Eppa Jr. broke up housekeeping and went back to live with his parents. For a while he seemed "unable to rally." Then little by little he began to recover his energy and his enthusiasm for the practice of law.

By 1899 he was strong enough to pull off a fairly remarkable feat in nineteenth-century transportation in order to see his father join the Episcopal Church: All day Saturday, his father wrote, "Eppa was engaged in the trial of two important will cases in Harrisonburg . . . but Saturday night he finished the argument of his cases, won them both, and at nine o'clock jumped into a buggy and drove to Staunton, twenty-odd miles; took the cars in Staunton at one o'clock A.M., reached Warrenton Junction about sun-rise, hired a buggy, and was home to breakfast"—in time to witness the baptism of General Hunton. Although the general's wife was very ill, she rallied enough to attend the service and was "very much gratified" by the event.[37]

On September 4, 1899, Lucy Caroline Wier Hunton died, and for the next two years the father and son, both widowers now, continued to live together in the house on Main Street in Warrenton.

Then came 1901, a year that was to initiate many happy changes in Eppa Jr.'s life. On April 24 he married Virginia Semmes Payne, the youngest sister of his first wife. In a letter of congratulation, Mrs. Jefferson Davis, who had befriended the younger Huntons and Paynes at Narragansett, wrote to the bride's parents: "I do not know a man to whom I should more willingly entrust a daughter's happiness or a girl more calculated to confer it in her turn than this same dainty, conscientious little daughter of yours."[38]

Earlier that same year, Eppa Hunton, Jr., had stood as a candidate for the Virginia Constitutional Convention from Fauquier County, and after a "very stiff fight" for the nomination, was elected by "a triumphant majority" in May.[39]

The next month he moved to Richmond—temporarily, he thought—to attend the convention, which began on June 12, 1901. It lasted until June 26, 1902, so lengthily did the one hundred delegates debate each revision of "the organic law" of the state, which they had inherited in the Underwood Constitution of 1869.

In the 1890s there was a movement throughout the South to dismantle the constitutions that the white Southerners had been forced to adopt—"at bayonet point," they used to say—in order to be readmitted to the Union. Virginia, which had been the first Southern state to adopt a Reconstruction constitution, was one of the last to get around to replacing it.

The product of the year-long effort, the now-infamous Constitution of 1901–2, disfranchised most of the blacks and many poor whites by literacy tests and poll tax laws, reducing the electorate to a very small group, less than 12 percent of the total population over twenty-one. This small group would control Virginia politics for the next six decades.[40]

The new constitution also created a model State Corporation Commission fully empowered to regulate corporations and utilities, particularly the railroads, which had been operating without effective restraint and spreading their wealth liberally in the state's elections to avoid it.

Although the members of the convention had been instructed by the General Assembly to present their constitution to the electorate for ratification, they ultimately decided to pass it by "proclamation," thus depriving the majority of black and many poor white voters of the chance to vote on their own disfranchisement. The validity of their action, unprecedented in Virginia in peacetime, was subsequently upheld in court.[41]

Yet many, if not most, members of the convention nevertheless saw themselves as reformers. By reducing the electorate, they believed they would finally put an end to the graft, bribery, and outright fraud that had characterized Virginia's elections in the last decades of the nineteenth century.

Politically, Eppa Hunton, Jr., was aligned with the Independent Democrats who opposed the tactics of Senator Tom Martin's increasingly efficient Democratic "machine." On the issue of disfranchisement, he fell in line with the majority of the members of the convention reflecting the attitudes of that particular decade, when race relations had reached their nadir and Jim Crow legislation was drafted. At one point during the campaign for election, Eppa

Hunton declared himself "in favor of disfranchising the ignorant colored people of the state, [and] of disfranchising no white man." He was promptly chastised by *The Spirit of the Valley* of Harrisonburg, Virginia, which said, "if this report of his speech is correct, it shows that Mr. Hunton's judgment has been badly warped by the unreasoning prejudice which seems to rule the hour in Virginia."[42]

Hunton's main work at that convention, however, was not in restricting the electorate, but in modernizing Virginia's judicial system, as chairman of the Courts of Justice Committee, and in helping to develop an efficient system for organizing and regulating corporations, as a member of the Corporation Committee. The chairman of the latter, A. Caperton Braxton of Staunton, made the most lasting contribution of any of the delegates at that convention, through his courageous insistence on a truly powerful Corporation Commission—which Eppa Hunton, Jr., initially thought too bold a plan but eventually supported.

The Independent Democrats controlled the Constitutional Convention and elected as president the venerable Colonel John Goode (who had served with General Hunton in the Secession Convention in 1861) over the "organization's" candidate, John Daniel. Goode then gave the most prestigious chairmanship—of the committee on the elective franchise—to Daniel and most of the other important committee assignments to Independents, like Hunton Jr.

General Hunton's long career in politics—which had ended with an interim appointment to the U.S. Senate from 1893–95—and Eppa Jr.'s own service on the Courts of Justice Committee in the General Assembly of 1893–94 helped him get two choice appointments, on the Courts of Justice and the Corporations committees.

Once appointed, he quickly established a reputation as a bold and articulate debater. Barely three months after the convention opened, Randolph Williams and Henry Anderson were eager to have him join their new law firm as senior partner with the same Beverley Munford whom Eppa Hunton, Jr., had opposed in 1896 on the free-silver issue.

The contrast between Eppa Hunton, who was progressive on the currency question but a conservative on social issues, and Beverley Munford, who seems to have been the direct opposite, provides a precedent for diversity of opinion at the very outset of the law firm.

Yet to modern eyes, those differences seem dwarfed by what the two senior partners had in common: a firsthand knowledge of the most tragic era of Virginia's history, a fierce loyalty to their state expressed in public service, and superior skills combined with tact and courtesy in the practice of law. In the years to come, the latter combination of qualities in Eppa Hunton, Jr., would win the confidence—and ultimately the business—of many Northern capitalists organizing corporations under Virginia's new corporation code or investing in its infant industries.

In 1901 Eppa Hunton's thirty-year-old junior partners-to-be, Williams and Anderson, must have been a little surprised when their white-haired, forty-six-year-old senior said he could not give them an answer until he had talked to his father. At that point, they would not have known that his life and the general's were "interwoven . . . more closely than is usual with father and son."[43]

On September 29, 1901, having secured his father's promise to move with him to Richmond, Eppa Jr. met with his future partners, Munford, Williams, and Anderson, in Washington, D.C., and one week later, the Richmond newspapers announced the formation of the new law firm, effective November 1, 1901.[44]

On the first official day of the firm's existence and the following day, Hunton is listed as "busy on brief in *Rowe vs. Dresgill*, Court of Appeals," a case that the firm had inherited from Munford & Anderson involving oyster rights in King and Queen County. Although he still had eight more months to serve in the Constitutional Convention, and later in the month would have to defend the proposed changes in the state court system before the whole convention, Eppa Hunton, Jr., had already decided to put the practice of law ahead of any career in politics he may at one time have considered.

He had made this fact clear to his father when they were discussing Randolph Williams's and Anderson's proposal:

47

"Have you given up all idea of politics?" his father had asked.

"Yes, absolutely."

"Then," said the old general, "you may form a law partnership in Richmond; but if you mean to go into politics, Warrenton is a better place for you than Richmond."[45]

In 1901, since four-fifths of the people of Virginia still lived in the country, city lawyers did not go very far in statewide elections. Beverley Munford, who had delivered minority reports in the last two Democratic state conventions, could have told him that.

In 1904 General Hunton concluded his autobiography with the report that

> Eppa's firm is doing a splendid business in Richmond and sur-rounding country. The partnership has proven even more bril-liant than was anticipated. The firm gets as much business as its members can attend to and the income is large and satisfactory —Eppa stands so very high both as a lawyer and gentleman. No one in Richmond stands higher. The move to Richmond was very judicious.

Then he adds a lament that would be echoed in the families of the law firm through the years: "I fear he has more work than he can stand and that his health will fail."[46]

On July 31, 1904, a son was born to Virginia Semmes Hunton and Eppa Hunton, Jr., who was then forty-nine. The baby was named Eppa Hunton IV, since the name Eppa had also belonged to General Hunton's father, and the eighty-three-year-old general slipped an extra page into the back of his autobiography wishing his grandson well:

> I hope he will grow to be a good and great man and reflect credit on the name he bears . . . always love and defend the Con-federate cause for which his grandfathers fought and bled . . . avoid the use of profane language, gambling and intemperate use of intoxicants, and be in all respects as good a man as his father is.

Four years later, on October 11, 1908, General Hunton died. The grandson, Eppa IV, grew up to be a lawyer, too, joined the firm his father had founded, and served for many years as its principal source of continuity and conviviality. He was host to the firm's fiftieth and seventy-fifth anniversary celebrations and, with Thomas Benjamin Gay, custodian of its history until his death in 1976.

After the general's death, Eppa Jr. continued to secure and build the reputation of the firm of Munford, Hunton, Williams & Anderson as its only active senior partner. Conspicuous at the Richmond bar with his snow-white hair, black eyebrows and mustache, handsome features, and regal bearing, Eppa Hunton had clearly become a leader in his adopted city.

In 1905 he had been appointed counsel to the receivers of the Virginia Passenger and Power Company.[47] Three years earlier, when John L. Williams & Sons ran into financial problems, they had sold their interests in local street railway and power companies to their competitor, George Fisher, who controlled Virginia Passenger and Power Company.[48] By the end of 1902, Fisher was in financial trouble himself, so he approached Frank Gould and his sister Helen, children and heirs of the legendary nineteenth-century financier, Jay Gould, and persuaded them to take over control of the companies and refinance them. Before a year had passed, however, George Fisher became antagonistic to the Goulds' management and began to bring suits against them all over the state.

At this point the law firm was retained by the Goulds, and the ledgers of Munford, Hunton, Williams & Anderson from 1904 to 1909 record many hours spent by each of its partners, and substantial fees collected, on matters related to the titanic struggle between Fisher and the Goulds.

After five years of legal warfare, the Goulds finally prevailed. In 1909 they merged the old Virginia Passenger and Power Company and other electric utility companies into the Virginia Railway and Power Company. Henry Anderson was named its general counsel and served in that capacity until 1917, when he went on a Red Cross mission to Rumania and was replaced by Randolph Williams.

Meanwhile Eppa Hunton was developing new business in other areas. In 1910 he became a director of the National Bank of Virginia, then after a merger in 1912, a director of the First National Bank of Virginia. When the latter bank merged with the Merchants Bank in 1925, he was appointed to the new First & Merchants Board and served until his death in 1932.[49]

Richmond's business leaders were ecstatic when the city was selected to be the Federal Reserve Center for the Fifth District. Eppa Hunton, Jr., had been among the Richmond leaders who had lobbied for the choice. In the winter of 1914–15, the banks of Baltimore challenged the choice of Richmond. At a hearing before the Federal Reserve Board in Washington, D.C., Eppa Hunton, Jr., and Legh R. Page successfully defended the choice of Richmond against a "mass of statistics and a flood of oratory."[50]

One year earlier, in 1914, Eppa Hunton had brought a new railroad client to the firm, when he was named general counsel to the Richmond, Fredericksburg and Potomac Railroad, to succeed A. Caperton Braxton. During World War I, when the federal government took over operation of the railroads, Hunton served as counsel to the director general.

Then there was the Freeport Texas Company on whose board Hunton served from April 28, 1920, until April 7, 1930. According to Thomas Benjamin Gay, who had been taken into the firm as its first new partner in 1916, "one of Mr. Hunton's few speculative investments" grew out of a personal loan of five thousand dollars to his Fauquier County friend, Frank R. Pemberton of the New York investment firm Pemberton & McAdoo. The loan, which enabled Pemberton to take up an option on rights to mine sulphur near Freeport, Texas, was converted into stock in the Freeport Texas Company. As a result of wartime purchases of sulphur, the stock became so valuable that in 1920 Hunton felt he could afford to retire from the practice of law and accept the presidency of the RF & P.[51]

During his nineteen years at the law firm, Eppa Hunton, Jr., worked almost as many hours for the community as he did for his clients. He was especially devoted to the Confederate Memorial Institute, the University of Virginia, and the Medical College of Virginia.

There was probably no man Eppa Hunton, Jr.'s age who had stronger ties to the Confederacy. Both his father and his father-in-law were Confederate generals and, since he had spent a winter with his father's brigade, he almost qualified as a veteran himself. The loyalty those ties inspired was expressed in his many efforts to help the few remaining Confederate veterans and honor them through institutions like the Confederate Memorial Association, of which he was president, and its Battle Abbey.[52]

In the archives of the Virginia Historical Society, there is a particularly interesting series of letters from 1910 in which Eppa Hunton, Jr., tries to prevent the irascible old ex-Confederate Colonel John S. Mosby from being fired from the Justice Department job he had received in return for his support of the Republican party. To do so, Hunton had to negotiate his way through a political minefield. First, he wrote to the Republican attorney general, George Wickersham, his partner Henry Anderson's friend, on June 6, 1910: "May I avail myself of my slight acquaintance to write you in behalf of Colonel John S. Mosby?" Then he tried to establish Mosby's credentials as "a loyal and earnest Republican" during Reconstruction. "When a boy, I lived in the same town with Colonel Mosby," he went on to say. "My earliest political recollections are of his active support of General Grant in the Grant-Greeley Campaign."

Wickersham replied that because Colonel Mosby was seventy-eight years old and no longer productive, he would have to let him go, despite the "sentiments" expressed in Hunton's letter. Various friends from Fauquier County then wrote to Hunton, pointing out that the colonel had no other means of support and asking him to persuade one of Virginia's senators to take up Colonel Mosby's cause. At the time, the only senator with whom Eppa Hunton, Jr., had close ties, John W. Daniel, had just had a stroke. So there was no alternative but to appeal to Tom Martin, whom Hunton disliked. He had opposed Martin since 1893, when, in Hunton's opinion, Martin had maneuvered his way into a U.S. Senate seat at the expense of Fitzhugh Lee. In the end, ironically, after Hunton had humbled himself and appealed to Martin and Martin had agreed to help, Colonel Mosby was "too proud" to stop by Martin's office to confer on strategy.[53]

In honoring Virginia's past through his work for Battle Abbey, Eppa Hunton, Jr., managed to enrich its future with the nucleus of the Virginia Museum of Fine Arts' collection. In 1916 he began to correspond with John Barton Payne, one of his wife's relatives who was then a lawyer in Chicago and wanted to leave his paintings to the state of Virginia if a proper home could be found for them.[54]

Hunton persuaded the directors of Battle Abbey to hang them there temporarily, and the gift was accepted by the governor in 1920. The paintings were then sent by rail to Battle Abbey, but were sidetracked on the way during a railroad strike, and for a while Payne was fearful that the works of art had "fallen among thieves."

Although Hunton's service to the future Museum of Fine Arts was an isolated occurrence, his service to education was a continuing commitment. In the early 1900s he was a strong supporter of the Progressive movement for reforms in education and attended a meeting organized by Mary Munford to plan the "May Campaign of 1905."[55] Governor Montague appointed him to the Board of Visitors of the University of Virginia and during his term of service, 1903–7, the board hired Edwin Alderman as the university's first president.[56] In December 1908 Hunton was elected to the Alumni Board of Trustees of the University of Virginia Endowment Fund and served on it until his death. For many years, as treasurer of that board, he raised money from alumni all over the state to support President Alderman's programs.

His closeness to the alumni and their desire to preserve the university as they had always known it brought him into a head-on collision with his late partner's wife, Mary Munford, when she was trying to persuade the legislature to establish a coordinate college for women at the University of Virginia. The struggle began in the fall of 1910 and gathered momentum through the 1912, 1914, and 1916 sessions. At one point, on February 4, 1914, the Richmond *Virginian*[57] ran a headline on the "pretty fight" between Eppa Hunton, Jr., and Mary Munford as spokesmen of opposing forces at a hearing in the Senate chambers. Despite Hunton's oratorical skills, the newspapers reported that Mrs. Munford won that particular battle. In the end, however, she lost the war—by just two votes in 1916—and women were not admitted as undergraduates to the University of Virginia until 1970, more than fifty years later.[58]

In the heat of the Coordinate College fight, Eppa Hunton also had to contend with Mrs. Norman Randolph, the president of the United Daughters of the Confederacy, who was as formidable in physique as she was in social influence.[59] Mrs. Munford's nephew and biographer, Walter Russell Bowie, describes a memorable contest in which:

> Mrs. 'Normous Randolph (to use the children's name) launched forth. She had been a childhood playmate and lifelong friend of Mr. Eppa Hunton . . . who had a son who was about the age of Mrs. Randolph's grandchildren. In a speech preceding Mrs. Randolph's arising, Mr. Hunton had pictured graphically the demoralization which he believed would come to the University of Virginia by the admission of women students to any connection there. He had pleaded his own love for the University, and his supreme ambition that his only son should go there, and declared that if the Coordinate College bill were passed his dearest hope would be destroyed, because he could never be willing to send his son to the University of Virginia then. Mrs. Randolph took indignant note of this, and when she had finished the main part of her speech to her satisfaction, she turned toward Mr. Hunton in a mood in which were mingled her old-time intimacy and the immediate fire of her ruffled spirit. "Eppie Hunton," she said, "you stood here a

few moments ago and said that if girls went to the University of Virginia it would spoil the University, and that your little son, your darling son, could never go there. The girls of Virginia have just as much right to go to the University as the boys have; and don't you dare stand there, Eppie Hunton, and tell me that the University would not be fit for your son to go to if my grand-daughters should go there." The galleries rocked with delighted amusement, and Mr. Hunton, who turned very pale, neverthe-less remembered to make Mrs. Randolph a profound, though very formal bow.[60]

Eppa Hunton's service to the Medical College of Virginia was probably even more important than his service to the University of Virginia. During the stormy sessions that preceded the merger of Dr. Stuart McGuire's University College of Medicine with Dr. George Ben Johnston's Medical College of Virginia in 1913, Eppa Hunton served as counsel to Dr. Johnston. Yet when the merger was about to be completed, and a new Board of Visitors created with nine members from each faction, Dr. McGuire suggested that a special nineteenth place be created for Eppa Hunton, Jr., his rival's counsel. Hunton always regarded it as one of the supreme compliments of his life.[61] In March 1925 he became chairman of that board and after his death, the Medical College commissioned a portrait of him, which hangs there still.

Hunton also served on the board of the Church Schools of the Episcopal Diocese of Virginia and was president of the local board of St. Christopher's School, after he had left the law firm.

In a letter to a friend on March 1, 1920, Hunton confessed that he had been recently "overwhelmed in an effort to merge the Washington-Southern Railway Company [the link from Quantico, Virginia, to Washington, D.C.] into the Richmond, Fredericksburg and Potomac Railroad" and that the merger had been completed the preceding Thursday.[62]

A few months later he was elected president of the merged rail-roads, to succeed William White. There was some controversy surrounding the selection. The Richmond *Times-Dispatch* at one time favored another candidate, while the *News Leader* refused to take sides between the two Richmond candidates: Norman Call, an executive who had risen in the ranks of the railroad, and Hunton, who was said to be White's choice as his successor.

On September 15, 1920, there is a break in the ledger to indicate Hunton's retirement from the law firm. On September 16 he became president of the RF & P and also the Richmond Terminal Company, which had just completed the sumptuous Broad Street Station, designed by architect John Russell Pope in the Roman Revival style.[63]

Why did Eppa Hunton, Jr., at the age of sixty-six, leave the law firm he had founded for a new career as a railroad executive? A later partner in the law firm speculated that accepting the presidency of a hundred-mile-long railroad, which was actually controlled by six other railroads, may have been a glamorous way of escaping "molestation by clients," as well as the pressures of a law firm expanding to meet the demands of the post–World War I "boom."[64]

At any rate, Hunton made the most of his new position, ruling the hundred-mile railroad from his offices in the Broad Street Station. His special combination of intellectual skill with a forceful but charming personality served him as well in his final career as it had served him at the bar, and he was popular among the railroad executives.[65]

Although Hunton began to show signs of heart disease in 1931, he continued to serve as president of the RF & P and to devote many hours to community endeavors, including the Richmond Civic Musical Association, of which he had just been elected president. Then on March 5, 1932, after only a few days of illness, he died from a heart attack.

Two days later, Douglas Southall Freeman introduced a grandiloquent editorial on Eppa Hunton, Jr., in the Richmond *News Leader*, with a quotation from 2 Samuel 3:38, "Know ye not that there is a prince and a great man fallen this day in Israel?" Then he went on to describe the qualities that Eppa Hunton had brought to his adopted city and his profession:

> Courage and duty stood first, but their possession never implied or suggested any lessening in that sense of obligation to oneself, to one's associates and to one's state and nation that gave a peculiar dignity and charm to the old Virginia Gentleman.
>
> Those characteristics were signalized in the life of Mr. Hunton. Wherever he went he was conspicuous for his innate courtesy and consideration. Nor was this a mere expression of an easygoing desire to avoid conflict. On the contrary, at the bar, on the hustings, in the constitutional convention, in the discharge of public duty, or in the daily tests of personal integrity, no one was more firm or unyielding. But as was to be seen by all who were thrown with him, Mr. Hunton's instinctive attitude towards his fellow-man in every walk of life was to be courteous and kindly. It was this rare combination of ability and charm that conferred on Mr. Hunton the unique and distinguished position that he held. And it also serves to emphasize for others the thought that no limits can be set to the achievements of one who, in addition to being a generous gentleman, also possesses moral courage and intellectual power. . . .
>
> The spirit of Eppa Hunton was so indigenously Virginian that there was neither pose nor provincialism in the familiar story of his reception by King George when the American Bar Association met in London [in 1924]. His Majesty was attracted by the fine, aristocratic face of Mr. Hunton and by his perfect poise; and when he heard the name he inquired, "Where are you from, Mr. Hunton?" To which, with a smile, Mr. Hunton immediately replied, "Fauquier, sir—upper end."[66]

All of the trains on the RF & P's tracks were stopped for a full minute at four o'clock on March 7, when Eppa Hunton, Jr.'s funeral service began. The active pallbearers were evenly divided —as Hunton's loyalties must have been—between the railroad and the law firm, which was represented by three new partners, Wirt Marks, Jr., Irvin Craig, and Edmund Preston.

In 1927 the law firm had changed its name to Hunton, Williams, Anderson & Gay, dropping Beverley Munford's name to honor Thomas Benjamin Gay, but still carrying into the future the names of three of the original senior partners and the old Virginia style that they brought to the practice of law.

FOUR

Edmund Randolph Williams

1871–1952

In September 1920, when Eppa Hunton, Jr., retired from the law firm, Randolph Williams became the firm's senior partner. His colleague Henry Anderson was not suited by temperament to serve as the firm's father figure. Moreover, Anderson was heavily involved in politics at the time, and he would run for governor, on the Republican ticket, the following summer.

Henry Anderson was, in fact, one of the problems Randolph Williams inherited. How should the firm deal with this brilliant, difficult man who had risen like a meteor in utility and railroad law, and then, at the peak of his career, abandoned it for a Red Cross mission to Rumania? Now he was about to abandon it again for a hopeless political campaign, because he said it was time for Virginia to wake up to the modern world. If he could resurrect the two-party system and inject some honest debate into the state's politics, he might at least start the process of reform.

Anderson's priorities had changed radically in the past five years. But he was still the law firm's greatest asset. When he chose to concentrate his energies on the law, he was, in his way, almost a genius. And despite fundamental differences in personality and style, Randolph Williams was very fond of Henry Anderson. Their friendship was the rock on which that law firm had been founded twenty years earlier, and the firm's future depended on keeping Henry Anderson interested in it.

The third and youngest partner, Thomas Benjamin Gay, would

be a great help, of course. He was bright and blessed with an almost inexhaustible store of energy. It was remarkable, in fact, that so much drive could be contained in that diminutive body, which he dressed impeccably and carried with high-chested pride, like a bantam rooster.

Gay had an excessively formal manner. It may have been a result of shyness, but a more relaxed manner would have eased his relationships with younger lawyers in the firm—the new man, Whiting Faulkner, and Henry Anderson's cousin Wirt Marks, who could be as difficult as he was intelligent.

Keeping the peace among the bright, ambitious, and basically contentious men who make up a law firm is never easy. But if any man had the temperament and the training to do so, it was Edmund Randolph Williams.

He had been born into a family of bright, ambitious, and frequently contentious brothers. Almost unconsciously, he had spent a large part of his early life smoothing the rough edges of their personalities, making contact between them less abrasive than it would have been if he had not been there. This was a natural gift in Edmund Randolph Williams for which his family, his law firm, and nearly everyone who met him was supremely grateful.

On May 1, 1871, one year after Virginia came out of Reconstruction, Randolph Williams was born at 609 East Leigh Street in Richmond. From his mother, Maria Ward Skelton Williams, a great-granddaughter of Washington's first attorney general, Edmund Randolph, he got his name and many of his Old Virginia values.[1] From his father, John L. Williams, he inherited his love of literature and a vein of iron that ran so deep beneath his gentle manner that only those closest to him could detect it.

Randolph's father was a complex man who tempered his ambition in the business world with a love of the classics, Shakespeare, and the Bible—and a deep religious faith. Originally he had planned to be a lawyer and actually practiced briefly, but he found "the work of this profession was not congenial to him." In the mid-1850s, he joined the Richmond banking house of John A. Lancaster & Sons and settled into his life's work.[2]

During the Civil War, the Lancaster firm—and consequently John L. Williams—served as fiscal agents for the Confederate government, a challenging, but ultimately hopeless task. After the war, John L. Williams began to build his career again, but suffered a severe reverse in the early 1870s.

Almost twenty years later, when Randolph was at the University of Virginia, his mother wrote him a letter that she asked him to keep "as a testimonial—in part—of some of the blessings of adversity." In it she described how during Randolph's early childhood, his father, "through no fault of his own," had been called upon to pay off large financial obligations and had to give up "everything he owned except the necessary household furniture and family responsibilities":

> With a wife and six children he began life again—with no capital except his character & experience—and an abiding faith in God's promises. There were years of struggle before us. . . . While he could not give us the indulgences which the world calls pleasures and even necessaries—your father gave us freely his dear companionship—strengthening [his] growing ones by his example—charming us with his conversation and filling every evening with all manner of innocent fun for you children—with games and stories.
>
> And when the lack of business at the office added to my work at home, he was always ready to aid me. . . . Don't you remember how he would tumble two or three of you little boys into the bath tub and rub you down while I dressed the baby for our early morning ride—in the street cars! Ennion every morning because he was [the] baby and you other six alternate days, three at a time. I wonder if you remember those rides—I never enjoyed any in my life more than those! . . .
>
> Three more babies came during those times. I won't call them "Hard Times"—and when Miss Mary Harrison grumbled about it, I told her the Baby was the only luxury we indulged in.
>
> I tell you all of this my darling boy that you may know your Father's character under circumstances you were too young to

appreciate and that you may see how independent of worldly riches and pleasures is the Home wherein dwell the righteous.[3]

To modern ears, Maria Williams's letter may sound a bit sententious, but it reveals a set of values in which the family was all-important. Those same values would be echoed in the life of the Williamses' third son, Randolph, who would extend the definition of "family" to the members of his law firm, and, in a way, to his whole community.

It was 1874 when John L. Williams started his own firm. Though its early years were lean ones, by the end of the century it had emerged as the leading investment-banking firm in Richmond, and possibly the Upper South. Four of John L. Williams's sons— John Skelton, Lancaster, Langbourne, and Berkeley—joined the family firm, whose name was changed to John L. Williams & Sons.[4] According to one family legend, the sons begged their father to install a modern chalkboard, like the one across the street at Thomas Branch & Sons or down on the next square, at Scott & Stringfellow—to help their customers keep track of stock quotations—but the father resisted it for years on the grounds that it "encouraged gambling."

As the firm began to prosper beyond his expectations, John L. Williams began to worry about the state of his sons' souls. Another family legend has him offering a prayer one Sunday morning in the early 1900s, asking the Lord to save his children from being corrupted by too rich a share of this world's goods. The next morning at his office he discovered that his prayer had been answered through the machinations of J. P. Morgan's agent, Thomas Fortune Ryan, which had brought the firm and the Seaboard Air Line Railway to the brink of bankruptcy.[5] Whether these stories are literally true or not, they testify to the ambivalence with which the Williamses viewed the wealth they were accumulating in the final years of the Gilded Age.

As his six sons and three daughters were growing up, John L. Williams filled their ears with moral precepts and wrote them page after pious page of fatherly advice. In August 1888, when Randolph and his younger brother Ennion went off to the University of Virginia to live away from home for the first time in their lives, their father wrote: "Be careful & watchful. Be sure that what you are going to say will be agreeable. Don't let them take trouble about you. Don't be helped to things that are scarce and constantly give place to others—take the seat that nobody wants."

Such advice may help explain the modest, almost deferential manner Randolph Williams developed, which sometimes disarmed rivals who did not take the time to assess the solid skills that lay beneath it.[6]

Once when he seems to have come perilously close to getting in a fight, his father gave him a tutorial in manners: "You can't undertake to teach people manners. Bad manners are the only kind some people have. And the high mission of a gentleman is not to be offended at such, but to show the extremest patience and propriety in their presence. Let your amiability, self control and good manners do the business. Contrast is very powerful."[7]

Forty years earlier John L. Williams had had great success at the same university, winning a degree of Master of Arts—the highest offered then. As his middle sons prepared for their examinations —Randolph, in the School of Law, and Ennion, in the School of Medicine—he wrote to Randolph: "I am especially anxious . . . both for you & dear Enn, that you will keep up a constant review, running back over all that you [have] done to the very first principles & beginnings of things and cultivating a familiarity with the most important elements, truths & facts. You are master only of what you are familiar with and have perfectly & thoroughly digested."[8]

He reminded Randolph in February 1893:

Your diploma will be of little importance except as an evidence that you have mastered the course. But in this the great matter is that the principles shall be imbedded and incorporated in your very soul. If they are true they should become a part of your being, the light of your professional life—not the tricks of your trade. The methods of the law themselves rest upon everlasting wisdom. In this way honouring your profession, it will honour you.

But study what is the meaning of temperance: self-government, self-control: that you may not be mastered or overloaded with the learning of the law, but control the law through familiarity with its governing principles.[9]

Randolph's mother's love was expressed in simpler terms. She worried constantly that he would work too hard and wreck his health: "I wish you would give up this examination, Darling Boy. You are not equal now to the strain of study, or examination. And the honor, of course, would not be worth the vital loss which might result. . . . Dr. Dabney will not tell you to leave. The professors never do this—for the sake of the University—It has already such a bad reputation for unhealthiness." [10]

Despite his mother's fears, Randolph Williams managed to survive his examinations and received his law degree in June of 1893. By the end of the summer he was in Northport, Long Island, working on the editorial staff of the Edward Thompson Publishing Company, which was producing *The American and English Encyclopedia of Law.*

The Panic of 1893 wreaked havoc in the firm of John L. Williams & Sons. In a letter that September, Randolph's mother described the cake at his younger brother Langbourne's twenty-first birthday party. It was decorated with roses and twenty-one geranium leaves each holding a bright penny. "We promise to redeem the coppers with gold dollars," she explained, "when times get easier." [11]

It would be a while before those coppers were redeemed. The country had plunged into a major depression, and the John L. Williams firm, like many others, was in trouble. Though Randolph was in no position to help them, at least he was self-sufficient, making nine hundred dollars a year, just enough, he said, to sustain him in New York.

In January, he wrote from Northport to his father: "Are not the clouds lifting a little bit and have not things begun to look brighter? Difficulties must sooner or later [give way] before the stout hearts and willing hands that man the family ship. Would that I could be a more efficient member of the crew—than at present I can be. I begin to think it unfortunate that I declared for the law in [that] when called upon I am wanting and see no betterment for some time to come."[12]

It was mainly John, the oldest son, working day and night on his imaginative schemes for Southern industry, who managed to bring the family ship safely into harbor, laden with unprecedented treasure.

John Skelton Williams was almost six years older than Randolph. Born in July 1865, three months after Appomattox, he was old enough to remember the hard times that his family and, in fact, his whole society had suffered in the 1870s. As a consequence, perhaps, he was driven by a fierce determination to draw Northern capital into the South and keep it there.

At the age of fifteen he went to work in his father's firm and within four years was putting together and publishing on behalf of John L. Williams & Son, an annual *Manual of Investments, Important Facts and Figures Regarding Southern Investment Securities.* "Our manual," according to the 1890 edition, "was the first publication of the sort issued in the South, and has now, we believe, the honor of being the largest work of its kind published by any banking house in the United States. It is fast getting to be regarded as *the* standard reference book on Southern Securities."[13]

After John Skelton Williams died in 1926, Douglas Southall Freeman painted a romantic picture of him:

> a tall, thin boy [sitting] on a high stool in a basement office on Main Street and patiently [making] his way through hundreds of financial reports issued by Southern corporations. It was tedious work, and complicated, too, for some of the reports were deceptive, and all were made according to the whim or distinctive accounting system of the railroad or manufacturer. But that lank boy seldom left his desk in daylight hours, and at night he came back to it and stayed till Main Street was silent and he could hear the police signal to one another from Seventh Street to the

Old Market, by beating on the pavement with their nightsticks. Little he heeded them or any sound that came into the office, for he had caught a vision among the trim-set tabular columns of those reports, and he pursued it through documents from many states. It was a vision of a South free from the ancestral threat of civil strife, bright with the promise of achievement, overcoming already the prostration of after-war days, and offering to every man who had an honest dollar an honest opportunity of increasing it. When the day's quest ended, that fine-browed boy would slip out of the office and run all the way home, for that was the only exercise he allowed himself.[14]

Freeman then went on to describe the celebration on July 2, 1901, when the first train of the Seaboard Air Line arrived in Richmond from Tampa, Florida. After the howitzers fired a twenty-one-gun salute, John Skelton Williams, the organizer and now the president of the new railroad, emerged from the car filled with dignitaries to watch his three-year-old son drive a golden spike into the last tie, as a symbol of completion of the road.

The final scene of Freeman's sketch is set in 1914 as a group of Richmond businessmen receive a long distance call from John Skelton Williams, now the comptroller of the currency in Wilson's administration, informing them that Richmond had been chosen as the site for a Federal Reserve bank.[15]

Early in the 1890s John was already gaining recognition for his bold schemes to revitalize Southern industries and his thoroughness in investigating their potential for investment. The letters Randolph received from his parents while he was in Northport are peppered with references to "Johnny's" successes—the acceptance "in every detail" of his railroad reorganization plan and finally, the groundswell of interest by Wall Street financiers in his Seaboard scheme.

In April 1894 Randolph rode the train in from Long Island to meet with John on one of his increasingly frequent business trips to New York, but his older brother gave him only a few minutes of his time. Their father tried to soothe Randolph's wounded spirit by explaining that John was "very excusable for his brief interview with you. The business he was on was most important and may be of big consequence to us." [16]

That fact was probably small comfort to Randolph, as he wandered from one Wall Street law firm to another looking for a job. At the offices of a Mr. Robinson, a friend of his father whom Randolph perceived as "a great swell and a leader at the bar here," he found a chance to work "as a student without pay for some time to come," but felt that he could not afford it. What he wanted was "a paying job" with a good New York law firm, but those were hard to come by in 1894.

Well, what did you expect, his father wrote, "to find a committee of reception awaiting you? . . . Pluck, trust in the good Lord who has been so loving and merciful to us all through life—is your policy . . . too easy success never was good for any man." [17]

He had received a raise to a thousand dollars a year in Northport, so the job on the encyclopedia was "not without its advantages," in the short run, anyway. He was storing up facts about the law and improving his writing, and occasionally he was allowed to sign his name to an article he had drafted. His superiors, however, claimed his best ones for themselves, including one on taxation of which he was particularly proud.[18]

Still, he must have been getting tired of sitting at a long table all day, poring over books, preparing drafts, correcting proof. Though ceiling fans had been installed to give him and his fellow workers some relief when the temperatures got up into the nineties in the summer, there was no stove close enough to protect them from the bone-chilling drafts that came with the winter.

The scholar's life was not for Randolph Williams. "I have decided," he wrote home in April 1894, "the sooner I can get into the active world the better." [19] His father, as always, counseled patience. "Why in the world can't young men have a little sense?" Then he softened and assured him that "John has you in mind and is looking for a foothold for you in Baltimore."

Apparently John was successful, because in the spring of 1895 Randolph moved to Baltimore and entered into a brief partnership with Thomas J. Michie. By the end of that year, the enterprises of John L. Williams & Sons had expanded to the point that they could virtually guarantee Randolph a continuing source of legal business. And so, early in 1896, Randolph returned to Richmond to begin a practice that would last for fifty-six years.

Initially he went into partnership with the venerable William Wirt Henry, the grandson and biographer of Patrick Henry, with whom Randolph had studied, off and on, while he was in law school. The association seems to have offered more prestige than clients at that late point in Henry's career.[20] But there was more than enough business coming from Randolph's own connection with the John L. Williams firm.

In 1896 Randolph Williams was appointed counsel and president of the Richmond Traction Company. With Williams financing, the company had built electric streetcar lines along Broad Street from Thirty-fourth Street west to Robinson, then south on Robinson to Reservoir Park and the carbarns at Robinson and Cary.[21]

Since 1888 the City of Richmond had been a leader in the development of electric street railway systems. That fact delighted Randolph's mother, who now wrote that she enjoyed "electric rides, flying through the fields" as she had once enjoyed early morning rides with her young family on the old horse-drawn streetcars.

By the early 1900s "the Williams interests" controlled three local companies: the Richmond Traction Company, the Virginia Electric Railway and Development Company (which had built an innovative hydroelectric power station on Twelfth Street), and the Westhampton Park Company. They had bitter controversies with "the Fisher interests," which controlled most of the other local streetcar companies, including the Richmond Passenger and Power Company with its highly desirable franchise on Main Street.[22]

Randolph Williams frequently appeared in court and before the city council on "street car matters" before the rival lines were finally merged into the Virginia Passenger and Power Company in 1904 and then reorganized in 1909 into the Virginia Railway and Power Company.[23] He also represented various small railroads that were merged eventually into the Seaboard system, including the Richmond, Petersburg & Carolina Railroad, in which he was associated with his Main Street neighbor Beverley Munford and Munford's younger partner, Henry Anderson.

On November 22, 1900, Randolph Williams married Maude Lathrop Stokes. Their evening wedding was described by the *Evening Journal* as "one of the most beautiful marriages that has ever taken place in Richmond." The best man was Randolph's brother Ennion, who by this time had become a pioneer in the use of the X ray and soon would be Virginia's first state health commissioner. One of the ushers was Randolph's new friend, Henry Anderson.[24]

Maude Stokes Williams was by no means as soft-spoken and tolerant of human frailty as her husband was, and Richmonders still love to quote her sharp, witty remarks. In the curious way that married couples have of using their partners' personalities as compensation, Randolph Williams may have relied on his wife to provide some spice in his life and to vent, perhaps, some less-than-positive thoughts about the people around him that he himself was much too kind to express.

After the wedding reception the young couple left by railroad, in a private car, for their wedding trip to Hot Springs. But Randolph was called back on December 5 to the deathbed of his senior partner, William Wirt Henry.[25]

As the year 1901 dawned, marking the official beginning of the twentieth century, Randolph was practicing alone, still in the State Bank building at 1111 East Main Street, with more business coming in from his brothers' enterprises than he could possibly attend to on his own.

It was at some point during that winter or spring of 1901 that he and Henry Anderson, whose senior partner, Munford, was now gravely ill, began the plans that resulted in the founding of Munford, Hunton, Williams & Anderson the following November.

The ledgers for the first two years (November 1901 to October

1903) show that the three active partners were extremely busy and were distributing the work load as evenly as possible.

In addition to his work for the Seaboard, the street railways, and the Old Dominion Iron and Nail Company, Williams represented two local newspapers, the *Dispatch* and the *News*, which the Williamses operated in competition with Joseph Bryan's *Times* and *Evening Leader* until January 24, 1903. On that day they signed a contract merging the two morning papers into the *Times-Dispatch*, to be controlled by the Bryans, and the evening papers into the *News-Leader*, controlled by the Williamses until they sold it to the Bryans in 1909.

On July 15, 1902, the Williamses' first child, Edmund Randolph Williams, Jr., died, and the next month Randolph Williams took his wife to England.[26] On the eve of his departure he wrote home from New York: "I already feel how glad I shall be to turn homewards."[27] Nevertheless, homebody that he was, he enjoyed his first trip abroad and the chance it gave him to recover, at least partially, from his grief over the baby's death and from the strenuous effort that had resulted in the sale of the "Williams interests" in the local streetcar and power companies to the rival "Fisher interests" in June of 1902.

It was fortunate that he was able to build up his strength, because as soon as he returned he had to deal with serious financial problems in the family business.

During the past few years John L. Williams & Sons had become overextended. When the Southern securities market collapsed in 1903, they found themselves perilously close to bankruptcy. The law firm's ledgers from 1902 to 1909 are filled with evidence of efforts by all four lawyers in the firm, including Munford, to help the Williamses resolve their financial problems. They accomplished this by appealing for more time from their creditors, selling the streetcar and the hydroelectric power companies to the Fisher interests, and then refinancing and finally surrendering control of the Seaboard Railway to John Skelton Williams's enemy, Thomas Fortune Ryan.

Ironically, the new management of both lost businesses ran into problems, too, and by the end of the decade, the firm's lawyers found themselves representing Frank and Helen Gould, who bought control of the Virginia Passenger and Power Company from Fisher in December 1902, and the Seaboard Railway, which went into receivership in 1908. Randolph Williams's brother, R. Lancaster Williams, was appointed as one of the receivers, and his oldest brother, John Skelton Williams, was the president.[28]

The decade from 1901 to 1911 was a tempestuous one in which the law firm did not grow much (it actually shrank with the death of Munford in 1910), but it certainly prospered. Of the four associates who came to work at the firm at various times during its first fifteen years—Lewis Williams, Randolph's brother-in-law; John Randolph Tucker, grandson and namesake of General Hunton's friend and fellow boarder; Thomas Benjamin Gay; and Andrew Christian—only Gay stayed long enough to be made a partner. The others left and founded other major Richmond law firms.[29]

In its early days, Munford, Hunton, Williams & Anderson was more like a nuclear family than a corporate family. And the Randolph Williamses' house at 826 West Franklin Street was its hearth. In the evenings, the Huntons frequently walked up from their house down the street, at 810 West Franklin. Henry Anderson, the only partner who worked regularly late into the night, often came for Sunday dinner, or sent his butler down from 913 West Franklin to borrow silver if he was entertaining a large crowd.

In 1916, the year that Thomas B. Gay became the first new partner, he was also married, and he brought his bride to live in the Chesterfield Apartments, on the northwest corner of Franklin and Shafer streets, just across the street from the Williamses.[30]

Eppa Hunton, Jr., a staunch member of the "old school" of Virginia lawyers, and Henry Anderson, an aggressive leader of the new, were not always congenial, and they seemed to have grown less so as the years—and Henry Anderson—advanced. But Randolph Williams loved them both, and he kept the peace between them with his gentle manner, his sense of humor, and his special gift for identifying and then nourishing the finest qualities in each man's personality. His value to the law firm, in this respect, was incalculable.[31]

When World War I came, it severely disrupted the "Happy Family," as the firm came to be called by employees at the post office who had to sort its mail. Ironically, it almost deserved that sobriquet during those early years when all four of its partners lived so close together.

In July 1917 Henry Anderson accepted an appointment as chairman of a Red Cross mission to Rumania and served there until March 1918. After the Armistice in November 1918, he returned to Eastern Europe for a second year's service as the Red Cross commissioner to all the Balkan States.[32]

When Anderson left, Randolph Williams succeeded him as general counsel to the Virginia Railway and Power Company, while Thomas Benjamin Gay took over the representation of the Southern Railway. Eppa Hunton, Jr., accepted an appointment as counsel to the director general of the railroads after President Wilson "proclaimed control" of them in December 1917, and Andrew Christian, the firm's only associate, went off to fight.[33]

While he was struggling with the heavy work load during the war, Randolph Williams suffered a personal blow from which neither he nor his wife would ever fully recover. In October 1918, his fifteen-year-old son, Jack, a leader in the local Boy Scouts' effort to transport victims of the terrible influenza epidemic to local hospitals, contracted the disease himself and died.

By the time Henry Anderson came back from the Balkans, and Eppa Hunton left the firm, Randolph Williams had changed from the mild-mannered but always eager and hard-working young lawyer who had founded the firm. The death of his second son, the mellowing of age, and the security provided by sound investments all contributed to his desire to spend less of his time fighting railroad and power company battles and more of it on philanthropic work.

In any case, the last half of Randolph Williams's career at the law firm was relatively quiet—in sharp contrast to that of Anderson. After the two years Henry Anderson spent in the Balkans, his unsuccessful race for governor of Virginia in 1921 and his service to the three Republican administrations in Washington, he came roaring back into the fight with imaginative solutions for corporations facing the Depression and the new world of legislation created by the Democrats' New Deal.

In 1920, when Eppa Hunton, Jr., assumed the presidency of the RF & P, Randolph Williams succeeded him as its general counsel. He continued to serve in that capacity until 1951, when he retired and his assistant, Wirt Marks, succeeded him. In 1925 the Goulds sold control of the Virginia Railway and Power Company to Stone & Webster and several investment firms who then organized a holding company, Engineers Public Service, to own and manage the Virginia Electric and Power Company (Vepco). An aggressive young trial lawyer who had served as house counsel for the old power company, T. Justin Moore, was then named general counsel of the new company, though Randolph Williams and his law firm continued to do a great deal of its corporate legal work.

By this time Williams had lost his taste for the knock-down-drag-out court fights of his younger days and began to rely more on his strengths "as a counsellor, who," as Lewis Powell put it,

> had good judgment and sought solutions rather than conflict. I thought he performed an excellent role as a family lawyer in particular. I am not talking about divorce or custody or things like that, but he was the sort of person you'd like to go to, just as you would like to have a family physician in whom you had total confidence. [In this way] he made a real contribution, in my view, not only to the harmony of the firm but to its growth and prestige.[34]

Younger lawyers like Powell, George Gibson, and later, John Riely, loved Randolph Williams because he was extraordinarily kind and considerate of them. He had "a wry, dry sense of humor," Powell remembered, "and a twinkle in his eye . . . so much of the time."[35] George Gibson recalled that he served as the "peacemaker in the firm. He had a great abiding love for his friends, partners and relatives and a great sense of humor" that enriched the stories

General Eppa Hunton was best friend as well as father of Eppa Hunton, Jr.

Erva Winston Payne, the oldest daughter of Confederate general William H. Payne, married Eppa Hunton, Jr., in 1884. She died October 9, 1897, and four years later Hunton married her younger sister, Virginia Semmes Payne.

Former Confederate general William H. Payne was the father of both of Eppa Hunton, Jr.'s wives and counsel for the Southern Railway. Large portraits of General Payne and General Hunton hung in the library at 6705 River Road, where Eppa Hunton IV often entertained his partners.

Brentmoor on Main Street, Warrenton, Virginia. The house was bought by General Hunton from Colonel John B. Mosby in 1877 and sold after the Huntons moved to Richmond in 1901.—*Virginia State Library*

Eppa Hunton, Jr., and Virginia Semmes Hunton posed in the spring of 1905 with their eight-month-old son, Eppa Hunton IV, whose father, grandfather, and great-grandfather all shared the name "Eppa."

Eppa Hunton, Jr., and his second wife, Virginia Semmes Payne Hunton, clearly enjoyed their honeymoon trip to Atlantic City in 1901.

"Prussianism is not a national matter but a state of mind," wrote artist, feminist, and ally of Mrs. Munford, Adele Clark, under her sketch of their opponent, Eppa Hunton, Jr., at the General Assembly's public hearing in 1918 on the Coordinate College.—*Virginia State Library*

With sword and horse, Eppa Hunton IV (c. 1908) prepares to follow in the military tradition of his grandfathers, Eppa Hunton and William Payne, both brigadier generals in the Confederate army. —*Virginia Historical Society*

Eppa Hunton IV as an
undergraduate at the
University of Virginia. Four
years later, in 1927, he
received a law degree from
that same university and
became associated with the
firm his father had founded.

Eppa Hunton, Jr., and Virginia Semmes Hunton in 1924, after he had
left the law firm to become president of the Richmond, Fredericksburg
and Potomac Railroad Company.—*Foster Collection, Virginia Historical
Society*

John L. Williams and his family in the late 1880s. Front, from left: Langbourne Meade Williams, William Berkeley Williams, John Langbourne Williams, Maria Ward Williams, Maria Ward Skelton Williams, Ennion Gifford Williams. Rear, from left: John Skelton Williams, Cyane Dandridge Williams, Charlotte Randolph Williams (who drowned off Old Point Comfort, Virginia, July 7, 1884, represented by her portrait), Edmund Randolph Williams, Robert Lancaster Williams.—*Virginia State Library*

William Wirt Henry, Randolph Williams's senior partner from 1896 until 1900. —*Virginia State Library*

E. Randolph Williams at his desk at Munford,
Hunton, Williams & Anderson in 1906.

Margaret Williams, about 1910.

Maude Stokes Williams in 1924.
—*Foster Collection, Virginia
Historical Society*

The architect William Lawrence Bottomley designed the house
Randolph Williams built at 4207 Sulgrave Road in 1927.—*Reid Freeman*

Randolph Williams playing checkers with his grandson, John L.
McElroy, Jr., in 1936.

that he used to tell. Gibson said he often asked Williams to write his stories down so that they could be preserved, "but he modestly or lazily refused to do so."[36]

When John Riely came to work for Randolph Williams, fresh from Harvard Law School in the early 1940s, he found in him the ideal combination of gentleness and strength: "He was a very courtly, old fashioned gentleman and he dealt with me that way. He was always charming, always agreeable, . . . often firm, and always a joy to be around."[37]

J. Harvie Wilkinson, Jr., former president of State-Planters (then United Virginia, now Crestar) Bank, says that:

> one of my most intimate, delightful remembrances of Mr. Randolph Williams was when I, a very young bank officer, asked Lewis Powell, a very young lawyer at Hunton, Williams, to conduct a case for me in suing Hartsville Print and Die Works under the indenture of a bond issue on which they had defaulted. This was a big case for my reputation, as to how it turned out, and I think it fair to say it was a big case for Lewis, being the first one that the firm had had in the way of corporate representation for the State-Planters Bank. . . .
>
> Lewis, Mr. Williams and I set off for Charleston, South Carolina, to try the case the next day. Lewis and I had a double room. Mr. Williams, of course, had a single room to himself, adjoining us. Next morning I was awakened and my first scene was Lewis sitting at a desk with a raincoat on because it was chilly, and Mr. Randolph Williams standing in his skivvies in the doorway saying, "Now, Lewis, it is always thus. We are up early trampling the vineyard, and the client lies abed."[38]

In 1928 Williams moved from West Franklin Street into the handsome Georgian house overlooking the James River on Sulgrave Road in Windsor Farms, a new suburb just west of the city limits.[39] There he continued to welcome the members of his law firm as members of his extended family. He also helped them out when they were in trouble.

During the Great Depression, he voluntarily took a substantial cut in his "take" from the law firm and began to devote more and more of his time to the Children's Home Society, the Virginia Historical Society, and the Episcopal Church. In his later years, the church became his principal interest, according to his junior partner and ardent admirer Archibald Robertson. Since 1923 Robertson had worked very closely with Williams on Virginia Electric and Power Company matters. He had also served with him on the vestry of St. Paul's Church and succeeded him as chancellor of the [Episcopal] Diocese of Virginia. Robertson recalled: [40]

> Randolph Williams did more unrecorded, unknown acts of generosity and kindness to get people out of jams than anybody I ever saw. . . . He was beloved by everybody that knew him. As an illustration of that: Cabell Lawton [a retired banker who had become the firm's office manager in the 1930s], his son had polio, . . . a perfectly heart-breaking illness. I got this from Mr. Lawton. And everybody in the firm was very sympathetic and would come in and be most solicitous and find out how his boy was getting on—he finally died—and Mr. Williams would come in and say, "Well, how is your boy getting along?" And he'd tell him. And he said, "Well, I reckon you can use that all right. And I just would like to leave that with you." And . . . Mr. Lawton would turn the thing over, and it would be a check for five hundred dollars. Everybody else talked, and Mr. Williams acted.[41]

According to his daughter, there were only two people in the world that Williams disliked: Harold Ickes and Franklin Delano Roosevelt.[42] In 1936 Williams plunged into politics to oppose Roosevelt's re-election, joining the Liberty League and the "Jeffersonian Democrats."[43] By 1937, when FDR's "court-packing" plan was aired, George Gibson reported that "poor Mr. Williams became so violently incensed at every headline about Franklin Delano Roosevelt that Mr. Anderson became quite protective in an effort to shield him from the public news, fearing it would give him a heart attack and put an end to him."[44]

The strong friendship between these two men, the original instigators of the law firm, who were, as Mrs. McElroy puts it, "poles apart in almost every way," is one of the most reassuring facts in the firm's history.

At the fiftieth anniversary party in November 1951, Randolph Williams and Henry Anderson sat by a roaring fire in Eppa Hunton IV's library swapping tales about the early days. Less than a year later, on June 9, 1952, Randolph Williams appeared before the Virginia Supreme Court of Appeals, *pro bono,* in a matter related to the Episcopal Church's endowment. He then went home to his house on Sulgrave Road and died in his sleep that night, from a heart attack.

His chief legacy to the law firm he had founded was an example of not only how to practice law, but how to live with consummate skill, humor, and humanity.

In 1986 Justice Powell still remembered "the wonderful warmth and good will about him. . . . When he died we were distressed, not only because everyone loved and admired him, but because he was a father figure of the firm. We lost that.

"And he never was replaced."[45]

FIVE

Henry Watkins Anderson

1870–1954

Where in the world did he come from? The subject of Henry Anderson's origins has been discussed by Richmonders for almost a century, though very few facts have emerged from the discussion. With his Republican politics and extravagant style of living, he defied the city's traditional restraints and aroused not a little bit of envy. More than thirty years after his death it was still impossible to get a completely unbiased report on him.

Probably the most *in*accurate one is the portrait offered in *Stuffed Peacocks* by the literary satirist Emily Clark, who introduces him as the "grandson of a shopkeeper in a small mountain town." The most helpful portrait is that offered by his niece Frances Richardson Shield, who lived with him in the 1930s after her mother died.[1]

The most penetrating analysis is provided by the novelist Ellen Glasgow, who made the study of character in his particular society the focus of her life's work. She also had the misfortune to fall in love with him. On the surface, her account of him is bitter, and understandably so, since he lost enthusiasm for their secret engagement after he met Marie, the queen of Rumania, during World War I. Yet he and Ellen Glasgow still remained friends. And beneath her irony, there is an understanding all too rare in accounts of Henry Anderson.[2]

They met on Easter Sunday, 1916. By that time Henry Anderson was at the peak of his pre-World War I career. As Ellen Glasgow puts it: "An unusual intellectual endowment, a constitution of iron and an infinite capacity for taking advantage, had enabled him to attain the highest peak but one in his profession. Only the Supreme Court was denied him, and delegations of prominent Virginians [had] attacked Washington, in the hope of correcting, during President Taft's administration, that error of circumstance."[3]

Through his friendship with Lady Hadfield, Attorney General Wickersham's sister, he had acquired the veneer of an English gentleman and filled his house with English servants.[4] Ellen was an Anglophile, too, just back from New York City, living alone and writing novels in her family's house at One West Main Street.

For years, she had heard Henry Anderson criticized—"not without a drop of envy," she suspected—and had consciously avoided meeting him. Described as "a pluperfect snob" by one old man she knew, he seemed to respect "all the things I looked down upon. Trivial honors, notoriety, social prominence, wealth, fashion, ladies with titles, an empty show in the world," she wrote:[5]

It was related that he had sprung from a vigorous stock in Southside Virginia, that he had worked his way through the law course at Washington & Lee University, and had come, in Richmond, to a boarding house kept by a decayed gentlewoman.[6] A man of outstanding ability and tireless energy, he was in that period, so eager to arrive somewhere that he injured his eyesight by studying all night in his hall bedroom and even, or so his landlady recounted, rose from a severe illness, against the orders of his physician, to attend the first important party to which he was invited. All these acts revealed a forthright spirit and a commendable zeal. When this same landlady added, however, that he always kicked away every rung of the ladder he mounted, and especially that he had never recognized her in the street since he had been able to afford a car of foreign make —when one heard these complaints, one, not unnaturally, reconsidered one's judgment, until one discovered that he was painfully nearsighted.

In later years, long before I knew him, he had reached the

top of his ladder and the ground below was liberally strewn—
or so malice remarked—with the rungs he had kicked aside. If
there is any social top in Richmond, he was standing upon it.[7]

Having drawn this unflattering portrait from rumor, she then
goes on to dismiss it as "half-truth":

> The man was not incapable of perception. He was, on the
> contrary, made of sensitive fiber. His too rapid climbing was
> little more than a successful struggle to overcome an early un-
> warranted sense of inferiority; and though he used people a
> little too obviously, he used them less for selfishness than for
> self-improvement, a different, and not an ignoble, pursuit. . . .
>
> People might laugh at him. . . . They might ridicule his slightly
> pompous manner and his too punctilious way of living. They
> might ridicule his English clothes, his valet, his footmen in plum-
> colored livery; but it was his accurate boast that only death kept
> them away from his dinners.[8]

Henry Anderson's later partners George Gibson and Archibald
Robertson did not remember the plum-colored livery but they
did remember the arrogance that the livery symbolized. Although
George Gibson's intellectual gifts were to draw praise from no less
than four Supreme Court justices,[9] Henry Anderson was not impressed by them at his recruitment interview in 1930, according
to George Gibson's account:

> The first preparation for the interview with "the Colonel," as
> he was called, was to go through a grilling by Thomas Benjamin
> Gay. And after I'd been grilled sufficiently and was deemed in
> trim, I was ushered into the august presence. The interview,
> while august, was very brief because Mr. Anderson looked at
> me and said, "Gibson, can you look up law?" It's the dreariest,
> most servile task that any lawyer can perform. It's not done now;
> machines do it. I said, "I think so, sir. I can certainly try."
>
> And his reply was: "Well, that is a good thing, for to put *me* to
> that task would be like putting a thoroughbred to the plow."[10]

Another partner, Lewis Powell, remembered getting into Colonel Anderson's long car after an elaborate lunch at Anderson's house at 913 West Franklin Street, and having the chauffeur come around and tuck a lap robe at their knees. When Powell made a remark to the effect that this certainly was luxurious living, the colonel replied, "I deserve it." [11]

Archibald Robertson, a fun-loving, rough-talking trial lawyer who came to the firm nearly every day until he died at age ninety-five, later explained that the stories "got more curlicues . . . as the years went on." Neighbors would describe in great detail the long car driving up, the colonel emerging from the house, and, if it happened to be raining, the chauffeur, in boots polished to perfection, holding an umbrella over the colonel's head. The chauffeur would then help him into his car, fuss with the lap robe, and finally drive him off to the office. [12]

Robertson defended the colonel's right to such behavior: "If you *like* to put on dog, and got the *money* to put on dog, and know *how* to put on dog, I think you ought to be able to put on dog without being ridiculed." [13]

To the sheltered, almost shabby, denizens of Richmond during the first part of the twentieth century, Henry Anderson seemed larger than life. No wonder they speculated wildly about his origins.

The facts would probably have disappointed them.

Henry Anderson was born in Dinwiddie County, Virginia, on December 20, 1870, at Hampstead, his family's farm, or "plantation," as Anderson later described it. His father, William Watkins Anderson, was a farmer and country doctor who had received his medical degree from the University of Pennsylvania in 1841. [14]

Henry and his twin sister, Laura, were born into the middle of a family of five children. According to their niece Frances Shield, Laura got the upper hand in the relationship at the outset, dominated him through his childhood, and continued to dominate him, as no other person could, until the day he died. [15]

The hard times that the Williamses experienced in Richmond

during the 1870s seem minor compared to the persistent poverty the Andersons endured in Southside Virginia in the aftermath of the Civil War and Reconstruction, when very few patients were able to pay their doctor.

Yet Anderson was a natural student. Eventually he overcame the limits of his early education at home and in the Dinwiddie County schools to fulfill his childhood ambition to become a lawyer. But it took a little time.

Since he could not afford to go to college and did not have a brother-in-law to say "Come live with me, and study law," as Beverley Munford did, he went to business school and learned shorthand and typing. With these skills he then began a lifelong association with the railroads, working as a stenographer, first in the claims department of the Richmond & Danville Railroad at West Point[16] and then for the Norfolk & Western in Roanoke, where he served for one year as secretary of the Board of Trade.

During the time that Henry Anderson worked as secretary to the officers in charge of the Richmond & Danville Railroad, he may have gotten to know their trial counsel, Beverley Munford. And surely Munford would have sympathized with this bright young man from Dinwiddie whose goal of practicing law seemed almost unreachable at this point in his life.

In any case, by the summer of 1897 Anderson was working as a clerk in Munford's firm, Staples & Munford, in Richmond. That fall, he moved to Lexington where he had accepted a job as a secretary to the president of Washington and Lee University in order to study at the law school there. Despite the demands of his jobs, by working almost incessantly, he managed to complete the law course in one year and received his LL.B. from Washington and Lee in 1898.[17]

The summer of 1898, Anderson returned to the office of Beverley Munford who was then practicing alone in the Merchants Bank building at the corner of Eleventh and Main streets in Richmond.

A year later, on October 1, 1899, Munford and Anderson formed a partnership. In one of that firm's account books, Anderson recorded—in his neat stenographer's handwriting—the payment of ten dollars on October 13 to a local sign painter "for painting signs on doors and at entrance." Presumably the signs were to display the new style of "Munford & Anderson."[18]

At age twenty-nine, Henry Watkins Anderson had finally arrived as a lawyer to be reckoned with on Main Street.

At the turn of the century, Richmond liked to think of itself as a "closed society." Actually, the way was wide open, and always had been, to an enterprising young man with good manners, style, and money, particularly if he married into an old Richmond family. If the statements imputed by Ellen Glasgow to his former landlady have any truth in them, Henry Anderson pursued this course initially. But as his view of the world broadened, he set his sights higher, began to court attractive women from all over the world, and lived exactly as he wanted to in Richmond.

Though he loved to give elaborate parties, and he invested enormous amounts of time, energy, and money in his social life, his work came first, especially in those early days.

The original partnership agreement of Munford, Hunton, Williams & Anderson assigned the smallest share of the profits to Anderson (one-fifth), while the other three partners were given one-third of the remaining four-fifths. There was, however, a provision that he would be raised to equal participation in two years.

In fact, he got there in one year. Between November 1901 and October 1902, Anderson worked very hard to hold on to old Munford & Anderson clients. Among them were the Southern Railway and the South Atlantic Insurance Company. He also consolidated the Norfolk, Portsmouth, and Newport News street-railway systems for the Williams firm. When the second partnership agreement went into effect on November 1, 1902, Anderson was allotted a full one-third of the profits, while Munford, still ill in Colorado, was cut out of participation altogether.

During the firm's second year, 1902–3, Lewis Williams, a young lawyer from Orange County who had married Randolph Williams's sister, became the first associate. He left the following fall, when Munford came back into the practice, and ultimately formed his own Richmond firm, Williams & Mullen.[19]

On May 25, 1904, there is a note in the firm journal under Anderson's name: "Went to NY with Northrop for conference with Frank J. Gould." This is the first evidence of an association that would catapult Anderson into a world of high finance, corporate management, and lucrative law suits involving electric utilities in Richmond, Petersburg, Norfolk, and Newport News, and railroads spread across the country.

Frank J. Gould was the son of the nineteenth-century railroad baron Jay Gould. Early in 1902, when he was only twenty-five, he became involved with street-railway systems in Virginia, a first step in his dream of building an electric railroad from Norfolk to Fredericksburg, via Petersburg and Richmond, with branches to the Northern Neck.[20]

Later that same year, when George Fisher ran into financial trouble with his newly consolidated streetcar companies, Frank Gould and his sister Helen—at Fisher's request—bought the controlling interest in them. In January 1903, the Goulds, who maintained their residence in New York, sent their cousin William Northrop down to Richmond to manage their interests.[21]

Though Northrop proved to be a brilliant manager, Fisher turned against him and the Goulds almost immediately, and instituted receivership proceedings, first in Petersburg and then in the federal court in Richmond, to regain control of Virginia's emerging electric-utility industry. The litigation lasted five years—a long time in those days—and was just the sort of test that the ambitious new law firm and its most ambitious partner, Henry Anderson, needed to prove their worth.[22]

In the beginning, Beverley Munford helped his junior partner. On June 7, 1904, he and Anderson took the night train to New York for a second conference with Frank Gould. Ten days later when Fisher filed the suit in Petersburg, Anderson met Gould in Washington and brought him down to Richmond to a conference at the Munfords' house.

By midsummer the companies were in receivership with William Northrop and Henry Wickham, general counsel of the C & O Railway, appointed as receivers; Eppa Hunton, Jr., and Henry Anderson were counsel to the receivers. Over the next five years, the receivers of the Virginia Passenger and Power Company and the Goulds, who were behind them, would replace John L. Williams & Sons as the law firm's major client.

By August 1904 Henry Anderson was immersed in the Goulds' problems, working regularly until ten o'clock at night, sometimes until two and three in the morning, and Sundays as well. According to the journals during that one month, he met Frank Gould in New York several times, spent three days with him in Greenwich, Connecticut, and accompanied him to Richmond and then to Old Point Comfort, near Hampton, Virginia.

In the meantime, Eppa Hunton, Jr., was working long hours, too, appearing in the federal court and preparing reports for the "Receivers of Va P & P Co." who were now on a retainer equal to that paid by the Seaboard Air Line and the Southern Railway.

Over the next five years the firm's ledgers are replete with references to the partners' efforts to protect the Goulds' interests in the increasingly complex street-railway litigation.

During the years from 1904 to 1909, when the street railways were in receivership, William Northrop emerged as an exceptionally effective manager and a firm opponent of graft, which had all too often been involved in the granting of the franchises. He also became one of Henry Anderson's closest friends.[23]

In 1906, after an arduous effort to consolidate three systems into the Norfolk, Portsmouth & Newport News Street Railway Company and then disentangle them for the Williams firm, Henry Anderson had been named director and general counsel of the Norfolk & Portsmouth Traction Company.

In a series of imaginative maneuvers, arguments, and legal tours de force—sometimes working around the clock—young Henry Anderson and the law firm managed to guide the Goulds to victory. When they finally created a new company, the Virginia Railway and Power Company, from the old Virginia Passenger and Power Company and several others, Northrop became its president, and Anderson, vice-president and general counsel.[24]

Two years later, Frank Gould retained Henry Anderson in the

reorganization of the International & Great Northern Railway, initiating a series of railroad reorganizations in which Henry Anderson earned a national reputation. In 1912 he was named general counsel of the International & Great Northern Railway and served in that capacity until 1914.[25]

During the first decade of the firm's existence, Henry Anderson had risen from the bottom of the partnership to the top; with his new responsibilities for the I & GN, whose lines ran from St. Paul, Minnesota, to Seattle, Washington, he was well on his way to becoming a national leader in railroad law.

Parallel to this spectacular rise in his profession was his emergence as a leader in Republican politics. In 1908, while Beverley Munford was writing articles from his sickbed urging local businessmen not to bolt the Democratic party to vote for Republican presidential candidate William Howard Taft, Henry Anderson, who had not yet officially left the Democratic party, was organizing the "Taft Democrats."[26]

On October 17 he introduced the future president to Richmond in the Old Horse Show Building and expressed his hope that a strong two-party system could be established in Virginia, because "the division of the people into parties representing different schools of thought, is essential to the intelligent discussion of political questions." It was also essential, he went on to say, to any real progress in the state of Virginia.[27]

Taft won the election of 1908, and though Henry Anderson was not able to deliver Virginia's electoral votes to him, he had become the new president's friend. Soon after Anderson moved into his handsome three-story house at 913 West Franklin, he hung a portrait of Taft above the mantelpiece in his library.[28]

The victory of Woodrow Wilson in the election of 1912 severed Anderson's ties to the White House—temporarily. He then became one of Wilson's most vehement critics, insisting that the idealistic professor was temperamentally unfit to be president of the United States, "an infliction upon the country of an angry God."[29]

When war broke out in Europe, Anderson was one of the first people in the state to become involved in organizing the relief effort. He was, in fact, serving as president of the Virginia War Relief Effort on that Easter Sunday in 1916 when he met and fell in love with Ellen Glasgow.

At the height of their romance the following spring, the United States entered World War I. Though he was forty-six years old, Anderson attempted to enlist. When he was turned down for medical reasons, probably poor eyesight, he accepted an appointment as chairman of a Red Cross commission to Rumania with the assimilated rank of lieutenant colonel.[30]

On July 18, 1917, Ellen Glasgow received an urgent note from him: "I *want to see you*. I decided finally to go to Roumania. Everyone seemed to think it my duty to go, a chance to render service for which I have been asking—but I shall go with a heavy heart."[31]

The following night they became engaged, and Henry Anderson left Richmond the next day for New York. As his train moved west to Chicago and on to Vancouver, Ellen Glasgow received almost daily telegrams and notes from him. As he sailed across the Pacific to Japan, then took a train across Russia, his communications became less frequent.[32]

Finally on the sixteenth of September he "vanished into the silence of Rumania." To him, at least as Ellen Glasgow saw it, "this particular war was not only a patriotic adventure, but a new and higher ladder to eminence."[33]

The majority of the commission sailed home in October, but Anderson stayed on for the winter in Jassy with a few members of his staff.

During the winter of 1917–18, Ellen Glasgow heard very little from Rumania except rumors, some of them concerning Henry's growing friendship with the queen. In March 1918, when the Germans moved into Rumania, a separate peace was negotiated and the Allied commission was forced to leave immediately. In her *Life Story*, Queen Marie describes a farewell scene in which a "Southern Colonel" from America falls on his knees to kiss the hem of her skirt, a gesture which Glasgow recognized as "the last act of chivalry."[34]

By June 1918 Henry Anderson was back in Richmond. His first

night at home, "he came down in his colonel's uniform, glittering with decorations," Ellen Glasgow wrote. "'I thought you would like to see me as I looked abroad,' he said with innocent vanity. But at my first glance I saw only the difference; I saw only that nothing would ever be again as it was before he had gone to the Balkans. Something had intervened. . . . He could talk of nothing but the Queen and, occasionally, of the Princess Ileana."[35]

On July 3, 1918, Henry Anderson came to dinner at Ellen Glasgow's house, and they had their first quarrel. Afterwards they went over the text of a speech he was going to make the next day containing the significant phrase: "Happiness comes only from the sacrifice of self in the crucible of service."

When he left, Ellen Glasgow, overcome with depression, went up to her bedroom and took an overdose of sleeping pills.[36]

A few years after her unsuccessful suicide attempt, she found a better way to cope with Henry Anderson. She wrote *Barren Ground*, a stoic novel and one of her finest, in which the heroine triumphs over the desertion of her lover by developing "the serenity of mind which is above the conflict of frustrated desires," and declares that she is "thankful to have finished with all that."[37]

When the book was published in 1925, the *New York Times* Book Review announced that "Southern romance is dead. Ellen Glasgow has murdered it." The phrasing seems particularly apt since Queen Marie, the source of her murderous mood, has been called "The Last Romantic." In murdering romance, Ellen Glasgow was striking at the queen, or, more accurately, the qualities in Henry Anderson that had responded to her.

"In fairness to all sides," Marie, the lively granddaughter of Queen Victoria, had said on one occasion, "I must admit that prudence was not my specialty."[38]

Ellen Glasgow gave Henry Anderson a copy of her novel, and he wrote her a pleasant note congratulating her on a fine piece of work but said he thought the heroine's reaction to her former fiancé's return was a little bit unnatural and melodramatic.[39]

A Balkan queen and an embittered novelist seem, like Henry Anderson himself, a little larger than life—stock characters, perhaps, from a melodrama—so there has been a tendency to laugh at the whole episode.

The reaction is unfair, as most of the reactions to Anderson seem to have been throughout his life. In 1919, at the end of his second mission to the Balkans, in a moving letter to Randolph Williams, Anderson referred to his "somewhat wrecked life."[40]

He was strongly attracted to two very different women, because each one appealed to a different side of his complex personality. Marie, the queen in distress, appealed to the romantic and also to the public servant in him who deserved respect. Anderson proved more than once that he was willing to sacrifice his fortune, his career, and if necessary, his own life for the public good—which, in World War I, he saw as intertwined with that of Rumania, America's ally in the Balkans. Ellen Glasgow appealed to the realist who rebelled against the sentimental decadence of the society in which they lived, and also to the literary amateur who once stayed up all night to write a "poem in Spenserian verse" in response to a poem that she had sent him.[41]

His behavior toward Ellen Glasgow was honorable to the end. Their secret engagement was never publicly announced, nor was it ever broken. Instead it was eroded by a change in feeling on both sides, exacerbated by Glasgow's depression.

When Anderson came back from his second, postwar mission to the Balkans in 1919, she asked him if he still considered himself engaged to her. "Of course I do," he wrote. "There has not been a word or suggestion to the contrary." Later in the same note he equivocates a little, saying that "we entered into the engagement in good faith by mutual agreement, and any change in status should be by mutual agreement." He then concludes with this moving and revealing statement: "I am distressed, my Dear, to have given you pain or distress. It has been the most painful experience of my whole life—I am sorry that the doom which seems to hang over my life has involved yours."[42]

Behind that fiercely ambitious and much-touted arrogance was a very shy and now unhappy man. He would thence "go forth," he wrote, "to face life as best I can shadowed by one great failure."[43]

In a note he wrote much earlier, Anderson had hinted at the dark side of his personality: "Mine is a cold and lonely path, . . . and those who cross it seem only to feel the chill—God grant me that I may not bring its chill to you, but only warmth and beauty."[44]

One must bear in mind, however, reading any of these letters, that Anderson may have been experimenting with Ellen Glasgow's literary style.

Almost every day for months a servant would carry a message from 913 West Franklin Street to One West Main Street and wait for a reply. Sometimes the message was just a line or two to say good morning, or a note that he would be coming down for dinner, which in summertime was served "by candlelight under the clustering vines of the back gallery, or porch" of the Glasgow House.[45]

As her notes became more and more strident and reproachful, he tried to clear the atmosphere by bringing his "sense of humor out of storage."[46] To one of them he replied, "Dear, *Dear,* DEAR! what a blast! If I am as bad as your last note says why bother with me at all? Anyhow, the withered and stricken remains of me will come down tonight and be converted into a metaphorical grease spot on the rug."[47]

From responses like this, one can only guess what Ellen Glasgow wrote to him. After his death, Frances Shield burned Glasgow's letters to him, on explicitly written instructions from her uncle, who was attempting to protect their privacy.[48] Of course, he did not know that Ellen Glasgow had already violated it in her autobiography, *The Woman Within,* because her literary executors held up publication of the book until after Anderson's death.[49]

When *The Woman Within* came out in November 1954, Henry Anderson's law partners were surprised to learn of his secret engagement to Ellen Glasgow. They had not heard a word about it, though they had been showered with anecdotes about the queen and Princess Ileana. Many of them concluded that the whole affair was just another work of fiction by Ellen Glasgow, until his letters to her, preserved in the archives of the University of Virginia, began to appear in print.

Inadvertently, Henry Anderson wrote his own defense in an undated note to Ellen Glasgow: "I am wondering if it has ever occurred to you that your judgment might be wrong. You judge me so freely and with such apparent sureness that your conclusions are right that it makes me strong in my belief that no human being is or can be capable of judging another." [50]

When the bond between these two frequently misunderstood and stubbornly original people began to weaken, both of them suffered. Still they managed to preserve a platonic friendship which lasted until Ellen Glasgow died in November 1945. [51]

If the First World War had not come when it did, they probably would have married. As it is, the world of letters is richer for the fact that they did not. The masterpieces that followed the abandonment of their engagement, *Barren Ground* in 1925 and *The Sheltered Life* in 1932, were Ellen Glasgow's consolation for the suffering that Anderson had caused her.

Henry Anderson's romance with Queen Marie has attracted so much attention that it has almost obscured the fact that he did a prodigious amount of work during his two missions to the Balkans. The glittering decorations and the testimonials accompanying them from the governments of Rumania, Bulgaria, Serbia, Montenegro, Russia, Greece, Czechoslovakia, Italy, and France are eloquent testimony to his achievement. [52]

With a staff of 150 doctors, nurses, and assistants under his command, he delivered desperately needed medical services and ultimately transported 25 million pounds of food to the starving populations in the Balkans.

Queen Marie, who was as bright as she was beautiful, quickly recognized the administrative talents of Henry Anderson and turned her castle at Jassy over to him and his staff. From there he supervised a vast relief operation, which was amazingly successful, considering the handicaps against which he was struggling.

When the Germans moved into Rumania in March 1918, the entire Allied Mission was forced to leave immediately. The only way out was through the port of Murmansk, twenty-five hundred miles northward across Russia, which was in the middle of a revolution.

The American officers, doctors, and nurses were put on an ancient train with a wood-burning engine and third-class sleeping cars without water supply or heating facilities. And they would have to spend forty-nine consecutive nights in those cars before they would find passage on a ship out of Murmansk.

They passed through Odessa into the Ukraine just a few hours ahead of the German troops who were bombarding the countryside half a mile away. As their train moved northward toward the Arctic Circle, it averaged less than a hundred miles a day since they had to stop at every station and negotiate with the station master, newly appointed by the Soviets, to let them through. They also stopped to chop down wood to feed the steam engine or to hunt down rabbits and reindeer to supplement their rations. At one point, Anderson set out on a hunting expedition at the frozen White Sea and came back with three turkeys, which the Americans shared with members of the French mission traveling with them.

The extraordinary story of that winter of hard work in Rumania, followed by the dramatic exodus through Russia is eloquently told in manuscripts preserved at the Virginia Historical Society. Small wonder that the man who came home to Ellen Glasgow in June seemed to have changed.

While he was in the Balkans, Anderson flew three flags on the front of his car: the flags of the Red Cross, the United States, and the Commonwealth of Virginia. He confessed in a letter to his friend Randolph Williams that he had come to feel "intensely American"—more specifically, Virginian. And the suffering that he had seen in Eastern Europe had made him aware of the evils that could overtake his own society if it did not move steadily forward.[53]

At the time, Virginia was still in the doldrums. Despite a few steps forward during the progressive Montague and Swanson administrations, very little progress had been made since 1861. The schools were bad, the roads were bad, and the politicians—in the tiny, patronage-peddling Republican party as well as the all-powerful Democratic organization—were all too often "crooked," as Anderson put it.[54]

As soon as Anderson came back from his second mission to the Balkans, he turned his attention to politics, using as his vehicle for reform the Republican party, which was still despised by most white Virginians east of the Shenandoah Valley.

Anderson's own mother could not overcome the distrust the very word "Republican" aroused in her Reconstruction-damaged heart. When he ran for governor in 1921, she did not vote for him. Nor did his brother. And the headmistress at St. Catherine's School, Miss Jennie Ellett, an otherwise enlightened educator, made his ten-year-old niece's life miserable when she came to school with the Republican candidate's buttons on her coat.

In Anderson's opinion, a viable two-party system was the only way to infuse honest debate, and through debate, reform, into state government. And so, with a reckless, almost chivalric courage that is hardly understandable today, he threw himself and his considerable skills into the political process.

At the Republican National Convention in 1920, the Virginia delegation nominated Henry Anderson for the vice presidency. He received the fourth-largest vote from the whole convention, eventually losing the nomination to Coolidge who, on Harding's death, would become president.[55]

The next July in Norfolk, Anderson won the state Republican party's nomination as candidate for governor of Virginia. In his acceptance speech, he analyzed major problems facing the state (including the need for more efficient government, better roads, and better schools). He then proposed "constructive remedies" for those problems on the theory that the state ought to be managed as efficiently and imaginatively as a modern corporation.

In this speech, Anderson also called for repeal of the poll tax and a general reform of the election laws, which since 1902 had perpetuated the Democratic oligarchy's control of the state. He spoke openly about the "Race Question . . . the existence of which is the chief excuse urged for the present Constitution. . . . I do not propose to follow the usual practice and evade it. . . . It is a delicate and difficult subject for discussion, but it is here and it must be met."[56]

Then he proceeded to give a brief history of the blacks in Virginia, drawing on the knowledge he had gained some twelve years earlier helping Beverley Munford with the final manuscript of *Virginia's Attitude toward Slavery and Secession*. He pointed out that the blacks "did not come to America of their own free will, but were brought for the iniquitous purpose of slavery (over the protest of Virginia)." Then he picked his way around positions that might further split the "black and tan" and "lily white" factions in his own Republican party. And finally he came down squarely with the statement that

> it must be recognized by any fair-minded person that justice to the people of both races requires that the white people of Virginia, constituting over two-thirds of the population and owning ninety-five per cent of the property of the State, with their long experience in self-government are morally charged with . . . the duty to see that there is but one standard of justice in Virginia which shall be applied to rich and poor, white and colored, without discrimination. No free government can be founded upon two standards of justice.[57]

There were very few black delegates at that particular Republican convention to applaud Henry Anderson's enlightened statement. In protest to their exclusion from the Republican party's deliberations, black Republicans met in Richmond on Labor Day and nominated a slate of black candidates headed by John Mitchell, Jr., editor of the Richmond *Planet*.

Anderson's Democratic opponent, E. Lee Trinkle, capitalized on the race issue, attacking the Republican record in Reconstruction, charging that the Republican plank to repeal the poll tax was a sop to the black voter, and finally expressing "fears that full Negro enfranchisement could set state progress back a half century."

"Thus," says Trinkle's biographer, L. Stanley Willis, "the race bogey, in spite of Anderson's protests, became *the* issue." Although Anderson had tried to keep the campaign "on a higher plane, the Democracy impaled him on the race issue."[58]

As the atmosphere became increasingly unpleasant, Henry Anderson continued to run a hard-hitting, "anti-machine" progressive campaign. Though he knew that as a Republican he had no chance of winning the election, he was determined to stir as many Virginians as possible out of their complacent acceptance of things as they were, and always had been, into serious thought about the future of their state.

It was an unusual campaign, to say the least. In small town after small town all over the state, Henry Anderson would arrive in his long, low chauffeur-driven town car. Meticulously dressed in smartly tailored clothes and with pince-nez perched upon his nose, he would mingle briefly with the party officials who had organized the event, deliver his address, then walk back to his limousine and wait for the chauffeur to open the door and whisk him away to his next engagement. Pressing the flesh with crowds of potential voters was clearly not Henry Anderson's style.[59]

In November 1921, as everyone expected, the Democratic candidate, Lee Trinkle, won, but Anderson managed to receive over 30 percent of the vote. It was a surprisingly successful showing for a Republican in Virginia at that time.[60]

Ironically, four years later, Harry Byrd (whose name would later become synonymous with that oligarchy and its resistance to change) initiated in his own administration many of the reforms that Henry Anderson had suggested. In that sense at least, Anderson's effort had not been in vain.

Meanwhile, the national Republicans, who controlled the White House and Congress, were quick to take advantage of the skills that Virginia had rejected. In Harding's administration Anderson served as special assistant to the attorney general, in charge of cases arising out of the Ordnance Department in World War I, including a suit against the Chemical Foundation of Wilmington, Delaware, which he argued in the Supreme Court. In Coolidge's administration he served as U.S. Agent on the Mexican Claims

Commission. And in Hoover's administration he was appointed to the National Commission on Law Observance and Enforcement. Former Attorney General Wickersham was chairman of that commission, which undertook a study of the effects of Prohibition.[61]

After extensive research, including a visit to Sweden at his own expense, Henry Anderson wrote the minority report for the Wickersham Committee. It was a beacon of clarity in the fog of rhetoric surrounding Prohibition and was widely publicized. Basically, the "Anderson Plan" recommended the repeal of the unenforceable Volstead (or Prohibition) Act and outlined a system that would turn over the profits from the sale of liquor to the government, very much like the system still used in Virginia today.[62]

In the 1920s Anderson was appointed by the U.S. Government trustee for all the stock of the stockyards of Swift & Company and Armour & Company under consent decrees for the administration of those interests in the "Packer's Dissolution Suit." He also represented, in private practice, the minority stockholders of the C & O Railroad before the Interstate Commerce Commission in their successful opposition to the "Van Sweringen Plan"; the plan would have consolidated that company with the Nickel Plate, the Erie, Pere Marquette, and Hocking Valley railroads.[63]

In 1930, when the Seaboard Air Line Railway went into receivership for the second time, Anderson was appointed counsel for the receivers. Two years later he became co-receiver with the former president, Legh Powell, Jr., and over the next fourteen years they virtually rebuilt the company. In 1946, when the Seaboard finally came out of receivership, Anderson was made chairman of the board.

In March of 1930 his name was mentioned once again as a possible candidate for the Supreme Court. President Hoover was reported to be considering him for nomination, as Harding had done six years earlier, but Anderson saved the president the embarrassment of a defeat. He pointed out that Virginia's Democratic senators, Carter Glass and Claude Swanson, were unlikely to approve him since he had severely criticized them and the "ring" they represented in the gubernatorial campaign that had just passed.[64]

Two years later, in 1932, Anderson was mentioned by the newspapers as a possible running mate for Hoover, because of "Mr. Hoover's personal friendliness" for him. But the Republican National Convention nominated Charles Curtis. In August Anderson gave the keynote address at the Republican State Convention, though he refused to let it draft him as its candidate for the Third District seat in Congress. During the next three months he campaigned all over the state for the Republican candidates in the election that swept the Democrat, Franklin Delano Roosevelt, into the White House.[65]

Ironically, the victory of the Democrats in 1932 and the radical changes they put through Congress in those first one hundred days provided Henry Anderson with the final, and probably the sturdiest, rung in his ladder to eminence.

During the Roosevelt era, he very quickly gained recognition as a leader in developing the strategies with which large corporations, particularly the railroads, would cope with the avalanche of New Deal legislation.

His experience with societies in crisis and his talent for rushing into a complicated legal situation, analyzing it quickly, and devising an imaginative solution began to be sought by railroad executives and insurance companies all over the country. As his associate George Gibson later explained, "He had no taste whatever for looking up law. . . . Or even for giving prolonged consideration to any legal question as such. But he loved to dash in and devise a solution and promulgate it and did it with extraordinary success."[66]

Anderson often told his junior partner that "the law is what is confidently asserted and aggressively maintained." The New Deal gave him a unique chance to put his theory into practice and to shape the law as it was applied to the railroads particularly. And he was one of the two principal authors of a new provision, chapter fifteen, of the Bankruptcy Act.[67]

As the country struggled to recover from the effects of the stock market crash of October 1929 and the Great Depression that followed it, the fact that Henry Anderson was not a Wall Street lawyer worked to his advantage. "Wall Street" and "New York" had become associated in the minds of certain judges with the financial disaster the country was now facing, and many corporate executives, aware of this fact, began to look elsewhere for first-rate lawyers to represent them.

Over the next fifteen years, Henry Anderson became a legend in the railroad industry.[68] At one point, he was reorganizing the financial structure of five large railroads at the same time.

While he was co-receiver of the Seaboard, he served as counsel for prior lien bondholders of the St. Louis–San Francisco Railway and negotiated with various committees and the Interstate Commerce Commission an acceptable plan for its reorganization. Simultaneously he represented a group of insurance companies holding securities of the Denver and Rio Grande Western Railroad and helped with the reorganization of that company. He also served as counsel for the Baltimore and Ohio Railroad in its recapitalization proceedings, and finally—when he was in his middle seventies—represented a small group of insurance companies holding bonds in the Boston Terminal Company in the reorganization of the New Haven Railroad.[69]

As busy as he was in his professional life, Anderson still found time to live life to the hilt in his hours off. For three years in the early 1930s, his niece lived with him at 913 West Franklin Street and had a chance to observe his dedication to pleasure, which was almost as intense as his dedication to the law and public service. He gave to the word "style" an entirely new dimension that made the term "bon vivant" seem curiously inadequate.[70]

First of all, there was the staff of English-trained servants waiting on him night and day: the butler, Mr. Mangan, and his wife, who was the cook; a chambermaid; and a valet who often traveled with him. Once in the late twenties, when he signed a hotel register: "Henry W. Anderson and valet," his associate then signed himself on the next line as "Jennings C. Wise and valise."[71]

The chauffeurs who drove those sleek-lined "automobiles of foreign make" that caused such a stir in conservative Richmond were not necessarily English. There was a "marvelous looking" chauffeur named Grey, who was half Indian and half black, as well as William Bristol, who was English.[72]

Depending on the occasion, the chauffeur would drive either the sports car or the town car. Mrs. Shield remembered a Flint, followed by a Packard Roadster and a Marmon town car, open in the front where the chauffeur sat, with a closed cab behind. Because there was no heat, the car was equipped with enormous fur robes—automobile robes—to be put over the passengers' laps.

The chauffeur would often drive Anderson and his niece to "Whippernock," a family farm in Dinwiddie County, which had been elaborately restored. They also went to Washington, D.C., to receptions at the White House while Hoover was in office, and westward to the spas at Hot Springs and White Sulphur Springs, where Henry Anderson, the ever-popular though aging bachelor, had apparently cut a wide swath in the late twenties.

He and his friends used to dance late into the night at "the Hot," he told his niece, then hire a band and start out toward "the White." Sometimes they would stop along the way beside a stream, and put the band on the rocks, dance there for a while and then go on to the White Sulphur.[73]

Archaeological evidence supports this legend. In 1985 an amateur historian, searching a Civil War battlefield near Byrd Airport with a metal detector, unearthed a dented silver funnel with the following inscription:

> Colonel Henry W. Anderson
> with Love from the Harem
> Hot Springs
> Virginia
> 1927[74]

There are photographs of Henry Anderson with his chauffeur in an open Pierce Arrow surrounded by fashionably dressed flappers. A later photograph shows him and his niece Frances in the elaborate eighteenth-century costumes that won them the first prize at the Everglades Ball in Palm Beach. Anderson had had his costume—black moire silk with lace, black buckled shoes with red heels, and white wig—made in New York. He had originally planned to wear it for a ball that he was going to give for Queen Marie on her visit to America in the fall of 1926.[75] The invitations were already out when she was suddenly called back to Rumania because the king was ill, and the ball was cancelled.[76] Later Anderson had a matching costume of white lace made for his niece, and he and she adorned their costumes with his decorations and won the prize.[77]

Unquestionably, Henry Anderson had a way with women. He was an attentive and immensely vital man who knew how to entertain them and to court them with flowers, flattery, and presents. "When you look at his life," said his niece, "they were all magnificent people. The first one that I know about was Lady Hadfield, and then of course Ellen Glasgow." There were also Queen Marie of Rumania, Molly McCrea of Carter's Grove, and Countess Szechenyi, née Gladys Vanderbilt, to mention just a few whose names came up in one interview.[78]

Though Anderson was in his fifties when the Roaring Twenties came, he was young enough in spirit to participate with gusto. "Law and his duty" came first in his priorities, but he managed to find ingenious ways of combining duty with pleasure. In the process he set an epicurean standard that even his junior partner, George Gibson—who was to carry that standard forward into the next generation—could not match.

In his Seaboard Railroad days, during the thirties and the forties, Anderson was given a private railroad car, or "business car" as he preferred to call it. It was beautifully appointed, with brightly polished brass rails, a handsome desk, luxurious chairs, and, when he took it down to Florida, a block of ice set up on the roof for air conditioning.[79]

When the car pulled in to Boca Grande or Palm Beach, the rich widows there—who were also large stockholders and faithful patrons of the railroad—showered him with invitations to their parties. When Anderson grew tired of them, he would have the locomotive pull him and his car out in the middle of the night, leaving word that he had been called away on urgent business.

Obviously he enjoyed his "business car." As his associate put it, he "took to it with the customary relish." But he was nevertheless "forthright in his conviction" that the custom of assigning private cars to railroad presidents and officers and allowing them to travel for free anywhere they wanted to go, was an abuse which should be terminated. In proceedings before the Interstate Commerce Commission, he attacked the assignment of the business car to railroad executives as "a vicious personal utilization of corporate resources."[80]

Through the 1930s and well into the 1940s, Anderson appeared on behalf of railroads and their bondholders in courts all over the country, as the railroads struggled to get back on sound footing during the Depression, and then to cope with the unusual demands of World War II.

By the time the war came to an end and the railroads began to complete their reorganizations, his younger partner, George Gibson, had assumed a great deal of leadership and visibility in the field of railroad law. Anderson, now in his middle seventies, may have felt displaced and perhaps slightly jealous.

In any case, by the time a small group of insurance companies holding bonds of the Boston Terminal Company asked Anderson to represent them in the reorganization of the New Haven Railroad, George Gibson had all the work that he could handle. So Anderson turned to another younger partner who had just come back from four years' service in the Air Corps, Lewis Powell.

The law firm had only a small part in the New Haven reorganization. And that was "just as well," Powell later explained, "because it was a *disaster*. I enjoyed it primarily because it was the only work I ever did with Mr. Anderson. . . . I'll never forget the first time I went with him, [on an overnight train] to New York. He was then a receiver of the Seaboard Air Line. . . . [and] he was treated, as he was, lord of the manor on the railroad and always had everything he wanted, including the best stateroom. And he took fairly good care of me, too."

When Anderson and Powell arrived in New York early the next morning, they were met by limousine at Penn Station and taken to the old Ritz-Carlton at Forty-Sixth Street and Madison Avenue. "And what I've always enjoyed thinking back on is that he would get out of the limousine and even at the early hour in the morning . . . there would be a doorman [saying,] 'Good morning, Colonel Anderson. Welcome to New York.' . . . And he would walk into the Ritz-Carlton and go straight up to the suite that they had reserved for him, not even stopping at the desk. In the dining room he did not bother to sign checks. The first time Powell ate with him there, he thought that Anderson had just forgotten. So I grabbed his elbow and I said, 'Don't we have to sign something?' And Anderson explained that he never signed a check or gave a tip. Instead, at Christmas time he would send half a freight car filled with produce—hams and turkeys—from his farm in Dinwiddie County to be divided among the service people at the hotel."[81]

Henry Anderson also had his own way of dealing with the matter of presenting his fees. He flatly refused to charge by the hour, "like a plumber or a bricklayer." His best ideas often came to him, he said, when he was shaving in the morning. In fact, he said, a single moment of his time, backed by his experience could be worth several days or even weeks of a less able lawyer's. His new assistant, Lewis Powell, then had the dubious honor of explaining this attitude to the Interstate Commerce Commission.[82]

By the late 1940s Anderson was beginning to lose ground in his battle against old age and colon cancer. He was making an argument in the Second Circuit before Judge Learned Hand and overran his allotted thirty minutes. When the judge said, "Colonel Anderson, your time is up," he retorted, "But I haven't finished my argument yet!" The judge just shook his head and allowed him to continue for another twenty minutes.[83]

By that time Anderson was dying, and he must have known it. Yet he still continued to go down to his office as often as his health would permit.

During this time of his life, he was still serving as president of the Virginia Museum of Fine Arts. The taste he had developed for the finer things of life included an appreciation of fine art refined during his frequent trips to Europe. Both he and Randolph Williams had served on the board since the museum was established in 1936 from that nucleus of paintings—many of them fakes, as it turned out—that John Barton Payne gave to the state in 1919, and which Eppa Hunton, Jr., had managed to transfer by rail, despite a railroad strike, from Chicago to the Battle Abbey.

In 1948 after Anderson hired Leslie Cheek, Jr., to replace Thomas C. Colt as the museum's director, he immediately enlisted him and his wife in his effort to develop potential donors of fine art. Anderson believed that Southerners had a great potential as collectors of fine art. Though poverty had starved their aesthetic sense, their fierce attachment to their silver, furniture, and portraits was evidence of that potential, he believed, and so their taste just needed to be broadened. He explained all this to the Cheeks as they rode down to Palm Beach with him in his business car to meet potential donors.[84] As a direct result of Anderson's efforts, Arthur Glasgow and the Adolph D. Williamses gave important collections, which helped begin the transformation of the Virginia Museum from a small provincial institution to the significant museum that it is today.[85]

By the time the firm's fiftieth anniversary came around on November 1, 1951, Anderson was so weakened by his illness and his most recent operation that he was "practically carried" by his chauffeur into the party at Eppa Hunton IV's house on River Road.[86]

After dinner, the firm's lawyers—there were twenty-two of them by that time, sixteen partners and six associates—retired to the library for cigars and Fulcher's Old Virginia Mountain Whiskey, a pre-Prohibition treat brought up from the Huntons' cellar for the occasion. Henry Anderson settled into one of the tall wing chairs that flanked the fireplace, and Randolph Williams into the other. And then the two old men, the founders of the firm, began swapping tales about the early days and the practice of the law when they had started out.

Colonel Anderson told a story from his railroad damage suit days. The company was being sued for injuries sustained by a traveler who had tried to cross its track at night. The railroad's lawyers

put an old watchman on the stand to establish the fact that he had
been guarding the crossing and had signaled with his lantern to
warn the traveler of the oncoming train.

The witness gave his evidence with so much apparent fairness,
and yet with such great decision, that after he got off the stand
the lawyers complimented him on his performance. "Well, I did
best I could," the old man said, "and I was telling the Lord's truth
when I said I waved that lantern at that man. But when they kept
on asking me how many times I waved it, I got mighty scared that
they were going to ask me was that lantern *lit*." [87]

The story was an old chestnut that Beverley Munford had written up in *Random Recollections*, but the younger lawyers seemed to
have enjoyed it, as they enjoyed the other stories that Anderson
and Randolph Williams told that night.

It was a happy anniversary. And it gave Anderson a chance to
bask in his time-tested friendship with Randolph Williams. He
considered that friendship one of the great blessings of his life. As
early as 1919, when he was on his second mission to the Balkans,
relying totally on Randolph Williams to look after his household
and his mother in Farmville, he tried to put his feelings into words:

> Here in Greece, [there is] no opportunity to relax in the
> warmth of friendship. My staff, now fifty, are splendidly helpful
> and loyal, but ... . none of them are friends of such long stand-
> ing as to give one that restful feeling of personal understanding.
> ... I thank you for what you write about my work out here, for
> the encouragement it gives, and for your attention to and in-
> terest in my personal affairs. Your loyal friendship has been so
> constant and abiding through the years that I take it as a matter
> of course, as a foundation stone in the structure of my personal
> life, yet I assure you I appreciate and value it more and more
> each year. Without it life would be a very different thing.[88]

When Henry Anderson came home that night to 913 West Franklin, he sat up for a while with his niece Frances Shield, who happened to be staying there, telling her how much he had enjoyed

the anniversary dinner and the chance to reminisce with Randolph Williams.

He pointed out that there never had been two more different people. "Randolph is a married family man, and I'm not. Randolph is a churchman, and I am not. Randolph is a Democrat, and I'm a Republican. And yet in all those fifty years," he said, "we have never disagreed."[89]

When his niece responded that he must be proud to see the law firm that he and Williams had started grow to be such a large, important one, he drew himself up in his chair and looked at her sternly.

"My dear child," he said, "nobody's interested in what you have done. They're always interested in what you're *going* to do. Remember that."

Over the next two years Henry Anderson grew steadily weaker. At the end he was bedridden, surrounded by mementos from his successful and unusually romantic life.

There were photographs of Queen Marie, the Princess Ileana, and Ellen Glasgow scattered through the house. Gladys Vanderbilt Szechenyi, a longtime friend from Washington, came down and spent a week at the Jefferson Hotel so that she could visit with him each day and read to him. On the bedroom mantelpiece was a single fresh rose delivered every other morning by a local florist who was not allowed to reveal the name of the woman who had sent it.[90] Above the rose was the life-sized portrait of Queen Marie, "the last thing that he saw when he went to sleep at night, and the first thing he saw when he woke up in the morning."[91]

Finally, on January 7, 1954, Henry Anderson, the last surviving founder of the law firm, died.

SIX

Thomas Benjamin Gay

1885–1983

In 1899 when Henry Anderson and Randolph Williams were fledgling lawyers practicing four doors apart on East Main Street, Thomas Benjamin Gay, a fourteen-year-old orphan, applied for a job across the street at John L. Williams & Sons. He presented his letter of introduction and was told to wait until Mr. Williams senior was free to see him.

He sat down on a bench and began to watch the men—brokers, customers, and messengers—rushing in and out. All day long he watched, until finally at closing time somebody noticed him and told him to come back the next day.

The next morning the boy presented himself and his letter once again. This time he got a job and began a lifelong association with the Williamses. Many boys, even orphans like himself who had to make some money, would have given up that first day, but Thomas Benjamin Gay was blessed with perseverance. Whether he was looking for a job, breaking in a horse, or researching a point of law, he added that extra measure of determination—"grit" might be a better word for it—that tips the balance to success instead of failure.

What was going through his mind as he sat there with his flat cap in his hand, swinging the short legs that protruded from his knickers, waiting for one of those tall, thin, and *powerful* Williamses to notice him, no one will ever know. Already life had made him taciturn. A stoic. He did not often talk about emotions.

He had been born May 22, 1885, near Hollywood Cemetery in Richmond, the son of Thomas Bolling Gay and Mary Ratcliffe Ellett Gay. When Gay was seventeen months old, his father, a mechanical engineer, died as a result of a chill he got hunting with his friend Dr. George Ben Johnston, chief surgeon at the Medical College of Virginia. It was Johnston from whom the infant Thomas Benjamin Gay got his middle name.[1]

After his father's death in October 1886, young Tom—or Ben, as he would be called later[2]—and his mother moved in with his grandmother Ellett and his Aunt Lou on Laurel Street, near the church that is now Grace and Holy Trinity. He spent a relatively happy childhood there, often playing in Monroe Park and sometimes in the open fields north of Lombardy Street.

When time came for him to go to school, he walked up West Main Street to Lombardy and climbed the steep granite steps to what was then the West End School (later Stonewall Jackson School). Since his mother was a teacher at the girls' school started by one of her relatives, "Miss Jennie" Ellett, she was able to supplement her son's education.[3] Eventually he entered Nolley's Preparatory School.[4]

In July 1899, when he had just turned fourteen, his mother died. For a while he continued to live with his maiden aunt Lou, then moved in with some family friends, the Craigs, on Church Hill.[5] Their son Pat[6] was his age, and their younger son, Irvin, would one day work for Gay and be a partner in his firm.[7]

The job at John L. Williams & Sons gave young Gay a little independence, a glimpse of what he liked to call "the Street" in action, as well as small change for his expenses and those of his aunt Lou, whom he now had to support.[8] For six years he worked there in the summer as a runner and clerk until, at the Williamses' urging, he entered the University of Virginia's Law School in the fall of 1904.

For years Dr. Johnston had been giving him a gold piece on his birthday. He had saved them all and, with them and the hundred dollars one of the Williams sons had offered him in exchange for a promise not to smoke until he was twenty-one, he went off to Charlottesville.[9]

Over the next two years he worked his way through the law courses there and was eventually elected to both Phi Beta Kappa and the Raven Society. But his life as a student was severely limited by lack of money. Since he knew shorthand and typing, he took careful notes in class, transcribed them, and subsequently sold them for ten cents a set.

At the University of Virginia, he lived on "the Lawn," in one of the student rooms designed by Jefferson, and took his meals at a boarding house for fifteen dollars a month. The price did not include dessert, except on Sunday, so he bought a pack of chewing gum each week, and made it serve as his weekday desserts.[10]

When he entered law school, it was understood that he would come back to Richmond afterwards and work for Randolph Williams's law firm. But by the time he got his license to practice law in 1906, his health had broken down.

Working out of doors, away from books for a while, might restore his health, the Williamses thought, so they sent him down to Georgia to help survey for a railroad—probably the Atlanta to Birmingham connection—that their firm was financing.[11] To his surprise Gay discovered that he loved working out of doors, and bit by bit he regained the strength that had been drained in law school.

On his way back to Richmond and his commitment to the law firm, he stopped off in Atlanta to see a friend from law school. As it happened, his friend's father was looking for a bright young lawyer to work for one year with a railroad in Tucson, Arizona— at the munificent salary of five hundred dollars a month.

Since young Gay had no money to speak of and the firm of Munford, Hunton, Williams & Anderson was not prepared to pay him his first year, this was an opportunity he could not afford to pass up. He asked for and received from Randolph Williams a year's reprieve from his commitment.

Tucson in the early 1900s was a fascinating town, combining frontier conditions with Eastern refinement; some houses actually had dirt floors with Oriental rugs on them, Gay told his wife in later years. Beverley Munford, a former Laurel Street neighbor, was in Tucson that same winter (1906–7) in a last vain attempt to reverse the progress of tuberculosis. The Munfords were kind to him there, and to the end of his life, Gay used to talk about the time that Mrs. Munford brought hot soup to him at his boarding house when he had the flu.[12]

Sometime in 1907 or 1908 he returned to Virginia and reported for work at Munford, Hunton, Williams & Anderson. The three active partners were then heavily involved in the struggle between Fisher and the Goulds for control of Virginia's electric-utility industry, a struggle that would not be finally resolved until 1909. Henry Anderson had been named director and general counsel of the newly organized Norfolk & Portsmouth Traction Company in 1906.[13] Since he needed to know more about the way the company was being run, he sent young Gay to Norfolk for a year to work directly for the traction company.[14] Late in 1908 Gay returned to Richmond and settled down at the law firm he would serve successively as associate, partner, managing partner, chairman, and historian for seventy-five years.

The first record of payment to Thomas Benjamin Gay in the firm journal appears on November 15, 1909: half payment of a salary of a hundred dollars a month. In his history of *The Hunton Williams Firm*, Gay gives November 15, 1908,[15] as the date he first came to the firm, thus corroborating the story that he worked that first year without payment.[16]

The other associate in 1908–9 was John Randolph Tucker, who had been at the firm since April 1906. When he left September 1, 1909, Gay became the only associate serving three increasingly active partners.

He was immediately put to work on Southern Railway litigation. A letter from John T. Wingo, dated January 28, 1972, admonished him for failing to mention in his history of the law firm

an important case in which you and I tussled in Law and Equity Court, then presided over by Judge John H. Ingram.

The case involved two deaths by wrongful act of the Southern Railway, the victims being two handsome, sound mules, of
great value, the property of I. J. Smith & Co. The careless act of
that terrible Railway Company took place in the yard near the
south end of the Ninth Street Bridge, where the victims were
invited guests and far too intelligent to be guilty of contributory
negligence.

But justice, [Wingo ruefully recalled,] did not prevail. The
jury must have been confused by too many instructions on negligence, contributory negligence, last clear chance, etc.

In his reply, Gay wrote that "I, of course, well remember the tort
action which you instituted against Southern Railway in behalf of
I. J. Smith Company, since it was the first jury case in which I alone
represented a party. Judge Ingram had some very kind words to
say to me after the case was over, of a prophetic nature concerning
my future as a railroad lawyer." [17]

Judge Ingram's prophecy was amply fulfilled over the next half
century. A later partner who tried cases with Gay recalled that
although he was only five foot six inches tall, [18]

he was like a bantam rooster. When he stood up in front of a
jury, you felt like he was tall. He was very forceful . . . [and also]
very conscious of eye contact with jurors. He'd look them right
in the eye . . . stand right in front of 'em, and I've seen him do
it, he'd pull out his handkerchief and wipe his face, and make
out like he was crying.

Oh, he had theatrics, [though he was] not the ham that Leith
Bremner used to [be]. Now Bremner, oh, he'd weep and wail
and moan. [19] . . . Mr. Gay didn't do that. Mr. Gay was very strait-
laced about the way he did it. But he had a consciousness of the
fact that he had to get their attention and hold it until he could
get into their head the point he wanted to make.

He was also very effective with judges. He intimidated judges.
. . . He brought with him, and took advantage of, his reputation
as one of the principal trial lawyers in that big firm down in
Richmond called Hunton, Williams, Anderson, Gay, whatever it

was. And some of the country judges were afraid of him. And he would begin to talk about taking on appeal or something, and they'd say, "Wait a minute, Mr. Gay. Now, let me make sure, what is your point in here?"

They didn't want to be reversed. And they thought he must be right, I mean, "This smart lawyer from Richmond, that big law firm, what do I know? And if he says that's the law, maybe that's the law." . . . Particularly when he was offering instructions.

He knew how to take full advantage of his reputation, and he was careful to make sure that his reputation preceded him. And . . . with that he made up for what he may have lacked in terms of intellectualization of the law. I mean he was not a *student* of the law. He knew a lot, but he wasn't a George Gibson.[20]

Though other lawyers might chuckle and his own associates squirm in their seats when he would turn his broad "a" on and off during oral argument, there was no doubt about the fact that Gay had a theatrical flair that was effective with jurors and with judges.[21]

In those early years when he was trying cases for the Southern Railway and for Standard Oil, Gay also became involved in representing an important client inherited from Munford, the Atlantic Life Insurance Company.[22] By April 1913 he was getting half the fee for that account in addition to his salary, which was now $150 a month.[23]

By this time Henry Anderson's practice had expanded so dramatically that he must have welcomed the assistance of this energetic, persevering, and exceedingly ambitious young associate. One of the most complicated cases in which young Gay assisted concerned the riparian rights of the Old Dominion Iron & Nail Works.[24] This company, located on Belle Isle in Richmond, was a longtime client of the firm dating back to the days when John L. Williams & Sons was developing hydroelectric power on the James River.

Eppa Hunton, Jr., had enlisted Gay in the effort to get the Federal Reserve Bank for the Fifth District located in Richmond, taking advantage of the fact that John Skelton Williams was now comptroller of the currency and was predisposed in Richmond's favor. In 1914, the year that the Federal Reserve Bank began its operations on East Main Street, Hunton had succeeded Caperton Braxton as general counsel to the Richmond, Fredericksburg and Potomac Railroad.[25] Under Hunton's direction, Gay now began to do the trial work for the RF & P.

Since 1910 Gay had been helping Randolph Williams, district counsel for the Seaboard Air Line, with both the office and the trial work for that railroad, and had been named local counsel for the Seaboard in Richmond.[26]

Though his future was brightening, it was still not secure enough, he felt, for him to take on the responsibility of a wife. By this time he had fallen in love with a young artist, Lenore Temple Skeen. She was a delicate and diminutive beauty who had many other callers, but once again Ben Gay's tenacity gave him an advantage. He simply "outsat" them all, he later said. Though they had become engaged, he did not think he should get married until he had been taken into the partnership. Lenore, in the meantime, was enjoying success as a commercial artist in Baltimore. In fact, she was then making more money as an artist than her fiancé was making as a lawyer.[27]

In those days Gay allowed himself few luxuries. Most of the time he worked, gradually making himself indispensable to the firm's three partners. And when he played, he generally played to win— clients as well as the silver trophies from steeplechase races, golf tournaments, and skeet-shooting contests that would eventually adorn his house.

On January 1, 1916, eight years after he had come into the firm and ten years after he had received his law degree, Gay became, at the age of thirty, the first associate to be taken into the original partnership.[28]

Now at last he could afford to get married, and on June 10, 1916, Lenore Skeen became Mrs. Thomas Benjamin Gay.

In keeping with his status as a partner at Munford, Hunton, Williams & Anderson, he had moved from rented rooms to an apartment at The Chesterfield at 900 West Franklin Street, at the intersection of Shafer and Franklin, just across the street from the Randolph Williamses.

As the year 1916 drew to a close, Gay must have felt he had his life under control. Literally and figuratively, he had moved into the world of his senior partners. He had just become a member of the American Bar Association, determined to extend his influence beyond Virginia. Most important, he had married the woman he loved, and now she was going to have a baby.

One night late in March 1917, the telephone rang at the Williamses' house. It was Gay calling from Grace Hospital. A son, Thomas Benjamin Gay, Jr., had been born, but his wife, Lenore, who was a Christian Scientist and had not wanted specialized prenatal care, had developed complications in childbirth, was in a coma, and was not expected to survive.[29] Randolph Williams happened to be out of town that night, and so his wife Maude got dressed immediately and walked over to the hospital, at 2:00 A.M., to be with him.[30]

On April 1, 1917, Lenore Gay died. Her funeral was held from the Williamses' house, and she was buried at Hollywood Cemetery —where her husband would be buried at her side sixty-six years later—in the lot adjoining the Williams family lot.

A nurse was hired to look after the baby. Often she would take him to the Williamses' porch for an airing or down to Monroe Park where his father used to play, since The Chesterfield was not an ideal place for raising babies.[31]

Mercifully, Gay had no time to nurse his grief. There was too much work to do down at the office. And Gay loved to work; in fact, he thrived on work; the more work there was to do, the better he liked it.[32]

When the United States entered World War I, he became a "Three Minute Man," giving brief patriotic speeches to sell war bonds.[33] In May the firm's only associate, Andrew Christian, went into the army, and two months later Henry Anderson left for Rumania. While Randolph Williams took over the representation of Virginia Railway and Power Company, Gay picked up the slack for

Anderson's other clients. In recognition of this fact, Anderson allocated two of his percentage points to Gay in 1917.[34]

At the beginning of the summer of 1917, two new associates were hired, Wirt Marks, Jr., to replace Andrew Christian; and Floridus Crosby, who left in 1919 to practice in his hometown of Staunton, Virginia, where he eventually became a judge.[35]

While Anderson was in the Balkans from 1917 to 1919, three partners and two associates were holding down the office. In the "boom years" of the twenties, the firm's growth accelerated; more associates were hired, and four of them were taken into the partnership: in 1925, Wirt Marks, Jr., Anderson's able but rather solitary cousin, who had been there since 1917; in 1928, Whiting Faulkner, who came in January 1920 and would leave in December 1930;[36] Edmund Preston, who came in 1921 and would help establish the firm's labor department; and Preston's classmate Irvin Craig, the son of the same Craigs with whom Gay had lived after his mother died.[37] By February 1928 there were seven partners and two new associates: Eppa Hunton IV, the son of the founder, who, in September 1927, had begun half a century of service to the firm;[38] and Jennings C. Wise, later described by this same Eppa Hunton IV, as "much older and engaged solely in politics. Republican, of the gutter type."[39] For a little less than two years, Wise worked for Colonel Anderson directly. He left the firm at the end of 1929.[40]

After the departure of Eppa Hunton, Jr., in 1920, Williams was clearly the leader of the firm. Henry Anderson ran for governor and was defeated in 1921, and then he began to spend more and more of his time in Washington, discharging the responsibilities he was given during three Republican administrations.

For this entire decade and the one preceding it, Thomas Benjamin Gay had no peer or partner in his age group. As the firm expanded, he became, in effect, the managing partner charged with the responsibility for hiring new lawyers, and he continued in that role for more than half a century.[41] No wonder one of his successors said, "Oh, Mr. Gay. He had been managing partner since the Ice Age."

As his influence in the law firm grew, so did his status in the community and at the bar. Though Gay was an unusually small man, his energy was gigantic. And he was also fastidious and dapper, always dressing neatly and appropriately for the occasion, whether it was working, hunting, shooting, yachting, or attending the races.

He worked very hard, and he played hard, too, putting the same intense determination, perseverance, and perfectionism he displayed as a lawyer into developing his skills as a sportsman. His partner Archibald Robertson expressed great admiration for this quality:

> I think Benny is a very remarkable character in a way that most people don't talk about. Now, they talk about Benny's ori gin on Church Hill and Benny's attainment to the Richmond German and so forth. All of which is true.[42] But I think that Benny is a very remarkable person . . . from the standpoint of putting up a physical fight. . . . Benny's got a very frail physique. And yet Benny . . . made himself [into] a good golfer . . . an excellent horseback rider . . . a good shot . . . and a good sailor.
>
> He and Jim Corbitt brought back their sailboat from up North somewhere and got in a terrible storm and brought it on through [in] an experience that would make your hair curl.[43]

Robertson also recalled a story that his friend and contemporary Virginius Shackelford[44] told him about Gay when he was spending a weekend on the Shackelford's farm in Orange County:

> Virginius was interested in horses and had two or three horses, and Benny had been very active out in the Deep Run Hunt Club. . . . And "V." said he had a young colt up there that had been broken, but that was about all. And that the colt was just as mean as hell. And all the people working around the stable were scared of him, but that Benny was a pretty good judge of horses, too. And so . . . they brought the horse out there to show him to Benny. And "V" told him that the boys up there were afraid of him. Benny said, "I'll ride him." . . . Everybody tried to

talk him out of it, but he said, "No, I'll ride him. You just hold him, so I can get on."

And so they held him, and Benny got on him and they turned the horse aloose. And he said Benny rode him till he conquered him, and it was the most wonderful exhibition of courage and skill that he, Virginius, had ever seen.[45]

Riding was probably Gay's favorite sport. Every Wednesday he would defy the firm's work ethic and take the afternoon off to go riding. Almost nothing was allowed to interfere with this weekly ritual, not even the fact that it infuriated his hard-working colleague T. Justin Moore.

In 1924 and 1925 Gay served as Master of Fox Hounds at the Deep Run Hunt Club, and from 1927 through 1931 as the club's president. He persuaded his friend and client Albert Rudduck to build a steeplechase course on his property, "Curles Neck," and then almost single-handedly, he raised the money to hold the First Renewal of the Deep Run Races on May 13, 1928. His horse "Lauvain" won the first race.[46]

For the first four years after the death of his wife Lenore, he was showered with invitations from the matrons of Richmond who could not bear to watch his small son growing up without a mother. They were determined that Ben Gay would not remain a bachelor long. One of them, Grace Bryan, the wife of the surgeon Dr. Robert Bryan, was finally successful when she introduced him to her former roommate from Stuart Hall, Mary Pattison from Baltimore. On November 25, 1921, Mary Pattison became the second Mrs. Gay and a loving stepmother to four-year-old Tom, who would grow up to be an artist, like his mother, Lenore. A daughter, Mary Frances, was born on April 3, 1923, but died three months later, and there were no more children after that.

In 1925 a group of local stockholders in the Chesapeake & Ohio railroad hired Gay to bring suit to prevent a proposed unification of the C & O with the Nickel Plate, Hocking Valley, Erie, and Pere Marquette railroads. The suit initiated major litigation in the railroad industry and earned Gay a national reputation.[47]

Henry Anderson (center) as a member of the senior law class,
1898, at Washington and Lee University.—*Washington and
Lee University*

Henry Anderson started
a new page in the ledger
and in his life in 1901.
—*A. R. Dementi*

Henry Anderson's chauffeur, Grey, sat in the back seat of the Pierce
Arrow with Helen Hamilton Bryan (1884–1967) and Thomas Pinckney
Bryan (1882–1920) while Anderson posed at the wheel with Mrs.
Bryan's sister, Sarah Hamilton (later Mrs. S. Boothe McKinney) beside
him, around 1909.

Henry Anderson at his desk in Queen Marie's castle in Jassy, during the
winter of 1917–18, supervising the work of the American Red Cross in
Rumania.—*Virginia Historical Society*

"I took Colonel Anderson about . . . and drove also far out into the country . . . so that, with his own eyes, he could see how terrible was the want in the villages," wrote Queen Marie in *The Story of My Life.* —*Virginia Historical Society*

Inscribed photographs from Marie of Rumania were all over Anderson's house at 913 West Franklin Street.—*Virginia Historical Society*

With the jewels that are mine no more

Marie

Ellen Glasgow, the novelist and, for a brief time, Anderson's fiancée, around 1920. Though their romance had cooled, she actively supported him in his campaign as Republican candidate for governor of Virginia in 1921.—*Virginia Historical Society*

When Henry Anderson ran for governor of Virginia as a Republican in 1921, his mother and brother, still smarting from Reconstruction, chose not to vote at all rather than vote Republican.

With his niece, Frances Richardson, Henry Anderson won first prize at the Everglades Ball in Palm Beach in 1931. Anderson's costume had been made in 1926 for a ball in Richmond to honor Queen Marie, but she was called home early and the ball was cancelled.

Randolph Williams receives a slice of turkey from his host and close friend, Henry Anderson, at "Whippernock," Dinwiddie County, Virginia, in the late 1940s.

Thomas Bolling Gay (1855–1886) was a mechanical engineer who died when his young son, Thomas Benjamin Gay, was only seventeen months old.

Mary Ratcliffe Ellett Gay (1860–1899), who married Thomas Bolling Gay on September 15, 1881, was a schoolteacher at the Virginia Randolph Ellett School. When she died, she left her fourteen-year-old son an orphan.

Thomas Benjamin Gay, age five, in 1890.

Thomas B. Gay, age fourteen, when he went to work for John L. Williams & Sons as a runner in 1899.

After Gay moved into the Chesterfield Apartments in 1916, he and his three partners, Eppa Hunton, Jr., Randolph Williams, and Henry Anderson, lived within one block of each other on West Franklin Street. Clockwise, from top left: Chesterfield Apartments, 900 West Franklin—*Reid Freeman*; Hunton house, 810 West Franklin—*Margo Peters Millure*; Williams house, 826 West Franklin—*Reid Freeman*; Anderson house, 913 West Franklin—*Reid Freeman*

Self-portrait of Lenore Temple Skeen Gay, Thomas B. Gay's first wife, who died April 1, 1917.
—*A. R. Dementi*

Gay was an avid horseman, Master of Fox Hounds (1924–25), then president of the Deep Run Hunt Club (1927–31), and an active promoter of steeplechase racing.

Thomas B. Gay had moved to 2712 Monument Avenue by 1924, and lived there for forty years.
—*Margo Peters Millure*

Thomas B. Gay helped organize the American Bar Association's Board of Governors and served as chairman of its House of Delegates from 1939 to 1941.

Captain Lewis F. Powell, Jr., in September 1943 upon his return from North Africa. He was assigned to the faculty at the Air Force Intelligence School, Harrisburg, Pennsylvania, then returned to England in January 1944 as an ULTRA officer.—*Curator's Office, Supreme Court of the United States*

Lt. Col. B. Warwick Davenport received the Legion of Merit for his service as assistant secretary to the General Staff and liaison to the White House.

On November 21, 1945, Col. H. Merrill Pasco received the Distinguished Service Medal from General George C. Marshall for his work as assistant secretary, then secretary of the War Department General Staff.

Francis V. Lowden, T. Justin Moore, Jr., H. Brice Graves, and John W. Riely during the early 1950s.

Merrill Pasco, Martha Davenport, and Warwick Davenport on the golf course at the Homestead Hotel in Hot Springs, Virginia, in the 1960s.

Thomas B. Gay at the races in the mid-1970s with his son, Thomas B. Gay, Jr., a poet and an artist like his mother, Lenore.

At age ninety-two, Thomas B. Gay married Miriam Riggs Harkrader, forty years his junior.

In recognition of that reputation and the burden of responsibility that Gay was now carrying, the law firm voted to add his name to its style and drop that of Munford, to become, on January 1, 1927, Hunton, Williams, Anderson & Gay. At that time there were eight lawyers in the firm.[48]

Gay had no rival in the firm until 1932 when T. Justin Moore, who had served as general counsel for the Virginia Electric and Power Company for the past seven years, came in laterally with two associates—Archibald G. Robertson and Norman Flippen—increasing the number of lawyers to twelve and changing the firm's style to Hunton, Williams, Anderson, Gay & Moore.

During the next decade, Gay and Moore, two men with radically different styles and aptitudes, vied for the position of leader of the firm. Gay remained the chief administrator, the detail man, and the managing partner, while Moore secured and controlled the lion's share of clients. During the 1930s four new partners were admitted: Eppa Hunton IV and George D. Gibson in 1934, Archibald G. Robertson in 1937, and Lewis F. Powell, Jr., in 1938.[49]

Early in 1934 the general counsel for the New York Stock Exchange retained Gay to represent it in hearings before the congressional committees that were drafting the Securities Exchange Act.[50] In challenging the bill's constitutionality, Gay called it "the most extreme and far reaching measure proposed under the Roosevelt administration," and he received a good deal of publicity in the *Wall Street Journal* and the *New York Times*.[51] The bill was nevertheless enacted in June 1934. "It has been said that 'Wall Street,' of which the New York Stock Exchange was a significant and essential part, was generally blamed for the five years of economic depression following the panic of 1929," Gay later wrote. "In such an atmosphere, the Board of Governors of the Exchange would seem to have had no effective choice but to comply with the Act." It decided not to test the act's constitutionality.[52]

During the 1930s and 1940s, Gay was at the height of his career. In 1936 he became president of the Richmond Bar Association, and that same year he began twenty-one years as state delegate to the American Bar Association. In 1939 Gay was elected chairman of the ABA's House of Delegates, the second most powerful position in that organization, and the following year was reelected for a second term.[53]

On the eve of World War II—the greatest challenge Gay would face as the firm's administrator—the city of Richmond and the surrounding county of Henrico locked horns in a bitter contest. When the city instituted annexation proceedings, Henrico County engaged Gay and the firm to try to defeat the annexation. Irvin Craig and Lewis Powell, Jr., as the second and third lawyers on Gay's team, worked almost around the clock to prepare a defense challenging the "necessity and expediency" of the city's proposal.[54]

In the end they lost the suit, and the city was allowed to annex over fifteen square miles of highly developed real estate in Henrico and Chesterfield counties.[55]

The strain of preparing for day after day of acrimonious hearings spread over several months had broken the health of Gay's assistant, Irvin Craig. And he never fully recovered.[56] Within the firm, there was criticism of Gay for not being sufficiently sensitive to the pressure he was putting on Craig, who did not have the temperament for such arduous, prolonged, and highly controversial litigation, despite the fact that he was an able lawyer and had been a star in the University of Virginia's law school class of 1921.[57] Lewis Powell, Jr., on the other hand, seemed to have suffered no ill effects from the ordeal, and Irvin Craig might well have recovered fully had not World War II come along right afterwards.[58]

On December 7, 1941, the Japanese bombed Pearl Harbor, and within a week the United States was at war with both Japan and Germany. As, one by one, the younger lawyers left for the service, Gay struggled to replace them and keep the law firm going. The strain of those war years on the lawyers left at home is hard to imagine now. Most of the associates[59] and two of the nine partners[60] went off to war. The situation at the office "was frantic," as George Gibson put it. "We had an undiminished number of things to do with a greatly diminished number of people to do them."[61]

The venerable Randolph Williams found himself going to police court once again;[62] Irvin Craig's health continued to deteriorate despite periodic vacations to restore it; and Edmund Preston drove himself so relentlessly that he died from a heart attack, at age forty-six, six weeks before the war in Europe ended.

The career of Edmund Preston is one of the most interesting in the history of the firm. At first, he combined a great deal of trial work with corporate work, then established for the firm an early national preeminence in labor law. And on his own time, he continued to do *pro bono* work in civil liberties and race relations.

Grandson of Major E. T. D. Myers, the first president of the Richmond, Fredericksburg and Potomac Railroad, and son of the Richmond lawyer William C. Preston, Edmund Preston grew up on West Franklin Street. He received the traditional education at McGuire's University School, the Episcopal High School, and the University of Virginia. Later he followed Gay as Master of Fox Hounds at the Deep Run Hunt Club. Yet despite his privileged and conservative upbringing, Preston was essentially an independent thinker who followed only his own conscience.

According to his contemporary Virginius Dabney, he was "one of the few people around here in his social stratum that was interested in race relations. It was hard to find *anybody* else, outside of the ministry, or journalism, or college faculties, who would even listen to you."[63] Specifically, Dabney recalled Preston's "defense, at his own expense, of a black sharecropper, Odell Waller, charged with murder in Pittsylvania County, in a very controversial trial" and his earlier defense of Alice Burke, who was said to be a Communist.[64] In an editorial the day after Preston's death, Dabney wrote: "Mr. Preston's wide human sympathy led him to espouse the cause of the weak and the underprivileged. He was a prominent member of the legal profession with clients among the great corporations, but he also was quick to help the most defenseless citizen, especially if he felt that that citizen's constitutional rights had been invaded."[65]

After serving in World War I and graduating from the University of Virginia Law School, Preston came to the law firm in 1921 and became a partner in 1928. Initially he worked for Randolph Williams, who had just succeeded Eppa Hunton, Jr., as counsel for the Richmond, Fredericksburg and Potomac Railroad. In time, Preston was named assistant general counsel to the RF & P and did a great deal of their trial work. When the National Labor Relations Board was created in the mid-1930s, Preston argued one of the first cases before that board and soon gained a national reputation for himself and his law firm.[66]

According to Archibald Robertson, the principal trial lawyer for Virginia Electric and Power Company and its transit operations (which were not separated from it until 1944), the firm's first labor case arose when the streetcar company was charged with unfair labor practices after firing a motorman caught breaking open the fare box at the end of the line.[67] Robertson was overloaded with damage cases at the time and Justin Moore asked another partner, Edmund Preston, to handle the case. From then on, Preston specialized in labor law and over the next seven and a half years, built up a substantial national practice in that field.[68]

In addition to the demands of his practice within the firm and in various *pro bono* cases, Preston found time to serve as counsel, then president, of the Children's Home Society of Virginia; as a member of the Executive Committee of the Richmond Commission on Inter-Racial Co-operation; as a member of the Executive Committee of the Southern Regional Council; and as legal adviser to the Society for the Prevention of Cruelty to Animals.

Strikingly handsome, with all of the charm and courtesy of the old school from which he came, Edmund Preston was a hardworking, hard-drinking, essentially solitary man, who died prematurely in 1945. He seems to have been driven by a vision of a just society reminiscent of the Munfords' many years before him and a zeal for political reform more radical than that which Henry Anderson had tried to infuse into the machine-controlled Virginia scene. Preston's presence would be sorely missed a decade later when that same political machine forced upon Virginia "massive resistance" to court-ordered integration of the public schools.

Through 1942 and well into 1943, Thomas B. Gay, as the firm's managing partner, struggled to find and hire able young associates, only to see them called into the service soon after their arrival at the firm.

By the summer of 1943, when both Frank Lowden and Ralph Ferrell, whom he had hired in 1942, received commissions in the navy, he must have been feeling fairly desperate. At any rate, it was then that he finally acted on a suggestion that Dean F. D. G. Ribble of the Virginia Law School had been making for the past two years; he hired the firm's first woman associate, Sarah Geer Dale, from the University of Virginia's law school class of 1941. Two months later, in October 1943, he brought in Nan Ross McConnell, a 1943 graduate of the University of Richmond's law school.

Sarah Dale was assigned to work for Edmund Preston in labor law, and Nan McConnell to work for George Gibson in the railroad and utility practice, which he was then developing under and *beyond* Colonel Anderson and Justin Moore.

Actually Mrs. Dale and Miss McConnell were not the first women lawyers to be hired by Gay. In the early 1920s, he had hired Elizabeth Tompkins, the first woman to graduate from the University of Virginia Law School, to work as a summer clerk in 1921 and 1922.[69] Initially, Eppa Hunton, Jr., criticized his former law firm for hiring a *woman* to do legal work. "And then the next thing I knew," Gay later recalled, "Mr. Hunton had her up there at the RF & P doing work for *him*."[70]

This anecdote is especially ironic in view of the fact that from 1910 through 1918, Gay had helped Eppa Hunton, Jr., block Mary Munford's effort to have women admitted to the University of Virginia at all levels. The most that was accomplished in Mrs. Munford's lifetime was the admission of women to the graduate and professional schools in 1921. Half a century later, when women were finally admitted as undergraduates—with a class-action suit pending—Gay was still arguing the "unwisdom" of coeducation at UVA.[71]

In an interview in 1985, Sarah Geer Dale (who had subsequently married a second time and become Mrs. Finley Gayle) recalled a time when she researched a case for Thomas B. Gay. "I finally wrote a resume of the whole thing and I put it on his desk. And in an hour or two he called me up and said, 'Mrs. Dale, that was an *excellent* piece of work you did for me. It was *excellent*.' I mean I think he couldn't believe it. And I couldn't either."

There had probably been "great dissension about whether to even *consider* a woman," Mrs. Gayle speculated. Some of the senior partners seem to have been "shocked" when it turned out that the women lawyers did a creditable job. After she came for an interview at Gay's request during the summer of 1943, the partner who actually called her up to offer her the job was Randolph Williams. "*Precious* man. . . . Oh, he was one of the loveliest people I ever knew in my life. He was quite elderly then. And he said, 'Mrs. Dale . . . I think we're going to let you come and join us, but I want to tell you Richmond is not ready for a woman lawyer. And we're going to be right behind you. And we're going to give you every help and so forth. . . . So don't be worried about it.' "

Was he implying that they might take her into the partnership eventually? "No," she answered. "No. Implying that they'd give me every chance to show that a woman could do law. I think they really had no *idea* that I was going to turn out to be much more than just a good secretary."

When the lawyers who had left for the war began to come back in the fall of 1945, Sarah Dale left the firm to get married and retired from the practice of law altogether. Nan Ross McConnell stayed on for two and a half years longer, then left in 1948 to marry Charles Appel, a lieutenant colonel in the air force. Later, she became a tax consultant in Marietta, Georgia.

Though the firm had lost two partners during the war with the death of Edmund Preston and the retirement of Irvin Craig, it had gained one, too. In 1943 Norman Flippen, the lawyer who had come into the firm with Justin Moore and Archibald Robertson in 1932 and still worked almost exclusively on Vepco matters, was finally elevated to the partnership.[72]

During the summer of 1945 Patrick Gibson, younger brother of George Gibson and a former Rhodes scholar and, since 1941, special assistant to the U.S. attorney general in the antitrust division, was brought in as an associate to do labor work; he was taken into the partnership two years later.[73]

On August 14, 1945, the Japanese surrendered, and World War II was over. One by one the lawyers who had left the firm to serve their country drifted back into the office, aged and broadened by their war experiences.[74]

Eppa Hunton IV, now a major in the army, brought back with him a bronze star and near blindness in one eye, as a result of an eye disease he had contracted in Africa and Italy, serving as adjutant in the Forty-fifth General Hospital, which had been formed by the Medical College of Virginia.[75]

Lewis Powell, now a colonel, had been awarded the Legion of Merit, the Bronze Star, and the Croix de Guerre with Palm for his service as an Army Air Force intelligence officer in the supersecret ULTRA operation.[76] Merrill Pasco, though still an associate at the firm, had been promoted to full colonel at the age of twenty-nine. For his work as assistant secretary and finally Secretary of the War Department General Staff and on the personal staff of General George C. Marshall, he received the Distinguished Service Medal and was made a member of the Order of the British Empire.

Pasco was one of a very few people in the War Department who knew about the "Manhattan Project" experiments in nuclear fission, and he was the person General Leslie Groves, head of the Manhattan Project, was to call if he needed to get in touch with General Marshall. The test explosion in New Mexico took place while Marshall was at the Potsdam Conference, so Pasco, in Washington, sent him word that it had been satisfactory. Soon afterwards, Colonel Pasco was directed to sign the order for a message to be sent to General Carl D. Spaatz, by that time commander-in-chief of the Strategic Air Force against Japan, to drop the atomic bomb:[77]

"I had nothing to do with it. I was just [part of] a mechanical process of conveying the messages when the decision was made to let it go to General Spaatz . . . who had the plane under his command [that] went and dropped the bomb," Pasco later recalled. "I just wonder about it, it worries me sometimes. . . . Oh, it saved

WE WISH TO ANNOUNCE

THAT THE FOLLOWING PARTNERS AND ASSOCIATES

OF OUR FIRM HAVE RETURNED TO THE

PRACTICE OF LAW,

AFTER SERVING WITH THE ARMED FORCES

OF THE UNITED STATES:

EPPA HUNTON, IV

MAJOR, MEDICAL ADMINISTRATIVE CORPS

LEWIS F. POWELL, JR.

COLONEL, ARMY AIR CORPS

H. MERRILL PASCO

COLONEL, GENERAL STAFF CORPS

JOHN W. RIELY

LT. COMMANDER, U. S. N. R.

FRANCIS V. LOWDEN, JR.

LIEUTENANT, U. S. N. R.

B. WARWICK DAVENPORT

LT. COLONEL, GENERAL STAFF CORPS

HUNTON, WILLIAMS, ANDERSON, GAY AND MOORE

RICHMOND, VIRGINIA
JANUARY 1, 1946

The law firm proudly announced the return of six lawyers who had served in the armed forces during World War II. Another, Ralph Ferrell, returned in March of 1946.

a million lives, I'm convinced of that. But of course it destroyed things terribly."[78]

Warwick Davenport, who had risen from second lieutenant to lieutenant colonel, had also served on the War Department General Staff under General Marshall. He was the liaison to the White House and eventually became Pasco's principal assistant.[79] John Riely was now a lieutenant commander in Washington, D.C.[80] Because of his poor eyesight he had been stuck behind a desk at the Pentagon in the Bureau of Naval Personnel, in the Discipline Section of the Officers Performance Division, as he put it, "looking after all of the liars, thieves and homosexuals in the navy."[81]

Also returning to the firm were those two associates who had been hired in January 1942 and received commissions as lieutenants in the navy the following year. Ralph Ferrell had actually worked at the firm twenty-two months before he left November 1, 1943, to serve as an aerial gunner and air combat intelligence officer.[82] Frank Lowden had been at the firm for only one year when he left to serve in the U.S. Naval Reserve with his principal assignment as Intelligence Officer, Commander Air Forces, Pacific Fleet.[83]

It was not easy for these men to come back and pick up the practice of law in the still-provincial city of Richmond, Virginia, as if the Second World War had never happened. They had trouble narrowing their focus so abruptly, and the firm had trouble, too, reabsorbing all of them, while struggling to develop enough business to support them.

Since the late thirties and early forties, the practice of law had changed radically. Federal regulations had multiplied, first under the New Deal and then during the war, and law firms were now having to change radically to cope with the new conditions.

One of the most dramatic differences was in income-tax law. "Before the war," Lewis Powell observed, "no one had worried much about it."[84] Now it was a crucial factor in advising clients. And the need for expertise in this field inspired the firm to hire their first true specialist, Brice Graves, in the fall of 1948 to start a one-man tax department.[85]

<table>
<tr><td>

EDMUND RANDOLPH WILLIAMS
HENRY W. ANDERSON
THOMAS BENJAMIN GAY
T. JUSTIN MOORE
WIRT P. MARKS, JR
EPPA HUNTON, IV
GEORGE D. GIBSON
ARCHIBALD G. ROBERTSON
LEWIS F. POWELL, JR.
NORMAN L. FLIPPEN
PATRICK A. GIBSON
H. BRICE GRAVES
H. MERRILL PASCO
RALPH H. FERRELL, JR.
JOHN W. RIELY
FRANCIS V. LOWDEN, JR
B. WARWICK DAVENPORT

LAWRENCE E. BLANCHARD, JR

</td><td>

HUNTON, WILLIAMS, ANDERSON, GAY & MOORE

ELECTRIC BUILDING

RICHMOND 12, VIRGINIA

September 27, 1950

</td></tr>
</table>

Firm's letterhead, 1950: Lawrence E. Blanchard, Jr., at the time the sole associate, was nicknamed "Atlas," for obvious reasons.

Meanwhile the "Rinky-Dinks," the five veterans who were still associates, waited not so patiently to be taken into the partnership. On January 1, 1949, the logjam broke, and all five were made partners along with Brice Graves. The total of six partners admitted at the same time doubled the previous record of three—Faulkner, Preston, and Craig—admitted in 1928 during the boom times of the 1920s. For a while, Lawrence Blanchard, Jr., was the only associate serving eleven partners.[86] His name stood alone below the thin, but all-important black line on the left side of the firm's letterhead.

In 1950 Gay celebrated his sixty-fifth birthday. He was still at the helm of the law firm as it entered a decade of phenomenal expansion. In the 1940s, as old age and illness had forced Williams and Anderson to slow down, Gay and Moore had emerged as the dominant figures. Now Lewis Powell and George Gibson were coming up behind them, and by the end of the 1950s would take control of the very different firm that was emerging.

In 1955 Powell and Gibson drafted the first formal partnership agreement since the early 1900s. Under its provision, a six-man Executive Committee was created and Gay became its first chairman on January 1, 1956. That same day he began the three-year process of cutting back to semiretirement, or, in the words of the agreement, "counsel status," which he attained on December 31,

1958. Merrill Pasco succeeded him as the firm's managing partner and Eppa Hunton IV as chairman of the Executive Committee.[87]

In 1965 Gay reached his eightieth birthday, and the Southern Railway, recognizing his service "in various capacities" since 1909, made him counsel emeritus and named Merrill Pasco to succeed him as division counsel in Virginia.[88]

After the war Powell had begun to build up an enormous client base of his own, and Pasco gradually replaced him as Gay's chief assistant. Paul Funkhouser came in as the second assistant in July 1950, and when he decided to return to Roanoke to practice, he was replaced by Robert Buford, whom Gay remembered favorably from an earlier interview.[89]

Both Pasco and Buford worked closely with Gay and found him exceedingly demanding, but never more demanding of them than he was of himself. In his own way, Gay was a superior teacher. He would always take the time to go over a brief that an associate had drafted line by line, explaining why he was making any changes he was making. And although Gay himself had a somewhat stilted style of writing, he was flexible in adopting the younger lawyers' language and willing to accept their suggestions. In other words, Buford said, "he wouldn't take a draft that I had tried to put in modern conversational English and go back and put 'whereases' and 'saids' and hackneyed expressions in it."[90]

Even more important was Gay's unique method of training the younger lawyer in court, the elbow-in-the-ribs technique, as Buford recalled it:

> When you would go with Mr. Gay to try a case, he never told you what role he wanted you to play, if any. You prepared *him*—you wrote the briefs, and you outlined the examination of witnesses, and you outlined probable cross-examination, and you got all the exhibits ready to go with him. But he never told you what part of the case he wanted *you* to try. . . . When you were sitting in the courtroom, all of a sudden, he'd give you a little punch in the ribs and say, "Bob, why don't you examine this witness?"

"Bob, why don't you cross-examine that person?" "Bob, I think you ought to make the closing argument in this case."

With *no* warning. And that happened to me one time. I was absolutely shocked. Scared me to death. I had no *idea* he was going to ask me to examine this next witness, but he did. Well, I learned that time. And the effect of that was when you went to the court with Mr. Gay, you were prepared to do the whole thing.[91]

Buford and Pasco's predecessor, Lewis Powell, emphasized that Gay had taught him "a lot about litigation." In 1935 Powell came to the firm thinking he was going to work for Justin Moore, but "Mr. Gay preempted me," he said. Initially, Powell was disappointed since he had come to admire Moore's decisiveness, drive, and adventurous spirit as a business lawyer and did not even know Gay. But eventually he was reconciled to the change in assignment since Gay was at that time "the principal big case litigator at Hunton, Williams," and Powell found him to be "a very skillful advocate." He was "very quick [and] made a brilliant appellate argument without doing what George Gibson can do . . . and that is, write one out and memorize it."[92]

There was a formality in their relationship that did not soften over the years. "He was never a warm person," Powell said. "And I doubt that Mr. Gay had many really close friends, people who felt entirely free to say anything they wanted to say in his presence. But I learned a great deal from him. Contrary to what you would have thought, he was a good trial lawyer. I did not think he was a gifted *business* lawyer [the way that Mr. Moore was, for example] although he did a lot of things. I think he organized Philip Morris."[93]

Years after Powell had gone to the Supreme Court, Gay stopped in to see him there one day, and Powell found himself still addressing him as "Mr. Gay." There was something in Gay's manner that prohibited informality and easy intimacy. Whether it was shyness, coldness, or an ingrained preference for formality, almost everybody in the firm responded to it. Even Archibald Robertson, his contemporary and, later a septuagenarian himself, had to make a conscious effort to call him "Ben" or "Benny."

Once a colleague in the American Bar Association said to Powell, "In the House of Delegates here, we all call your senior partner 'Ben.' You know him better than we do. Why do you insist on calling him 'Mr. Gay'?"

"Because I know him well enough to know what he is *thinking* when you call him Ben," Powell answered.[94]

During the late sixties, in order to preserve the knowledge of the firm's beginnings and the sense of continuity that Gay alone was able to provide, the firm urged him to write a history. He brought to the task his formidable energy and his meticulous methods, and also his rather dry literary style. The result was *The Hunton Williams Firm*, an invaluable sourcebook on the history of the firm's early years and its major cases between 1901 and 1951. The book was published in 1971.

Five years later the law firm celebrated its seventy-fifth anniversary at the house of Eppa Hunton IV, who had succeeded Gay as chairman of the Executive Committee. The habit of command is a hard one to give up, even in retirement. After Eppa Hunton IV, first, and then John Riely succeeded to the chairmanship of the firm, Gay still insisted on wielding the gavel at the monthly partners' meetings, and the younger men were generous enough not to press the point.

Finally one day Gay looked around the room at a gathering of the partners and realized that he could no longer readily identify each one of them by name. As chairman of the ABA's House of Delegates, he always took great pride in the fact that he could instantly identify every man in that entire body. When he discovered that he could no longer do this at his law firm, he set the gavel down and never took it up again.

In May of 1980, Gay gave himself a lavish ninety-fifth birthday party and invited his partners to celebrate with him and his new wife, Miriam Riggs Gay.[95]

In 1968, Mary Pattison Gay, his wife of forty-seven years, had died, and for a while Mr. Gay was a bachelor again, a bon vivant in his semiretirement, chartering a sailboat or going to the Deauville races in France in the summer and to the "Hot"—The Homestead Hotel in Hot Springs—at Christmastime.

At the age of ninety-two, he married Miriam Riggs Harkrader, who was forty years his junior.[96] It turned out to be a very happy marriage that brought life and fun and humor to his final years.[97]

Until his last few weeks, Thomas Benjamin Gay lived his life as fully as he could manage to do it. Every day he went down to the office, unless he was ill or traveling, and he continued to direct the University of Virginia Law School's Endowment Fund.

When death finally came on October 13, 1983, at age ninety-eight, he could go to rest assured that he had made the most of the talents given to him and, through his special blend of perseverance, stoic courage, and just plain grit, he had reversed setbacks that would have stopped a less determined man.[98]

SEVEN

Thomas Justin Moore

1890–1958

Thomas Justin Moore, the first partner in the firm who was not a native Virginian, was born on August 28, 1890, in Liberty Hill, Louisiana. His mother was Carrie Lelia Preslar; his father, Jeptha Thomas Moore, a tall, scholarly Baptist minister and teacher who named his oldest son for his friend Thomas Justin, a judge in nearby Shreveport.[1]

Justin Moore was a bright, determined boy who excelled in school, especially in mathematics and the classics. He received his first undergraduate degree from Louisiana College at the age of sixteen,[2] then traveled a thousand miles northeast to get a second one at the University of Richmond.[3]

Though he was a long way from home and had very little money, Moore enjoyed his experience at the University of Richmond. He threw himself wholeheartedly into the student as well as the academic life there and played on the baseball team with Willis Robertson, a future U.S. senator.[4]

After his graduation in 1908, Moore stayed on in Richmond, living at the college and teaching at Richmond Academy, a preparatory school for the University of Richmond. He was also courting Caroline Irvin Willingham, a 1908 graduate of The Woman's College and daughter of his father's friend, Robert J. Willingham, who was secretary of the Southern Baptist Foreign Mission Board and a leader in Richmond's Second Baptist Church.[5] The Willinghams lived in a handsome antebellum house on the northeast corner of Fifth and Cary streets.[6]

Harvard intervened between Justin and Caroline's engagement and their marriage. Moore had won a scholarship to work for a graduate degree in English and prepare for a career as a teacher. "But he got up there," his son recalled, "and literally, at Harvard, . . . said, 'I can't go through with this thing,' like the guy that gets cold feet at the altar, 'I really don't want to be a teacher the rest of my life.' Then he went over to see the law school and said to himself, 'This is really what I want to do and this is the place I want to do it.'"[7]

He had no money, of course, and his scholarship was for studying English, but he met with the dean, explained his situation and worked out a deal with him. In return for a scholarship to the law school, he agreed to teach full-time for several years and pay the university back.

True to his word, Justin Moore came back to Richmond with an LL.B. in 1913, passed the bar exam, and joined the faculty of the University of Richmond's T. C. Williams Law School. As a full-time professor from 1913 to 1919, and part-time until 1925, he relied on the Socratic method, teaching courses in torts, real property, bankruptcy, municipal corporations, private corporations, and bailments and carriers. He was best known, however, for his lively course in torts.[8]

On December 18, 1913, he married Caroline Willingham. For their wedding trip, he took her by boat, the cheapest means of travel then, to Boston and Cambridge, where he showed her his old haunts at Harvard and his room at 15 Kirkland Street.[9]

When they returned to Richmond and settled down at 1721 Hanover Avenue, they asserted their independence from the Willinghams by joining the First Baptist Church. Caroline, who had been a stalwart worker at Second Baptist, now became a mainstay of First Baptist, first as a teacher in the Sunday school, and then as its director.

Almost immediately her husband was elected to the Board of Deacons, serving from 1914 until his death in 1958. From 1919 through 1925 he was superintendent of the Sunday school, and for many years afterwards, he taught a popular men's Bible class there. A fellow lawyer who was a student in that class for fifteen years marveled at Moore's rare "capacity to make people think" by asking the right questions.[10]

While he was still in law school, Moore had decided that the electric-utility industry was going to expand dramatically during his lifetime and would offer him the greatest opportunity as a lawyer.[11] By 1914 he had secured a part-time job as assistant to Captain Guigon, the general attorney of the Virginia Railway and Power Company,[12] and office space on the fourth floor in the new Electric Building, where he would spend his entire career as a lawyer.[13]

At that time the Virginia Railway and Power Company was still engaged mainly in transportation, but its shift in emphasis to electric light and power was predicted, and its high hopes for the future were dramatized on the roof of its new building with iron towers shooting jets of steam into the sky, illuminated by spotlights at night.[14]

The firm of Munford, Hunton, Williams & Anderson had just settled into the offices designed for it on the tenth floor of that same building. At some point Moore applied for a job there, and Henry Anderson, the power company's general counsel from 1909 to 1917, is said to have turned him down.[15]

Captain Guigon, on the other hand, was quick to take advantage of the skills of this aggressive young redhead from Louisiana.[16] At that stage, Moore must have been a bull in the genteel china shop that was the old Richmond bar, and his immense energies and drive disturbing to its more indolent members.[17]

As the years passed, however, Moore became "the wheelhorse," among Guigon's assistants, taking on more and more responsibility for Virginia Railway and Power Company's day-to-day legal work: claims against the streetcar companies, acquisitions of rights of way, and condemnation proceedings.[18]

By the early 1920s Henry Anderson had been replaced as general counsel by the more amiable but less ambitious Randolph Williams. Captain Guigon, the general attorney, was hopelessly ill with cancer. Meanwhile the Virginia Railway and Power Company had won the right to have its rates regulated by the State Corporation Commission, rather than by local city councils, and had begun to expand rapidly. The volume of work that fell on Justin Moore, who was still teaching law part-time and trying to build up an independent practice, was more than even *he* could manage.

In 1923 he asked Archibald Robertson, then city attorney, to come over to his office and help him. After some tense negotiations over salary, which presaged a strained relationship between the two men through the years, Robertson accepted.[19]

When he came into Moore's office, which was still on the fourth floor of the Electric Building, Robertson found him on the verge of a breakdown from overwork. "Very few people could have stood the strain that Moore was under," he said. In that office, with a western exposure and no air-conditioning, the temperature would climb to a hundred degrees in summertime, and by the end of the day, Moore would be "looking like a corpse."

"But the next day he'd come back looking like a college boy," according to Robertson. If the office started heating up again,

> he'd take off his coat. Nobody could ever say he was a stuffed shirt. And nobody could ever say that he drove anybody else any harder than he drove himself. . . . He'd come down here—in some of these hearings before the State Corporation Commission—he'd come down and work all night to be ready for the hearing the next day. And I said for years that he loved the practice of law more than anybody that I've ever known.[20]

At that time Frank Gould was trying to sell the Virginia Railway and Power Company, and his instructions were "that any responsible people . . . interested in the possible purchase of the control of the Virginia Railway stock be given all the information on the business . . . upon one condition: that they give [the company] a copy of the report that was made upon their examination."[21] After reading the report, the company officials would try to correct those weaknesses, and Gould would raise the price.

In 1924 Stone & Webster, a New York engineering and consulting firm, was showing interest in the company, but "Mr. Randolph Williams had already made his plans [to go] abroad that summer. And Moore was here and knew that company from A to Izard," Robertson recalled.

And Moore was never one to block his own progress, and in a perfectly legitimate way he just worked like a dog, morning noon and night with those, I reckon you've seen that volume . . . that describes all the ins and outs of the organization [of the various companies that became Virginia Passenger and Power Company in 1901] before it went into receivership [in 1904] and then when it came out [as Virginia Railway and Power Company in 1909].

And Moore just knew it backwards and forwards and could satisfy the most complicated questions just like that, and he developed [into] the most important contact man for the Vepco people.[22] And when they bought the thing out it was just perfectly obvious who was the best qualified person to be the general counsel.[23]

Moore was made assistant general counsel for a while, "by euphemism," Robertson said, and then he was advanced to general counsel. "Mr. Williams was a very remarkable person. He apparently never had any resentment" of the fact that Moore had replaced him as general counsel. Five years later, in fact, he led the effort to persuade Justin Moore to come into the law firm, and they became good friends.[24]

On April 15, 1925, the same day that Moore was made assistant general counsel of the power company, his only son, Justin Jr., was born. The son's hair turned out to be almost as red as his father's, but his personality was much more affable and easygoing. Though he was very able and ambitious, too, Justin Jr. was blessed with an extraordinary gift for making other people feel at ease.[25] Eventually, he would become a partner in his father's law firm, and then chairman of the Virginia Electric and Power Company, a job his father had turned down at least three times.[26]

The relationship that Justin Moore developed with his son rivaled that of General Hunton with Eppa Jr. "I don't know whether it was because of the war or something of that sort, but we had a very, very close relationship," said Justin Jr., "more of a friend relationship than a typical father-son kind of thing."[27]

> We'd take walks every afternoon when I was at St. Christopher's. . . . He'd come back from the office and we'd go over and putt around and play on that little golf course at the Country Club or take a walk, or . . . just go out in the yard and throw a baseball. . . .
>
> You would see him, at home, with my mother, at night, and . . . it was almost like he'd gone through a time warp. I mean he would . . . be sitting there talking about what the children were doing, and whether the dog had fleas, or whether the guy had fixed the swimming pool.
>
> He lived a fairly spartan, simple life. . . . My mother did not like to entertain. She thoroughly disapproved of drinking, you know, [although my father] said that once I went to Princeton, that sanctified drinking in the family.[28]

Caroline Moore's abhorrence of alcohol, even after Prohibition was repealed in 1933, was the only serious source of conflict in an otherwise idyllic marriage. When she refused to go with her husband to the traditionally "wet" conventions of the Virginia Bar Association at the Greenbrier and the Homestead hotels, Moore took his oldest daughter, Carolyn. She served as his hostess there from the time that she was five years old until she married a fellow medical student, Howard McCue, in 1941.

Carolyn McCue's relationship with her father was as remarkable and close, in its way, as her brother Justin's. When she decided to pursue a career in medicine, her mother thought it was "unladylike," but her father encouraged her, while he steered her away from the law, because he thought that a woman lawyer still would not be treated equally in the early 1940s.[29]

By 1932 Moore had emerged not only as a powerful general counsel of Virginia Electric and Power Company, but also as a tremendously effective business lawyer and business getter in the middle of the Depression. Henry Anderson was now receptive to the idea of having Justin Moore in the firm and joined his partners in inviting, indeed begging, Moore to join them.[30] Moore, in turn, was ready to spread his wings beyond the world of Vepco.[31] And so he moved six floors up in the old Electric Building and came into the law firm as a partner, on April 1, 1932.

The style was changed immediately to Hunton, Williams, Anderson, Gay & Moore. "And more and more and more," sang the lawyers in a Richmond Bar Association skit poking fun at the expansionist tendencies of the firm whose ranks had now swelled to a total of twelve lawyers.[32]

When Moore came in as a partner, he brought with him two associates who would continue to work almost exclusively on Virginia Electric and Power Company matters, Archibald Robertson and Norman Flippen, a quiet but hardworking lawyer who had started as a clerk for Captain Guigon, studied law at night, and passed the bar exam in 1917. Robertson recalled that Moore's original plan had been to leave the two of them "downstairs at Vepco" until Robertson himself persuaded Randolph Williams to take them into the law firm as associates.

Archibald Robertson was a year older than Moore, and his personality was equally combative.[33] Though his competitive instincts served him well in court, they also caused some friction in the firm —as did Moore's.

Justin Moore seems to have had two personalities. With his family, his friends, and close associates, he was kind and supportive. In the business world, however, he could be perceived as excessively aggressive and demanding—as "a rough and tough guy who would ride roughshod over people without batting an eye."[34]

As a result, Moore was not universally loved, though he was widely respected. Tough and hardworking, he had an almost magical ability to attract clients. In the unvarnished words of his associate and later partner, John Riely, it was like "the aroma of a bitch in heat. He could walk into a room, and every businessman would take him over in the corner and say 'I want you to do my work.'"[35]

In the central personality that Riely, like Moore's children, came to know and love, "Moore was a surprisingly gentle man." And Riely said he found it touching and, in a way, inspiring to work with a man "so anxious to do well, so anxious to do good, to be a success."[36]

In the early 1930s the firm's bright new associate, George Gibson, was "pirated" by Moore from Anderson for a long succession of Virginia Electric and Power Company financings. Gibson found his new mentor to be

a person of enormous power, energy and determination . . .[37] [who showed] indomitable courage in facing up, with all effort, to any challenge. Whatever the time of day or night, he championed, adopted and carried to victory the cause of any client— to the absolute astonishment and delight of the client himself. Just what a client would like a lawyer to be. . . .

Mr. Moore had an unfailing sense for the practical necessity. And that controls, in most cases, in the end. [Gibson's other mentor] Mr. Anderson was intent . . . on looking at things in a *big way*, and that meant knowing only the people of importance and staying only in places of importance. And being the exponent of a grand philosophy, he wouldn't bother with anything of less moment. Mr. Moore, on the other hand, was intensely devoted to the facts of the problem before him and getting the best out of them for his client. Whatever the facts were.[38]

I remember once a friend of Moore's came into his office with a red face of *fury*, and said, "Justin, will you represent me? So and so has called me a son-of-a-bitch!"

"Sit down," said Mr. Moore, "and tell me the facts."

Nothing was too unimportant for him. The only important thing was getting the job done well.[39]

When Congress was preparing the Public Utilities Holding Company Act of 1935, Moore was selected by fellow utility lawyers to present the industry's arguments against it. Though they lost "by just one vote in the Senate, . . ." his son recalled, "that long, hard fight . . . propelled him up in utility circles nationally."[40]

By World War II, Moore, with Edmund Preston, had also built up a substantial labor practice, representing not only Virginia Electric and Power Company, but the Newport News Shipbuilding and Drydock Company, Allied Chemical, and various clients from Mississippi to New Jersey.

Justin Jr. found his father's versatility his most impressive quality as a lawyer:

> I never really saw him in front of a jury, but Archie Robertson used to tell me that he was a very clever courtroom lawyer. . . . Knowing when a witness is lying, and knowing when he's not, knowing how to cross-examine him, and seeing the effect of all of this on individual jurors, knowing what line of questioning to pursue and knowing when to start and when to stop. He was extremely good at that.
>
> But he moved on [from] trial lawyer to appellate lawyer . . . arguing cases in the Supreme Court of Virginia, and became particularly skilled at the way you deal with the judge on appeal, with a printed record [rather than] a jury hearing the witnesses. It is quite a separate skill, and he was able to do both.
>
> And then he turned around and started doing all this corporate work. . . . He practically invented utility corporate law in Virginia and wrote some of the early part of the corporation code, this thing George Gibson keeps updating[41] . . . and the public utility law and that famous rule about the right to work law and no striking against public utilities. He wrote a lot of that when Bill Tuck was governor of Virginia. . . . They got away with that largely by his legal skill and Bill Tuck's ability to bluff.[42]
>
> I don't know of anybody else who could make so many transitions in the law, from . . . that basic trial work to the appellate work, and then to the general corporate work and finally, zeroing in on the utility work.[43]

In the spring of 1951, the state of Virginia asked Moore to defend the School Board of Prince Edward County in a suit in which lawyers from the Legal Defense Fund of the National Association for the Advancement of Colored People (NAACP) were challenging the constitutionality of the state's segregated school system. Eventually that case, *Dorothy E. Davis, et al. v. the County School Board of Prince Edward County, Virginia, et al.*, would go to the Supreme Court as one of five cases in the historic *Brown v. Board of Education of Topeka Kansas* group.

The decision that would come down in 1954 outlawing segregation by race in the public schools would wrench the South out of the segregated society that had been sanctified by law since the turn of the century. But few lawyers foresaw that in the spring of 1951.

Nobody at the firm wanted to take the segregation case, Moore Jr. recalled. But Governor John Battle and Senator Harry F. Byrd said the state, which was intervening in the case, needed a strong appellate lawyer to represent the Prince Edward County School Board, and in a series of meetings and telephone calls, they persuaded the senior Moore to take it on, though he was "anything but inspired over the thought of doing this."[44]

First of all, Moore was afraid that this controversial case would be disruptive to the firm, since he would have to put together a temporary team to handle it, "just like a team to deal with the tornado [that] blows through once and [then] it is all over," Justin Jr. said. Robertson, the veteran trial lawyer, was recruited for interviewing witnesses and proving facts, along with his assistant, Justin Jr. Moore then chose John Riely, a junior partner in his mid-forties then, to do research and write the briefs.

In the beginning, the firm's lawyers believed they were dealing with a relatively simple legal case, so they concentrated on the principle of *stare decisis*, that what has been decided in the past will continue to be the law. The decision in *Plessy v. Ferguson* in 1896 held that facilities for blacks and whites could be separate if they were equal, so they decided to argue that that was still the law, and that if the time had come to outlaw segregation, the Constitution of the United States would have to be changed by amendment.

The Prince Edward case was argued first in February 1952 before a three-judge panel in the Federal District Court, which upheld the segregation laws but found that the facilities were unequal and the black schools had to be improved. On appeal, the cases were then grouped with four other cases and heard by the Supreme Court for three days in December 1952. In June of 1953, the Court sent the cases down for reargument, asking counsel to brief five questions.[45]

When Justin Moore reargued that case in the Supreme Court the following December, he was sixty-three and "right at his prime," according to his son. The lead lawyer for the group was John W. Davis, senior partner at the Davis, Polk firm in New York. Davis, who had been solicitor general from 1913 to 1918, and had run against Calvin Coolidge in the 1924 presidential election, was then eighty years old. He had argued more cases in the U.S. Supreme Court than had any other lawyer in the twentieth century.[46]

Opposing them were the three black lawyers from the NAACP's Legal Defense Fund: Thurgood Marshall, the future Supreme Court Justice; Spottswood W. Robinson III, Richmond attorney and future judge on the U.S. Court of Appeals for the District of Columbia; and Robert Lee Carter, future judge of the U.S. District Court of Southern New York.

Each side was given two hours to make its arguments. In the reargument on December 7, 1953, Robinson and Marshall argued first, then Davis and Moore were to follow. As Justin Moore, Jr., recalled, Davis made a strong argument in spite of his age and failing health:

> And he left something like three or four minutes at the end of the first day. And he sat down, and Daddy got up, and I remember he said, "I assume the court would like to adjourn until tomorrow morning." And they said, "No. This court sits until four-thirty and you may proceed for five minutes."
>
> And you talk about an awkward spot for a lawyer to be in! With five minutes before they adjourned. Then he had all this other stuff he was supposed to talk about. And again being a good old rough and tumble trial lawyer helped. And he got up, and he said, "Well, fine. I have one little procedural matter to mention to the Court that will take exactly five minutes, and

I will get that out of the way, and then we'll all start off fresh tomorrow morning." Just made it sound nice and smooth.

The next day Moore gave the best argument his son had ever heard him make. When he finished, "Thurgood Marshall thought that they were sunk," and came up and told him that.[47] The argument that had impressed Marshall was the product of Riely's brief, communicated through oral argument "in about the most effective way I'd ever seen," the younger Moore explained.

Oliver Hill, the dean of the black lawyers in Richmond who led the NAACP Legal Defense Fund's fight in Virginia, was less enthusiastic about Moore's performance.[48] In an interview in November 1985, he would not even say that Moore had been fair, though he said that he had held his temper better than Archibald Robertson had. "Old man Robertson . . . made no bones about the fact he was a segregationist. But Mr. Moore, I think he was just as much a segregationist, but he was more polished."[49] John Riely and particularly Justin Jr.—the younger generation, which had fought in World War II—seemed to the black lawyers less prejudiced and more accessible.

"Oh, we were battling," said Oliver Hill. And it was a bitter battle, Hill recalled:

> But you might say *this* now, in all fairness, there was a different relationship among lawyers back in those days. If a lawyer told you he would do something . . . or he had done something or [that] you could count on his not opposing something, I never had any one of them to ever go back on his word. And I've had them to just accept *my* word on a thing like that. You didn't have to write everything down, dot every 'i'. I'm talking about when you're just dealing, lawyers just dealing with themselves. But today you don't find that. At least I don't.

In the 1940s and early 1950s among lawyers, Hill said, "there was a different spirit in Richmond anyway; I can't say it was, you know, general. . . . And so far as the *practice* was concerned, it was a pleasure."[50]

John Riely spent weeks during the summer of 1953 working with the Davis, Polk lawyers in New York, researching the background of the Fourteenth Amendment, first at the New York Public Library and then at the Virginia State Library in Richmond, ruining his suits with dust from the decaying calf that bound old copies of *The Congressional Globe*.[51]

In the end he produced a historically accurate review of the legislative history in a 217-page brief. But from hindsight, he viewed it as a futile effort. "The heart of the case," he said, "was discrimination on the basis of race and the fact that the mores of the country had reached the point that such discrimination could no longer be tolerated. It had nothing really to do with constitutional law."

Justin Moore, he explained, "was defending a way of life to which he was used and which he thought was a highly desirable way of life. And that involved segregation of the black people. It was not really quite as outrageous as they try to make it sound, now. It had been going on for quite some time. . . ."[52]

The first *Brown* decision came down on May 17, 1954. Most Southerners, black and white, can remember exactly where they were when they first heard about it. Instinctively they sensed the segregated world they had grown up in had come to an end. In August of that same year, Justin Moore took office as president of the Virginia Bar Association. In his acceptance speech at the annual meeting, he outlined to his fellow lawyers ways the state might minimize the impact of the decision in Virginia but said, unequivocally, that "duty requires that the decision be accepted."[53]

While Hunton, Williams lawyers were negotiating an arrangement to keep the Prince Edward County schools open for a year during which their client, the county school board, would work out plans to integrate them, the Board of Supervisors stepped in and closed the schools without warning. "This action was entirely unjustified, and we resigned our representation of the county's school board," wrote Riely thirty years later.[54]

During the early 1950s Justin Moore was at the peak of his influence not only in the firm and the organized bar, but in the community as well. In 1951 he succeeded Douglas Southall Freeman as rector, or chairman, of the University of Richmond's Board of Trustees and served until his death in 1958. From 1952 to 1953 he was a chairman of the Legal Committee of the Edison Electric Institute, the utility industry's trade association, and the following year, president of the Virginia Bar Association. When asked why he would take on so many chairmanships, his answer was: "I have always thought that if an organization is worth belonging to, it is worth running."[55] As George Gibson expressed it, "Justin Moore was never content to occupy an office idly. Everywhere he went he brought the full resources of his personality, his experience, and judgment." And his community, his university, and especially his church were stronger as a result.[56]

For twenty years, Moore was chairman of the First Baptist Church's Board of Deacons and of the search committee that brought in from Ohio Dr. Theodore Adams, one of the most effective ministers in Richmond's history and a strong voice for reason and humanity during the integration and civil rights crises of the late 1950s and early 1960s. According to his son, Moore agreed to chair the search committee only if he could look anywhere in the country for the right man, despite the expressed preference of other church members for a "staunch Southern Baptist."[57]

Yet his primary allegiance was to his family, with which he had an unusually close relationship. "He was absolutely devoted to my mother," said Justin Jr. "And he was interested in her and the children as A-Number One on the totem pole.

"And the law firm and building it up was Number Two."[58]

There is no doubt that at a crucial point in the 1930s Justin Moore brought to the firm the extra vigor and the solid client base it needed. And through the 1940s and the 1950s, he continued to supply that vigor and to expand that client base.

Eventually he also expanded the teams of lawyers that would serve those clients, though his loyalty to his family left him open, on occasions, to criticism in the firm for not pushing to hire more associates earlier and then for proposing, after Justin Jr. was made partner in 1954, that a few of his own percentage points be transferred to his son, without reference to the firm's general policy. For one tense weekend, the Executive Committee feared that Moore would leave the firm, taking his son and his clients with him, but that fear quickly dissipated when Justin Jr. refused to have anything to do with any effort to secure preferential treatment for himself.

In 1956 Moore suffered a mild heart attack, though few of his colleagues were aware of it. He then began to cut back on his work, but remained the dominant lawyer at the firm until his death from a second heart attack in March of 1958.[59]

"Eager and dynamic as he was," George Gibson wrote, "he departed this life as he would most have liked, swiftly, mercifully, at the height of his powers and influence."[60] And he was mourned by a broad group of people whose lives he had touched. That group ranged from the elevator operators at the Electric Building, who took up a collection to send flowers to his wife, to executives all over the country who had come to rely not only on his legal skills but on his friendship and his practical judgment. "He had so much good common sense," observed Lloyd Noland, Jr., his client and a leading Virginia businessman. "Good common *business* sense, which not many lawyers have. That's what was special about him."[61]

He had lived only sixty-seven years, but into those years he had packed at least two normal lifetimes' worth of work. And the law firm that he left behind him was far more vigorous, more broadly staffed, and widely focused than the elite and potentially static one he had entered in 1932.

EIGHT

Lewis Franklin Powell, Jr.

1907–

When Lewis Powell was a long-legged adolescent, the best hitter, in fact, on the McGuire's School baseball team, his first interest was athletics—baseball and basketball. His second was history.

"I read an enormous amount of history," he recalled. First, a series of romantic novels by G. A. Henty based on history, "which would be viewed as trash by many people, but it aroused my interest." Then, *The Boy Allies*, set in World War I. And "a fair amount" of biography. "It was clear to me from reading history that the people who *made* history were military people and lawyers. I decided I didn't want to be a military person. So I was a lawyer."

Lewis Franklin Powell, Jr., was born on September 19, 1907, in Suffolk, Virginia, where his father, a Richmond businessman originally from Southampton County, and his mother, a Gwathmey from Hanover County, happened to be living at the time.[1] When they returned to Richmond, his parents built the rambling white house in Chesterfield County, where Lewis and his younger sisters, Eleanor and Zoe, and his brother Angus, Zoe's twin, grew up.

The old Powell house is still standing on what is now Forest Hill Avenue. When Lewis was growing up, it was an isolated farmhouse with two horses and fifteen of his father's foxhounds in the backyard and a dirt road running in front.[2] His formal education began at a small school run by a Miss Morton on that same dirt road. He and his younger sister Eleanor walked there together until Lewis was old enough to ride the streetcar to the Powhatan School.[3]

Three-quarters of a century later, he remembered all too vividly his first day as a new boy entering the fourth grade of that fairly rough public school:

> Powhatan was located in South Richmond on Twelfth Street, which even then was not the most society-minded part of the city [nor that] with the most elegant homes. . . . Mother had fixed me a great lunch; she was in tears to send me off to school. The first day at recess the other boys gave me a hell of a beating and took my lunch away. And so my teacher—a lady named Miss Webb—offered to keep me in school, in her room, to eat lunch.
>
> Happily, I declined to do it. And I was finally accepted. But I took very small lunches after that.[4]

After Powhatan, Lewis went first to Bainbridge Junior High and then to McGuire's University School, though he didn't want to go to private school—particularly one that required riding streetcars more than an hour each way, taking the Forest Hill car across the James River, then changing to the Main Street line at Seventh Street.

But Lewis was an adaptable boy and soon began to enjoy the advantages McGuire's offered, not the least of which was Byrd Park as its athletic field. He went out for four sports and earned a varsity letter for three years in both basketball and baseball. Finally, the last year, he also earned a longed-for letter in football, despite his lanky frame, though the honor was diminished by the fact that "McGuire's quit football before the season was over; we had such a poor team."

At McGuire's he met his lifelong friend, Harvie Wilkinson. They traded sandwiches at lunch and over the years developed one of those rare friendships between bright, ambitious men where communication is almost absolute, and goals are fused as each is drawn closer to his full potential by the unconditional support of the other.

"I can see him now playing first base," Wilkinson said in 1985. "The [baseball] uniforms were handed down from year to year. Lewis was very tall and there was a gap between the stockings and the bottom elastic band around the leg of his baseball uniform. And when he would stretch out, his flesh would show."[5]

Initially Lewis had trouble with Latin, but luckily he had his great-uncle Edward Gwathmey to tutor him during the summers. Gwathmey was a Latin scholar who ran a school as well as the Gwathmey farm at Bear Island in Hanover County. With "a lot of help" from his Uncle Ned in Latin and from his sister Eleanor in mathematics, Lewis managed not only to survive, but to excel academically, winning the purple ribbon for the top grade at McGuire's every year.[6]

In 1925, his last year, he was awarded the school's highest honor, the Jack Gordon Medal, which Wilkinson had won two years before him. The citation that accompanied it reflects the romantic, almost chivalric ideals in which that school and that society were steeped: "bestowed in recognition of the highest traits of manly character: dauntless courage and stainless integrity. . . . [The winner] must be a strong and recognized force in the school for what is high and noble."[7]

By this time Powell had made up his mind to become a lawyer, but athletics was still his primary interest, and it dictated his choice of colleges. Wilkinson was urging him to come up to the University of Virginia in Charlottesville, where the majority of McGuire's boys went, but the baseball coach at Washington and Lee in Lexington had shown more interest in Lewis than Virginia's coach had. So he chose W & L, but, he later recalled with a laugh, "I didn't make the baseball team!"

What he did make was a whole new set of friends, and he says he never, for a moment, regretted his decision. His years in Lexington were, in many ways, the most relaxed and carefree years of his life.

Though his father wanted him to go to the Harvard Law School, Lewis managed to prolong his stay in Lexington by enrolling in a six-year program for both the undergraduate and law degrees.

His uncanny ability to manage time was already well developed as he worked and unabashedly played his way through six happy years. At W & L, he combined the courses for a B.S. in Commerce and Administration and the LL.B., and participated in the theater group and various dance committees. He also served as manager of the football team, managing editor of the college paper, associate editor of the annual, and president of the student body and honor council.

His quiet but effective qualities of leadership were already apparent to his peers and his professors. In 1929, the year he received his undergraduate degree, he was awarded the Algernon Sydney Sullivan Medallion "for one who excels in high ideals of living, in spiritual qualities and in generous and disinterested service to others." [8]

During the Christmas vacation of 1929–30, he took a train to California to attend the midwinter conference of the National Student Federation of America (NSFA) at Stanford University. There he formed a friendship with Edward R. Murrow, the future CBS broadcaster, from Washington State. Together they helped organize a winning slate with Murrow as president; Eleanor Wilson, from Hollins College, as vice president; and Powell as representative of the Southern district.

In July 1930 Powell sailed for Europe with four other delegates from the NSFA to an international meeting of student leaders in Brussels.[9] After a stormy two-week session with the highly politicized European students, Powell and Murrow traveled through northern Europe together. In the eyes of Murrow, a lanky boy who had grown up in the timberlands of the Northwest and worked his way through Washington State, Lewis Powell, the law student, may have seemed rather bookish, privileged, and formal. In any case, Murrow promptly—and presciently—nicknamed him "The Judge." [10]

The following year, 1931, Powell graduated from Washington and Lee Law School, first in his class. His father then insisted that he go to Harvard for a Master of Laws degree. "I was outraged by that," Powell said. He had passed the bar exam and was eager to start practice, and he also realized that although his father was doing well with David Lea, the wood-products manufacturing firm he now owned, there were three younger children to be educated and an extra year for Lewis would be a strain financially.[11]

Nevertheless, being "a very obedient child, like most children" in those days, Powell dutifully went to Harvard. There he found himself stimulated by seminar courses with Felix Frankfurter and Dean Roscoe Pound and by an intellectual competition fiercer than any he had ever known. As a result, he became far less "activities prone" than he had been at Washington and Lee. "I worked *hard* at the Harvard Law School," he says, "on nothing but law," though he did find time occasionally to go to dances at the Copley-Plaza with the Southern Society in Boston.[12]

At Easter time, the former solicitor general, John W. Davis, a trustee of Washington and Lee whom Powell had met in Lexington, invited him down to New York for an interview at Davis, Polk, which then offered him a job at $150 a month.[13]

But Powell wanted to come back to Richmond and Virginia. "I'm proud of Virginia. And of my family on both sides. The roots are deep here," he explained in 1984.[14]

He applied at Hunton, Williams, which he had been told was the leading law firm between Washington and Houston. But Hunton, Williams turned him down, offering their only opening to another Harvard graduate, Virgil Randolph, who had just received his LL.B. Powell then offered to work without salary for the McGuire firm in Richmond, where he had been a summer clerk, but they turned him down, too, explaining that they did not want to have to pay for his office space and secretarial help. It was 1932, the bottom of the Great Depression, and most law firms were worried about their overhead.

Finally, the Richmond firm of Christian, Barton & Parker hired him, at a salary of fifty dollars a month, to work for Andrew Christian, a tough but talented trial lawyer who had begun his career as an associate at Munford, Hunton, Williams & Anderson. In 1917 Christian had left to serve in World War I and afterwards came back to the firm briefly, but found its "bureaucracy" oppressive.[15] So he left a second time, taking with him a major client, the Atlantic Life Insurance Company.[16]

When President Roosevelt declared a bank holiday in March 1933, the American Bank & Trust Company in Richmond closed its doors and never opened them again. Andrew Christian's firm was appointed counsel to the receivers, and he and his young assistant plunged into the flood of law suits that ensued.

When he started with Christian, Barton & Parker, Powell resolved to be the first lawyer to arrive at the office and the last lawyer to leave. Since he was a relatively slow worker, he felt he had to make up for that fact with unflagging industry.

His industry was soon rewarded. When the receivers of the American Bank brought suit against the directors and hired Andrew Christian to represent them, Christian let Powell make the principal argument. His careful preparation and obvious ability impressed a lot of people in that courtroom—including the clients.[17]

The most aggressive and, to Powell, impressive of the three receivers struggling to collect the American Bank's debts and pay its creditors was a hard-driving, red-headed lawyer from Louisiana named T. Justin Moore, who had joined Hunton, Williams just a few months before Powell began to practice.

Late in 1934 Moore invited Powell to come over to his firm and work for him. It was a tough decision. Should he leave Andrew Christian, his mentor whom he not only admired but genuinely loved, to work for this up-and-coming business lawyer, Justin Moore, at Hunton, Williams? If he stayed where he was, Christian said that he would make him a partner right away, putting his name—the name of a twenty-eight-year-old three years out of law school—into the *style* of the law firm. But Andrew Christian had added, with characteristic generosity, "If you can stand the bureaucracy over there, Hunton, Williams can offer you a broader practice."[18]

As he would do with almost every major decision of his life, Powell took some time—six weeks in this case—to weigh the pros and cons. Then he made the more ambitious and adventurous choice. The kind of lawyer he had set out to be, the kind who "makes history," would need that broader practice and the national exposure that lawyers like Justin Moore, Henry Anderson, and Thomas B. Gay could offer him.

So Powell came to Hunton, Williams in January 1935. He came as an associate, though he had been assured that he would be made partner in three years.

His first experience at his new firm was disappointment. He learned that he would not be working for Moore after all, but had been assigned instead to Gay, a formidably formal senior partner whom he hardly knew. The fact was, "Mr. Gay had pre-empted me," Powell said, by asserting his seniority—the final word in those hierarchical days—claiming that "Moore was hogging the staff." [19]

Initially Powell did classic railroad tort work for the Southern Railway: accidents at crossings, minor labor problems, the kind of work that Messrs. Munford, Hunton, Williams, and Anderson had cut their teeth on in the last years of the nineteenth century. But he also got a sampling of modern corporate practice when Gay asked him to file, for a small local company, the first registration statement in Virginia under the new Securities Exchange Act.

"When I was in law school," Powell observed in 1987, "none of the legislation that people now think of as important, with the exception of the Interstate Commerce Commission and the Federal Trade Commission, existed. The Securities Acts were passed after I finished law school, the Labor Relations Act, Social Security Act, every major statute that we deal with up here [at the Supreme Court]." [20]

In this new world, neither Powell's law school training nor his senior partners could help him. How did he manage, then, to prepare that first registration statement? Like any well-trained scholar he sought the primary source. He took a train to Washington, borrowed a couple of registration statements from the Securities and Exchange Commission, wrote the registration statement, and oversaw its printing. [21]

As a result, he became known locally as a securities "expert." After that there was more securities work, a charter change for

Philip Morris, and one early labor case, but for the most part Powell spent his prewar years on litigation. Usually it was local litigation, but in his spare time he was planning for a broader future.

At least once a week he saw Harvie Wilkinson, his old friend from McGuire's who was now at the State-Planters Bank. They would meet at the Occidental Restaurant for a twenty-five-cent lunch over which they planned a future in which Wilkinson and Powell would be leaders, and Virginia would move from its static position in the 1930s into full participation in the business world of the Northeast.[22]

The Depression had virtually paralyzed that business world for the moment, but there was no harm in dreaming. One of Wilkinson's dreams was to have Powell as general counsel of State-Planters Bank, about the time that he would be emerging, he hoped, as its president.[23] During the next decade he managed to persuade the bank's president, Harry Augustine, that State-Planters needed separate counsel for the bank and the trust department, and then he worked to get Thomas B. Gay appointed to the board and named general counsel to the bank, knowing that Powell was still too young to be considered.[24]

The two young men "were clearly driving for the top," Wilkinson recalled in 1985. "To each other we never pretended anything else. I hope that we kept it sufficiently under cover so as not to be obnoxious." During their lunches together, which Wilkinson regarded as "the highlight of my young manhood here in Richmond," they talked over plans "in every conceivable arena of life."[25]

Powell was always conscious of his responsibilities to the community, a fact Wilkinson attributed to the strong religious commitment of his parents and the values they transferred to him. Most of the other lawyers and doctors at that time were "not very participatory," Wilkinson said. "They had the view that they had to absorb a number of bad credits in the practice of law and . . . medicine and that was their social contribution. Lewis never had any such idea as that."[26]

The Depression began to bottom out in 1933, although Richmond didn't really recover until World War II, Wilkinson recalled. "We had up blips and down blips and the recovery was very slow, but we seemed to have no economic impetus to really propel us into anything called a sharp recovery. But we were improving, there's no question about that. We weren't dead flat bottom. We were making upward curves, making progress."

In the 1930s Powell and Wilkinson served together on the boards of several local businesses, and that experience gave them invaluable training for the larger corporate boards that lay ahead. They could see there, as they could never have seen on the board of a large corporation, all the facets of each business and "what made one business tick and another one fall on its face."[27]

As bachelors, the two of them joined the "Lonely Hearts Club," a coeducational discussion group. Its intentions were purely intellectual, though a local wit is said to have remarked when they took in one young woman with an exceptionally nice figure, "Well, I see you've changed your emphasis from the engine to the chassis." In a society as anti-intellectual and antifeminist as Richmond was in those days, a serious coeducational discussion group was a bold experiment. Yet no marriages ever came from it, a fact that Powell viewed, in retrospect, as a reflection on the men.[28]

In choosing his wife, as in choosing his college, Lewis Powell's interest in athletics was the catalyst. When his twin sister and brother were about to be born in 1914, the only doctor who would struggle through a snowstorm to Chesterfield County to deliver them was a young Doctor Rucker.[29] Afterwards he became the Powells' family doctor. When Lewis came back to Richmond from Harvard, his mother urged him to look up Dr. Rucker's daughter Josephine, a Sweet Briar graduate who was then a model at the local department store Miller & Rhoads.

Initially Powell ignored his mother's suggestion until one day at a party he heard somebody say that Jo Rucker held the record for the broad jump at Sweet Briar. "How far did she jump?" he asked. Twenty-two feet, was the answer. "You're mistaken," he said. "No woman's ever jumped twenty-two feet." A day or two later he saw

"Courtship Days. Before the Sea of Matrimony, Buckroe Beach," reads the scrapbook caption on this picture of Justin Moore and Caroline Irvin Willingham, who were engaged January 9, 1910, when he was only nineteen years old, and married December 18, 1913, after he finished Harvard Law School.

In 1907, Caroline's father, Robert J. Willingham, Secretary of the Southern Baptist Foreign Mission Board, crossed the Pacific with William Howard Taft, then U.S. Secretary of War. Reporters who photographed the impressive pair called them "Secretary of War and Secretary of Peace."

Justin Moore with his father, Jeptha, and his daughter Carolyn, who was born June 16, 1916.

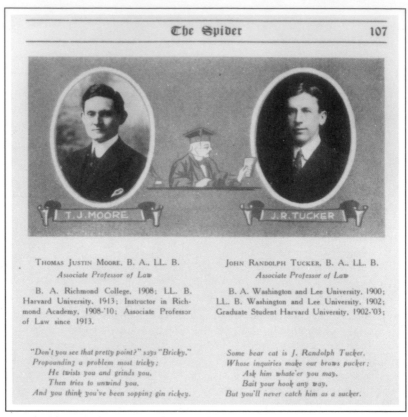

THOMAS JUSTIN MOORE, B. A., LL. B.

Associate Professor of Law

B. A. Richmond College, 1908; LL. B. Harvard University, 1913; Instructor in Richmond Academy, 1908-'10; Associate Professor of Law since 1913.

"Don't you see that pretty point?" says "Bricky,"
Propounding a problem most tricky;
He twists you and grinds you,
Then tries to unwind you,
And you think you've been sopping gin rickey.

JOHN RANDOLPH TUCKER, B. A., LL. B.

Associate Professor of Law

B. A. Washington and Lee University, 1900; LL. B. Washington and Lee University, 1902; Graduate Student Harvard University, 1902-'03;

Some bear cat is J. Randolph Tucker,
Whose inquiries make our brows pucker;
Ask him whate'er you may,
Bait your hook any way,
But you'll never catch him as a sucker.

Justin Moore, nicknamed "Bricky," for his red hair, taught full-time in the University of Richmond Law School from 1913 until 1919, and part-time until 1925. His colleague, John Randolph Tucker, later a senior partner at Tucker, Bronson, Satterfield and Mays, had been an associate at Munford, Hunton, Williams & Anderson from January 1, 1906, until September 1, 1909.—University of Richmond Yearbook

As a child, Carolyn Moore often accompanied her father to Virginia Bar Association meetings and served as his hostess there. Here they are on the Homestead Hotel's golf course in Hot Springs, Virginia, in the early 1920s.

As soon as the Electric Building at Seventh and Franklin was completed in 1913, the law firm moved in on the tenth floor, and stayed there until February 1967. Within a year, T. Justin Moore had moved into room 403 as assistant to the general attorney of the Virginia Railway and Power Company.
—*Virginia State Library*

Justin Moore and Norman Flippen. Flippen worked for Moore when he was general counsel at the Virginia Electric and Power Company and came with him to Hunton, Williams, Anderson, Gay & Moore in 1932.

Archibald G. Robertson (left), with his parents, Margaret Briscoe Stuart Robertson and Alexander Farish Robertson in August 1917. Robertson also came to the firm with Moore in 1932. As a lieutenant during the First World War, he was cited for extraordinary heroism in action and awarded a Distinguished Service Cross and the Croix de Guerre.

Justin Moore, Jr., was born on April 15, 1925, the same day that Stone & Webster bought control of the Virginia Railway and Power Company from the Goulds and made his father assistant general counsel of the new Virginia Electric and Power Company.

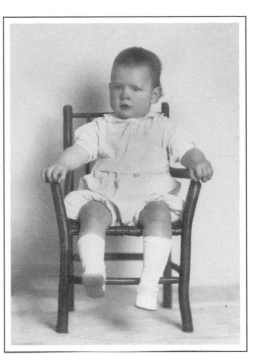

T. Justin Moore, Sr., and his son, T. Justin Moore, Jr., who is preparing to leave the reception after his marriage to Mary Elizabeth Pearson, October 22, 1954.

Justin Moore (standing, center), looks on as Vepco executives Miles Cary, David Davenport (of Stone & Webster), Jack Holtzclaw (sitting), Montell C. Smith, and "Red" Fitz dust off plans for the 200,000-kilowatt hydroelectric dam at Roanoke Rapids, North Carolina, in 1953. A U.S. Supreme Court decision had just ended a long and bitter fight over whether the U.S. Government or Vepco should build the dam.

Governor J. Lindsay Almond of Virginia, John W. Davis of Davis, Polk, Wardwell, Sunderland & Kiendl, and T. Justin Moore, Sr., in the cloak room of the U.S. Supreme Court in December 1952 when the Court was hearing arguments in *Brown v. Board of Education of Topeka, Kansas*.

Justin Moore, Sr., and his grandson, Scott McCue.

Justin Moore, Sr., reading to his grandchildren, Scott McCue, Jim Hall, Laura Hall, Sally Hall, Carol McCue, and Polly Moore, December 1955.

In September 1957, more than four decades after they embarked on the "sea of matrimony," Mr. and Mrs. T. Justin Moore, Sr., took a boat trip to Europe.

her picture in the paper, and his curiosity overwhelmed him. He called her up, introduced himself, and asked if she had broad-jumped twenty-two feet.

She had not. She was a high jumper, in fact, and held the record in *that* sport. But before the conversation ended, Lewis had asked her for a date.[30]

On May 2, 1936, Josephine Pierce Rucker became Lewis Powell's wife and, in every sense of the word, his partner for life. Her forthrightness, intelligence, and natural grace would prove to be, over the next fifty years, one of his richest resources.[31] Jo Powell had the knack of making everybody, from the youngest associate's wife to the most senior executive or judge, feel completely at ease, thereby compensating on occasions for a certain austerity in her husband.

For underneath the gentle and unfailingly courteous style of Lewis Powell, there was the steel of his determination. In later years, younger lawyers in the firm who were not close enough to feel, also, the warmth of his concern for them, nicknamed him "The Ice Man." To ordinary mortals, his self-discipline and drive combined with his rapidly accumulating power could be slightly overwhelming. When this reaction occurred, his easygoing wife, Jo, often served as a bridge.

In the early years it was her job to manage their relatively modest income while he supplemented it by teaching economics in the University of Richmond's evening business school. In turn, she gave him an allowance of a dollar a day for carfare, lunches, and expenses, until the price of lunches at the Occidental rose, and Harvie Wilkinson wrote her a letter to get his friend a raise.[32]

Meanwhile Powell was putting in legendary hours at the law firm. He arrived at the office by eight o'clock each morning, including Saturday and usually Sunday. And he almost always took home a briefcase filled with work.

Yet he still found time to participate in numerous community endeavors, charities, and legal-aid societies. He later recalled that one of his first and least successful speeches was to the night shift at the DuPont plant in 1933, urging the employees to contribute to the Community Fund. As time went on, however, he became more effective in community service, particularly in legal aid, and by the end of the decade was elected president of the Family Services Society as well as head of its subsection, the Legal Aid Society.

Building a strong reputation locally was not enough, however, for Lewis Powell. "I decided early that there were tens of thousands of able local and state lawyers in our country. I wanted to establish a national reputation. The ABA afforded one way to acquire a wider acquaintance."[33]

In the summer of 1937 he went to Kansas City to attend his first annual meeting of the American Bar Association and immediately became involved with the Junior Bar Conference, later called the Young Lawyers' Section, drawing on the quiet skills he had developed as a campus politician and NSFA leader. By 1938 he was a member of the Junior Bar Council, and in 1941 he was its chairman.

During that same period, his colleague George Gibson, at the age of thirty-six, served as chairman of the ABA's Public Utilities Section and his senior partner, Thomas B. Gay, then in his mid-fifties, was chairman of its House of Delegates.[34]

At the firm Powell continued to do securities work and a great deal of trial work. Though he was a Democrat in state elections and remained so throughout his life, when Franklin Roosevelt ran for his third term in 1940, Powell helped organize local support for the Republican candidate, Wendell Willkie.[35] Powell also organized a speakers' bureau in the ABA's Junior Bar section to alert the country to the Nazi menace and, after the fall of France, gave numerous speeches urging that the United States get into the war in support of Great Britain before Western civilization was destroyed.

When Pearl Harbor was bombed on December 7, 1941, Powell was thirty-four, well over the draft age, and the father of two small daughters.[36] Yet because of all of those speeches and his strong feeling about the war, he felt an obligation to volunteer for the service.

His wife, Jo, reluctantly supported his decision. When he sought advice from his senior partners, Gay was "vehemently," and Moore "strongly," against his going off to war, saying in effect that he was crazy even to think of it at his age, with his family obligations. Randolph Williams, "was in the middle—typically," weighing Powell's obligations to his family and his firm against those to his country. At the other extreme was Henry Anderson, the great adventurer in World War I, who advised Powell to get into this war, saying, "Lewis, in all probability, this war will be the greatest event of the United States during your lifetime. . . . If you sit it out in Richmond, Virginia, practicing law, you'll regret it."[37]

As it turned out, Powell had an "exceptional career" in World War II, which fully challenged him and opened many doors to him later. "There's so much luck in life that, secretly to myself, I don't claim anything except being at the right place at the right time. . . . [But] I look back on that with a good deal of satisfaction."[38]

When the navy turned him down because of his poor eyesight, he managed to get into the Army Air Corps' combat intelligence group. By May 1942 he was in officers' training camp in Miami; by July, in air intelligence school in Harrisburg; and by early September he was sailing across the Atlantic on the Queen Mary with 17,000 other men, sardined with fifteen in a stateroom built for two.

Powell's bomber group, the 319th, initially was stationed near Norwich (East Anglia), England.[39] And there the group underwent further training. In October Powell was sent to a Royal Air Force intelligence school on the Isle of Man and was leading his class there, when he got an emergency call to return to his base in England.

Soon afterwards Powell found himself in a British convoy sailing through the Strait of Gibraltar as part of the Allied invasion of northwest Africa. As he was landing under fire on a beach east of Oran on November 8, 1942, he thought to himself, "What a damn idiot I was to leave a wife and two little girls. I thought I would be doing some *office* work somewhere."[40]

In February 1943 he did get an office job and a promotion to captain when he was transferred from his air group to a combat intelligence unit at the headquarters of the Twelfth Air Force.[41] He described his new job in a letter to the law firm, written on April 24, 1943, saying that though he missed living and working directly with the combat crews, he found his civilian training "in study, analysis, evaluation and draftsmanship" was being put to better use. "Anyway, I am now fighting a 'paper' war with a desk, a secretary (not a WAAF), books, reports *and reports,* maps, pins, colored pencils, etc., etc. . . . working an average of about fourteen hours a day, with no client against whom to charge the time. It reminds me, in this respect, of the battle for Henrico County."[42]

After the invasion of Sicily in August 1943, Powell was sent back to the United States to share his combat experience with the intelligence school in Harrisburg and to rewrite its basic manuals. Early in 1944 he was summoned to the Pentagon to meet with Colonel Alfred McCormack, formerly a senior partner in the Cravath firm in New York, who was then directing the Special Branch of the Military Intelligence Service. McCormack invited Powell to become a field representative of ULTRA, the super-secret British operation that was breaking top-level German codes and virtually reading the German army's mind.[43] The ULTRA operation was so secret, in fact, that Powell was not allowed to tell even his wife about it until the archives were released thirty years later.

"[W]hen I asked him, 'Why me?'" Powell recalled that McCormack said he was selecting "primarily lawyers," on the theory that they could combine clarity of thought with the practical judgment and tact that would be needed to convey the very sensitive ULTRA information to senior officers in the field.[44] According to Ronald Lewin, McCormack was trying "to evolve an entirely new breed of animal—the 'ULTRA adviser' or 'representative.'"[45] His Special Branch was soon nicknamed 'the best law firm in Washington.'"[46]

Though Powell was "given the large picture by Al McCormack," he did not understand "the full scope of ULTRA information" until he actually went to Bletchley Park, the Victorian estate between Oxford and London where British cryptographers, analysts, and translators were working round the clock on messages intercepted from the Germans on the airwaves.[47]

"For the most part the people who worked on ULTRA in Hut 6 [at Bletchley] could fairly be called geniuses. They were the best mathematicians in Great Britain. There were some physicists and even some philosophers, on the theory that you needed a sort of mixed quality of intellectual giants. Bletchley had them."[48]

After several weeks at Bletchley where he was trained not as a cryptographer, but as an intelligence officer, Powell was sent to Italy to see how ULTRA information was being used in combat operations. He was then returned to England where he had been assigned to serve as ULTRA adviser to General Carl ("Tooey") Spaatz.[49]

It was a heady experience, to say the least, since General Spaatz commanded all American bomber forces in the European theater, and the Allies were preparing for the invasion of Normandy in June. Every morning Powell briefed the officers in the U.S. Strategic Air Force war room, folding in information received from ULTRA (on the precise location of German oil supplies, air bases, or troop movements) with information derived from other sources, so that a listener who was not initiated into the ULTRA secret would not suspect the information's source.[50] Gaining control of the air over Western Europe was the primary objective and "by D-Day, that had almost totally been accomplished," Powell recalled. "Our victory in the air made the land invasion possible on D-Day."[51]

By August of 1944 Powell was a lieutenant colonel and chief of the Operational Intelligence Division at USSTAF's headquarters which, after the invasion, were moved from England to St. Germaine in France. "As you know from the newspapers," he wrote to Thomas B. Gay in March 1945, "this war is rapidly approaching final disaster for the Germans." But with forty officers and an equal number of enlisted men under his command he was still "kept fully occupied on about a ten or twelve-hour day basis, seven days a week."[52]

Gay wrote back immediately, urging him to come "back to the fold" as soon as possible. With the sudden death of Edmund Preston in March and the breakdown of Irvin Craig's health "due to overwork," the few partners at home were finding it "difficult if not almost impossible to hold together the firm's practice with the staff we now have available."[53]

At the end of October 1945 Powell arrived back in Washington. He then took one of the few vacations, and possibly the longest, of his adult life—three weeks at Sea Island, Georgia—before he came back to the law firm early in December.[54]

The adjustment back to relatively dull work in private practice was difficult for him. As a sympathetic colleague put it: "He who had been hurling thunderbolts on three continents," was back where he had been four years earlier, at the beck and call of an exceedingly harassed and demanding senior partner.[55]

Powell seriously considered accepting an offer from E. R. Squibb & Son, the drug company in New York of which his army friend, Lowell Weicker, was president.[56] The job as the vice president and general counsel there would have tripled his income, but he decided finally against it. "My primary concern *always* was to be a highly competent lawyer," he explained to his children. And he did not want to give up the independence that he prized in private practice, where "if I really didn't like the way that things were going in the firm, I could always put my hat on and walk out."[57]

He also turned down the chance to serve as general counsel to the agency that administered the Marshall Plan for the rehabilitation of Western Europe and Japan, though he later told his children, "had I fully realized the importance to Western civilization of the Marshall Plan, I probably would have accepted."[58]

"I knew what he was going through," his partner George Gibson said of this difficult time in Lewis Powell's life. Since he could do nothing to help him, Gibson was "immensely relieved to see that he worked out his own solution."[59]

That solution was to work even harder than he had worked before, extending his influence in the community to the point that he was well known to its business leaders, trusted by them all and eventually given a lion's share of their business. As he moved beyond the practice of Gay, and younger lawyers took his place in serving Gay's clients, Powell became a great "rainmaker" for the firm and, finally, the dominant partner.

Some of Powell's friends believe that he came back from the war a changed man, more driving and ambitious than he had been before.[60] His accomplishments over the next five years seem to support that observation: his election in 1947 to the Special Charter Commission, which, under his chairmanship, established the city-manager form of government in Richmond; his presidency of the Richmond Bar Association, 1949–50, and of the Chamber of Commerce, 1950–51; and finally his chairmanship of the Richmond City School Board from 1952 to 1961.[61] Yet his really close friends saw no basic change in him.[62] He had just gone public with his lifelong ambition.

In the South these men grew up in, raw ambition was considered not just impolite but downright unattractive. So the smart young Southerners, if they did not strike off for New York and become part of the "brain drain," learned to mask their ambition with a casual, even jovial manner, downplaying their cleverness. But Lewis Powell, who was naturally soft-spoken and considerate of other people's feelings, did not now have the time or the need to play that particularly Southern game of deception, as he was rising steadily, bringing in more business than any lawyer in the firm, save Justin Moore.

In 1954, after Henry Anderson's death, the firm acknowledged Powell's contribution by putting his name into its style, and dropping Anderson's, to make it Hunton, Williams, Gay, Moore & Powell.

At the time the change seemed right, based as it was on economics and the size of the business empire Powell was now building in the law firm. The younger partners, who were not consulted by their seniors in those predemocratic days, did not question the decision, although Powell's name had been moved ahead of that of George Gibson, whom they all acknowledged as the most brilliant lawyer in the firm.[63]

Building on the client base that Anderson and Moore had established, Gibson had become a national leader in railroad reorganization, utility and corporate law. To his credit, Powell asked that *both* names be put into the style, but Gay and Moore demurred, perhaps thinking six names would be too many for anybody to remember.

"They might have gone for just the two names—Hunton and Williams—at that point, like the big Wall Street firms," former partner Lawrence Blanchard speculated later. But that would have meant taking out the names of Gay and Moore, an unlikely prospect in 1954 when those two men were at the height of their power in the firm, and "Powell's star was rising," Blanchard observed, "so I guess they just decided to make the most of it."[64]

During the 1950s the law firm changed dramatically after the death of the last founding partners: Randolph Williams, the great stabilizer and peacemaker, in June 1952; and Henry Anderson, the arrogant but magnetic railroad reorganizer, in January 1954.[65]

Gay and Moore were the dominant partners as the decade of the 1950s opened. Both were in their sixties, and Gay would reach seventy and begin to cut back to semiretirement in 1955. By this time Moore had surpassed Gay by the sheer force of his personality, as well as by the volume of the business he controlled. But Powell was coming up rapidly behind him with a commanding presence in the community and a host of new clients.

The law firm had by that time overcome its postwar fear of expansion. To accommodate future growth, Moore proposed that two new associates be hired every year—"whether we need them or not."[66] With the hiring of Justin Moore, Jr., and Paul Funkhouser in the summer of 1950, the bold new policy was initiated. Three months later a prominent local lawyer, Royall Cabell, died, and the executives of three of his clients—Albemarle Paper, the Chesapeake Corporation, and Miller & Rhoads—came to Powell and asked if he would represent them.

The firm's phenomenal growth had started. In January 1950 there had been only eleven lawyers in the firm: ten partners and Larry Blanchard, the lone associate, nicknamed "Atlas" since he was presumably holding up the firm all by himself. By the end of the decade the number of lawyers had almost tripled.

Next to Gay, Wirt Marks had been at the firm longer than any other partner. Marks was an exceptionally able lawyer, but a combative one, not a team player by Powell's standards.[67] In fact, his personality could hardly have been more different from Powell's. For years there had been tension between Marks and Justin Moore, and now tension had developed between Marks and Powell.

In March 1953 a dispute arose involving Marks's client, the Virginia-Carolina Chemical Corporation, and an opinion Marks had given it without consulting his partners. It conflicted with an opinion the firm had just given to another client in a similar situation. Marks argued that a lawyer, even in a partnership, has the right to his own opinion—a reasonable argument, theoretically, but an impossibility in a large law firm where every partner is legally responsible for the opinions given by the others. Tempers flared. A special meeting of the partners was called on a Sunday afternoon, and this time there was no Randolph Williams to diffuse the anger and reconcile the differences. It came down to a choice between Powell's view or Marks's, and the partners stood behind Powell. For the first time in the firm's history the partnership was dissolved, and then reorganized—without Wirt Marks.[68]

The time had clearly come for the firm to put down in writing the principles and policies it had been operating under for more than fifty years. Among them would be the requirement that any controversial opinion given to a client reflect a consensus of the partners in the firm. Another would set guidelines for the distribution of the profits. Distribution was a thorny matter that caused disruption in the firm whenever a new lawyer was elevated to participating partnership. Under the strict percentage system, used from 1901 until the late 1970s, the senior lawyers had to give up some of their own percentage points of ownership to make them available for the newcomers.

In the past, Randolph Williams had set an example and eased the situation by giving up his own points freely and continuously, though his colleague Henry Anderson showed no such inclination. In 1951, the year that Anderson was eighty, he was still drawing almost 15 percent of the firm's net profit, the same share that Gay and Moore were drawing, while Williams, one year younger, had cut back to 7 percent.

In 1955 Powell and Gibson drafted a written partnership agreement. It was the first one since those relatively simple documents in the early 1900s, and it provided for an Executive Committee which would be elected by the partnership, and mandatory retirement which would begin to be phased in at the age of seventy. George Gibson always said that Powell contributed most of the ideas to the agreement while he gave them expression, beginning with an eloquent statement of the "purposes and principles":[69]

1.01. *The Practice of the Law.* The practice of the law is a service to society. While an aid to business, it is concerned also with the public welfare. It is informed by the past, dedicated to the future and governed by justice. It is in the light of these principles that this Agreement shall be interpreted and applied.

1.02. *The Purposes of the Partnership.* The client cannot be served by an individual so well as by a team. It is only a team that can offer special abilities in innumerable fields and co-ordinate them for the discharge of important responsibilities. Promoting in this way the interest of clients, the partnership promotes also the interests of partners and renders a broader public service. It strengthens each with the judgment of all. It builds and maintains a position of public respect. It provides the volume of work that permits the development of specialized competence and tends to stabilize the level of receipts. All the partners accordingly pledge their best efforts to aid the professional advancement of each to the end that with just recognition for achievement and ability each shall receive from the others a fair opportunity to use his best abilities for the common benefit and shall receive an approximate, if not complete or perfect, compensation for his abilities and industry, out of the partnership funds, so far as such funds will go. It is in the light of these purposes that this Agreement shall be interpreted and all questions that arise from time to time be resolved.[70]

A vote of "two-thirds in interest" of the partners and a majority would be necessary for the dissolution of the partnership or a change of the partnership agreement. The "in interest" concept empowered the seniors with a vote proportionate to the draw they took from the firm and presumably staved off insurrection by impatient junior partners.[71] The agreement also provided for gradual retirement, beginning on December 31 of the year a member turned seventy and resulting three years later in "counsel status" in which he would be "relieved, so far as he may desire, from the practice of law" and "further obligation to work" but still retain his office.[72]

Gay, Moore, Powell, and Gibson were to serve as permanent members of the Executive Committee, with two rotating members.[73] On December 31, 1958, after Gay had retired from the Executive Committee and Moore had died, the number of the rotating members was increased to three and the permanent members reduced to two: Powell and Gibson.

By this time Eppa Hunton IV had been elected to a rotating membership and, in deference to his seniority, made chairman of the Executive Committee. Though he was not as single-mindedly devoted to the practice of law as Powell or Gibson, Hunton was so beloved as a unifying force in the firm, as well as the custodian of the firm's social traditions, that he was reelected continuously until his retirement in 1974.[74]

"Sufficiently democratic" is the phrase that George Gibson applied to the form of government that he and Lewis Powell had devised.[75] But it was a *limited* democracy, particularly when it came to the division of the firm's profits. Looking back from the perspective of the late 1980s, the ratio between the distribution of profits to the highest-paid participating partner and that to the lowest seems a little bit excessive if not downright exploitive. Yet it was in line with, even moderate compared to, the ratio in some of the Wall Street firms.

The team concept, so carefully spelled out in the new partnership agreement, played a vital role in the organization of the burgeoning law firm. By the 1950s government regulations had proliferated to the point that even the most diligent generalist, like Powell, could no longer keep abreast of all of them. Specialists were required, and this decade of the 1950s saw the formal organization of a labor team, a tax team, and finally a litigation team as entities within the firm, available to clients whenever they were needed.

Teams were also organized the traditional way, by the partner in charge of the client. For the "Powell team," Powell assembled a gifted group of younger lawyers, beginning with Warwick Davenport, Lawrence Blanchard, Joseph Carter, and Robert Buford. Each lawyer was assigned specific responsibilities for Powell's clients. One of Powell's greatest strengths was his ability to delegate authority, encouraging initiative in his subordinates yet still keeping himself fully informed and in control.[76] Powell's disciplined work habits and careful budgeting of his time were not lost on the lawyers who worked for him. Without his having to say a word to them, they quickly realized that the same kind of dedication and performance was expected of them.

The younger lawyers also learned from his example a great deal about the care and the keeping of clients. It was Powell's policy to go to his client's office, rather than have the client come to his. "I tried to do that from the very beginning," he explained. "I didn't see any reason to put the client to the difficult problem of coming to see me. I wanted to keep the client." Usually, he took an associate lawyer with him. His purpose in doing so was twofold, to broaden the base of representation within the firm, and to help the client get acquainted with the associate, so that he would be comfortable working with him when Powell himself was not available. The latter was an essential consideration given the number of clients Powell had and the depth of his commitments in the community.[77]

The late 1950s was a turbulent time in the South, particularly for Powell, the chairman of the Richmond School Board, as Virginia's legislators reacted to the Supreme Court's order to integrate the races in the public schools with a policy of "massive resistance." This policy was based on a quasi-legal "doctrine of interposition" urged by the Richmond newspaper editor James Jackson Kilpatrick and adopted by Senator Harry Byrd, Sr., whose political organization still controlled the state legislature.[78] Powell made a special trip to Washington to try to convince the senator that there was no sound legal basis for "interposition," and when Byrd insisted on espousing it, Powell broke with him politically on this issue.

In a letter to Edward R. Murrow, who was filming a television documentary on the closing of the Norfolk public schools as a result of the "massive resistance" laws, Powell wrote:

> A climate of intolerance now exists in the South which, in my opinion, far exceeds, both in intensity and danger to our country, the type of intolerance which came to be known as McCarthyism. . . . I hope your forthcoming program can help to some extent to solve the present, and much more acute, problem . . . to bring out the truth and dispel the illusion that the Court decision can be circumvented . . . to restore reason to the point where we do not in effect abandon public education for most, if not all, of our children.[79]

Powell quelled a potentially dangerous demonstration at a public meeting called to discuss desegregation of the public schools. The meeting was held in the auditorium of the old John Marshall High School, next door to the house of Chief Justice Marshall, and as chairman of the Richmond City School Board, Powell served as moderator. The two speakers were Oliver Hill, the prominent black lawyer and civil rights leader, and a white lawyer who was counsel for and one of the founders of a segregationist organization known as the Defenders of State Sovereignty and Individual Liberty.[80]

The latter spoke first, and Hill later remembered the following scene:

> His highly emotional fervor worked the largely segregationist audience into such a frenzy that when I rose to speak, there was an uproar of boos, catcalls and epithets. It was obvious that this audience had no intention of permitting me to speak. A typical moderator would have suggested that I retire hastily for my own safety, but Lewis stood up beside me and, with calm demeanor and a steady voice, insisted upon the restoration of order. His doing so reminded me of depictions of Jesus calming the stormy

Sea of Galilee. The audience quieted down, I began to speak, and there was no further disorder.[81]

Under Powell's leadership, the members of the Richmond School Board tiptoed gingerly around the legislation passed by the Virginia General Assembly, which was still taking orders from Senator Byrd in Washington, to close the public schools rather than integrate them. As a result, the Richmond schools stayed open, while schools in Norfolk, Charlottesville, and Warren County were closed for several months, and in Prince Edward County for four years, before peaceful integration of the races was finally accomplished.

Powell and his friend Wilkinson were aware of the adverse effect that "massive resistance" was having on Virginia's efforts to attract industry to the state, and they joined Frank Batten, publisher of Norfolk and Portsmouth newspapers, and Stuart Saunders, vice president of the Norfolk & Western Railway, on a committee of business leaders that eventually persuaded Governor Lindsay Almond to do an about-face, defy the Byrd machine, and integrate the schools.[82]

If the 1950s was the decade of Powell's ascendancy to leadership in the law firm and the city of Richmond, the 1960s marked his ascendancy to national leadership, through his service as president of the American Bar Association in 1964–65.[83]

As president-elect, he had announced that he would concentrate on reforms in three areas of the bar: criminal justice, legal aid for the poor, and professional ethics. And he lived up to his promises, eventually making himself an expert in criminal law, despite his previous inexperience in the field, and bringing "an initially distrustful ABA into active partnership with the Johnson administration in providing free legal services to the poor."[84]

In 1966 President Johnson appointed Powell to his Commission on Law Enforcement and Administration, and he also appointed him to the National Advisory Committee on Legal Services for the Poor. Since 1961 Powell had been serving on the Virginia State Board of Education, and in 1968 he became its chairman.

Governor Mills Godwin then appointed him to the Constitutional Commission, which undertook a thorough revision of the Virginia Constitution in 1969.[85] In that last year of the decade Powell also served as president of the American College of Trial Lawyers (1969–70) and of the ABA's research agency, the American Bar Foundation (1969–71).

Considering the range and depth of Powell's commitments to boards, commissions, and bar activities in the late fifties and the sixties, one cannot help but wonder how much time he had left to give to his family, particularly to his postwar children, Molly and Lewis.[86] Yet the Powell family is an exceptionally close one, at the top of Powell's priorities. Somehow, he found or made the time to develop a strong bond with each of his four children.

Despite his quiet manner and generally serious nature, Powell has some of the characteristics of an extrovert. He loves being with people, relaxing with them in a duck blind or on a tennis court, as well as organizing and directing them in business, bar, or community activities. In his own law firm he was perceived more as a first-rate lawyer and leader than as a legal scholar like George Gibson or John Riely, whose deepest satisfaction came from the intellectual delights of practicing.[87]

When Richard Nixon first began to search for a Southerner to appoint to the Supreme Court, in 1969, Powell was approached indirectly but he stated firmly that he was not interested, in a letter to the attorney general, John Mitchell. He had no desire to be a judge, not even a Supreme Court justice, but preferred being a lawyer, he wrote.[88] It was the same answer he had given earlier to Senator Byrd when asked if he would accept an appointment to the Fourth Circuit and to Governor Mills E. Godwin concerning the Virginia Supreme Court.[89]

Two years later, in October 1971, the president himself telephoned Powell and told him that he thought it was his duty to accept a Supreme Court appointment. Powell then asked for twenty-four hours to think the matter over. At an emergency meeting of the Executive Committee the next day, his partners urged him to accept the highest honor an American lawyer can receive, despite his reservations because of his age (he was then sixty-four) and the fact that he was "not robust."[90]

It was an agonizing decision for Lewis Powell, torn between his strong belief that one does not say "no" lightly to a president's request and his genuine preference for the lawyer's life.

At 5:00 P.M., the deadline, he telephoned the attorney general and accepted. But in the middle of the night he woke up convinced that he had made "a hell of a mistake." The next morning he called Attorney General Mitchell and said that on reflection he had decided he could not accept, but Mitchell held him to his commitment by saying, "Mr. Powell, you can't treat the President of the United States that way. A lot of his advisors now know you have accepted."[91]

An irrevocable process had started. At a meeting of the law firm later that afternoon, Powell told his partners of his nomination, swearing them to secrecy until the president's announcement on television that evening.

"He's clean as a hound's tooth," said Watkins Abbitt, a plain-speaking congressman from Southside Virginia, who anticipated no problem in the confirmation process, despite the fact that the Senate had rejected two previous Southern candidates of Richard Nixon.[92] Judge Clement Haynsworth, the first of those rejected and a man who was "eminently qualified to serve," in Powell's view, was less optimistic.[93] In fact, he came by to see Lewis Powell at his office and advised him to prepare for the Senate hearings as thoroughly as he would prepare for the most important case of his life.[94] He himself, Judge Haynsworth said, had made the mistake of assuming that he could stand on his record as a judge and had gone up to the hearings virtually unprepared, with a single law clerk.

Powell took Haynsworth's advice and mobilized a four-man "confirmation team" within the firm. Two young associates were assigned the responsibility of collecting everything that he had ever written, reading it and identifying anything that might be subject to attack by anyone seeking to block his nomination. One partner was to deal with the Justice Department, Senator Eastland, and

Senator Thurmond, and another was to marshal Powell's ABA-related supporters and deal with the senators who had blocked the last two Nixon nominees from the South.[95] After they had combed through Powell's past and read the text of the hundred-odd speeches he had delivered through the years, the four young lawyers grilled him in practice sessions, hurling hostile questions at him. When he went into the Senate hearings, he found that he was "better prepared than necessary," and he breezed through in two easy sessions. "There was not," he later said, "a single question asked which my confirmation team had not asked me before."[96]

William Rehnquist, who had been nominated with him, had a rougher time, as the Richmond *News Leader*'s Jeff MacNelly poignantly recorded in a cartoon showing the two former athletes and future Supreme Court justices as football players coming out of a tussle: Powell, spotless; Rehnquist, bruised and bloodied.[97] What carried Powell through so easily was not just his preparation by the "Powell confirmation team" but his calm, reasonable, always "lawyerly" responses to even the most hostile questions. It was also his long record of achievement in the practice of law, in the organized bar, and in public service, where he had shown time and again a clear and penetrating mind, practical judgment, and a sense of fairness that went back to the playing fields of Byrd Park.

On January 3, 1972, Powell withdrew from the firm that now became Hunton, Williams, Gay & Gibson.[98] To avoid any hint of impropriety, new firm stationery without Powell's name on it was distributed immediately. And lawyers checking in at airport weighing stations with those huge, black, boxlike briefcases the firm provided for their papers noticed that the gilded initials by the handle that used to read "H. W. G. P. & G." now had a blackened smudge before the ampersand, rather like a missing tooth.

NINE

George Dandridge Gibson

1904–1988

When Lewis Powell went to the Supreme Court in January 1972, George Gibson became the ruling senior partner of the law firm.[1] His personality was fundamentally different from Powell's.

As a boy and a young man, Gibson had never been one of the gang, let alone the star athlete and student leader that Powell was. He lacked Powell's gift for easy relationships with his peers, but he made up for that lack with a small circle of close friends and a quick mind that produced an astonishing precision of expression. From his boyhood Gibson was clearly an intellectual and an elitist. Even then, he set the highest standards for himself in his dress, in his speech, and in his determination to live up to Lord Chesterfield's ideal of the perfect gentleman.[2]

For forty years Gibson would be viewed as a brilliant eccentric. Then in middle age, to the surprise of both his colleagues and his friends, he undertook a rigorous course of self-improvement to reach out to a broader group of people.

On May 8, 1904, George Dandridge Gibson was born into a well-established Richmond family. He was the first of the four children of Alice McClung and George Armistead Gibson. His father was a cousin of Randolph Williams and a groomsman in his wedding. As unpretentious as an old shoe himself, George senior used to poke fun at his oldest son's pretensions, when young George took to carrying a cane and wearing yellow spats at age fifteen, for instance, or composing poems with alternate lines in French and Latin.[3]

In New England, perhaps, where the intellect and the well-ordered life were valued more highly, George Gibson might have had an easier childhood. But in the provincial, rather sloppy world of Richmond and Virginia in the first two decades of this century, classmates at the Chamberlayne School and Episcopal High School laughed at his meticulous speech and his devotion to form, although secretly they must have envied his precocity.[4]

Like most Southern families at that time, the Gibsons had their share of financial problems. George's father had not been able to afford but one year of college for himself, and he was determined to do better by his children.[5] Sticking to a job with an insurance company, which he did not particularly enjoy, he managed to send all four of his children to college—George and Patrick to both the University of Virginia and Harvard Law School; Elizabeth to Bryn Mawr; and Stuart, the youngest, to Virginia.[6]

Despite the differences in temperament and interests that separated the father from his oldest son, in later years the younger George came to appreciate the elder for his good nature, his love of literature, and his loyalty to his family. He also realized that his ebullient mother, who exasperated him with her inability to arrive any place on time, had given unconditional love to each of her four very different children.

At the University of Virginia in the early 1920s, Gibson had two memorable teachers, Albert Lefevre in philosophy and Fiske Kimball in art, but he found little else to interest him there intellectually. In retrospect, he claimed that he had not received "*any* instruction in what study was all about. . . . The only studying I did there was exactly what I'd done at the Chamberlayne School: that is, way into the night before an examination, I'd spend a couple of hours looking over my notes of lectures, [then remember] the high points of those notes [and get] an undeservedly good mark the next day." In the process, he learned nothing about "independent inquiry or balancing of merits. . . . It was an enormous handicap to me at law school. I was certainly not awake intellectually."[7]

Nevertheless he earned a B.A. in philosophy and was elected to Phi Beta Kappa, after only three years at Virginia. He then went on to Harvard for an M.A. in history and philosophy in 1925 and an LL.B. in 1928.

At Harvard, he recalled, his greatest pleasure was his membership in the Signet Society, an eating club where students with an interest in fine arts and literature dined with members of the faculty or notable alumni like T. S. Eliot, or Ellery Sedgwick, editor of the *Atlantic Monthly*, who became one of George Gibson's mentors. In 1935 Gibson would marry Sedgwick's niece Edith Ludlow Sedgwick.

In the meantime, however, he set out to establish himself as a lawyer. Though he recognized that the most challenging and financially rewarding practice was in New York, where many of his classmates were going, "the arguments in favor of Richmond, I felt, were controlling. . . . Family was here. Friends were here . . . and people without money, going to New York to earn their way, had an awfully hard time."[8]

So George Gibson returned to his hometown, although it turned out "there wasn't a damn thing to do" in it. He applied at Hunton, Williams, Anderson & Gay, but was told that with seven lawyers there already, they had no room for another. So, he went to work for Williams, Mullen & Hazelgrove on "most uninspiring terms of no salary at all."

His only fee for the year 1928 was five hundred dollars from Frederic W. Scott, father of his University of Virginia roommate, for supervising distribution of some real estate in Nelson County. At the end of his first year, Williams & Mullen agreed to pay him a hundred dollars a month. Soon afterwards, Robert Tunstall, general counsel of the Chesapeake & Ohio Railway, offered him a job at triple that salary. He accepted it with alacrity and spent the next year and a half in the C & O's offices at Ninth and Main, immersed in research on Great Lakes cargo coal rates.

One rainy afternoon in the fall of 1930, he got a telephone call from his cousin, Randolph Williams. Was he still interested in working for Hunton, Williams? If so, Williams said, he and his partners would like to talk to him. "But don't hurry up in all this rain," he added.

Paying no attention to the warning, George Gibson picked up his umbrella and practically ran the three blocks up Main and then up Seventh Street to the Electric Building at Franklin. There he was interviewed first by Thomas B. Gay and, when "deemed in trim," was "ushered into the august presence of Henry Anderson." The latter had just been named counsel to the receivers for the Seaboard Railway and had announced to his partners that he needed an assistant. The now legendary interview followed, with George Gibson meekly agreeing to "look up law" and play the draft horse to Anderson, the self-styled legal "thoroughbred."[9]

Officially, Gibson came into the firm on January 1, 1931, the day after Whiting Faulkner, a partner who had worked on local Seaboard Railway matters, withdrew. A cubicle next door to Anderson's corner office on the tenth floor of the Electric Building now became Gibson's "vest pocket office."[10]

It wasn't long before Gibson learned that serving as assistant to Henry Anderson involved a whole lot more than simply looking up law. It was, in fact, a way of life requiring frequent trips to Palm Beach in Anderson's private railroad car or to Washington and New York where they stayed in only the best hotels, or in private clubs that met the colonel's sybaritic standards.

For the first fifteen months, George worked exclusively for "Mr." Anderson, whom he steadfastly refused to call "Colonel"; the colonelcy was after all only "an honorary *lieutenant*-colonelcy granted by the Red Cross." When it was pointed out that neither Lewis Powell nor Merrill Pasco, both full colonels in the army during World War II, expected afterwards to be addressed as "Colonel," Gibson said laconically, "Real colonels don't."[11]

Despite Anderson's anticipation of new responsibilities from his position as counsel to the receivers and, after 1932, as the receiver of the Seaboard Railway, there was relatively little work, at first, for his assistant to do. "The Seaboard was not a reorganization effort," Gibson later explained. "It was a *management* effort and therefore did not involve legal questions to the extent that Mr. Anderson had expected." [12] He then pointed out that

> his employment of me was not coincidental with the [Seaboard's] employment of him as counsel. It was causally, vitally related. He imagined that he would have, or could produce, occasions for legal work in that capacity. He certainly didn't want any trouble of *doing* the legal work. That would have taken the whole fun out of it. And that's why he demanded an assistant.
>
> And when I went to him the first year I had rather sketchy responsibilities, in large part undefined. Going with him on so-called inspection trips of the line in Florida—during the winter, of course—with Frances Richardson, his niece. And a few odds and ends which could quite well have been done by inside counsel, if they'd had one, in Norfolk.[13] So I was quite disappointed in *that*, but was bound to be impressed and exhilarated by the breezy hauteur with which the Colonel, as he was always called, managed to propel himself through the Universe.[14]

In the mid-thirties, Anderson was retained by the Prior Lien Bondholders Committee of the St. Louis–San Francisco Railway, and he and his assistant were suddenly immersed in the first reorganization under the new federal Railroad Bankruptcy Act. As the reputation of Anderson and, gradually, Gibson, spread, other railroad reorganizations followed, including the complicated one of the Denver & Rio Grande Western.

For a lawyer with Gibson's appetite for intellectual challenge, the 1930s was an exhilarating time. "With the old order collapsing in the wreckage of the Great Depression," he later explained, "stones had to be laid for new foundations and the law was soon rewritten in . . . revolutionary statutes." [15] Those statutes were then, almost immediately, tested in the courts.

At the time, George Gibson's attitude toward the New Deal legislation reflected that of his elders Randolph Williams, the Liberty Leaguer;[16] Henry Anderson, the staunch Republican; and Justin Moore, the vigorous opponent of the Public Utility Holding Com-

pany Act. In short, he believed that Franklin Roosevelt was destroying the country.

By 1986, however, Gibson's attitude was "greatly altered"; he then
thought that Roosevelt's program had been "the safeguard for the
country. Otherwise there would have been revolution, or at least,
very sharp disagreement culminating in disorder." At the time,
however, he was "violently against it." [17]

After Anderson argued the case for the Prior Lien Bondholders
Committee against the Reconstruction Finance Company [which
sought priority for its lien] before the court in St. Louis, the case
was remanded to the Interstate Commerce Commission.[18] Gibson
later described their work:

> So then we started all over again with a long review of the earn-
> ings and so on. That was the time when Mr. Anderson found
> it feasible and desirable to let Leonard Adkins and me do the
> work, which was great fun.[19]
>
> When the Denver & Rio Grande Western Railway also filed
> for reorganization under the Railway Reorganization Act . . . a
> composite institutional group including Prudential, Metropoli-
> tan, New York Life, and others asked Mr. Anderson to represent
> it for them. And that's how we got into the very long and very
> *complicated* reorganization of the Denver Rio Grande Western.
>
> Everything about it was tantalizing, I thought: in the first
> place, the location of the railroad, spanning the Rockies, and
> the location of the court, in the city of Denver which I'd never
> known before.[20]

And then, of course, there was the intellectual challenge. The
Denver & Rio Grande Western case turned out to be infinitely
more complex than the "Frisco" case. Ultimately Gibson argued it
twice before the U.S. Supreme Court.[21]

There was also work for the Baltimore & Ohio, based on the
"very simple idea of seeking a very moderate bankruptcy relief, quickly administered."[22] As a result, Henry Anderson, with

George Gibson's help, developed a new provision of the Bank-ruptcy Act to allow short-term reorganizations.[23]

In the B & O effort, George Gibson again had a chance to work with Leonard Adkins, an "extremely brilliant, facile and pleasant" senior partner in the Cravath firm in New York who became a lifelong friend.[24] Adkins's supreme confidence in dealing with his powerful clients inspired nothing less than awe in Gibson. He said that Adkins

> always had an answer to every question put to him on the tele-phone, no matter how novel or complicated. Having been a slave to looking things up, I timidly inquired of him one day . . . did he ever look it up, later? And he said, yes, if he remembered to think about it. I said, "What happens if you find you are wrong?"
>
> "Oh," he said, "I call up the client and say I was absolutely right and some damn fool court has decided to the contrary." [25]

Working for Anderson exposed Gibson to fascinating people up and down the Eastern seaboard.[26] He found it stimulating to participate in Anderson's "confident, buoyant sense for the big." [27] But the experience was not always pleasant. As he grew older, Henry Anderson became increasingly arrogant and overbearing. He and his assistant had to spend many days together in New York, working with the large insurance companies and law firms on Wall Street, and in Washington preparing for hearings before the Interstate Commerce Commission and other regulatory agen-cies.

Through a friend from Harvard, George Gibson struck up a friendship with retired justice Oliver Wendell Holmes, Jr. One of his greatest pleasures in the early 1930s was calling on the justice at his house in Washington until one afternoon Henry Anderson insisted that he be allowed to come along, too.

The visit took a turn toward disaster, Gibson recalled, when Anderson remarked "in a condescending grandiloquence: 'So now you're writing your autobiography are you, Justice Holmes?' Holmes turned on him in fury and said, 'I'd see the earth cracking flames beneath me before I would touch such a thing!'" Gibson felt humiliated by the incident, and since he had more or less forced Anderson on Justice Holmes, he never went back to see the justice again, because, he said, "I felt I had forfeited my *persona grata* status."[28]

Justice Holmes was "the idol of our generation in law school," Gibson explained. "He wrote all of his opinions by hand, standing up, at a desk that he inherited from his father and still used in Washington," and his prose, as a result, perhaps, was "lean and to the point." Gibson admired Holmes not only for his prose style, and his "majestic, rich and charming personality," but also for the fact that he "had read widely. And understood deeply, [and] could look through the formalities of legal speech and come down to some human conclusion."[29]

By comparison, Anderson had "a more romantic notion of the law, as sort of a tournament."[30] And in that tournament Gibson was expected to serve as his squire.

During the spring of 1932, Justin Moore had arrived at the law firm with "a host of new things" for Gibson to do, in addition to his work for Anderson. In his own blunt way, Moore could be as demanding as Anderson, although "their visions were on different planes. Anderson tended to take the Olympian view, while Moore went right at the immediate terrain."[31]

By that time, Anderson's work "had become exclusively railroads. In the case of the Seaboard, it was railroad administration and management. In the case of the other railroads, it was reorganization, in bankruptcy or equity." Mr. Moore's work was utility financing. "And utility planning and acquisition," Gibson explained. "He took me from Mr. Anderson in order to conduct the legal aspects of Vepco financing which was important, new, continuing business, wholly unfamiliar to the firm. But it continued for decades."[32]

Around the office Justin Moore was famous for being a prodigious worker and expecting others to work just as hard as he did. "I don't want excuses," he used to say, "I want *results*." And he got them very quickly, when he "pirated" Gibson from Anderson.[33]

But there was a price. Under the pressure of meeting the demands of both Anderson and Moore, Gibson became excessively exacting with the secretaries in the office. They literally trembled when his buzzer summoned one of them into his office.[34]

One day, not very long after Moore arrived at the firm, he called Gibson in and informed him that the Virginia Electric and Power Company had decided to make its first public offering and sell ten million dollars' worth of bonds. Would George please prepare the necessary papers?

"What should I do?" Gibson asked.

Have the money ready to be turned over to Vepco at a specified time and place in New York, Moore told him. Then he added, humanely, that since Vepco would be working through Stone & Webster, there might be someone there who could advise him.[35]

There was. And Gibson was launched into a long career in corporate financing. Over the next forty years he would supervise the legal aspects of numerous financings for Vepco.[36]

By 1934 Gibson had become indispensable to both Moore and Anderson. In recognition of that fact, on June 1, 1934, he was elevated to the partnership with his childhood friend Eppa Hunton IV, though he had been at the firm only three and a half years compared to Hunton's seven.

The following year, in February 1935, he married Edith Sedgwick, a quiet but exceptionally intelligent young woman from an old New England family known for its eccentricity as well as for its brilliance. It was a winter wedding in Stockbridge, Massachusetts, and the bride and groom rode away from the reception in a sleigh.[37]

After a wedding trip to Mexico, the Gibsons settled down in Richmond on Park Avenue in the neighborhood that would later be called the Fan District. They stayed there with their daughters—Pamela, born in 1936, and Alice, born in 1938—until 1943 when they moved to River Road.[38]

When America entered World War II at the end of 1941, George Gibson was ineligible for the service, not only because of his age (thirty-seven) but because of a problem with his back and neck, which grew more serious as he grew older.[39] Years later, he would preface his remarks about the practice of law in the early 1940s with the statement that "that was when anybody of any *account* was in the war."[40] The fact is that the firm of Hunton, Williams might not have survived had George Gibson not stayed at home and carried an enormous work load through those four war years when the firm was woefully understaffed and losing new associates to the service within months of hiring them.[41]

Richard Emory, who had served ably as Gibson's assistant since July 1940, left for the service in February 1942 and was later replaced by Nan Ross McConnell, the firm's second woman associate. She came to work for Gibson in October 1943 and stayed until her marriage in 1948.[42]

Final action on most of the railroad reorganization plans had to be postponed until after the war. But there was more than enough other work to fill Gibson's time as the nation's railroad and electric utility industries strained to meet the new demands of wartime.

Before the war George Gibson had emerged as a leader in public-utility law with his election to the chairmanship of the American Bar Association's Public Utility Section in 1940, when he was only thirty-six. With his typical blend of modesty and irony, he attributed this "premature honor" to Harold J. Gallagher, counsel to the receivers of the Seaboard, who "needed somebody to put into the top ranks of the utility council [and] happened to think of me, as somebody who would not deplete his own working force to get a job done."[43]

By the time the war was over, Anderson was in his middle seventies and spending more and more time giving speeches all over the country, with less and less time at the office, where Gibson and his brilliant postwar associate John Riely were struggling to complete various railroad reorganizations. Also, in the late 1940s, Anderson's previously robust health had begun to fail.

When it was clear that the Denver & Rio Grande Western Railway case was going to be heard by the Supreme Court in 1946, the lawyers involved selected George Gibson, rather than Henry Anderson, to make the principal argument. Anderson was understandably hurt and became increasingly sensitive to real or imagined slights by George Gibson.[44]

By this time George Gibson had become a superb appellate lawyer. His brevity, clarity, and unique phrasing delighted the justices, and more often than not, won them to his point of view.

In oral argument Gibson appeared to be speaking spontaneously. Actually, he always wrote out his argument beforehand, honing it down to its most laconic form and committing it to memory so thoroughly that he could depart from it and return to it with ease should a new thought occur to him or should a judge interrupt him with a question.[45]

Justin Moore, Jr., who succeeded John Riely as Gibson's junior assistant in the middle 1950s, recalled one time, however, when George Gibson did not want to be diverted from his line of reasoning and parried Justice Felix Frankfurter's sudden question from the bench: "Mr. Gibson, will you tell the Court the date of that case?" Without skipping a beat, Gibson replied, "It was 1892, Mr. Justice, give or take thirty-five years."[46]

According to Moore, the justice simply laughed and let him argue on.

In appellate court, particularly the U.S. Supreme Court, Gibson was in his element. On separate occasions three Supreme Court justices—Reed, Harlan, and Frankfurter—commended him on his performance in oral argument.[47] At Gibson's eightieth birthday party, Justice Powell read a list of the cases Gibson had argued in the Supreme Court and recalled that Felix Frankfurter, sitting in a wheelchair at a meeting of the American Law Institute in the last year of his life, had told him Gibson was "one of the half dozen" best lawyers to appear before the Supreme Court in his time on it.[48] George Freeman, a former law clerk to Hugo Black, as well as assistant to George Gibson, then added that although it wasn't often Justice Black and Justice Frankfurter agreed, Black had said to him: "That fellow from your office, George Gibson, ranks with Dean Acheson and John W. Davis as one of the three most effective oral arguers before this Court."[49]

Small wonder that Henry Anderson's clients began to seek Gibson out.

In addition to their work on the Frisco and the Denver & Rio Grande reorganizations, Gibson and Riely did a number of financings for the Virginia Electric and Power Company as that company expanded in the postwar period. They also argued a series of rate cases for the Chesapeake & Potomac Telephone Company as well as for Vepco.[50] Then there was the merger of the Chesapeake & Ohio and Pere Marquette in 1948, followed by the formation of the holding company for the C & O, called the Chessie System.[51]

Soon after the law firm moved into the second half-century of its existence, the founding partners died—Williams in 1952, Anderson in 1954—and the second generation began to fade away. Gay moved into semiretirement in 1956, the year after his seventieth birthday, and Justin Moore suffered a heart attack and died in 1958.

Powell and Gibson were now the leaders of the law firm. They had prepared for the transition by drafting the formal partnership agreement that was adopted in December 1955 after a year of extensive discussion and revision.

Powell had come back from World War II determined to achieve independence by building his own empire of institutional clients. By 1954 he had amply achieved his objective, and the firm's name was changed to "Hunton, Williams, Gay, Moore & Powell."

Instead of being jealous of Powell's ascendancy into the law firm's style, George Gibson actively supported it, recognizing that Powell had built a solid base of clients and a reputation in the city and the state that surpassed his own.[52] In the nation, however, Gibson's reputation in the field of railroad law was preeminent. But the era of reorganizations, indeed, the era of the railroads, was coming to a close. More railroad work would come to him, of course, from the C & O particularly, but it was always on a case-by-case basis.[53] George Gibson did not yet have major institutional clients of his own.

By the 1950s his marriage to Edith Sedgwick, which would end in divorce in the 1960s, had become a source of stress and tension. To alleviate that tension, Gibson threw himself into his work and took on several demanding community projects.

In 1952, at Randolph Williams's urging, Gibson went on the board of the Virginia Museum of Fine Arts. Initially he enjoyed the opportunity it gave him to expand his own knowledge of art and to foster the arts in the state. And he continued to take pride in furnishing his house with eighteenth-century French furniture, fine porcelain, sculpture, and paintings. When the museum's theater wing was being constructed, he worked tirelessly as chairman of the building committee, and for this work he was awarded the Webster S. Rhoads medal.

In 1957 he was elected president of the museum. Soon afterwards, he locked horns with the museum's talented but controversial director, Leslie Cheek, Jr. In a bitter jurisdictional dispute, Cheek submitted his resignation rather than submit to Gibson's authority, thereby sparking an editorial battle between James Jackson Kilpatrick of the *News Leader*, supporting Cheek, and Virginius Dabney of the *Times-Dispatch*, supporting Gibson.

In the end, George Gibson and his vice president, Horace Gray, conceded that they were not prepared to run the museum if Cheek left it, and submitted their own resignations to the board. No resignations were accepted, and Gibson remained on the museum's board until 1963, but the controversy had destroyed any pleasure that he might have derived from the association.

With the Business Law Section of the American Bar Association, Gibson had a more continuously productive and pleasant association.[54] Here, in his profession, senior partners from the leading law firms and general counsel of corporations all over the country fully appreciated, indeed delighted, in Gibson's ability to cut to the heart of a legal problem, his strikingly original mode of expression, his irony, and his urbanity. In 1957 he was elected secretary of the section and over the next three years moved "through the chairs" of office, as secretary and editor of *The Business Lawyer*, 1957–58, vice chairman, 1958–59, and finally chairman of the section from 1959–60.

At the end of 1959 he made another attempt to serve his own community as chairman of a commission to review the City of Richmond's tax structure. In that capacity, as in every task that he ever undertook, George Gibson did a thorough job and came up with the recommendation that the city levy a tax on county residents who made their living in the city. But he had no success at all in winning the politicians' support for his recommendation.

The fact was that George Gibson had difficulty communicating with people who were outside his profession or who did not share his intellectual and cultural interests. His prowess with the English language and his clipped, almost British, phrasing of it tended to intimidate and alienate them.[55]

For the first half of his life, Gibson seems to have accepted this fact as an unalterable condition of his existence. What he once said of Henry Anderson could have been applied to himself: "He was not one to suffer fools gladly. Indeed, he was not disposed to suffer them at all."[56]

In the postwar decade, John Riely found Gibson "extremely difficult" to work for. Though Riely had a powerful intellect himself, he was "absolutely terrified" of George Gibson at that time. Years later he remembered standing at Gibson's door with his hand on the doorknob, phrasing and rephrasing his opening sentence because "if there were one *word* in that sentence that Gibson found inappropriate, he would stop listening to me." As a result, he claimed, Gibson had the shiniest brass doorknob in the Electric Building.[57]

Two younger associates came to work for Gibson and left very quickly.[58] Then an almost perfect match was made when Justin Moore's son became Gibson's assistant in 1956. With a personality that could put anyone at ease, Justin Moore, Jr., served as Gibson's interpreter, sometimes even his protector, when Gibson would enrage New York cab drivers with remarks like, "By this time it should be apparent even to you that out of the six available lanes of traffic you have managed to choose the slowest."[59]

It was during this period that George Gibson decided to make a dramatic "mid-course correction." He suddenly focused both his mind and his energy on lowering the barriers to communication that had built up through the years.

An incident early in Moore's association with Gibson dramatized the problem. Gibson had written a petition for appeal asking the Virginia Supreme Court of Appeals to hear a case involving the common law doctrine known as the Statute of Frauds. His petition had reviewed old English cases as well as more recent American and Virginia ones and concluded that "the foregoing brings the Statute of Frauds from the thickets of accumulated sophistication into the light of present day policy."

"And I read that thing three times," Moore recalled, "and thought, 'What in the hell is he talking about?'"

When at the last minute Gibson was unable to make the oral argument for granting appeal, Moore went over to the court and did the best he could. Finally one of the judges directed Moore's attention to the sentence that included the "thickets of accumulated sophistication," and said, "Would you mind explaining to the court what that sentence means?" At that point, Moore recalled:

> I said, "Your Honor, that is the best reason I can think of for granting this appeal, because if you grant that appeal, Mr. Gibson will come over here and not only tell *you* what it means, but he may even tell *me* what it means. And I can't wait to hear."
>
> And they started laughing, and [the justice] said, "Granted" on the spot. And I went back, and there was a big smile on my face and George said, "Did you get the petition granted?" And I said, "Yes, but I'm not going to tell you *how*."
>
> That was his writing style—in "the thickets of accumulated sophistication"—and when he realized . . . he was working himself into a box where he wouldn't be able to communicate with anybody, . . . that he was drifting in that direction, he just took a mid-course correction, a self-imposed course correction.[60]

"It was the most remarkable change I ever saw," John Riely used to say.[61] And the change probably began when Gibson enrolled in the Dale Carnegie Course in Effective Speaking and Human

Relations.[62] Though he was kidded about it at the office, Gibson persisted, and was elected valedictorian of his class.[63]

Some of the habits Gibson formed as a result of the Dale Carnegie course he recommended to his new assistant George Freeman who arrived in July 1957: one, always begin a letter with the pronoun "you," rather than "I"; two, never let your introduction of a speaker exceed one minute; three, extend your hand immediately upon meeting a stranger, or someone whose name you cannot remember, and give your own name in the hope that the other person will return the courtesy.[64]

Gibson also shared with his assistants the civilized life that he so assiduously pursued. When they went to New York to work on financings, for instance, he insisted that all business be completed at the close of the working day. To the consternation of many Wall Street lawyers with whom they worked and who were used to a work routine that started at noon and ended at midnight, Gibson insisted that the conferences start promptly at 10:00 A.M. and end by 5:30 P.M. He would then take his Hunton, Williams colleagues, but hardly ever his clients, to a superb dinner at one of his four New York clubs: the Brook, the Knickerbocker, the Century, or the Coffee House. The conversation there was as stimulating as the fine wines he ordered, and no business was ever discussed. Afterwards they would go on to a French film, perhaps, or to the ballet.[65]

Gibson could never have been accused of being a "workaholic." He would not allow his life to be dominated by his work the way that Lewis Powell's or John Riely's was. Almost every year he took a trip to Europe or the Orient and at home insisted on a disciplined schedule that allowed time for social pleasures, tennis, and even painting lessons, as well as his wide reading in French and English literature. Fortunately, he had been blessed with a mind so swift and so precise that it could accomplish in a single hour work that would have taken most lawyers several days to accomplish.

More important than any practical habits Gibson had learned in the Dale Carnegie course was the psychological discipline he developed, putting himself in the other person's shoes, trying to imagine what he or she would be interested in hearing and discussing. Obviously, the course did not work its effect overnight, but it started a process that would continue until the end of Gibson's life and enabled people who had once been intimidated by him to relax, finally, and learn to love him.

At the same time he was working to improve his ability to communicate in ordinary conversation in the late 1950s, Gibson also worked to improve it through the written word. The lean, spare prose style that distinguished the letters, speeches, articles, and briefs he wrote in his later years, began to be perfected at this time.

One can almost pinpoint the date, since the sentence on the Statute of Frauds that perplexed Moore and the judges was written in 1956, and by mid-1957 Gibson was insisting on "simple Anglo-Saxon words wherever possible and simple sentences, the shorter the better."[66] The "thickets of accumulated sophistication" had been cleared.

When George Gibson became the editor of the *Business Lawyer*, in the summer of 1957, he put his principles of composition into practice. Ten years later that same review published his article explaining the "Elements of Legal Style"; several senior lawyers in the ABA's Business Law Section still hand it out routinely to younger lawyers the day they come to work for them.[67]

Two samples of George Gibson's prose are offered here. The first one shows his blending of simplicity, erudition, and gentle irony in a speech to the Woman's Club of Richmond in 1965, after a trip to Japan:

> As for time, the Japanese always claim to be an old country, as if we could hardly understand that distinction. But in fact, it is not so very old—the Goths were pillaging the riches of Rome a thousand years before there was any recorded history in Japan. But in October 552 A.D. a Buddhist mission was sent across the narrow sea from Korea, bringing a religious tradition, an artistic style and a written language. That was the beginning of historic

Japan. Recent though that may seem, it was almost exactly a thousand years before the beginning of civilization in Virginia. So we may accept it as a respectable origin.[68]

The second example is from a talk on "Effective Legal Writing and Speaking," in 1980, to the lawyers in his firm:

> Each of you may wonder, "Why should I listen to a talk on the use of English? I took a course on that in school and passed the examination. Besides, I speak English. It is only when I go abroad that I have trouble."
>
> That, of course, is a natural attitude. But in fact a common complaint about lawyers, by leaders of the Bench and Bar, is that their writing is so poor . . . even graduates of our best law schools do not speak or write well, and are often unintelligible. . . . the spoken or written word is the key to our livelihood and the survival of our profession. True enough, we are employed to think. But that is not enough. The result of our thinking must be communicated. . . . Clients want results. Our thinking is useful . . . only if we can make use of it to explain or persuade. . . .
>
> Ability to speak simply and clearly confers tremendous power. It is the power to lead a court to a desired judgment. It is the power to build reputations and to influence public affairs. It is the power to attract a client. . . . Inevitably he responds to him who can summarize in short and simple terms. The more complicated the subject, the more welcome the simplicity. Giving an answer once to Mr. Justice Frankfurter in terms we lawyers had agreed on in conference, I was interrupted by a sharp inquiry, "Mr. Gibson, will you answer my question in short and simple terms?" You may be sure that I did. Promptly.[69]

In April 1958, after the death of Justin Moore, Sr., Gibson was named general counsel of the Virginia Electric and Power Company, then the largest client of the firm. By that time he had also inherited the Noland Group clients and acquired some important new ones of his own, including the C & O Railway, New York Life, and Freeport Sulphur.

As John Riely moved into his own sphere, Justin Moore, Jr., and George Freeman became George Gibson's principal assistants.[70] Moore was named associate general counsel of Vepco and worked with Gibson on its affairs, while Freeman worked for Gibson's other clients. These included the Carolinas-Virginia Nuclear Power Association's expansion into atomic energy, financings in Virginia and South Carolina for New York Life, the C & O's acquisition of the B & O and Western Maryland and its brief affair with the Norfolk & Western. Freeman also assisted him in his bar and civic work.

When Moore left the firm in 1967 to become senior vice president, then president, of Vepco and later chairman of the board, Evans Brasfield replaced him as assistant general counsel of Vepco and became Gibson's principal assistant for this client.[71] By this time the business Gibson controlled was so extensive that the so-called Gibson team was divided into two discrete subteams, which would become the Utility team, led by Brasfield, and the Energy and Environmental team, led by Freeman.[72]

On January 1, 1960, the law firm's style was changed to "Hunton, Williams, Gay, Powell & Gibson," and George Gibson entered the decade that would bring him increased recognition in his profession. It also brought him happiness in his personal life with his marriage to Roberta Pearson Grymes in August 1966.

The marriage required some courage, since Gibson was sixty-two at the time, and she was only thirty, the age of his eldest daughter. At first the friends of both felt uncomfortable, not knowing how to bridge the generation gap. They were soon put at ease at a party given by Gibson's lifelong friends, the Tennant Bryans, to celebrate the Gibsons' marriage. Guests were instructed to choose from four sets of cocktail napkins, imprinted with "Mr. and Mrs. Gibson," "Mr. Gibson and Pearson," "George and Miss Grymes," and "George and Pearson"—whichever names made them feel most comfortable.

The next two decades were probably the happiest of George Gibson's life, the result of both his mid-course correction and what John Riely used to call his "beatific marriage." Pearson Gibson's

Lewis F. Powell, Jr., 1909.

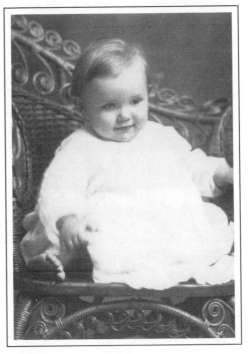

Lewis Powell's father built this house for his family around 1908.
Powell lived in this house from a few months after his birth in 1908
until his marriage in 1936. It is still standing at 4103 Forest Hill Avenue
in Richmond, Virginia.—*Margo Peters Millure*

The McGuire's University School baseball team of 1923 with Powell at the far left of the back row.—*Curator's Office, Supreme Court of the United States*

Lewis F. Powell, Jr., and Miss Sally Barret led the Opening Figure in the 1929 Fancy Dress Ball at Washington and Lee University. — *Washington and Lee University*

LEWIS FRANKLIN POWELL, JR.

RICHMOND, VA.

Φ Κ Σ. Φ Β Κ. Ο Δ Κ. Σ. Π Δ Ε. Φ Δ Φ. Π Α Ν
"13," C. C., Α Σ

President Student Body, '30; Manager Football, '30; "Ring-tum Phi," '25, '26, '27, '28, Assistant Editor, '29; "Calyx," '26, '27, '28, '29, University Editor, '29; Troubadours, '28, '29; Publicity Manager, '29; Political Science Scholarship, '28; Secretary-Treasurer Fancy Dress, '29; Finals Week Committee, '29, '30.

The 1930 *Calyx* lists many of the activities that Lewis Powell crowded into his six years at Washington and Lee.—*Washington and Lee University*

Captain Lewis F. Powell, Jr., beside a Nazi warplane shot down by his group in Tunisia, North Africa, in 1943.

Josephine and Lewis Powell at the Greenbrier Hotel, White Sulphur Springs, West Virginia, during the August 1948 Virginia State Bar Association Meeting.— *Curator's Office, Supreme Court of the United States*

Richmond School Board Chairman Powell and school superintendent H. I. Willett, September 10, 1958.
— *Richmond Newspapers*

Justice Powell after his
appointment to the U.S.
Supreme Court.—
*Curator's Office, Supreme
Court of the United States*

Powell and future Chief
Justice William Rehnquist
made the cover of *Time*
November 1, 1971.—
*Copyright 1971 Time Inc.
Reprinted by permission.*

'Great blocking in there, Bill!'

The Senate Judiciary Committee was much rougher with William Rehnquist than it was with Lewis Powell during the hearings on their nominations to the U.S. Supreme Court. This cartoon by Jeff MacNelly appeared on the editorial page of the Richmond *News Leader*, November 24, 1971.—*Reprinted by permission: Tribune Media Services*

Justice Powell and Justice Stewart in front of the Supreme Court.—*Richmond Newspapers*

Eppa Hunton IV served as chairman of the Executive Committee from 1960 until 1974.—*Virginia Historical Society*

George, Patrick, Stuart, and Elizabeth Gibson at Easter, 1911.

The house at 2514 Monument Avenue, Richmond, Virginia, where George Gibson grew up.

George Armistead
Gibson, from an album his
son George Dandridge
Gibson kept as a boy.

George Gibson and Eppa
Hunton IV, later senior partners at
Hunton & Williams, as schoolboys
at the Chamberlayne School.

George Gibson and Walter Russell
Bowie on a trip to the Grand
Canyon in Arizona in the 1920s.
Bowie, Mrs. Munford's nephew,
was by that time a minister at St.
Paul's Church in Richmond, and
he tried to persuade Gibson to
enter the ministry.

Edith Ludlow Sedgwick Gibson cuts her wedding cake on February 23, 1935, under the eye of her new husband.

Gibson and his daughters Alice and Pamela in 1938 or 1939.

Pearson (far left) and George Gibson (far right) had been married less than a month when this photograph was taken in September 1966 at the Greenbrier Hotel, White Sulphur Springs, West Virginia. On Mrs. Gibson's left is Vepco president Alfred ("Pete") McDowell, and opposite her is Vepco vice-president Edward Ratcliffe.

George Gibson on his wedding trip to Greece in 1966.

Pearson and George Gibson study a guide to Florence, Italy, in 1979.

George Gibson and Josephine Powell celebrate the Fourth of July in 1976.

George Gibson in his office at Hunton & Williams in November 1984.
—*Tim Wright*

Justice Powell waves good-bye at the end of the press conference June 26, 1987, at which he announced he would retire from the Supreme Court.—*Wide World Photos*

John W. Riely was chairman of the Executive Committee from 1974 until 1986, the year he died.—*Dementi-Foster*

Hunton & Williams's Richmond office will move to Riverfront Plaza (the twenty-story East Tower, on right) in 1991. The present office building, at 707 East Main Street, is immediately to the left of the twin towers. The Gothic clock tower of old City Hall and the roof of the Capitol are still visible to the right. Other buildings are, left to right, the Federal Reserve Building, Dominion Resources, Wheat First Securities (West Tower), Crestar Bank, Central Fidelity Bank, Omni Hotel, and Sovran Bank.—*Lee Brauer*

combination of serenity, kindness, and good humor turned out to be the perfect counterpoise for her husband's personality.

The same year that Gibson was married, the law firm opened a small office in Washington, initially as a convenience for the Richmond lawyers dealing with the regulatory agencies there. With Gibson's backing, the firm was becoming one of the national leaders in the atomic energy licensing field.

From 1966 to 1976, George Gibson was at the peak of his influence in the law firm. He shared the leadership with Lewis Powell for the first five years. Then, after Powell left, Gibson became the only remaining permanent member of the Executive Committee and the unquestioned leader of the firm intellectually. Eppa Hunton IV continued to serve as chairman of the Executive Committee until 1974, and as the firm's social leader until his death in 1976.

Though Gibson reached his seventieth birthday on May 8, 1974, he did not officially retire, or become "counsel," until April 1, 1976. As that date approached, John Riely, who had succeeded Eppa Hunton IV as chairman of the Executive Committee, became increasingly concerned about the future of the law firm's style.

The time had come, Riely decided, to reduce "Hunton, Williams, Gay & Gibson" to the first two names, "Hunton" and "Williams," which the telephone operators had been using for the past fifty years. Riely's decision was as magnanimous as it was practical, since his name would probably have been the next to go into the style.

In the past no lawyer's name had been removed from the style during his lifetime, except in the case of Lewis Powell when he resigned to serve on the U.S. Supreme Court. When Riely discussed the idea with Gibson, Gibson responded positively, recognizing the precedent in large New York firms like Sullivan & Cromwell, Shearman & Sterling, or White & Case, as well as the discord that could be avoided in the future. Gibson then asked Hunton to go with him to discuss the proposal with Thomas B. Gay, who was then ninety-one and had had his name in the firm's style for half a century.

Initially Gay was opposed to the change, but gradually he "drifted around" and "finally agreed to our proposal," Eppa Hunton reported. "With the growth of the firm and at a time when no individual partner was seeking to have his name added, the time for this move . . . was most propitious," Hunton added. [73]

On April 1, 1976, the firm sent out an engraved announcement that Messrs. Gay, Robertson, Hunton IV, and Gibson would become "counsel" to the firm and that henceforth the firm's name would be "Hunton & Williams." [74]

In a sense, April 1, 1976, was the birthday of the modern law firm. During the next decade, John Riely would preside, with energy and occasional expletives, over the expansion of the firm from 112 lawyers in 1976 to almost 350 in 1986. During those same years, the Washington office expanded, and new offices were established in Norfolk in 1979; Raleigh, North Carolina, 1980; New York City and Knoxville, Tennessee, 1983; and Fairfax, Virginia, 1984. [75]

But the greatest change of all was the gradual democratization of the law firm, a policy to which John Riely was deeply committed and for which Powell and Gibson had allowed when they drafted the partnership agreement of 1955, providing for a constantly rotating membership on the Executive Committee of the future.

Democracy generates its own problems, of course. And so does geographical diversity and geometrically multiplying size. As future leaders of the firm deal with these and other problems, and devise solutions for them, they can draw strength from the roots established over eighty-five years and the eight very different men who set the law firm's style.

Epilogue

In a sense, 1976–86 could be called the Riely Decade. After George Gibson's retirement, John Riely, as chairman of the Executive Committee, presided over the enormous expansion of the firm, the enlargement of the Washington office, the opening of five other branch offices, and the dramatic growth of the firm's practice.[1]

George Gibson continued to exert a strong influence within Hunton & Williams with his towering intellect, his passion for perfection, and his commitment to the civilized life. As long as his health permitted, he came into the office regularly. For a while he continued to work with Evans Brasfield, who had succeeded him as general counsel for Virginia Electric and Power Company, on utility financings, and with George Freeman on national energy and environmental practice. He also took a number of trips abroad with his wife, Pearson.

In the ABA's Business Law Section he continued to attend the council meetings where he and his wife were immensely popular, and his colleagues treasured his flashes of wit and his imaginative leaps to the problems they will encounter in the next century.

Gibson foresaw most of the changes that are now transforming large law firms into aggressive, international organizations, which the staid firms of fifty, or even fifteen, years ago would hardly recognize. Yet of all the attributes of the law firm of the future, Gibson insisted that "the most important is quality. That stands out like a beacon. It is recognized at once in conference. It is conspicuous immediately in oral argument. It composes the perfect corporate document. Its results endure."[2]

During the decade of his retirement Gibson devoted a large proportion of his time to the venerable, but relatively static, Virginia Historical Society. As a member of its Board of Trustees and chairman of its nominating committee from 1978 to 1985, he rewrote the society's bylaws to allow for an infusion of new ideas through rotating board memberships. Thus, he laid the foundations for the institution's survival in a changing world, as he and Powell had done thirty years earlier when they drafted the new partnership agreement for their law firm.

During that same decade, 1976–86, Lewis Powell, the firm's most illustrious alumnus, emerged as a powerful force on the Supreme Court.[3] The first justice since Louis D. Brandeis to come straight from private practice, he brought with him the careful reasoning, the practical judgment, and the tact of the successful business lawyer who concentrates on solutions rather than theory. He also brought the independent thinking of the true conservative whose roots go deep enough into the past to enable him to withstand the temporary winds of opinion. And finally, he brought the values of the old team player for McGuire's School who cared more about the game and the way that it was played than the public's perception of his role in it.

Once he got on the Court, Powell fulfilled his boyhood dream of making, or at least strongly influencing, a small part of history. As a justice he worked the only way that he had ever known how to work, which was with all his might.

One of his former law clerks, now a professor at the University of Virginia Law School, John Jeffries, saw him as the most "lawyerly" of the justices on the Court at the time. By that term he meant to suggest the "absence of doctrine and great appreciation for situational context." Compared to other justices, Jeffries said,

> I think Powell was more disinclined to become involved with theoretical conceptualization and was much more inclined to

look at the case, look at the kind of situation, look at institutional alignments and in every instance, ask whether this was a problem that he, as a justice, ought to be concerned about. Very contextual, very situational, very pragmatic. I think of those as being very lawyerly virtues, with the willingness to look at what actually is involved in this situation rather than give it a label which may not entirely fit. He did that very well.[4]

The lawyerly quality that Jeffries saw as a great strength may also have been a limitation. As Powell's former law clerk J. Harvie Wilkinson III, now judge of the U.S. Court of Appeals for the Fourth District has said:

He will have his critics. Some of his votes are not easy to reconcile. Some of his theory is not seamlessly consistent. Not surprisingly, his retirement touched off a debate about what the nation wanted from its highest court. For those who seek a comprehensive vision of constitutional law, Justice Powell will not have provided it. For those who seek a perspective grounded in realism and leavened by decency, conscientious in detail and magnanimous in spirit, solicitous of personal dignity and protective of the public trust, there will never be a better justice."[5]

Gerald Gunther, a professor at Stanford Law School, concluded that Powell's tenure on the Court was "truly distinguished" because of

traits he brought to the bench and cultivated there. His superb fitness for his position stemmed ultimately from qualities of temperament and character; these, not any obsession with results, made it possible for him, more than any contemporary, to perform his tasks in accordance with the modest, restrained, yet creative model of judging. He displayed a genuine capacity to listen to and learn from both sides of an argument; he approached the cases before him with remarkable openmindedness, unblinded by overarching ideological commitments; he eschewed the crusader's zealotry and preferred the thoughtful, gentle voice of reason.

[Powell provided] the much needed replacement [for Justice John Marshall Harlan]. In retrospect, we have reason for gratitude that each came to the Court without a fully developed constitutional ideology, that each was temperamentally averse to extremism and Grand Theories, that each listened hard and studied hard, that each explained his judgments with minimum flamboyance and maximum persuasiveness. It would be rash to draw from this the lesson that the wisest Supreme Court appointments come from the corridors of corporate law firms. Still, the Powell story, like that of Justice Harlan, may contain a cautionary tale. I have suggested elsewhere that an appointee who has *not* spent his career brooding about constitutional questions "might well prove to have better judicial qualities"—qualities of "openmindedness, of listening to both sides of an argument" —than the "constitutional philosopher" who has thought about most of the issues for a long time and who therefore has a well set, ready made answer to most. The opinions of Justice Powell, like those of Justice Harlan, at least remind us that lack of a developed constitutional philosophy in an appointee, like lack of significant judicial experience, does not bar judicial greatness; indeed, it may facilitate it.[6]

On the eve of his retirement from a distinguished career as "swing man" on an evenly divided court, Powell estimated, with characteristic modesty, that "in the long reach of history," he would probably be a "footnote somewhere."[7] His fellow justice William J. Brennan, Jr., would not agree with that estimate. Responding to a law review article on Powell's constitutional opinions, Brennan wrote the author, "You are so very right [in] stating that his opinions have had 'special significance in determining the constitutional law of his day.' But I would speak more broadly. His opinions will continue to have special significance for many decades to come."[8]

At any rate, it is clear that in the history of the Hunton & Williams firm Lewis Powell was a giant. He and George Gibson, with the impetus supplied by Gay and Moore before them, and by Munford, Hunton, Williams, and particularly Anderson at the start, managed to enlarge and establish the firm's national prominence in many different areas of the law.

John Riely then inherited the leadership of the burgeoning firm that they had energized, and he guided it through a tumultuous decade of transition. Riely was later struck down by cancer, and he died on September 14, 1986, at the age of sixty-nine.

The day after John Riely died, a delegation of senior partners from McGuire, Woods & Battle, the firm's major Richmond rival and the firm of Riely's father, paid a condolence call on the Hunton & Williams partners. For more than an hour some twenty lawyers from both firms traded stories about the intellect and courage, the cultivated abrasiveness and wry humor that John Riely had added to their world.[9]

Riely himself, with one eye always on the balance sheet, would have been appalled at the number of otherwise billable hours that were spent honoring him that afternoon and the next morning at St. Stephen's Episcopal Church. Well before the memorial service began, the church where Riely had served as vestryman was completely filled, except for the front section on the right. Those pews had been reserved for members of his law firm, now gathering outside for the procession.

Inside the stone, cathedral-like structure, the small noises of the crowd were absorbed into the high-vaulted ceiling. Then at eleven o'clock, a resonant voice from the back of the church intoned the words, "I am the Resurrection and the Life, saith the Lord: he that believeth in Me, though he were dead, yet shall he live. . . ."

The congregation turned and looked down the long aisle toward the entrance where a crucifer had entered with a bright silver cross, followed by two priests in long white cassocks. There was a pause in the procession. Then into the vaulted doorway stepped the two silver-haired giants of the law firm, Lewis Powell and George Gibson, fragile now with age, looking more like figures from a Greek play than veterans of Main Street.

An almost perceptible shock ran through the congregation. Nearly everybody there knew who these men were and what they stood for. And suddenly it seemed that the sequence had been wrenched apart. These old men should not have to be burying their protégé. But they were doing that now, and with a dignity that can hardly be described.

Lewis Powell, on the left, stood ramrod straight and tall, though thinner than he had been when he left for Washington fifteen years earlier. He was thin almost to the point of emaciation, as if he were sustained now not by body but by spirit. Beside him, bent with age, George Gibson leaned unsteadily on a wooden cane. They started walking down the aisle, Powell carefully restraining his stride to match the hesitant steps of his longtime friend and partner, Gibson.[10]

Over their shoulders appeared the dark face of John Charles Thomas, the first black partner in the firm, now a justice on the Virginia Supreme Court, and the pale, furrowed face of Taylor Reveley, the managing partner. Behind them came John Riely's own contemporaries, Merrill Pasco and Warwick Davenport, now retired. Then, after a small cluster of senior partners, the ranks broke—as Riely, the democratizer, would have had them break—into a long, spontaneous stream.

Down the aisle flowed the Hunton & Williams lawyers in all of their diversity—tall and short, fat and thin, the men in somber suits, some bearded, some mustached, most of them clean-shaven, and the women generally more brightly dressed, one of them obviously pregnant.

As the verses of the hymn rolled on, they filled the pews that had been reserved for them, and still they kept on coming. Lawyers from the offices in Richmond, Washington, and Raleigh; Norfolk, Knoxville, Fairfax, and New York funneling, two by two, down the center aisle, then splitting at the transept into two thin streams that lined the side walls of the church in tribute to John Riely, their chairman for the past twelve years.

These lawyers represented the future of Hunton & Williams. Their story will be told in a subsequent volume as the firm approaches its second century in the year 2001. It will be a broader, more diverse, more democratic story than the one that has been told in these pages. That second volume will begin with Riely, who presided, although not without some strongly voiced objections, over more than a decade of expansion and the transition to the huge institution that the law firm has become.

Let us hope that the future story will reflect the values of the two white-haired patriarchs who were leading them that day: Lewis Powell and George Gibson, Virginians to the bone who became national leaders. Those men grew beyond the prejudices and provincialisms of their beloved, although sometimes benighted, region. And yet they still retained what was best in its tradition: a deep respect for the past and their roots in English law; a strong sense of honor and of duty, and finally, an insistence on fair play and courtesy, particularly in a litigious situation.

Lewis Powell and George Gibson—and John Riely whom they honored now—were gentlemen in the broadest sense of the word. Intellectually they were the equal of lawyers anywhere, but they tempered their cleverness with courtesy and consideration, setting an example that the younger members of the firm would now try to emulate.

Two days after John Riely was buried in Richmond, the *Times-Dispatch* reported that Hunton & Williams had become the seventeenth-largest law firm in the nation, with a total of 349 lawyers in its seven offices. It had come a long way from the day, eighty-five years earlier, when four lawyers signed the papers to form the largest firm in Richmond.

What the future holds for the new generation of Hunton & Williams lawyers, drawn not only from the South, but from the entire country—indeed, from the world—no one can predict. The law firm's Southern heritage has now been enriched with many other heritages. Its provincialisms have been left behind forever. Yet it still retains its original spirit of camaraderie and intellectual adventure, as well as its commitment to a higher purpose in the practice of law than victory in court or a six-digit income, a commitment which can civilize an exacting and competitive profession.

APPENDIX I

Sources

Books

Bar Register, Annual 1983. Summit, N.J.: Bar Register Co., 1983.

Baskervill, P. Hamilton. *The Skeltons of Paxton, Powhatan County, Virginia and Their Connections*. Richmond: Old Dominion Press, 1922.

Bowie, Walter Russell. *Sunrise in the South: The Life of Mary-Cooke Branch Munford*. Richmond: William Byrd Press, 1942.

Bryson, W. Hamilton. *Legal Education in Virginia, 1779–1979: A Biographical Approach*. Charlottesville: University Press of Virginia, 1982.

Cheek, Richard, and Zehmer, John G. *Old Richmond Today*. Richmond: Historic Richmond Foundation, 1988.

Christian, W. Asbury. *Richmond: Her Past and Present*. Richmond: L. H. Jenkins, 1912.

Clark, Emily. *Stuffed Peacocks*. New York: Borzoi, 1927.

Couture, Richard T. *To Preserve and Protect: A History of the Association for the Preservation of Virginia Antiquities*. Dallas: Taylor Publishing Co., 1984.

Dabney, Virginius. *Mr. Jefferson's University: A History*. Charlottesville: University Press of Virginia, 1981.

——— . *Richmond: The Story of a City*. Garden City, N.Y.: Doubleday & Co., 1976.

——— . *Virginia Commonwealth University: A Sesquicentennial History*. Charlottesville: University Press of Virginia, 1987.

——— . *Virginia: The New Dominion*. Garden City, N.Y.: Doubleday & Co., 1971.

Davis, Burke. *The Southern Railway: Road of the Innovators*. Chapel Hill: University of North Carolina Press, 1985.

Davis, William C., ed. *The End of An Era*. Vol. 6 of *The Image of War, 1861–1865*. Garden City, N.Y.: Doubleday & Co., 1981.

Dew, Charles B. *Ironmaker to the Confederacy: Joseph R. Anderson and the Tredegar Iron Works*. New Haven: Yale University Press, 1966.

Eminent Judges and Lawyers of the American Bar, 1951. San Francisco: C.W. Taylor, Jr., 1950.

Ferrell, Henry C., Jr. *Claude A. Swanson of Virginia, A Political Biography*. Lexington: University Press of Kentucky, 1985.

Foote, Shelby. *The Civil War: A Narrative*. Vol. 3. New York: Random House, 1958.

Forster, Reginald Bishop, ed. *American Bar: The Professional Directory of Leading Lawyers Throughout the World*. Minneapolis: James C. Fifield Co., 1958.

Freeman, Douglas Southall. *Lee's Lieutenants: A Study in Command*. 3 vols. New York: Charles Scribner's Sons, 1942–44.

Gay, Thomas B. *The Hunton Williams Firm and Its Predecessors, 1877–1954*. Richmond: The Lewis Printing Co., 1971.

Gildersleeve, Basil L. *The Creed of the Old South, 1865–1915*. Baltimore: The Johns Hopkins Press, 1915.

Glasgow, Ellen. *Barren Ground*. Garden City, N.Y.: Doubleday & Co., Page and Co., 1925.

———. *The Woman Within*. New York: Harcourt, Brace and Co., 1954.

Godbold, E. Stanly, Jr. *Ellen Glasgow and the Woman Within*. Baton Rouge: Louisiana State University Press, 1972.

Griffin, William E., Jr. *One Hundred Fifty Years of History: Along the Richmond Fredericksburg and Potomac Railroad*. Richmond: Whittet & Shepperson, 1984.

Hankins, DeWitt. *The First Fifty Years: A History of St. Christopher's School, 1911–1961*. Richmond: Whittet & Shepperson, 1961.

Hanson, Robert P., ed. *Moody's Industrial Manual*, 1980. Vol. 2. New York: Moody's Investors Service, 1980 and 1986.

Hofstadter, Richard. *The Age of Reform*. New York: Vintage Books, 1955.

Hoyt, Edwin P. *The Goulds: A Social History*. New York: Weybright and Talley, 1969.

Hunton, Eppa. *Autobiography of Eppa Hunton*. Richmond: William Byrd Press, 1933.

Kluger, Richard. *Simple Justice: A History of Brown v. Board of Education and Black America's Struggle for Equality*. New York: Vintage Books, 1977.

Kousser, J. Morgan. *The Shaping of Southern Politics: Suffrage Restriction and the Establishment of the One-Party South, 1880–1910*. New Haven: Yale University Press, 1974.

Kull, Irving S., and Nell M. *An Encyclopedia of American History*. New York: Eagle Books, 1965.

Kurland, Philip B., ed. *The Supreme Court and the Constitution: Essays in Constitutional Law from the Supreme Court Review*. Chicago: University of Chicago Press, 1965.

Lewin, Ronald. *ULTRA Goes to War: The First Account of World War II's Greatest Secret Based on Official Documents*. New York: McGraw-Hill, 1978.

Lewis, Williams Draper, ed. *Great American Lawyers*. Vol. 7. Philadelphia: The John C. Winston Company, 1909.

Lisagor, Nancy, and Frank Lipsius. *A Law unto Itself: The Untold Story of the Law Firm Sullivan & Cromwell*. New York: William Morrow and Co., 1988.

Lutz, Francis Earle. *Chesterfield: An Old Virginia County*. Richmond: William Byrd Press, 1954.

McDanel, Ralph Clipman. *The Virginia Constitutional Convention of 1901–1902*. Baltimore: Johns Hopkins Press, 1928.

McKenney, Carlton Norris. *Rails in Richmond*. Glendale, Calif.: Interurban Press, 1986.

McPherson, James M. *Battle Cry of Freedom: The Civil War Era*. New York: Ballentine Books, 1989.

Manarin, Louis H., and Clifford Dowdey. *The History of Henrico County*. Charlottesville: University Press of Virginia, 1984.

Marie, Queen of Roumania. *Ordeal: Story of My Life*. New York: Charles Scribner's Sons, 1935.

Mays, David. *The Pursuit of Excellence, A History of the University of Richmond Law School*. Richmond: University of Richmond, 1970.

Meagher, Margaret. *Education in Richmond*. Richmond: Works Progress Administration Adult Education Project, 1939.

Mitchell, Mary H. *Hollywood Cemetery: The History of a Southern Shrine*. Richmond: Virginia State Library, 1985.

Moger, Allen W. *Virginia: Bourbonism to Byrd, 1870–1925*. Charlottesville: University Press of Virginia, 1968.

Moody's Industrial Manual, 1980, 1986.

Munford, Beverley B. *Random Recollections*. Privately printed, 1905.

———. *Virginia's Attitude toward Slavery and Secession*. New York: Longmans, Green, and Co., 1909.

Munford, Robert Beverley, Jr. *Richmond Homes and Memories*. Richmond: Garrett and Massie, 1936.

Of Two Virginia Gentlemen and Their McGuire's University School. Richmond: The McGuire's School Alumni Association.

O'Neal, William B., and Christopher Weeks. *The Work of William Lawrence Bottomley in Richmond*. Charlottesville: University Press of Virginia, 1984.

Pakula, Hannah. *The Last Romantic: A Biography of Queen Marie of Roumania*. New York: Simon and Schuster, 1984.

Peters, John O. *The Tale of the Century: A History of the Bar Association of the City of Richmond: 1885–1985*. Richmond: Bar Association of the City of Richmond, 1985.

Pulley, Raymond H. *Old Virginia Restored: An Interpretation of the Progressive Impulse, 1870–1930*. Charlottesville: University Press of Virginia, 1968.

Putney, Diane T., ed. ULTRA *and the Army Air Forces in World War II: An Interview with Associate Justice of the U.S. Supreme Court Lewis F. Powell, Jr.* USAF Warrior Studies. Washington, D.C.: U.S. Government Printing Office, 1987.

Richmond City Directories. Richmond: Hill Publishing Co., 1899, 1900, 1901, 1902, 1904, 1906, 1908, 1914.

Richmond: The City on the James: The Book of its Chamber of Commerce and Principal Business Interests. Richmond: George W. Englehart, 1903.

Rouse, Parke, Jr. *Living by Design: Leslie Cheek and the Arts, a Photobiography*. Williamsburg: Society of the Alumni of The College of William and Mary, 1985.

Sands, Oliver Jackson, Jr. *A Story of Sport and the Deep Run Hunt Club: What It Is and How It Came to Be*. Richmond: Whittet & Shepperson, 1977.

Sanford, James K. *Richmond: Her Triumphs, Tragedies and Growth*. Richmond: Metropolitan Richmond Chamber of Commerce, 1975.

Schwartz, J. C., ed. *Who's Who in the Law*. New York, 1937.

Scott, Mary Wingfield. *Houses of Old Richmond*. New York: Bonanza Books, 1941.

———. *Old Richmond Neighborhoods*. Richmond: Whittet & Shepperson, 1950.

Shaw, Adam. *The Sound of Impact: The Legacy of TWA Flight 514*. New York: Viking, 1977.

Sheerin, Maria Williams. *The Parson Takes a Wife*. New York: Macmillan, 1948.

Sperber, A. M. *Murrow: His Life and Times*. New York: Bantam, 1987.

Stover, John F. *The Railroads of the South, 1865–1900: A Study in Finance and Control*. Chapel Hill: University of North Carolina Press, 1955.

Tyler, Lyon G., ed. *Encyclopedia of Virginia Biography*, Vol. 3. New York: Lewis Historical Publishing Co., 1915.

———. *Men of Mark in Virginia: Ideals of American Life: A Collection of Biographies of Leading Men in the State*. Washington, D.C.: Men of Mark Publishing Co., 1906.

———. *Men of Mark in Virginia*. Richmond: Men of Mark Publishing Co., 1936.

U.S. Congress. Senate. Committee on the Judiciary. *Hearings on the Nominations of William H. Rehnquist, of Arizona, and Lewis F. Powell, Jr., of Virginia, to Be Associate Justices of the Supreme Court of the United States*. 92d Cong., 1st sess., November 3, 4, 8, 9, and 10, 1971. Washington, D.C.: U.S. Government Printing Office, 1971.

Virginia State Bar Association Reports, Richmond, 1897–1972.

Ward, Harry M. *Richmond: An Illustrated History*. Northridge, Calif.: Windsor Publications, 1985.

Who's Who in America. Chicago: A. N. Marquis, 1916–17; 1936–37; 1938–39; 1954–55; 1964–65; 1980–81; 1982–83.

Who Was Who in America. Chicago: A. N. Marquis, 1943.

Wilkinson, J. Harvie III. *From Brown to Bakke: The Supreme Court and School Integration: 1954–1978*. New York: Oxford University Press, 1979.

———. *Harry Byrd and the Changing Face of Virginia Politics 1945–1966*. Charlottesville: University Press of Virginia, 1968.

———. *Serving Justice: A Supreme Court Clerk's View*. New York: Charterhouse, 1974.

Wolters, Raymond. *The Burden of Brown: Thirty Years of School Desegregation*. Knoxville: University of Tennessee Press, 1984.

Woodward, C. Vann. *Origins of the New South: 1877–1913*. Louisiana State University Press, 1971.

Younger, Edward, and James Tice Moore, eds. *The Governors of Virginia, 1860–1978*. Charlottesville: University Press of Virginia, 1982.

Pamphlets, Newspaper and Magazine Articles

Anderson, Henry W. "Beverley Bland Munford." *Virginia State Bar Association Reports* (1910): 94–99.

———. "Freedom in Virginia." Speech as nominee for governor of Virginia before the Republican State Convention at Norfolk, July 14, 1921.

Bearss, Sara. "Marie of Rumania and Henry Anderson of Virginia." *Virginia Country* 10 (April 1987): 20–28.

Black, Elizabeth S. "Hugo Black: A Memorial Portrait." *Yearbook 1982, Supreme Court Historical Society*: 72–94.

Borock, H. I. "Southern Romance is Dead." Review of *Barren Ground* by Ellen Glasgow. *New York Times*, Book Review section, April 12, 1925, 2.

Boyer, Richard O. "The Gentleman in the Pulpit." *New Yorker* (October 22, 1938): 27–33.

Cheek, Mary Tyler. "In Praise of Idiosyncrasy." *Richmond Quarterly* 6 (Summer 1983): 17–26.

Cleary, Ben. "T. Justin Moore, Jr., A Different Kind of Virginia Gentleman." *Style Weekly* 2 (December 11, 1984): 42–45.

Freeman, Anne Hobson. "Mary Munford's Fight for a College for Women Coordinate with the University of Virginia." *Virginia Magazine of History and Biography* 78 (October 1970): 481–91.

Freeman, George Clemon, Jr. "A Tribute to Justice Lewis F. Powell, Jr." *Harvard Law Review* 101 (December 1987), 404–9.

————. "Justice Powell's Constitutional Opinions." *Washington and Lee Law Review* 45 (Spring 1988): 411–65.

Gay, Thomas B. "Henry Watkins Anderson." *Proceedings of the Sixty-fourth Annual Meeting of the Virginia Bar Association*. Richmond: Richmond Press, 1954.

Gibson, George. "Elements of Legal Style." *The Business Lawyer* 22 (April 1967): 547–55.

————. "Effective Legal Writing and Speaking." *The Business Lawyer* 36 (November 1980): 1–9.

————. "The Practice of Law in 1998." *The Business Lawyer*, 33 (July 1978): 2115–2127.

Gunther, Gerald. "A Tribute to Justice Lewis F. Powell, Jr." *Harvard Law Review* 101 (December 1987), 409–14.

Heinemann, Ronald L. "Virginia in the Twentieth Century: Recent Interpretations." *Virginia Magazine of History and Biography* 94 (April 1986): 131–60.

Hill, Oliver W. "A Tribute to Justice Lewis F. Powell, Jr." *Harvard Law Review* 101 (December 1987): 414–16.

Holt, Wythe Whiting, Jr. "The Virginia Constitutional Convention of 1901–1902: A Reform Movement Which Lacked Substance." *Virginia Magazine of History and Biography* 76 (January 1968): 67–102.

Moore, Thomas Justin. "School Segregation in Virginia." Address at the sixty-fourth annual meeting of the Virginia Bar Association, August 12–14, 1954, reprinted in *Virginia Reports*. Richmond: Richmond Press, 1954.

Munford, Beverley Bland. "Our Times and the Men for Our Times." Address before the Alumni of the College of William and Mary, July 4, 1889. Richmond: J. W. Fergusson and Son, 1889. (Munford Family Papers, Virginia Historical Society, Richmond.)

New York Times, October 18, 1926; February 24, 1934; December 4, 1968.

"On Facing Death in Time of Peace," *The Survey*, newspaper of The Charity Organization of the City of New York, June 18, 1910.

Peters, John O. "The Early Years." *Virginia Bar Association Journal* 14 (Summer 1988): 5–14.

Powell, Lewis F., Jr. Interview by Bill Moyers in the series "Moyers: In Search of the Constitution," June 25, 1987, transcript. New York: Public Affairs Television, Inc.

————. "Reflections." *Virginia Magazine of History and Biography* 96 (July 1988): 315–32.

Pulley, Raymond H. "The May Movement of 1899: Irresolute Progressivism in the Old Dominion." *Virginia Magazine of History and Biography* 75 (April 1967): 186–217.

Renda, Lex. "The Advent of Agricultural Progressivism in Virginia." *Virginia Magazine of History and Biography* 96 (January 1988): 55–82.

Republican State Executive Committee of Virginia. "Henry W. Anderson of Virginia for Vice-President: Foremost Anti-Sectionalist and Advocate of a More Perfect Union," Virginia Historical Society Collection, 1928.

Ribblett, David. "From Cross Creek to Richmond, Marjorie Kinnan Rawlings Researches Ellen Glasgow." *Virginia Cavalcade* 36 (Summer 1986): 4–15.

Richmond *Dispatch*, August 17, 1893; June 5, 1896; June 6, 1896.

Richmond *Evening Journal*, June 1, 1910.

Richmond *Evening Leader*, November 22, 1900; December 5, 1900.

Richmond *News*, December 15, 1885; November 22, 1900; October 7, 1901.

Richmond *News Leader,* June 14, 1920; November 5, 1926; March 12, 1930; March 7, 1932.

Richmond *Times,* June 4, 1896; June 5, 1896; June 6, 1896; August 21, 1897; October 22, 1899; November 10, 1899; October 8, 1901.

Richmond *Times-Dispatch,* October 15, 1908; October 16, 1908; October 17, 1908; October 18, 1908; October 19, 1908; October 21, 1908; October 23, 1908; October 26, 1908; June 1, 1910; June 12, 1912; March 23, 1914; January 7, 1915; June 13, 1920; October 4, 1929; October 31, 1929; March 22, 1932; August 11, 1932; March 22, 1945; June 17, 1960; June 26, 1981; October 11, 1983.

Richmond *Virginian,* February 4, 1914.

Riely, John W. *"Brown v. The Board:* A Very Personal Retrospective Glance." *State Education Leader* 3 (Spring 1984): 3–4.

Roanoke *Times,* June 5, 1896.

Siepel, Kevin H. "The Gray Ghost in Mufti." *Virginia Cavalcade* 36 (Autumn 1986): 74–87.

Southern Workman, June 1910.

The State, June 5, 1896.

The Survey, June 18, 1910.

Temple, K. Richmond. "John Skelton Williams, Richmonder of Vision." *The Richmond Quarterly* 7 (Fall 1984): 38–42.

"Two Virginians Recall Women's Role in War." Richmond *Times-Dispatch,* May 6, 1985.

Underhill, Marjorie Fay. "The Virginia Phase of the Ogden Movement: A Campaign for Universal Education." Master's thesis, University of Virginia, 1952.

Wall Street Journal, February 24, 1934.

Warrenton *Virginian.*

Wilkinson, J. Harvie III. "A Tribute to Justice Lewis F. Powell, Jr." *Harvard Law Review* 101 (December 1987): 417–20.

Will, Erwin H. *The Past—Interesting, the Present—Intriguing, the Future—Bright: A Story of Virginia Electric and Power Company.* New York: Newcomen Society, 1965.

Wooldridge, William C. "The Sound and Fury of 1896: Virginia Democrats Face Free Silver." *Virginia Magazine of History and Biography* 75 (January 1967): 97–108.

Unpublished Sources

Anderson, Henry W. Papers. Virginia Historical Society, Richmond.

Gibson, George D. "Asian Pot-Pourri." Address to the Woman's Club, Richmond, December 1, 1965.

———. "Comments on the Firm of Hunton and Williams." Talk at partnership retreat at Wintergreen, Virginia, October 10, 1986.

———. "Effective Legal Writing and Speaking." Remarks to the firm of Hunton and Williams, May 24, 1980.

Glasgow, Ellen. Papers. Alderman Library, University of Virginia, Charlottesville.

Hunton-Payne Family. Papers. Virginia Historical Society, Richmond.

Hunton & Williams files, journals, and ledgers: 1901–1989.

Hunton, Williams, Gay, Moore & Powell Partnership Agreement, December 29, 1955.

Montague, H. W. "Beverley B. Munford, an Appreciation." Munford Family Papers. Virginia Historical Society, Richmond.

Munford & Anderson Journal (including Munford, Hunton, Williams & Anderson Record after November 1, 1901), October 1, 1899 to September 30, 1904.

Munford Family. Papers. Virginia Historical Society, Richmond.

Munford, Hunton, Williams & Anderson Journals. October 1904–March 1962.

Munford, Hunton, Williams & Anderson Ledgers, 1901–1926.

Powell, Lewis F., Jr. "Unrecorded Biographical Facts About Your Father." December 15, 1981.

Riely, John W. "The Firm's Involvement with *Brown v. Board of Education*." Luncheon talk, Richmond, January 28, 1985.

Williams Family. Papers. Virginia Historical Society, Richmond.

Interviews

William W. Archer, Jr.
John Austin
Lawrence E. Blanchard, Jr.
Lewis Booker
Evelyn Brown
Amanda Bryan Kane
David Tennant Bryan
Robert Pegram Buford
Joseph Carter
Leslie Cheek, Jr.
Mary Tyler Freeman Cheek
James Cremins
Virginius Dabney
Donald Evans
Sheila Evans
Pamela Gibson Farrar
George Clemon Freeman, Jr.
Miriam Riggs Gay
Thomas B. Gay
Thomas B. Gay, Jr.
Sarah Geer Dale Gayle
George D. Gibson
Pearson Grymes Gibson
Dorothy Grady
Brice Graves
Ira Michael Heyman

Therese Heyman
Oliver W. Hill
Joseph Reid Anderson Hobson, Jr.
Helen Pettway Craig Jefferson
John Calvin Jeffries, Jr.
Elizabeth Taylor Little
Carolyn Moore McCue
Margaret Williams McElroy
Wirt Marks III
George Modlin
T. Justin Moore, Jr.
David Nelson
Elizabeth Nelson
H. Merrill Pasco
Lewis F. Powell, Jr.
John W. Riely
Archibald G. Robertson
George Seward
Frances Richardson Shield
John Subak
Mary Corcoran Subak
William Webster
J. Harvie Wilkinson, Jr.
John Page Williams
Langbourne Meade Williams

APPENDIX II

Partners of Hunton & Williams, 1901–1991, and Counsel in 1991

Beverley Bland Munford. Born September 10, 1856. (University of Virginia, Summer Course, 1877) Staples & Munford, 1887–1897, Munford & Anderson, 1899–1901, Munford, Hunton, Williams & Anderson, *founder*, November 1, 1901; *left*, October 1, 1902; *returned*, October 1, 1903; *left*, July 5, 1906. Died May 31, 1910.

Eppa Hunton, Jr. Born April 14, 1855. (University of Virginia, B.L. 1877) Hunton & Son, 1877–1901, Munford, Hunton, Williams & Anderson, *founder*, November 1, 1901; *left*, December 31, 1920. Died March 5, 1932.

Edmund Randolph Williams. Born May 1, 1871. (University of Virginia, B.L. 1893) Edward Thompson Publishing Company 1893–1895, Michie & Williams 1895–1896, Williams & Henry, 1896–1900, Munford, Hunton, Williams & Anderson, *founder*, November 1, 1901. Died June 9, 1952.

Henry Watkins Anderson. Born December 20, 1870. (Washington and Lee University, LL.B. 1898) Munford & Anderson 1899–1901, Munford, Hunton, Williams & Anderson, *founder*, November 1, 1901. Died January 7, 1954.

Thomas B. Gay. Born May 22, 1885. (University of Virginia Law School, 1906) *Came to firm*, November 15, 1908; *partner* January 1, 1916. Died October 13, 1983.

Wirt P. Marks, Jr. Born November 4, 1893. (University of Virginia, LL.B. 1917) *Came to firm*, June 1, 1919; *partner* January 1, 1925; *left*, March 1, 1953. Died June 1, 1963.

Irvin G. Craig. Born September 4, 1896. (University of Virginia, LL.B. 1921) *Came to firm*, September 1, 1921; *partner* January 1, 1928; *left*, April 1, 1945. Died October 19, 1973.

Edmund M. Preston. Born October 9, 1898. (University of Virginia, LL.B. 1921) *Came to firm*, September 1, 1921; *partner* January 1, 1928. Died March 21, 1945.

Eppa Hunton IV. Born July 31, 1904. (University of Virginia, B.A. 1925, LL.B. 1927) *Came to firm*, September 1, 1927; *partner* June 1, 1934; *left*, May 15, 1942; *returned*, September 30, 1945. Died November 24, 1976.

George D. Gibson. Born May 8, 1904. (University of Virginia, B.A. 1924; Harvard

University, M.A. 1925, LL.B. 1928) *Came to firm,* January 1, 1931; *partner* June 1, 1934. Died April 3, 1988.

Norman L. Flippen. Born January 14, 1895. (Attended University of Richmond) *Came to firm,* April 1, 1932; *partner* July 1, 1943. Died July 15, 1950.

T. Justin Moore, Sr. Born August 28, 1890. (University of Richmond, B.A. 1908; Harvard University, LL.B. 1913) *Came to firm,* April 1, 1932, *as a partner.* Died March 10, 1958.

Archibald G. Robertson. Born October 6, 1889. (University of Virginia, LL.B. 1914) *Came to firm,* April 1, 1932; *partner* January 1, 1937. Died September 23, 1985.

Lewis F. Powell, Jr. Born September 19, 1907. (Washington and Lee University, B.S. 1929, LL.B. 1931; Harvard University LL.M. 1932) *Came to firm,* January 1, 1935; *partner* January 1, 1938; *left,* May 1, 1942; *returned,* December 1945; *left,* January 3, 1972.

H. Merrill Pasco. Born October 7, 1915. (Virginia Military Institute, B.A. 1937; University of Virginia, LL.B. 1940) *Came to firm,* June 15, 1940; *left,* February 28, 1941; *returned,* November, 1945; *partner* January 1, 1949.

B. Warwick Davenport. Born August 18, 1916. (Yale University, B.A. 1938; University of Virginia, LL.B. 1941) *Came to firm,* June 16, 1941; *left,* June 23, 1941; *returned,* January 1, 1946; *partner* January 1, 1949.

John W. Riely. Born March 9, 1917. (University of Virginia, B.A. 1938; Harvard University, LL.B. 1941) *Came to firm,* August 1, 1941; *left,* March 31, 1942; *returned,* December 20, 1945; *partner* January 1, 1949. Died September 14, 1986.

Ralph H. Ferrell, Jr. Born July 26, 1912. (University of Richmond, B.A. 1933; Harvard University, LL.B. 1936) *Came to firm,* January 1, 1942; *left,* November 1, 1943; *returned,* March 12, 1946; *partner* January 1, 1949. Died September 20, 1968.

Francis V. Lowden, Jr. Born August 27, 1915. (Dartmouth College, B.A. 1937; University of Virginia, LL.B. 1942) *Came to firm,* April 1, 1942; *left,* 1943; *returned,* January 1, 1946; *partner* January 1, 1949. Died August 29, 1977.

Patrick A. Gibson. Born July 7, 1907. (University of Virginia, B.A. 1928; Harvard University, LL.B. 1931; Oxford University, B.A. 1933) *Came to firm,* August 1, 1945; *partner* January 1, 1948. Died September 17, 1973.

Lawrence E. Blanchard, Jr. Born March 7, 1921. (Duke University, B.A. 1942; Columbia University, LL.B. 1948) *Came to firm,* July 1, 1948; *partner* March 1, 1953; *left,* December 31, 1966.

H. Brice Graves. Born September 1, 1912. (University of Virginia B.S. 1932, M.S. 1933, Ph.D. 1938, LL.B. 1938) *Came to firm,* November 15, 1948; *partner* January 1, 1949.

T. Justin Moore, Jr. Born April 15, 1925. (Princeton University, B.A. 1947; University of Virginia, LL.B. 1950) *Came to firm,* July 1, 1950; *partner* January 1, 1955; *left,* April 4, 1967; *returned,* May 1, 1985, *as counsel.*

Joseph C. Carter, Jr. Born June 3, 1927. (University of Virginia, B.A. 1948, LL.B. 1951) *Came to firm,* July 2, 1951; *partner* January 1, 1958.

Robert P. Buford. Born September 7, 1925. (University of Virginia, LL.B. 1950) *Came to firm,* January 1, 1952; *partner* January 1, 1958.

E. Milton Farley III. Born October 26, 1927. (University of Notre Dame, LL.B. 1952) *Came to firm,* February 1, 1952; *partner* January 1, 1959. Died September 4, 1991.

Harry Frazier III. Born September 13, 1928. (Williams College, B.A. 1951; University of Virginia, LL.B. 1954) *Came to firm,* July 6, 1954; *partner* April 1, 1965.

Lewis T. Booker. Born September 22, 1929. (University of Richmond, B.A. 1950; Harvard University, LL.B. 1953) *Came to firm,* November 1, 1956; *partner* April 1, 1963.

James A. Harper, Jr. Born December 18, 1929. (University of Virginia, B.S. 1951; University of Richmond, LL.B. 1957) *Came to firm,* February 1, 1957; *partner* April 1, 1965; *left,* January 31, 1988.

George Clemon Freeman, Jr. Born January 3, 1929. (Vanderbilt University, B.A. 1950; Yale University, LL.B. 1956) *Came to firm,* August 5, 1957; *partner* April 1, 1963.

Waller H. Horsley. Born July 2, 1931. (University of Virginia, B.A. 1953, LL.B. 1959) *Came to firm,* March 2, 1959; *partner* April 1, 1965.

Evans B. Brasfield. Born September 21, 1932. (University of Virginia, B.A. 1954, LL.B. 1959) *Came to firm,* July 1, 1959; *partner* April 1, 1965.

John J. Adams. Born November 12, 1934. (Denison University, B.A. 1956; University of Virginia, LL.B. 1959) *Came to firm,* January 1, 1960; *left,* March 19, 1965; *returned,* November 1, 1967; *partner* April 1, 1969.

Richard G. Joynt. Born July 24, 1936. (Hampden-Sydney College, B.A. 1958; University of Virginia, LL.B. 1961) *Came to firm,* June 30, 1961, *partner* April 1, 1968.

Norman A. Scher. Born October 21, 1937. (University of Pennsylvania, B.S. 1959; University of Virginia, J.D. 1962) *Came to firm,* July 2, 1962; *partner* April 1, 1969; *left,* July 1, 1989.

Joseph M. Spivey III. Born August 10, 1935. (Virginia Military Institute, B.S. 1957; Washington and Lee University, LL.B. 1962) *Came to firm,* September 4, 1962; *partner* April 1, 1969.

George W. Sadler. Born May 15, 1922. (University of Richmond, B.A. 1946, LL.B. 1948) *Came to firm,* March 1, 1963; *partner* April 1, 1967; *left,* December 31, 1983.

Hugh V. White, Jr. Born July 24, 1933. (Virginia Military Institute, B.S. 1954; Washington and Lee University, LL.B. 1961) *Came to firm,* April 23, 1963; *partner* April 1, 1969.

James W. Featherstone III. Born September 19, 1938. (Yale University, B.A. 1960; University of Virginia, LL.B. 1963) *Came to firm,* July 1, 1963; *partner* April 1, 1971.

R. Kenneth Wheeler III. Born July 25, 1934. (University of Richmond, B.A. 1957, LL.B. 1963) *Came to firm,* September 10, 1963; *partner* April 1, 1971; *left,* January 3, 1988.

Jack H. Spain, Jr. Born January 24, 1939. (University of North Carolina, B.A.

1960; Harvard University, J.D. 1963) *Came to firm*, January 3, 1964; *partner* April 1, 1971.

William A. Pusey. Born March 17, 1936. (Princeton University B.A. 1958; University of Virginia, J.D. 1962) *Came to firm*, May 11, 1964; *partner* April 1, 1969.

Robert F. Brooks. Born July 13, 1939. (University of Richmond, B.A. 1961, LL.B. 1964) *Came to firm*, June 15, 1964; *partner* April 1, 1971.

George H. Hettrick. Born August 15, 1940. (Cornell University, B.A. 1962; Harvard University, J.D. 1965) *Came to firm*, July 19, 1965, *left* February 11, 1966, *returned* March 1, 1968; *partner* April 1, 1973.

Michael W. Maupin. Born July 9, 1937. (Virginia Military Institute, B.S. 1959; University of Virginia, LL.B. 1964) *Came to firm*, August 16, 1965; *partner* April 1, 1971.

John H. Shenefield. Born January 23, 1939. (Harvard University, B.A. 1960, LL.B. 1965) *Came to firm*, August 25, 1965; *partner* April 1, 1971; *left*, March 31, 1977.

Paul M. Thompson. Born August 30, 1935. (Loras College, B.A. 1957; Georgetown University, J.D. 1959) *Came to firm*, March 1, 1966; *partner* April 1, 1971.

James E. Farnham. Born February 28, 1942. (University of Tennessee, B.S. 1963; Yale University, LL.B. 1966) *Came to firm*, May 23, 1966; *partner* April 1, 1973.

David F. Peters. Born August 15, 1941. (Washington and Lee University, B.A. 1963; Duke University, LL.B. 1966) *Came to firm*, July 5, 1966; *partner* April 1, 1973.

Walter F. Witt, Jr. Born February 18, 1933. (University of Richmond, B.S. 1954, J.D. 1966) *Came to firm*, October 3, 1966; *partner* April 1, 1974.

Dewey B. Morris. Born September 15, 1938. (University of Virginia, B.A. 1960, LL.B. 1965) *Came to firm*, June 19, 1967; *partner* April 1, 1973.

Guy T. Tripp III. Born April 9, 1939. (University of Virginia, B.A. 1962, LL.B. 1965) *Came to firm*, July 10, 1967; *partner* April 1, 1974.

Hill B. Wellford, Jr. Born April 30, 1942. (Davidson College, B.A. 1964; University of North Carolina, J.D. 1967) *Came to firm*, October 16, 1967; *partner* April 1, 1974.

Gordon F. Rainey, Jr. Born April 26, 1940. (University of Virginia, B.A. 1962, LL.B. 1967) *Came to firm*, March 14, 1968; *partner* April 1, 1975.

Allen C. Goolsby III. Born October 19, 1939. (Yale University, B.A. 1961; University of Virginia, LL.B. 1968) *Came to firm*, July 1, 1968; *partner* April 1, 1975.

Turner T. Smith, Jr. Born December 16, 1940. (Princeton University, B.A. 1962; Harvard University, LL.B. 1968) *Came to firm*, July 1, 1968; *partner* April 1, 1975.

William L. Bramble. Born August 27, 1903. (University of Virginia, LL.B. 1927) *Came to firm*, October 1, 1968, *as a partner; left*, September 26, 1975. Died November 21, 1981.

Harry J. Warthen III. Born July 8, 1939. (University of Virginia, B.A. 1961, LL.B. 1967) *Came to firm*, October 1, 1968; *partner* April 1, 1976.

Randolph F. Totten. Born June 20, 1943. (Yale University, B.A. 1965, University of Virginia, LL.B. 1968) *Came to firm*, June 23, 1969; *partner* April 1, 1976.

Thomas G. Slater, Jr. Born March 15, 1944. (Virginia Military Institute, B.A. 1966; University of Virginia, J.D. 1969) *Came to firm*, June 30, 1969; *partner* April 1, 1976.

T. S. Ellis III. Born May 15, 1940. (Princeton University, B.S.E. 1961; Harvard University, J.D. 1969; Oxford University, Diploma in Law 1970) *Came to firm*, July 7, 1969; *left*, August 9, 1969; *returned*, October 19, 1970; *partner* April 1, 1976; *left*, August 28, 1987.

Guy K. Tower. Born October 29, 1941. (University of Virginia, B.A. 1964, LL.B. 1967) *Came to firm*, August 4, 1969; *partner* April 1, 1975; *left*, January 1, 1981.

Lathan M. Ewers, Jr. Born May 26, 1941. (University of Virginia, B.A. 1963, LL.B. 1966) *Came to firm*, December 1, 1969; *partner* April 1, 1976.

Virginia H. Hackney. Born January 11, 1945. (Hollins College, B.A. 1967; University of Richmond, J.D. 1970) *Came to firm*, February 2, 1970; *partner* April 1, 1977.

C. Porter Vaughan III. Born August 26, 1945. (Yale University, B.A. 1967; University of Virginia, J.D. 1970) *Came to firm*, July 13, 1970; *partner* April 1, 1977.

Benjamin C. Ackerly. Born August 25, 1942. (University of Virginia, B.A. 1965, LL.B. 1968) *Came to firm*, August 3, 1970; *partner* April 1, 1977.

Mark S. Dray. Born February 8, 1943. (Mount Union College, B.A. 1965; College of William and Mary, J.D. 1968, M.L. & T. 1969) *Came to firm*, August 3, 1970; *partner* April 1, 1977.

John B. Ashton. Born February 14, 1944. (Williams College, B.A. 1966; University of Virginia, LL.B. 1969) *Came to firm*, August 30, 1970; *partner* April 1, 1977.

W. Taylor Reveley III. Born January 6, 1943. (Princeton University, B.A. 1965; University of Virginia, J.D. 1968) *Came to firm*, August 31, 1970; *left*, September 1, 1972; *returned*, October 1, 1973; *partner* April 1, 1976.

Arnold H. Quint. Born January 3, 1942. (Haverford College, B.A. 1963; Yale University, LL.B. 1966) *Came to firm*, November 16, 1970; *partner* April 1, 1974.

G. H. Gromel, Jr. Born February 27, 1946. (University of Virginia, B.S. 1968, J.D. 1971) *Came to firm*, August 2, 1971; *partner* April 1, 1978.

Donald P. Irwin. Born October 15, 1944. (Princeton University, B.A. 1965; Yale University, M.A. 1971, LL.B. 1971) *Came to firm*, August 16, 1971; *partner* April 1, 1978.

Daniel A. Carrell. Born January 2, 1941. (Davidson College, B.A. 1963; Oxford University, B.A. 1965, M.A. 1969; Stanford University, J.D. 1968) *Came to firm*, September 8, 1971; *partner* April 1, 1979.

Robert S. Parker, Jr. Born April 7, 1943. (University of Virginia, B.S. 1967; College of William and Mary, J.D. 1970) *Came to firm*, November 1, 1971; *partner* April 1, 1979; *left*, August 31, 1984.

Thomas J. Manley. Born January 23, 1946. (University of North Carolina, B.A. 1968; Harvard University, J.D. 1972) *Came to firm,* May 20, 1972; *partner* April 1, 1980.

J. Waverly Pulley III. Born May 19, 1946. (University of Richmond, B.A. 1968, J.D. 1972) *Came to firm,* July 24, 1972; *partner* April 1, 1979.

Manning Gasch, Jr. Born January 25, 1943. (Cornell University, B.S. 1966; University of Virginia, J.D. 1972) *Came to firm,* August 9, 1972; *partner* April 1, 1979.

Patrick J. Milmoe. Born October 2, 1937. (College of William and Mary, B.A. 1959; University of Virginia, J.D. 1962) *Came to firm,* September 5, 1972, *as a partner.*

Johnnie M. Walters. Born December 20, 1919. (Furman University, B.A. 1942; University of Michigan, LL.B. 1948) *Came to firm,* June 1, 1973, *as a partner; left,* March 31, 1979.

William L. S. Rowe. Born March 31, 1948. (Washington and Lee University, B.A. 1970; University of Virginia, J.D. 1973) *Came to firm,* July 2, 1973; *partner* April 1, 1980.

Joseph C. Kearfott. Born September 24, 1947. (Davidson College, B.A. 1969; University of Virginia, J.D. 1972) *Came to firm,* July 16, 1973; *partner* April 1, 1980.

James A. Jones III. Born June 16, 1944. (Yale University, B.A. 1966; University of Virginia, J.D. 1973) *Came to firm,* August 27, 1973; *partner* April 1, 1980.

James N. Christman. Born March 23, 1948. (University of Illinois, B.S. 1970; University of Michigan, J.D. 1973) *Came to firm,* October 8, 1973; *partner* April 1, 1980.

Robert Dean Pope. Born March 10, 1945. (Princeton University, B.A. 1967; Cambridge University, Diploma in Historical Studies, 1971; Yale University, M. Phil. 1972, J.D. 1972, Ph.D. 1976) *Came to firm,* January 2, 1974; *partner* April 1, 1980.

Abram W. VanderMeer, Jr. Born March 20, 1947. (University of Virginia, B.A. 1969; Georgetown University, J.D. 1974) *Came to firm,* May 20, 1974; *partner* April 1, 1981.

Christine H. Perdue. Born March 18, 1949. (Oberlin College, B.A. 1971; Duke University, J.D. 1974) *Came to firm,* May 21, 1974; *partner* April 1, 1981.

Douglas W. Davis. Born July 19, 1945. (University of Richmond, B.A. 1967; Boston University, M.A., 1971; Georgetown University, J.D. 1974) *Came to firm,* May 29, 1974; *partner* April 1, 1981.

Jack E. McClard. Born May 13, 1946. (Rice University, B.A. 1968; University of Texas, J.D. 1974) *Came to firm,* June 10, 1974; *partner* April 1, 1981.

Gregory N. Stillman. Born April 29, 1948. (University of Richmond, B.A. 1970; Washington and Lee University, J.D. 1974) *Came to firm,* July 1, 1974; *partner* April 1, 1981.

Richard D. Gary. Born April 25, 1949. (University of North Carolina, B.A. 1971; University of Virginia, J.D. 1974) *Came to firm,* August 26, 1974; *partner* April 1, 1981.

Thurston R. Moore. Born December 10, 1946. (University of Virginia, B.A. 1968, J.D. 1974) *Came to firm,* September 9, 1974; *partner* April 1, 1981.

Andrea B. Field. Born November 30, 1949. (Yale University, B.A. 1971; University of Virginia, J.D. 1974) *Came to firm,* September 16, 1974; *partner* April 1, 1981.

Virginia W. Powell. Born February 9, 1948. (University of South Carolina, B.A. 1970; University of North Dakota, J.D. 1974) *Came to firm,* January 13, 1975; *partner* April 1, 1985.

D. Alan Rudlin. Born November 4, 1947. (University of Virginia, B.A. 1969, J.D. 1973) *Came to firm,* May 27, 1975; *partner* April 1, 1982.

William L. Rosbe. Born February 17, 1944. (Yale University, B.A. 1966; Cornell University, J.D. 1975) *Came to firm,* June 16, 1975; *partner* April 1, 1982.

Charles J. Brown III. Born August 20, 1947. (Virginia Polytechnic Institute and State University, B.S.I.E. 1970; Washington and Lee University, J.D. 1975) *Came to firm,* July 28, 1975; *partner* April 1, 1982; *left,* July 31, 1982.

John C. Thomas. Born September 18, 1950. (University of Virginia, B.A. 1972, J.D. 1975) *Came to firm,* August 11, 1975; *partner* April 1, 1982; *left,* April 12, 1983.

A. Neal Barkus. Born July 17, 1949. (University of Virginia, B.A. 1969; Washington and Lee University, J.D. 1974) *Came to firm,* August 15, 1975; *partner* April 1, 1982.

Ray V. Hartwell III. Born June 19, 1947. (Washington and Lee University, B.A. 1969, J.D. 1975) *Came to firm,* August 25, 1975; *partner* April 1, 1982.

Edgar M. Roach, Jr. Born January 2, 1948. (Wake Forest University, B.A. 1969; University of North Carolina, J.D. 1974) *Came to firm,* September 8, 1975; *partner* April 1, 1981.

Michael L. Teague. Born October 3, 1948. (University of Virginia, B.S.N.E. 1970, M.S.N.E. 1972, J.D. 1976) *Came to firm,* June 1, 1976; *partner* April 1, 1984.

Henry V. Nickel. Born August 8, 1943. (University of Virginia, B.A. 1965; George Washington University, J.D. 1968) *Came to firm,* June 4, 1976, *as a partner.*

Michael B. Barr. Born July 24, 1948. (Georgetown University, B.S. 1970, J.D. 1973) *Came to firm,* June 7, 1976; *partner* April 1, 1980.

Gregory B. Robertson. Born April 2, 1951. (Washington and Lee University, B.A. 1973; University of Richmond, J.D. 1976) *Came to firm,* July 7, 1976; *partner* April 1, 1984.

Kathleen DuVal. Born October 8, 1949. (Brooklyn College, B.A. 1970; University of Louisville, J.D. 1973) *Came to firm,* July 12, 1976; *partner* April 1, 1983.

Robert M. Rolfe. Born May 16, 1951. (University of Virginia, B.A. 1973, J.D. 1976) *Came to firm,* July 14, 1976; *partner* April 1, 1983.

William H. McBride. Born August 8, 1948. (Princeton University, B.A. 1970; University of Texas, J.D. 1976) *Came to firm,* August 18, 1976; *partner* April 1, 1983.

James M. Rinaca. Born December 12, 1950. (University of Virginia, B.S. 1973, J.D. 1976) *Came to firm,* August 30, 1976; *partner* April 1, 1984.

Thomas J. Flaherty. Born November 14, 1950. (Yale University, B.A. 1972; Boston College, J.D. 1975) *Came to firm*, September 13, 1976; *partner* April 1, 1984.

Anne Gordon Greever. Born April 22, 1949. (Mary Washington College, B.A. 1971; College of William and Mary, J.D. 1976) *Came to firm*, April 4, 1977; *partner* April 1, 1985.

William A. Walsh, Jr. Born March 17, 1949. (University of Maryland, B.S. 1972; University of Richmond, J.D. 1977) *Came to firm*, June 20, 1977; *partner* April 1, 1985.

William F. Young. Born January 6, 1948. (University of Virginia, B.A. 1970; Harvard University, J.D. 1977) *Came to firm*, June 20, 1977; *partner* April 1, 1985.

John A. Lucas. Born August 1, 1943. (U.S. Military Academy, B.S. 1969; University of Texas, J.D. 1977) *Came to firm*, July 1, 1977; *partner* April 1, 1984.

J. William Gray, Jr. Born June 21, 1950. (Rutgers University, B.S., B.A. 1973; University of Virginia, J.D. 1977) *Came to firm*, August 15, 1977; *partner* April 1, 1985.

K. Dennis Sisk. Born April 4, 1952. (Vanderbilt University, B.A. 1974, J.D. 1978) *Came to firm*, May 22, 1978; *partner* April 1, 1985.

F. William Brownell. Born July 18, 1952. (Georgetown University, B.S. 1974, M.S. 1978, J.D. 1978) *Came to firm*, May 30, 1978; *partner* April 1, 1985.

L. Neal Ellis, Jr. Born August 1, 1948. (U.S. Military Academy, B.S. 1970; University of Virginia, J.D. 1975) *Came to firm*, July 3, 1978; *partner* April 1, 1985.

R. Noel Clinard. Born November 1, 1946. (Washington and Lee University, B.A. 1968, J.D. 1976) *Came to firm*, September 20, 1978; *partner* April 1, 1986.

Jack A. Molenkamp. Born October 1, 1952. (Michigan State University, B.A. 1974; University of Michigan, J.D. 1979) *Came to firm*, May 29, 1979; *partner* April 1, 1987.

John J. Beardsworth, Jr. Born November 10, 1954. (University of Pennsylvania, B.A. 1975; George Washington University, J.D. 1979) *Came to firm*, June 4, 1979; *partner* March 1, 1987.

Douglas W. Kenyon. Born April 15, 1954. (University of Notre Dame, B.A. 1976, J.D. 1979) *Came to firm*, June 4, 1979; *partner* April 1, 1987.

Anthony F. Earley, Jr. Born July 29, 1949. (University of Notre Dame, B.S. 1971, M.S. 1979, J.D. 1979) *Came to firm*, June 5, 1979; *partner* March 1, 1985; *left*, May 31, 1985.

Charles King Mallory III. Born November 16, 1936. (Yale University, B.A. 1958; Tulane University, LL.B. 1961) *Came to firm*, July 1, 1979, *as a partner*.

Charles D. Ossola. Born August 3, 1953. (Williams College, B.A. 1975; Villanova University, J.D. 1978) *Came to firm*, September 24, 1979; *left*, September 4, 1981; *returned*, March 7, 1983; *partner* April 1, 1988.

Lewis F. Powell III. Born September 14, 1952. (Washington and Lee University, B.A. 1974; University of Virginia, J.D. 1978) *Came to firm*, October 15, 1979; *partner* April 1, 1986.

Mark G. Weisshaar. Born April 1, 1950. (Yale University, B.A. 1972; George Washington University, J.D. 1977) *Came to firm,* January 2, 1980; *partner* April 1, 1986.

Lee B. Zeugin. Born December 30, 1952. (University of Kansas, B.S.Ch.E. 1974; University of Michigan, J.D. 1979) *Came to firm,* January 7, 1980; *partner* April 1, 1989.

L. Anthony Joseph, Jr. Born July 13, 1940. (University of Texas, B.A. 1963, LL.B. 1968) *Came to firm,* January 10, 1980, *as a partner; left,* August 31, 1984.

Edward S. Finley, Jr. Born March 24, 1949. (University of North Carolina, B.A. 1971, J.D. 1974) *Came to firm,* April 1, 1980, *as a partner.*

William M. Flynn. Born June 21, 1949. (Georgetown University, B.S.F.S. 1971; College of William and Mary, J.D. 1977) *Came to firm,* April 1, 1980; *partner* April 1, 1989.

Robert C. Howison, Jr. Born July 26, 1915. (University of North Carolina, B.A. 1937, J.D. 1939) *Came to firm,* April 1, 1980, *as a partner.*

Walton K. Joyner, Jr. Born April 1, 1933. (University of North Carolina, B.A. 1955, J.D. 1960) *Came to firm,* April 1, 1980, *as a partner.*

William T. Joyner, Sr. Born April 11, 1891. (Harvard University, LL.B. 1916) *Came to firm,* April 1, 1980, *as a partner.* Died December 30, 1981.

Henry S. Manning, Jr. Born June 8, 1938. (University of North Carolina, B.A. 1960, LL.B. 1965) *Came to firm,* April 1, 1980, *as a partner; left,* August 1, 1987.

Odes L. Stroupe, Jr. Born March 10, 1946. (North Carolina State University, B.A. 1968; University of North Carolina, J.D. 1971) *Came to firm,* April 1, 1980, *as a partner.*

James E. Tucker. Born September 14, 1914. (Wake Forest University, J.D. 1939) *Came to firm,* April 1, 1980, *as a partner; left,* December 31, 1983.

Jerry E. Whitson. Born June 15, 1955. (State University of New York, B.A. 1977; Boston University, J.D. 1980) *Came to firm,* May 27, 1980; *partner* April 1, 1988.

Cheryl G. Ragsdale. Born September 25, 1946. (Mary Washington College, B.A. 1968; University of Richmond, J.D. 1980) *Came to firm,* June 2, 1980, *counsel* April 1, 1988.

John Jay Range. Born March 28, 1955. (University of Michigan, B.A. 1977; University of North Carolina, J.D. 1980) *came to firm,* June 2, 1980; *partner* April 1, 1989.

William M. Richardson. Born October 8, 1952. (College of William and Mary, B.A. 1975; University of California, J.D. 1978) *Came to firm,* July 7, 1980; *left,* May 4, 1984; *returned,* March 11, 1985; *partner* April 1, 1988.

Gregory E. May. Born September 17, 1953. (College of William and Mary, B.A. 1975; Harvard University, J.D. 1978) *Came to firm,* July 14, 1980; *partner* April 1, 1986; *left,* April 12, 1989.

B. Cary Tolley III. Born July 17, 1949. (Yale University, B.A. 1972; Washington and Lee University, J.D. 1975) *Came to firm,* August 25, 1980; *partner* September 1, 1984.

Jennings G. Ritter II. Born March 9, 1953. (University of Virginia, B.A. 1975; University of Richmond, J.D. 1979) *Came to firm,* September 15, 1980; *partner* April 1, 1987.

Matthew J. Calvert. Born April 24, 1953. (Washington and Lee University, B.A. 1975, J.D. 1979) *Came to firm,* October 1, 1980; *partner* April 1, 1987.

Paul E. Mirengoff. Born April 17, 1949. (Dartmouth College, B.A. 1971; Stanford University, J.D. 1974) *Came to firm,* March 23, 1981, *counsel* April 1, 1988.

Jessine A. Monaghan. Born May 5, 1953. (Wellesley College, B.A. 1975; Washington and Lee University, J.D. 1979) *Came to firm,* April 27, 1981, *counsel* April 1, 1989.

Edgar H. MacKinlay. Born September 16, 1936. (Washington and Lee University, B.S. 1958, LL.B. 1964) *Came to firm,* May 1, 1981, *as a partner; left,* June 30, 1981.

William Jeffery Edwards. Born December 3, 1955. (Washington and Lee University, B.A. 1978, J.D. 1981) *Came to firm,* June 22, 1981; *partner* April 1, 1989.

Patricia M. Schwarzschild. Born January 15, 1950. (Virginia Polytechnic Institute and State University, B.S. 1972; Vanderbilt University, J.D. 1975) *Came to firm,* July 6, 1981; *partner* April 1, 1985.

Thomas McN. Millhiser. Born March 30, 1949. (Georgetown University, B.S. 1971; Washington and Lee University, J.D. 1981) *Came to firm,* August 3, 1981; *partner* April 1, 1989.

Phyllis M. Rubinstein. Born March 31, 1945. (Pennsylvania State University, B.A. 1966; Temple University, J.D. 1977) *Came to firm,* August 31, 1981, *counsel* April 1, 1989.

Alfred R. Light. Born December 14, 1949. (Johns Hopkins University, B.A. 1971; University of North Carolina, Ph.D. 1976; Harvard University, J.D. 1981) *Came to firm,* September 1, 1981, *counsel* April 1, 1989.

Kathy E. B. Robb. Born November 14, 1954. (University of Texas, B.A. 1976; University of Virginia, J.D. 1980) *Came to firm,* September 14, 1981; *partner* April 1, 1988.

Richard W. Goldman. Born July 2, 1947. (Yale University, B.A. 1969; Harvard University, J.D. 1973) *Came to firm,* October 1, 1981; *partner* April 1, 1985. Died October 18, 1989.

James T. Tilton. Born December 22, 1943. (Duke University, B.A. 1966; Emory University, J.D. 1969) *Came to firm,* October 19, 1981; *partner* September 1, 1984.

Robert S. Rausch. Born February 15, 1952. (University of Virginia, B.A. 1966; College of William and Mary, J.D. 1981) *Came to firm,* October 26, 1981; *partner* April 1, 1989.

E. Peter Kane. Born February 13, 1947. (State University of New York, B.S. 1969; Washington and Lee University, J.D. 1975) *Came to firm,* January 4, 1982; *partner* April 1, 1986.

Martin J. Barrington. Born July 16, 1953. (College of St. Rose, B.A. 1977; Albany Law School, J.D. 1980) *Came to firm,* March 29, 1982; *partner* April 1, 1990.

Gregory G. Little. Born January 7, 1955. (Drew University, B.A. 1977; University of Tennessee, J.D. 1982) *Came to firm,* May 24, 1982; *partner* April 1, 1990.

Robert J. Muething. Born April 24, 1957. (Harvard University, B.A. 1979; University of Notre Dame, J.D. 1982) *Came to firm,* May 24, 1982; *partner* April 1, 1990.

James F. Bowe, Jr. Born May 17, 1955. (Williams College, B.A. 1977; Northwestern University, J.D. 1982) *Came to firm,* June 1, 1982; *partner* April 1, 1990.

Edward B. Koehler. Born May 10, 1954. (University of Notre Dame, B.S. 1976, M.A. 1977, J.D. 1982) *Came to firm,* June 1, 1982; *partner* April 1, 1990.

Kristy A. Niehaus. Born July 20, 1957. (University of Detroit, B.A. 1979; Boston University, J.D. 1982) *Came to firm,* June 1, 1982; *partner* April 1, 1990.

B. Darrell Smelcer. Born October 6, 1955. (Washington State University, B.A. 1979; Tulane University, J.D. 1982) *Came to firm,* June 1, 1982; *partner* April 1, 1990.

Vicki O. Tucker. Born August 20, 1950. (West Virginia University, B.S. 1977, J.D. 1980) *Came to firm,* June 1, 1982; *counsel* May 13, 1991.

Linda L. Najjoum. Born June 15, 1946. (Ohio State University, B.S.N. 1970; University of South Carolina, J.D. 1981; Medical College of Virginia/Virginia Commonwealth University, M.S. 1983) *Came to firm,* July 20, 1982; *counsel* June 1, 1990.

George C. Howell III. Born June 27, 1956. (Princeton University, B.A. 1978; University of Virginia, J.D. 1981) *Came to firm,* September 20, 1982; *partner* April 1, 1989.

John R. McArthur. Born January 5, 1956. (Davidson College, B.A. 1977; University of South Carolina, J.D. 1981) *Came to firm,* September 28, 1982; *partner* April 1, 1989.

William F. Kennedy. Born February 19, 1918. (Fordham College, B.S. 1939, LL.B. 1943) *Came to firm,* March 1, 1983, *as counsel.*

Richard E. May. Born February 5, 1946. (University of Maryland, B.A. 1967; Georgetown University, J.D. 1975) *Came to firm,* July 18, 1983, *as a partner.*

Lucinda Minton Langworthy. Born January 2, 1956. (Bucknell University, B.A. 1978; George Washington University, J.D. 1981) *Came to firm,* August 8, 1983; *counsel* June 1, 1990.

Debbie G. Seidel. Born December 3, 1955. (West Virginia Wesleyan College, B.A. 1977; University of Pittsburgh, J.D. 1983) *Came to firm,* August 8, 1983; *counsel* April 1, 1991.

Donald L. Creach. Born May 9, 1953. (University of Kansas, B.A. 1975; Stanford University, J.D. 1982) *Came to firm,* September 19, 1983; *partner* April 1, 1990.

William D. Johnson. Born January 9, 1954. (Duke University, B.A. 1978; University of North Carolina, J.D. 1982) *Came to firm,* October 3, 1983; *partner* April 1, 1990.

John C. Baity. Born June 21, 1933. (University of Michigan, B.A. 1955, J.D. 1958) *Came to firm,* October 4, 1983, *as a partner; left,* August 31, 1984.

Joseph P. Congleton. Born June 8, 1947. (Centre College, B.A. 1969; University of Virginia, J.D. 1972) *Came to firm,* October 10, 1983, *as a partner.*

T. Justin Moore, III. Born November 26, 1956. (Princeton University B.A. 1979; University of Virginia M.B.A. 1983, J.D. 1983) *Came to firm,* October 31, 1983; *partner* April 1, 1991.

Laurence E. Skinner. Born March 23, 1956. (College of William and Mary, B.B.A. 1977; University of Richmond, J.D. 1984) *Came to firm,* December 19, 1983; *partner* April 1, 1991.

Grady K. Carlson. Born February 19, 1953. (Duke University, B.A. 1975; University of Virginia, J.D. 1978) *Came to firm,* July 1, 1984; *partner* April 1, 1987.

Thomas J. Cawley. Born October 7, 1943. (University of Scranton, B.S. 1966; University of Virginia, LL.B. 1969) *Came to firm,* July 1, 1984, *as a partner.*

Randolph W. Church, Jr. Born November 6, 1934. (University of Virginia, B.A. 1957, LL.B. 1960) *Came to firm,* July 1, 1984, *as a partner.*

Edward M. Barrett. Born July 18, 1920. (Princeton University, B.S. 1942; Brooklyn College, LL.B. 1949) *Came to firm,* July 1, 1984, *as counsel; left,* December 31, 1988.

Stephen M. Sayers. Born May 19, 1953. (Oxford University, B.A. 1975, M.A. 1979; University of Toronto, M.A. 1976; Georgetown University, J.D. 1983) *Came to firm,* July 1, 1984; *partner* April 1, 1991.

L. Raul Grable. Born August 14, 1955. (Yale University, B.A. 1977; University of California, J.D. 1980) *Came to firm,* July 2, 1984; *partner* April 1, 1989.

Stephen R. Romine. Born May 27, 1955. (University of Richmond, B.A. 1977, J.D. 1980, M.B.A. 1983) *Came to firm,* September 4, 1984; *counsel* April 1, 1991.

Patricia K. Epps. Born March 21, 1952. (University of Virginia, B.A. 1974, M.A. 1977, J.D. 1983) *Came to firm,* September 24, 1984; *partner* April 1, 1991.

C. Christopher Giragosian. Born October 15, 1951. (Washington and Lee University, B.A. 1973; University of Richmond, J.D. 1976) *Came to firm,* October 15, 1984; *partner* April 1, 1987.

Jeffrey N. Martin. Born June 26, 1952. (Lawrence University, B.A. 1974; Harvard University, J.D. 1978) *Came to firm,* October 22, 1984; *partner* April 1, 1988.

H. Barton Clark, Jr. Born August 22, 1956. (Washington and Lee University, B.A. 1978; University of Texas, J.D. 1981) *Came to firm,* December 10, 1984; *partner* April 1, 1991.

David F. Brandley, Jr. Born November 6, 1954. (University of Virginia, B.A. 1977; Washington and Lee University, J.D. 1980) *Came to firm,* March 20, 1985; *partner* April 1, 1990.

George V. Cook. Born February 14, 1927. (Columbia University, B.A. 1949, LL.B. 1952) *Came to firm,* April 1, 1985, *as counsel; left,* March 31, 1990.

David O. Ledbetter. Born March 16, 1950. (University of Redlands, B.A. 1972; University of California, J.D. 1977) *Came to firm,* July 15, 1985; *counsel* April 1, 1991.

John J. Rhodes. Born September 18, 1916. (Kansas State University, B.S. 1938; Harvard University, LL.B. 1941) *Came to firm,* April 1, 1985, *as counsel.*

Pauline A. Schneider. Born May 25, 1943. (Glassboro State College, B.A. 1965; Howard University, M.U.S. 1972; Yale University, J.D. 1977) *Came to firm,* July 22, 1985; *partner* April 1, 1987.

Myron D. Cohen. Born May 19, 1935. (Harvard University, B.A. 1957, LL.B. 1960) *Came to firm,* January 6, 1986, *as a partner.*

David Rees Davies. Born November 30, 1947. (Cambridge University, B.A. 1969, M.A. 1971) *Came to firm,* January 6, 1986, *as a partner.*

David Fink. Born November 16, 1947. (University of Pennsylvania, B.A. 1968; Columbia University, J.D. 1973) *Came to firm,* January 6, 1986, *as counsel.*

Anthony L. Fletcher. Born December 23, 1935. (Princeton University, B.A. 1957; Harvard University, J.D. 1962) *Came to firm,* January 6, 1986, *as a partner.*

Donald Fried. Born February 28, 1936. (College of the City of New York, B.A. 1956; Harvard University, J.D. 1959) *Came to firm,* January 6, 1986, *as a partner; left,* January 4, 1988; *returned,* January 1, 1992, *as a partner.*

Kathleen Imholz. Born May 3, 1944. (Cornell University, B.A. 1965; Harvard University, J.D. 1969) *Came to firm,* January 6, 1986, *as a partner; left,* July 31, 1986.

John T. Konther. Born December 13, 1946. (Muhlenberg College, B.A. 1967; Brooklyn College, J.D. 1971; New York University, LL.M. 1974) *Came to firm,* January 6, 1986; *partner* April 1, 1987.

George P. Kramer. Born February 22, 1927. (Harvard University, B.A. 1950, LL.B. 1953) *Came to firm,* January 6, 1986, *as a partner.*

Harrison D. Maas. Born September 24, 1945. (University of Iowa, B.A. 1967, J.D. 1970) *Came to firm,* January 6, 1986, *as a partner.*

Thomas V. McMahon. Born October 19, 1924. (Princeton University, A.A. 1946; St. John's University, LL.B. 1950) *Came to firm,* January 6, 1986, *as counsel.*

Axel P. Scyler. Born March 14, 1927. (Northwestern University, Ph.B. 1958; Harvard University, J.D. 1961) *Came to firm,* January 6, 1986, *as a partner.*

James W. Shea. Born July 10, 1936. (St. Peter's College, B.S. 1957; Fordham University, J.D. 1962; New York University, LL.M. 1965) *Came to firm,* January 6, 1986, *as a partner.*

Charles S. Robb. Born June 26, 1939. (University of Wisconsin, B.A. 1961; University of Virginia, J.D. 1973) *Came to firm,* February 1, 1986, *as a partner; left,* December 30, 1988.

T. Lawrence Jones. Born November 19, 1920. (University of Texas, B.B.A. 1944, J.D. 1948) *Came to firm,* May 1, 1986, *as counsel.*

Philip M. Battles III. Born April 10, 1944. (Syracuse University, B.A. 1967; Georgetown University, J.D. 1973) *Came to firm,* September 29, 1986, *as a partner.*

Francis A. McDermott. Born December 21, 1943. (Holy Cross College, B.A. 1965; University of Virginia, J.D. 1970) *Came to firm*, October 1, 1986, *as a partner.*

James L. Ritzenberg. Born October 29, 1957. (Yale University, B.A. 1979; University of Virginia, J.D. 1982) *Came to firm*, October 30, 1986; *partner* April 1, 1990.

James W. Dyke, Jr. Born November 25, 1946. (Howard University, B.A. 1968, J.D. 1971) *Came to firm*, March 23, 1987, *as a partner; left*, January 12, 1990.

Richard T. Robol. Born February 8, 1952. (University of Virginia, B.A. 1974; Harvard University, J.D. 1978) *Came to firm*, May 18, 1987; *partner* April 1, 1989.

Robert M. Hughes III. Born February 18, 1929. (University of Virginia, B.A. 1951, LL.B. 1957) *Came to firm*, May 19, 1987, *as counsel.*

A. Jackson Timms. Born July 13, 1938. (Yale University, B.A. 1960; University of Virginia, LL.B. 1963) *Came to firm*, May 26, 1987, *as a partner.*

Franklin H. Stone. Born October 19, 1951. (Hollins College, B.A. 1974; University of Virginia, J.D. 1977) *Came to firm*, November 16, 1987; *partner* April 1, 1989.

O. Julia Weller. Born September 21, 1949. (McGill University, B.A. 1970, LL.B. 1978; Georgetown University, LL.M. 1979) *Came to firm*, February 26, 1988; *counsel* April 1, 1991.

Jerry R. Marlatt. Born April 13, 1942. (University of Southern California, B.A. 1967; Southwestern University, J.D. 1977) *Came to firm*, October 10, 1988, *as a partner.*

Jeffrey P. Brown. Born December 30, 1955. (University of North Carolina, B.S. 1978, J.D. 1981) *Came to firm*, November 7, 1988, *as a partner.*

J. William Gibson. Born November 11, 1931. (Emory University, B.A. 1953, J.D. 1956) *Came to firm*, November 7, 1988, *as a partner.*

Kent E. Mast. Born July 12, 1943. (Princeton University, B.A. 1965; Duke University, J.D. 1968) *Came to firm*, November 7, 1988, *as a partner, left*, April 31, 1990.

C. L. Wagner, Jr. Born October 5, 1944. (Emory University, B.A. 1966; University of Virginia, J.D. 1969) *Came to firm*, November 7, 1988, *as a partner.*

Robert E. R. Huntley. Born June 13, 1929. (Washington and Lee University, B.A. 1950, J.D. 1957; Harvard University, LL.M. 1962) *Came to firm*, December 1, 1988, *as counsel.*

Rick J. W. Riggers. Born January 27, 1954. (Brigham Young University, B.A. 1978, M.B.A. 1982, J.D. 1982) *Came to firm*, December 15, 1988; *partner* April 1, 1990.

D. Whitten Joyner. Born February 8, 1957. (Auburn University, B.S. 1979; University of Georgia, J.D. 1982) *Came to firm*, January 16, 1989; *partner* April 1, 1990.

Robert H. Brumley II. Born July 19, 1948. (East Tennessee State University, B.S. 1974; University of Tennessee, J.D. 1977) *Came to firm*, February 24, 1989, *as a partner; left*, February 24, 1991.

John R. Fallon, Jr. Born February 18, 1955. (State University of New York, B.A. 1977, M.P.A. 1981, J.D. 1981) *Came to firm,* March 6, 1989, *as counsel; partner* April 1, 1991.

Robert G. Fitzgibbons, Jr. Born June 13, 1954. (Colby College, B.A. 1976; Georgetown University, J.D. 1980) *Came to firm,* March 20, 1989, *as counsel; partner* April 1, 1991.

Timothy J. Pfister. Born April 24, 1952. (University of Virginia, B.A. 1974; University of Louisville, J.D. 1978) *Came to firm,* April 1, 1989, *as counsel; partner* April 1, 1991.

L. Traywick Duffie. Born February 13, 1947. (Wofford College, B.A. 1969; University of South Carolina, J.D. 1972) *Came to firm,* May 13, 1989, *as a partner.*

Caryl Greenberg Smith. Born December 15, 1956. (University of Georgia, B.A. 1979, J.D. 1982) *Came to firm,* July 24, 1989; *partner* April 1, 1991.

Scott J. McKay Wolas. Born April 18, 1949. (Georgetown University, B.S.F.S. 1971; Fordham Law School, J.D. 1976) *Came to firm,* August 1, 1989, *as a partner.*

David F. Geneson. Born August 29, 1947. (Rensselaer Polytechnic Institute, B.S. 1969; University of Miami School of Law, J.D. 1974) *Came to firm,* January 2, 1990, *as counsel.*

Gerald L. Baliles. Born July 8, 1940. (Wesleyan University, B.A. 1963; University of Virginia, J.D. 1967) *Came to firm,* February 5, 1990, *as a partner.*

Ira L. Freilicher. Born August 5, 1937. (Columbia College, A.B. 1959; Harvard Law School, J.D. 1963) *Came to firm,* February 5, 1990, *as counsel.*

Richard L. Aguglia. Born July 11, 1945. (University of Toronto, B.A. 1967; Catholic University, J.D. 1970) *Came to firm,* February 12, 1990, *as counsel.*

Jean Gordon Carter. Born July 30, 1955. (Wake Forest University, B.S. 1977; Duke University, J.D. 1983) *Came to firm,* May 16, 1990; *partner* April 1, 1991.

William D. Patterson. Born July 16, 1947. (Wake Forest University, B.A. 1969; University of North Carolina, J.D. 1973) *Came to firm,* May 17, 1990, *as a partner.*

Christopher J. Valianos. Born November 25, 1937. (Cornell University, B.S. 1959; George Washington University, J.D. 1967) *Came to firm,* June 1, 1990, *as special counsel.*

Mark B. Bierbower. Born May 26, 1951. (Northwestern University, B.A. 1976; Georgetown University Law Center, J.D. 1979) *Came to firm,* September 10, 1990, *as a partner.*

Charles A. Perry. Born November 22, 1948. (Hampden-Sydney College, B.A. 1971; Samford University, J.D. 1974) *Came to firm,* October 8, 1990, *as a partner.*

Robert W. Hawkins. Born September 24, 1949. (Amherst College, B.A. 1971; Cambridge University, LL.B. 1973; University of Virginia, J.D. 1976) *Came to firm,* October 9, 1990, *as a partner.*

Lejb Fogelman. Born June 21, 1949. (Warsaw University School of Law, 1967–69;

Moscow University, 1978; Columbia University, M.A., M. Phil. 1977; Harvard Law School, J.D. 1981) *Came to firm,* October 22, 1990, *as a partner.*

David H. Williams. Born September 21, 1945. (Denison University, B.A. 1967; Columbia University, M.A. 1969; Ohio State University Law School, J.D. 1973) *Came to firm,* January 24, 1991, *as a partner.*

David C. Wright. Born November 20, 1955. (University of Virginia, B.A. 1978, J.D. 1981) *Came to firm,* February 20, 1991, *as counsel.*

Thomas M. Melone. Born September 5, 1957. (Fairleigh Dickinson University, B.S. 1979; Rutgers Law School, J.D. 1983; New York University School of Law, LL.M., 1989) *Came to firm,* April 1, 1991, *as a partner.*

Alexander W. Suto. Born July 24, 1945. (University of Virginia, B.S. 1967; Emory University School of Law, J.D. 1971) *Came to firm,* September 16, 1991, *as a partner.*

James D. Levine. Born December 1, 1956. (University of North Carolina, B.A. 1979; Yale Law School, J.D. 1982) *Came to firm,* September 30, 1991, *as a partner.*

Bradley B. Brooks. Born July 4, 1945. (University of Virginia, B.A. 1967, J.D. 1970) *Came to firm,* October 9, 1991, *as counsel.*

Endnotes

1   Main Street, 1901

1 Richmond *News*, October 7, 1901. The use of the word "style" to denote the name of a firm, though it was more common in the nineteenth century, continued through the twentieth.

2 Ibid.

3 Unfortunately the way the convention's leaders chose to regularize elections was to limit drastically the number of eligible voters by imposing literacy tests and a poll tax. In effect, they disfranchised most of the black voters, who had usually supported the Republican party, as well as many poor whites, and turned Virginia into a one-party state for the next six decades.

4 Archibald G. Robertson, interview with author, October 7, 1983, Richmond, Virginia.

5 W. Asbury Christian. *Richmond, Her Past and Present* (Richmond: L. H. Jenkins, 1912), 479–80.

6 Robertson, interview, October 7, 1983.

7 Henry W. Anderson, entry in his handwriting for September 29, 1901: "Sunday—In Washington with Messrs Munford, Hunton and Williams," *Munford & Anderson Journal*, 167. Munford was convalescing in the North. The journal records visits by Henry Anderson with him in August and September at "Mizzen-Top" and in Lakewood, New Jersey. Washington may have been chosen as the place for the firm's first partners meeting because rail connections from Washington to Richmond were difficult at this time, and Munford's strength was limited.

8 The *News* article of October 7, 1901, reports that "Beverly [sic] B. Munford is not in Richmond at this time, and, on account of his health, he will not return to active practice before the early spring. He and Mrs. Munford will spend the winter in the West."

   As it turned out, Beverley Munford spent two winters in the West and did not return to Richmond until the spring of 1903, and to his law practice until October 1903, a year and a half later than the newspaper's prediction.

9 Richmond *News*, October 7, 1901. At that time Hunton was still a resident of Warrenton, Virginia, but he had been staying in Richmond since June 1901, serving as Fauquier County's representative to the Constitutional Convention of 1901–2.

10 Munford & Anderson Journal, entry for November 1, 1901, 174. The case involved oyster rights in King and Queen County.

11 Richard Cheek and John G. Zehmer, *Old Richmond Today* (Richmond: Historic Richmond Foundation, 1988), 127. By the end of the nineteenth century, tram rails, which consisted of wood with a thin strip of iron nailed to the top and were suitable for the slow-moving horse-drawn trolley car, had proved inadequate for electric streetcar traffic and had been replaced by solid-steel girder rails. Carlton Norris McKenney, *Rails in Richmond* (Glendale, Calif.: Interurban Press, 1986), 147–49.

12 The Main Street Station was opened to passengers on November 27, 1901. Workmen were struggling valiantly, and noisily, to finish it during the last weeks of October and the first weeks of November 1901, according to the newspapers.

13 Between Thirteenth and Ninth streets all the buildings on the north side of Main Street were destroyed by the Evacuation Fire, April 3, 1865, except the old Customs House, which was used during the war as the Confederate Treasury and afterwards as the Federal Court House and Post Office. In 1910 the buildings on either side of the old Customs House, including the Shafer building in which John L. Williams & Sons had its offices, were razed, and wings were added. Today the expanded building is still being used as a post office as well as for the federal courts.

2   Beverley Bland Munford (1856–1910)

1 Beverley B. Munford, *Random Recollections*, privately printed, 1905, 12. All of the quotations in this chapter are from this source unless otherwise noted.

2 Munford, *Random Recollections*, 17–21.

3 Munford, *Random Recollections*, 21–23.

4 Munford, *Random Recollections*, 25.

5 Munford, *Random Recollections*, 27.

6 Munford, *Random Recollections*, 27–28.

7 Munford, *Random Recollections*, 43.

8 Munford, *Random Recollections*, 42–44.

9 Munford, *Random Recollections*, 45.

10 Munford, *Random Recollections*, 42.

11 Munford, *Random Recollections*, 55–56.

12 Ibid.

13 Munford, *Random Recollections*, 58, 68–69. John D. Munford died of kidney failure at the age of sixty-six on October 8, 1876, and was buried on the Greenfield estate near Amsterdam, Botetourt County, Virginia, beside his third wife, Beverley Munford's mother, Margaret Copland Munford. His fourth wife, who survived him, was his first cousin's daughter, Elizabeth (Lizzie) Radford, the sister of Peter Copland's wife. A daughter, Minnie Radford Munford, was born from that marriage. Beverley B. Munford, Data on Family History, Munford Family Papers, Virginia Historical Society, 2.

14 Munford, *Random Recollections*, 69.

15 Munford, *Random Recollections*, 71.

16 Munford, *Random Recollections*, 73.

17 At that time in Virginia any two judges of the circuit courts could issue licenses to practice law with or without an informal examination. One of the reforms

the Virginia Bar Association (formed in 1888) pushed through the legislature was a bill that gave to the Supreme Court of Appeals the right to grant licenses "under such rules and regulations, and upon such examination, both as to learning and character, as may be prescribed by the said court." The first formal bar examination was given on January 8, 1897, but there were no educational requirements for admission to the bar until 1934. John O. Peters, "The Early Years," *The Virginia Bar Association Journal* 14 (Summer 1988) 11.

18 Munford, *Random Recollections*, 74.
19 Munford, *Random Recollections*, 75–76.
20 Munford, *Random Recollections*, 133–34.
21 Munford, *Random Recollections*, 126–27.
22 See Governor McKinney, "Special Message Transmitting Report of the Commission Appointed on the Public Debt," January 14, 1892, House Document, no. II; Munford, Speech presenting the Draft of House Bill no. 368, *Journal of the House of Delegates, 1891–92*, Virginia State Library; and Allen W. Moger, *Virginia: Bourbonism to Byrd, 1870–1925* (Charlottesville: University Press of Virginia, 1968) 18–20, 36–45. The three sources named above provide brief but lucid explanations of the history of the state debt problem and the attempts to solve it. In March 1871 an honorable but unrealistic Funding Bill was passed by an inexperienced legislature. The next legislature repealed the Funding Bill's provision for coupons that could be used instead of cash to pay state taxes, but the Virginia Supreme Court voided that repeal (despite a vigorous dissent from Waller Staples, Beverley Munford's future partner, who held that the Funding Act was unconstitutional because it diverted for other purposes funds specifically designated for education by the constitution, and that one legislature could not so bind succeeding legislatures and the public revenue). The McCulloch Act of 1879 provided some relief by reducing the interest rate, and the Readjuster's Riddleburger Act of 1882 provided more significant relief by reducing Virginia's accepted share of the principal, as well as the interest, and by eliminating tax-paying coupons. In the Olcutt Settlement of 1893 a final resolution and compromise was worked out with the bondholders, who were mainly Northerners and Englishmen. It wasn't until 1918, however, that the United States Supreme Court ruled that West Virginia was liable for one-third of the debt and the legislature of that state made arrangements to pay its share.
23 Beverley B. Munford, Manuscript of "Speech Delivered at Richmond, November 20, 1884," Munford Family Papers.
24 The Richmond *News*, December 15, 1885, called the speech "an oratorical triumph." U.S. senators were still chosen by the state legislature at that time.

Mahone had been elected to a six-year term in the Senate in 1879 by the first of the two Readjuster-controlled legislatures, and the Democrat-controlled legislature was now replacing him with Daniel. In the U.S. Senate, Mahone generally voted with the Republicans, receiving their support and patronage in return and finally in 1884 he formed an official coalition between the Virginia Republicans and Readjusters using the name of the "Republican Party of Virginia," Moger, 50, 57.

Direct election of senators was one of the reforms championed in the 1890s first by the Populists and then by the Progressives, though it was not until 1913 that the Seventeenth Amendment made it obligatory in all states. After the Virginia Constitution of 1902 restricted the electorate, a one-party system developed in all but the southwestern section of the state, and Democratic candidates were virtually guaranteed victory in statewide contests. Thus the Virginia Democratic party's decision in 1904 to adopt a statewide primary to choose their senatorial candidates was far more important, practically, than the direct general election required by the Seventeenth Amendment after 1913. Richard Hofstadter, *The Age of Reform* (New York: Vintage Books, 1955), 108, 257; and Moger, 183, 204–6, 214.

John Warwick Daniel, U.S. senator from 1887 until his death in 1910, had received a wound in the Battle of the Wilderness that crippled him and earned him the nickname, "the lame lion of Lynchburg." He was a leader of the free silver block in Virginia and delivered the keynote address at the Democratic National Convention in 1896. In the 1901–2 Virginia Constitutional Convention, he served as chairman of the committee on the elective franchise.

25 Munford first met Staples in the electoral college in 1884 when both were serving as electors on the Cleveland-Hendricks ticket. Judge Staples's twelve-year term on the Virginia Supreme Court had expired January 1, 1883, at which time he and the entire court were replaced by Readjuster-chosen judges who held office until 1895, when they were replaced by the Democrats' choices. The two men who drafted the Code of 1887 with Staples were another former justice, E. C. Burke, and a future one, John W. Riely, grandfather of the John W. Riely (1917–86) who became a leading partner in the law firm Munford was to found.

26 Munford, *Random Recollections*, 88. Moger, 83, 99, 100.

27 Munford, *Random Recollections*, 103–6.

28 Munford, *Random Recollections*, 123–24.

29 The measure proposed by the Readjusters that Munford considered most dangerous was a bill to create the office of General Commissioner of Sales for the counties and cities of the Commonwealth, investing the governor with authority to appoint one hundred commissioners, each with exclusive right to sell all real estate decreed to be sold by his court and to receive for his services 2 percent of all moneys coming into his hands. "The political influence of such an official, holding the bonds of innumerable land purchasers can be readily appreciated," Munford wrote in 1889. The bill passed the House but was amended in the Senate and finally defeated, as was a bill to rearrange the judicial circuits in a way that would legislate each incumbent out of his circuit and thus out of office before the expiration of his term. Beverley B. Munford, "Mahone as Master! The Record in Evidence," September 12, 1889. Virginia State Library.

30 Richmond *Dispatch*, August 17, 1893. See also Richmond *Times-Dispatch*, June 1, 1910, Henry W. Anderson, "Beverley Bland Munford," in *Virginia State Bar Association Reports* (1910), 94–99; and Moger, 40–42.

31 William C. Wooldridge, "The Sound and Fury of 1896: Virginia Democrats Face Free Silver," *Virginia Magazine of History and Biography* 75 (January 1967), 97–108.

32 The Huntons were closely tied to their rural constituency in Fauquier and Loudoun counties, where the demand for free silver was very strong. Munford, on the other hand, had left his rural practice in 1887 and was tied by professional interests and marriage to Richmond's financial leaders, staunch supporters of the gold standard.

33 Richmond *Times*, June 4, 5, and 6, 1896; Richmond *Dispatch*, June 6, 1896; and *The State*, June 5, 1896. After Munford's strong plea for the gold standard at

the Staunton convention, it is doubtful that he could have been elected to state-wide office. Even U.S. Senator Tom Martin, a fiscal conservative and former railroad lawyer, but the ultimate political realist and the emerging party boss, switched over to support free silver and Williams Jennings Bryan at the Staunton convention. Martin actually called Cleveland "a wrecker" of his party, while the silver men cheered, and the gold men hissed at him. Wooldridge, 97–108. Moger, 157–58. Richmond *Dispatch*, June 5, 1896, and Roanoke *Times*, June 5, 1896.

34 See Beverley B. Munford, "Vindication of the South," an address at the unveiling of a Confederate monument at Parksley on the Eastern Shore, reprinted in the Richmond *Times*, October 22, 1899; and his speech at the unveiling of the monument to Winnie Davis, Jefferson Davis, and Jefferson Davis, Jr. (an event attended by 15,000 to 20,000 people in Hollywood Cemetery), reprinted in the Richmond *Times*, November 10, 1899.

35 See Walter Russell Bowie, *Sunrise in the South* (Richmond: William Byrd Press, 1942); and Beverley B. Munford, "Our Times and the Men for Our Times," Address before the Alumni of the College of William and Mary, July 4, 1889 (Richmond: J. W. Fergusson & Son, 1889), Munford Family Papers.

36 Munford, *Random Recollections*, 230.

37 She was a granddaughter of Thomas Branch, a successful banker who established the brokerage firm Thomas Branch & Sons, and was president of the Merchants National Bank, predecessor of the First & Merchants Bank and today's multistate Sovran Bank. Her father, James Read Branch, had been killed in an accident July 2, 1869, while working for the Conservative party candidate for governor, Gilbert Walker.

38 Munford Family Papers and Munford, *Random Recollections*, 233.

39 Munford, *Random Recollections*, 233.

40 Moger, 155, refers to a law promoted by Mary Cooke Branch and enacted in 1890 to prohibit employment of children under fourteen, and of women for more than ten hours a day. See also Bowie, 28–29, and Anne Hobson Freeman, "Mary Munford's Fight for a College for Women Co-ordinate with the University of Virginia," *Virginia Magazine of History and Biography* 78 (October 1970) 481–91.

41 Undated note from Claude Swanson in Munford Family Papers.

42 Bowie, 85–87. Walter Russell Bowie was the son of Mrs. Munford's sister Elizabeth Bowie, who could not afford to support him after her husband's death. He was an excellent student and formed a deep attachment to the Munfords, who nourished his love of books and commitment to social reform. In 1904 he graduated from Harvard and became an Episcopal minister, serving as rector of St. Paul's Church in Richmond, from 1911 to 1923, and Grace Episcopal Church in New York City, from 1923 to 1939. He joined the faculty of Union Theological Seminary in New York City from 1939 to 1950, and later the faculty of the Virginia Seminary, in Alexandria. A profile of Dr. Bowie in the *New Yorker* magazine, in 1938, stated that while the liberal social views that had made him "the leader of the [Episcopal] Church's liberal wing" had been generally accepted by the congregation of St. Paul's in Richmond (because the people knew him and his aunt), those same views caused a fairly dramatic exodus of the conservative members from Grace Church in New York. Richard O. Boyer, *New Yorker*, October 22, 1938, and correspondence of Mary Cooke Branch

Munford and Walter Russell Bowie at the Virginia Seminary Library.

43 Mary Wingfield Scott, *Houses of Old Richmond* (New York: Bonanza Books, 1941), 189. Munford, *Random Recollections*, 221.

44 Mary Safford Munford (later Mrs. Hester Hoogewerf) was born on November 22, 1895, and Beverley Bland Munford, Jr., on February 26, 1899. Munford's four-year term as senator from the city of Richmond was from December 1897 to December 1901.

45 Bowie, 77.

46 Munford & Anderson Journal, and Thomas B. Gay, *The Hunton Williams Firm and Its Predecessors, 1877–1954* (Richmond: The Lewis Printing Co., 1971) 51–52.

47 Munford Family Papers.

48 Bowie, 84, and correspondence of Beverley B. Munford with his children, Munford Family Papers.

49 On November 1, 1902, the four partners signed a "memorandum of suggestions as to the business of the firm of Munford, Hunton, Williams & Anderson, looking to the prolonged absence of Mr. Munford." The terms of the agreement were that Munford's name would continue in the firm, that all old business would be handled to completion by the firm, and that he would receive one-fourth of those proceeds. The duties of various positions held by Munford would be discharged by the resident members of the firm, and he would receive one-fourth of those receipts. His interest in all other business of the firm, past and future, would cease. Upon his return, the business of the firm was to be treated as if a new firm were being formed. When Munford did return to part-time work October 1, 1903, a new agreement was made that he would receive 16 percent of the revenue while the other three would each get 28 percent.

50 Phrase used by Eppa Hunton, Jr., in the debates at the Constitutional Convention of 1901–2, discussing judges' compensation.

51 The conference was held in Richmond April 22–24, 1903. Afterwards, the group adjourned for further meetings at the University of Virginia and the Hampton Normal and Industrial Institute in Hampton, Virginia.

52 See Bowie, and Raymond H. Pulley, *Old Virginia Restored: An Interpretation of the Progressive Impulse, 1870–1930* (Charlottesville: University Press of Virginia, 1968), 133–51, for an assessment of the contributions of Beverley and Mary Cooke Branch Munford to the reform of the state's education system and the child labor laws. An excellent portrait of Ogden and description of the educational odyssey that brought Northern philanthropists and Southern leaders together once a year and fueled major reforms in education for blacks and whites throughout the South can be found in Bowie, 63–68, and Marjorie Fay Underhill, "The Virginia Phase of the Ogden Movement: A Campaign for Universal Education" (Master's thesis, University of Virginia, 1952).

53 Munford Family Papers. Robert Ogden wrote the eulogy of Beverley Munford that the Hampton board published after Munford's death in 1910.

54 In time to drape the house with flags and bunting for President Theodore Roosevelt's visit to Richmond in mid-October. Beverley B. Munford to Beverley B. Munford, Jr., October 17, 1905, Richmond, Virginia, Munford Family Papers.

55 Henry C. Ferrell, Jr., *Claude A. Swanson of Virginia, A Political Biography* (Lexington: University Press of Kentucky, 1985), 66–68. The election of 1905 was the

first in which the Virginia Democratic Party chose its candidates for the U.S. Senate by statewide primary.

56 To escape the coal dust in the air of downtown Richmond and the cold drafts in the Grace Street house, the Munfords rented a frame house on Hermitage Road in Henrico County on the north side of Richmond and stayed there until Munford's death in May 1910.

57 Beverley B. Munford, "Should Business Men, Members of the Democratic Party, Vote for the Republican Candidates in the Ensuing Elections?," a series of seven articles, Richmond *Times-Dispatch*, October 15, 16, 17, 19, 21, 23, and 26, 1908.

58 "C. F. Adams on Virginia" clipping with reprint of letter from Charles Francis Adams, Boston, November 26, 1909, to Beverley B. Munford in Munford Family Papers. See also the Hunton chapter for a similar view expressed by General Eppa Hunton, who attended the secession convention of 1861.

59 Beverley B. Munford to Honorable J. Taylor Ellyson, president of the Senate of Virginia, March 10, 1901, quoted in Gay, 24.

60 *Southern Workman* (published by the Hampton Normal and Agricultural Institute), June 1910.

61 "On Facing Death in Time of Peace," *The Survey*, June 18, 1910. *The Survey* was published by The Charity Organization Society of the City of New York from 1909 to 1937.

62 Beverley B. Munford, "Resolution Concerning the John Marshall House," Munford Family Papers.

63 Mary Cooke Branch Munford to Walter Russell Bowie, June 2, 1911, Bowie Papers, Virginia Seminary Library, Alexandria. "More light, more light," were reputed to have been the last words of the German author Goethe. Mary Munford and her nephew, both of whom read constantly and widely, often made literary references and recommended books to one another in their correspondence.

64 James Branch Cabell, the poet and novelist, was the son of Mary Munford's sister, Annie Branch Cabell. At Beverley Munford's funeral he gave his aunt, Mary Munford, the following sonnet:

> Most blithe and sage and gentle, and most brave!
> O true clear heart, so quick to wake and war
> Against despondency, lest questioning mar
> One hour of living, or foiled hopes enslave
> And sour another's living! not to the grave
> Did we relinquish you, whose mourners were
> As mariners that mark, with hushed demur,
> Night's lordliest star sink in the insatiate wave,
> And so elude us, only to arise
> Elsewhere with equal lustre,—even as thus
> Today unfearingly, in Paradise,
> And near the inmost court of Heaven's house,
> A gentleman to God lifts those brave eyes
> Which yesterday made life more brave for us.

A lifelong friend, H. W. Montague, wrote, "I shall always consider it one of the great pleasures of my life to have known Beverley Munford, to have watched the expanding and developing of that clear mind, that gracious and serene spirit. . . . [He was a man] in whose nature the elements of life were so harmonized, whose soul was so clear that one might almost see the very process by which our feelings and our thoughts are transfused and interchanged, and thereby catch a note of that mysterious and far away harmony which underlies the world of sense & fact." Munford Family Papers.

65 Walter Russell Bowie, Manuscript of Sermon at Grace Episcopal Church, New York City, Munford Family Papers.

3 *Eppa Hunton, Jr. (1855–1932)*

1 The Democratic organization chief, Senator Thomas S. Martin, was listed in the morning paper, the Richmond *Times-Dispatch* of June 1, 1910, as an honorary pallbearer. However, an article in the same day's Richmond *Evening Journal* said that Martin stopped in Richmond only briefly on June 1, on his way to the wedding of his wife's sister in Isle of Wight County, so he must not have been at the funeral. He is not listed among the honorary pallbearers in the *Evening Journal*.

2 Hollywood Cemetery, rising on Hollywood Hill above the James River in Richmond, is an outstanding example of a carefully designed and landscaped nineteenth-century cemetery. Two U.S. presidents, James Monroe and John Tyler, as well as the president of the Confederate states, Jefferson Davis, are buried there along with twenty-one Civil War generals (including J. E. B. Stuart, John Pegram, and Eppa Hunton) and 18,000 Confederate soldiers. Six of the eight name partners of Hunton, Williams—Beverley B. Munford, Eppa Hunton, Jr., E. Randolph Williams, Henry W. Anderson, Thomas B. Gay, and T. Justin Moore—are also buried there.

3 Eppa Hunton, Jr.'s first wife, Erva Winston Payne, whom he had married in 1884, had poor health almost all of her married life. She died in October 1897. His mother, Lucy Caroline Weir (Mrs. General Hunton), died in September 1899.

4 Eppa Hunton, *Autobiography of Eppa Hunton* (Richmond: William Byrd Press, 1933), 232 (hereafter referred to as simply Hunton, *Autobiography*).

5 Hunton, *Autobiography*, 233.

6 They were married on April 24, 1901. Virginia Payne was the younger sister of his first wife, Erva Winston Payne.

7 The Mechanics' Institute, on Ninth Street near Main, was used for the Secession Convention while the legislature was in extra session at the Capitol. Hunton, *Autobiography*, 13. Later the convention moved to the Capitol and was meeting there when it voted to secede on April 17, 1861. Charles B. Dew, *Ironmaker to the Confederacy: Joseph R. Anderson and the Tredegar Iron Works* (New Haven: Yale University Press, 1966), 84. Virginius Dabney, *Richmond: The Story of a City* (Garden City, N.Y.: Doubleday & Co., 1976), 161.

8 Hunton, *Autobiography*, 16–17.

9 "Mr. Allen Howison, a very estimable Whig gentleman of the county, [Prince William], was a candidate against me. I was for immediate secession. Mr. Howison was unconditionally for the Union." Hunton, *Autobiography*, 11. (Robert C. Howison, Jr., current counsel in Hunton & Williams's Raleigh office, said in a

conversation on September 16, 1986, that this Allen Howison is probably his relative, since his family used to live near Fredericksburg.)

10 Hunton, *Autobiography*, 11. Charles Francis Adams, the historian, expressed the same opinion in his letter to Beverley Munford quoted in the previous chapter.

11 Hunton, *Autobiography*, 22.

12 Hunton, *Autobiography*, 42.

13 Hunton, *Autobiography*, 63.

14 Hunton, *Autobiography*, 104.

15 Douglas Southall Freeman, editorial, Richmond *News Leader*, March 7, 1932. Dr. Freeman's spelling of "Chafin's" is probably a misprint, as the name is spelled Chaffin's in his *Lee's Lieutenants: A Study in Command* 3 vols. (New York: Charles Scribner's Sons, 1942–44), on the contemporary maps; and in General Hunton's *Autobiography*.

During the Battle of Gettysburg, in the famous charge of Pickett's Division, Colonel Hunton was wounded and consequently was absent for six weeks from his regiment, the Eighth Virginia. Soon after returning to it he received his commission as Brigadier-General, dating from Gettysburg.

> I was directed to take my brigade, which had been almost annihilated in the Gettysburg Campaign, down to Chaffin's Farm, about eight miles below Richmond, and rest and recuperate and reorganize it. General Henry A. Wise had occupied that position for a long time previous, and had built very comfortable log cabins for his brigade, so my weary, gallant men of the 8th, 18th, 19th, 28th and 56th, as well as the 32nd Regiments, went right into these cabins prepared by General Wise. (Hunton, *Autobiography*, 103.)

16 Hunton, *Autobiography*, 105.

17 Hunton, *Autobiography*, 106.

18 Hunton, *Autobiography*, 110.

19 General Hunton did not surrender his sword. When one of Custer's staff officers demanded it, "I threw it as far as I could into the sassafras bushes. It may be in that spot today," he wrote in his *Autobiography*. Many years later it turned up for sale in Nebraska.

In a footnote to this passage in the *Autobiography*, Eppa Hunton, Jr., explains that his father eventually returned General Custer's kindness. After the senior Hunton was elected to Congress in 1872, "some charges were brought against General Custer, the nature of which I do not recall; but I know my father thought they were inspired by the fact that Custer was a Democrat. [When those] charges were referred to the Military Committee . . . [on which General Hunton was serving, Custer] put his defense and all his papers in my father's keeping. I never saw him more deeply and earnestly interested than in Custer's defense." Hunton, *Autobiography*, 123–24.

20 Hunton, *Autobiography*, 130.

21 Ibid.

22 Eppa Hunton to Bettie Weir, May 27, 1865, Fort Warren, Boston Harbor, Hunton Family Papers.

23 Hunton, *Autobiography*, 139.

24 Hunton, *Autobiography*, 136.

25 Hunton, *Autobiography*, 144.

26 John Randolph Tucker (1823–97), former attorney general of Virginia, had

been born in Winchester. After the Civil War, he moved to Middleburg, where he went into private practice. In 1870 he became a professor in the law school of Washington College in Lexington, Virginia, which became Washington and Lee University the next year. He was elected to Congress in 1874. After his retirement, he practiced law in Washington, D.C., and then returned to the Washington and Lee Law School, where he became the dean. He was president of the Virginia Bar Association in 1891 and of the American Bar Association in 1893. His grandson John Randolph Tucker (1879–1954), was associated with Munford, Hunton, Williams, & Anderson from April 1, 1906, until September 1, 1909.

27 Hunton, *Autobiography*, 145.

28 Ibid.

29 According to Freeman, *News Leader*, March 7, 1932.

30 Hunton, *Autobiography*, 206.

31 The list is in Thomas B. Gay, *The Hunton Williams Firm and Its Predecessors, 1877–1954* (Richmond: The Lewis Printing Co., 1971), 2.

32 Hunton, *Autobiography*, 212.

33 Hunton, *Autobiography*, 205.

34 Hunton, *Autobiography*, 227.

35 Ibid.

36 Hunton, *Autobiography*, 228.

37 Hunton, *Autobiography*, 230.

38 Mrs. Jefferson Davis to Mr. and Mrs. William H. Payne, May 9, 1901, Hunton-Payne Papers, Virginia Historical Society.

39 Hunton, *Autobiography*, 231.

40 "In 1900, 147 votes were cast for each thousand of the population; four years later the number was 67, and in the next three presidential elections the number remained at either 67 or 68." Allen W. Moger, *Virginia: Bourbonism to Byrd, 1870–1925* (Charlottesville: University Press of Virginia, 1968), 192.

41 *Taylor v. Commonwealth*, 101 Va. 829 (1903).

42 *Spirit of the Valley*, Harrisonburg, Va., April 12, 1901, quoted in Gay, 4.

43 Hunton, *Autobiography*, 9.

44 See *Munford & Anderson Journal*, September 1901; Richmond *Times*, October 8, 1901; Richmond *News*, October 7, 1901. Also the Warrenton *Virginian* and the Richmond *Dispatch*.

45 Hunton, *Autobiography*, 232.

46 Hunton, *Autobiography*, 233.

47 "Mr. Hunton was appointed counsel for the receivers and served in that capacity throughout proceedings in the consolidated cause." By an order of the U.S. Circuit Court on March 7, 1905, a number of proceedings against Virginia Passenger and Power Company, and Richmond Passenger and Power Company were consolidated under the name *Bowling Green Trust Company, Trustee v. Virginia Passenger and Power Company and others, Consolidated Cause*. Gay, 108–9.

48 The Virginia Electrical Railway & Development Company, the Richmond Traction Company, and the Westhampton Park Railway, which had been strong and aggressive competitors of Fisher's Richmond Passenger and Power Company, were now controlled by the Virginia Railway and Power Company. Gay, 98–100. At different times between 1899 and 1901, George E. Fisher of New York controlled the Richmond Railway Company, the Richmond and Petersburg Railway Company, the Southside Railway and Development Company,

the Virginia Internal Improvement Company (Petersburg utility supplier), and eventually the Virginia Passenger and Power Company. Fisher was very unpopular in Richmond, so he used agents and kept a relatively low profile. Carlton Norris McKenney, *Rails in Richmond* (Glendale, Calif.: Interurban Press, 1986), 62, 63, 81, 179, 180.

49 First & Merchants National Bank merged with Virginia National Bank on December 12, 1983, forming the Sovran Financial Corporation.

50 Richmond *Times-Dispatch*, January 7, 1915.

51 This is George Gibson's view, expressed in an interview with author, May 10, 1984, Richmond, Virginia. Langbourne Williams, interview with author, November 11–12, 1986, Richmond, Virginia, suggested that the $25,000 salary paid to the president of the RF & P may have been an inducement. It represented a 25 percent increase for Eppa Hunton, Jr., who had received $19,545.51 as his share of the firm's profits for the year 1919 in which E. Randolph Williams received $21,032.17; Henry W. Anderson (who was in the Balkans most of the year), $4,821.92; and Thomas B. Gay, $12,296.71. Munford, Hunton, Williams & Anderson Journal *#3*, 200.

52 Battle Abbey is the informal name for the Confederate Memorial Institute, which was constructed in three stages between 1912 and 1959. Since 1946 it has also been the home of the Virginia Historical Society, which merged with the Confederate Memorial Association that year. In addition to an extensive research library of materials related to Virginia, the building contains galleries with Confederate murals and weaponry, as well as special exhibits.

53 Correspondence concerning Colonel Mosby, Hunton-Payne Papers.

54 During the negotiations, Payne moved to Washington to become Secretary of the Interior in Woodrow Wilson's cabinet.

55 Moger, 245. See also Munford chapter.

56 Until Alderman accepted the position of president in 1904, the University of Virginia was governed under the chairman of the faculty system. The faculty opposed changing to the new system, although every other leading institution of higher learning in the country had by then adopted it. By the 1890s there was much debate on the issue, and in the end, the Board of Visitors, the alumni, and the school newspaper, *College Topics*, supported the change. Woodrow Wilson, then a professor at Princeton, was the first to be offered the presidency, but he declined it. Virginius Dabney, *Mr. Jefferson's University: A History* (Charlottesville: University Press of Virginia, 1981), 42.

57 Richmond *Virginian*, February 4, 1914.

58 Mary Washington College in Fredericksburg was affiliated with the University of Virginia as a coordinate college in 1944. Because the campus was sixty miles away from the professors, classrooms, and libraries of the University of Virginia, it was regarded by Mary Munford's followers as a compromise that would not have satisfied her.

59 Janet Weaver Randolph, who died in 1922, was the founding president of the Richmond chapter of the United Daughters of the Confederacy in 1897. She was later honorary president of the national organization.

60 Walter Russell Bowie, *Sunrise in the South* (Richmond: William Byrd Press, 1942), 107.

61 Resolutions of the Medical College of Virginia on the Death of Eppa Hunton, March 14, 1932, and Gay, 8–9.

62 Hunton-Payne Papers, Virginia Historical Society.

63 Broad Street Station, as Union Station of Richmond was informally called, was completed in 1919. It is the only major commercial structure designed by John Russell Pope, who was the architect for the National Gallery and the Jefferson Memorial in Washington, D.C., and the John Kerr Branch House in Richmond. The last train departed from the station on November 15, 1975, and the structure was sold to the Commonwealth of Virginia the following year. It was immediately given to the Science Museum of Virginia, which opened its doors in January 1977.

64 Gibson, interview, May 10, 1984. On July 31, 1901, the RF & P and the Washington Southern Railways were taken over by the Richmond-Washington Company owned equally by the Pennsylvania Railroad Company, Atlantic Coast Line Railroad Company, The Southern Railway Company, the Chesapeake & Ohio Railway Company, Seaboard Air Line Railway Company, and the Baltimore & Ohio Railroad Company. William E. Griffin, Jr., *One Hundred Fifty Years of History: Along the Richmond, Fredericksburg and Potomac Railroad* (Richmond: Whittet and Shepperson, 1984), 27–28.

65 L. M. Williams, interviews, November 11–12, 1986; and Gay, 9. Hunton regretted his decision to leave the law firm when he had the painful duty in the early 1930s of laying off RF&P employees and cutting back the salaries of those who stayed on, according to Lawrence Blanchard who was told so by Thomas B. Gay. Lawrence E. Blanchard, Jr., interview with author, July 28, 1987, Richmond, Virginia.

66 Freeman, *News Leader*, March 7, 1932. This anecdote appears in Dr. Freeman's editorial of March 7, 1932. Since it dramatizes a rather endearing provincial pride in Eppa Hunton, Jr., which the cosmopolitan Colonel Anderson is said to have viewed less charitably as "a narrow, Warrenton mind," it is included here, although the copy of the editorial in the Hunton Scrapbooks has a note on it signed by "V. P. H." (Virginia Payne Hunton), his wife: "We have often wonder[ed about] the origin of this incident which *never occurred*."

4 Edmund Randolph Williams (1871–1952)

1 Edmund Randolph was appointed attorney general in 1789 and secretary of state in 1794. He was governor of Virginia at the time of the Philadelphia Convention of 1787, to which he was also a delegate. Maria Williams's mother, Charlotte Randolph Skelton, was the daughter of Peyton Randolph the younger (1780–1828), the son of Edmund Randolph.

2 Lyon G. Tyler, ed., *Men of Mark in Virginia: Ideals of American Life: A Collection of Biographies of Leading Men in the State* (Washington, D.C.: Men of Mark Publishing Co., 1906), 409.

3 Maria Ward Skelton Williams to Edmund Randolph Williams, February 9, 1890, Richmond. Williams Family Papers, Virginia Historical Society.

4 John Skelton Williams (1865–1926) is discussed at length in this chapter. Robert Lancaster Williams (1869–1935) was a member of John L. Williams & Sons until 1911, when he went to Baltimore and became a partner in the investment firm of Middendorf, Williams & Company. Langbourne Meade Williams (1872–1931) joined John L. Williams & Sons in 1892 and remained with the firm until his death. Berkeley Williams (1878–1954) worked as an investment broker from 1906–13, a partner in John L. Williams & Sons from 1918 to

1928, and was postmaster of Richmond from 1931–33, appointed by Hoover.

5 The Seaboard Air Line Railway first went into receivership in 1908. J. P. Morgan controlled its rival, the Southern Railway. The Williams family legends were supplied by Langbourne Williams, Jr., interviews with author, November 11 and 12, 1986, Rapidan, Virginia, and by Dr. Lockhart McGuire and Dr. Hunter H. McGuire, Jr., in conversation.

6 John L. Williams to E. R. Williams, August 18, 1888, Richmond, Virginia, Williams Family Papers.

7 J. L. Williams to E. R. Williams, April 3, 1889, Richmond, Virginia, Williams Family Papers.

8 Tyler, 409. J. L. Williams to E. R. Williams, December 16, 1892, Richmond, Virginia, Williams Family Papers.

9 J. L. Williams to E. R. Williams, February 16, 1893, Richmond, Virginia, Williams Family Papers.

10 M. W. S. Williams to E. R. Williams, undated, Williams Family Papers. Dr. Richard Heath Dabney was the father of Virginius Dabney, Virginia historian and editor of the Richmond *Times-Dispatch*.

11 M. W. S. Williams to E. R. Williams, September 16, 1893, Richmond, Virginia. Williams Family Papers.

12 E. R. Williams to J. L. Williams, January 20, 1895?, Northport, Long Island, Williams Family Papers.

13 The first edition appears to have been issued in January 1885, before John Skelton Williams turned twenty, as the introduction to the 1890 edition describes it as the sixth annual edition, and it is dated January 1890.

14 Richmond *News Leader*, November 5, 1926.

15 Representatives of the Baltimore banks protested formally against the location of the Fifth District Bank in Richmond, and the Federal Reserve Board gave them a hearing on January 6, 1915. At that hearing, the attorneys for Baltimore interests opened their argument by asking that the secretary of the treasury, William Gibbs McAdoo, and the comptroller of the currency, John Skelton Williams, be excluded from the hearing since they were members of the organization committee that had chosen Richmond over Baltimore, but no action was taken on their request. Legh R. Page and Eppa Hunton, Jr., successfully defended the choice of Richmond by arguing that the majority of the banks in the Fifth District favored Richmond as the location, that Richmond was in closer touch with the cotton, tobacco, and peanut industries and had a better freight rate from the South, and that there were already two Federal Reserve banks (in Philadelphia and New York) relatively close to Baltimore. Richmond *Times Dispatch*, January 7, 1915.

16 J. L. Williams to E. R. Williams, April 30, 1894, Richmond, Virginia, Williams Family Papers.

17 J. L. Williams to E. R. Williams, April 19, 1894, Richmond, Virginia, Williams Family Papers.

18 "Thank you for your hasty congratulations, although for so small accomplishments. I have much better work in the preceding volume which I am not credited with, but which indeed is credited to someone else. The words and phrases and definitions in the volume which you saw were all done by Mr. Boggs and myself, every word of them and we should have been credited there, but it looks very much as if Mr. Ed in chief would like them to appear as his work. One half of the article "Dover" is my own. . . . I have also two sections in the

article *Taxation* which are carefully done by myself but credited to someone else. . ." E. R. Williams to M. W. S. Williams, December 1894, Northport, Long Island, Williams Family Papers.

19 E. R. Williams to J. L. Williams, April 8, 1894, Northport, Long Island, Williams Family Papers.

20 M. W. S. Williams to E. R. Williams, March 23, 1894, Richmond, Virginia, Williams Family Papers.

21 Sometime before 1901, E. L. Bemiss, a utility lawyer from New Orleans who had married Randolph Williams's sister, Cyane, took over as president of the Richmond Traction Company, and Randolph then became vice-president.

22 Carlton Norris McKenney, *Rails in Richmond* (Glendale, Calif.: Interurban Press, 1986), 140, 143.

23 The parent company of what was called Virginia Electric and Power Company (Vepco) from 1925 to 1985, which was owned and operated until the late 1930s by the holding company, Engineers Public Service. In 1983 Dominion Resources, Inc., was organized as the new holding company of Vepco, and two years later changed the name of Virginia Electric and Power Company (Vepco) to three names—Virginia Power, North Carolina Power, and West Virginia Power—to reflect the fact there were really three companies, operating in three states. On March 1, 1987, Dominion Resources sold West Virginia Power.

24 "In the Social World," Richmond *Evening Leader*, November 22, 1900.

25 Richmond *News*, November 22, 1900, and Richmond *Evening Leader*, December 5, 1900.

26 The baby died at nine months of "infant cholera," which took the lives of many babies the summer after they were weaned, Margaret Williams McElroy explained in a conversation December 23, 1988. The Williamses were to have three other children: John Langbourne Williams (1903–18); Margaret Pickett Williams (Mrs. John L. McElroy) b. 1905 and Maude Stokes Williams (Mrs. Thomas Urmston) b. 1907.

27 E. R. Williams to M. W. S. Williams, August 5, 1902, New York City, Williams Family Papers.

28 Frank and Helen Gould were the children and heirs of the nineteenth-century financier Jay Gould. Although they continued to live in New York, they sent down a cousin, William Northrop, to be the manager, and then receiver, of Virginia Passenger and Power Company. In 1909 Northrop became the president of the newly organized Virginia Railway and Power Company. See McKenney.

29 Lewis C. Williams founded Williams & Mullen (now Williams, Mullen, Christian & Dobbins) in 1909; John Randolph Tucker founded Tucker, Bronson, Satterfield & Mays (now Mays & Valentine) in 1923; and Andrew Christian founded Christian, Barton & Parker (now Christian, Barton, Epps, Brent & Chappell) in 1926.

30 For a short while before and during World War I, the four partners lived within a block of one another on West Franklin Street: the Huntons at 810; the Williamses up the street at 826 on the northeast corner of Shafer and Franklin; Henry Anderson to the west, next to the Frederic W. Scotts, at 913; and the Gays, more modestly, at the Chesterfield Apartments at 900, on the northwest corner of Shafer and Franklin.

31 In the years to come, Williams's gift as a peacemaker did not diminish. Nor did the need for it. In the 1930s and 1940s he frequently served as the intermedi-

ary between the two name partners of the next generation, T. Justin Moore and Thomas B. Gay. As one of their junior partners put it, "Both Moore and Gay were very, very strong personalities with strongly held views, and if and when they differed—that was not infrequently—Randolph Williams was the peacemaker. And he did that very well, always with . . . a light touch and a twinkle and usually came up with some sort of compromise solution." Justice Lewis F. Powell, Jr., interview with author, August 25, 1986, Richmond, Virginia.

32 Henry W. Anderson was appointed chairman of a Red Cross commission to Rumania with the assimilated rank of lieutenant colonel and served from July 1917 until March 1918. He was then commissioner of the Red Cross for all the Balkan States from October 1918 until October 1919 and returned to the practice of law in late 1919.

33 On the theory that the government could operate them more efficiently, Woodrow Wilson "proclaimed federal control over the nation's railroads" in December 1917. The United States Railroad Administration (USRA) was then formed under William Gibbs McAdoo who "became the virtual czar of the transportation system in the nation." Federal control was ended on February 29, 1920. Burke Davis, *The Southern Railway: Road of the Innovators* (Chapel Hill: University of North Carolina Press, 1985), 59–60.

Andrew Christian was replaced a few weeks after his departure by Wirt Marks, Henry Anderson's cousin, in June of 1917.

34 Powell, interview, August 25, 1986.

35 Ibid.

36 George D. Gibson, interview with author, July 24, 1986, Richmond, Virginia.

37 John W. Riely, interview with author, April 30, 1986, Richmond, Virginia.

38 J. Harvie Wilkinson, Jr., interview with author, November 14, 1985, Richmond, Virginia. The name of the United Virginia Bank was changed to the Crestar Bank in 1987.

39 The Williams house was designed by William Bottomley in 1927. The design for the north entrance door was taken from the south entrance door at Westover plantation, and there are some other exterior similarities to that house. The house at 6705 River Road, the first house Bottomley designed in Richmond, has two associations with the law firm. It was built for Colonel Jennings Wise, who worked at the firm for Henry Anderson in 1928 and 1929. Later the house was sold to Eppa Hunton IV, who often entertained members of the law firm there. William B. O'Neal and Christopher Weeks, *The Work of William Lawrence Bottomley in Richmond* (Charlottesville: University Press of Virginia) 1985, 134–45, 183. Conversation with Ellen Wise Oppenhimer Fleming, October 23, 1988.

40 Archibald Robertson left his job as assistant city attorney of Richmond in 1923 to enter private practice working for T. Justin Moore on Virginia Railway and Power Company damage suits. After the company changed ownership in 1925, he continued to specialize in Virginia Electric and Power Company litigation and worked closely with Randolph Williams both before and after he and Moore came to the law firm in 1932.

41 Archibald G. Robertson, interview with author, October 7, 1983, Richmond, Virginia.

42 Harold L. Ickes (1874–1952) was a leader in the Progressive Republican party until 1932, when he left the Republican party to support Franklin D. Roosevelt

and John N. Garner. As U.S. Secretary of the Interior from 1933 until 1946, he was an aggressive administrator of the New Deal and controlled the production and distribution of petroleum products during World War II.

43 The American Liberty League was a national organization formed in 1934 to unseat President Roosevelt and end the New Deal. The "Jeffersonian Democrats" was a group of Virginia Democrats who were opposed to Roosevelt's reelection.

44 Memo from George Gibson, July 31, 1986, on a conversation with Margaret Williams McElroy; and Gibson, interview, July 24, 1986.

45 Powell, interview, August 25, 1986.

5   Henry W. Anderson (1870–1954)

1 Emily Clark, *Stuffed Peacocks* (New York: Borzoi, 1927), 69. Emily Clark was the founder and editor of a small magazine, *The Reviewer* (1921–25), which fostered a short-lived literary renaissance in Richmond. Among the authors who supported it were James Branch Cabell, Ellen Glasgow, and H. L. Mencken. Since Henry Anderson had collaborated with Ellen Glasgow on the early chapters of her political novel, *The Builders*, and was often seen with her, Emily Clark considered him fair game for her satire. In 1924 she married a rich Philadelphian named Edwin Swift Balch and became a patron of literary causes.

2 In this love triangle, central to the lives of both Henry Anderson and Ellen Glasgow, but of relatively minor importance in that of Marie, all three participants were in their forties. Marie was born on October 29, 1875; Ellen Glasgow, on April 22, 1873; and Henry Anderson, on December 20, 1870.

3 Ellen Glasgow, *The Woman Within* (New York: Harcourt, Brace, 1954), 220. He was also mentioned as a possible nominee during Harding's and Hoover's administrations.

4 One of the earliest memories that Randolph Williams's daughter, Margaret McElroy, has of Henry Anderson is of him in her living room, where the rugs had been rolled back, dancing with Lady Hadfield to the tune of "Too Much Mustard" on the Victrola. Margaret Williams McElroy, interview with author, November 7, 1984, Richmond, Virginia. In an interview with author, June 13, 1985, Manakin-Sabot, Virginia, Henry Anderson's niece, Frances Hadfield Richardson, said that she was named for Frances Wickersham Hadfield, at her uncle's suggestion.

5 Glasgow, *Woman Within*, 221, 225.

6 According to the Richmond *City Directories*, 1899, 1900, 1901, and 1902, Henry Anderson lived at 203 West Grace Street with Mrs. N. D. Werth and H. H. Werth in 1899; at 311 West Grace Street with Dr. W. R. Jones in 1900 and 1901; and at 507 West Franklin with Jackson Guy, a lawyer, in 1902.

7 Glasgow, *Woman Within*, 219.

8 Glasgow, *Woman Within*, 219–221.

9 The four justices were Hugo Black, Felix Frankfurter, John Harlan, and Stanley Reed. See note below in the chapter on George Gibson.

10 George D. Gibson, interview with author, May 10, 1984, Richmond, Virginia.

11 Lewis F. Powell, Jr., interview with author, July 27, 1984, Richmond, Virginia.

12 Since Archibald Robertson was born October 6, 1889, he was just two weeks away from his ninety-sixth birthday when he died on September 23, 1985.

13 Archibald G. Robertson, interview with author, October 7, 1983, Richmond, Virginia.

14 Henry W. Anderson, "Freedom in Virginia." Speech as nominee for governor of Virginia before the Republican State Convention at Norfolk, July 14, 1921, 19.

15 Frances Richardson Shield, interview with author, June 13, 1985.

16 In 1886 the Richmond & Danville Railroad was brought under control of Richmond & West Point Terminal Railway & Warehouse Company, which had launched a movement of consolidation to eliminate competition and reorganize failing lines. In 1894 it came out of bankruptcy as part of the Southern Railway, J. P. Morgan's railroad, which soon became the largest system in the South. Burke Davis, *The Southern Railway: Road of the Innovators* (Chapel Hill: University of North Carolina Press, 1985), 25–31.

17 Richmond *Times*, August 21, 1897.

18 Thomas B. Gay, *The Hunton Williams Firm and Its Predecessors, 1874–1954* (Richmond: The Lewis Printing Co., 1971), 36.

19 Lewis Williams was a partner of A. Caperton Braxton from 1907 to 1909, then formed the parent firm of Williams, Mullen, Christian & Dobbins of Richmond in 1909. Though he was not related to Randolph Williams's family, he was closely connected to it after his marriage to Randolph's youngest sister, Maria. Henry Anderson had also courted Maria Williams.

20 Carlton Norris McKenney, *Rails in Richmond* (Glendale, Calif.: Interurban Press, 1986), 93.

21 By 1904 Henry Anderson was living at the Chesterfield Apartments, where William Northrop also lived. From 1906 through 1908 he and Northrop shared a house, first at 218 Shafer Street, then at 503 East Grace Street—the Beverley Munford house, which the two bachelors must have moved into after the Munfords moved out to Hermitage Road. Richmond *City Directories*, 1904, 1906, 1907, 1908.

22 Obituary of William Northrop, Richmond *Times-Dispatch*, June 12, 1912.

23 The Richmond *Times-Dispatch*, June 12, 1912. William Northrop's sudden death in 1912, as a result of his Pierce Arrow running over him as he was cranking it, ended his very successful ten-year career representing the Gould interests in Virginia. At the time of his death, the Virginia Railway and Power Company's stock had been put on a dividend-paying basis, and Northrop had secured the consent of the board of directors to expend more than $1 million in improvements in Richmond. Those improvements included erection of an annex to the main power plant at Twelfth Street and the twelve-story office building at Seventh and Franklin streets.

24 McKenney, 31; Richmond *Times-Dispatch*, June 12, 1912; Gay, 97–114; and Journal 2, (1904–15).

25 Journal 2. Frank Gould (1877–1954) is listed as chairman of the board of both the Virginia Railway and Power Company and of the International & Great Northern Railway Company in *Who's Who*, 1916–17. He was also listed as a member of the Westmoreland and Country Clubs in Richmond, Virginia, although he had been living a profligate life in Europe since 1909. At the age of forty, Frank Gould, after a bout with alcoholism, suddenly stopped drinking and launched a spectacular comeback as an investor in real estate, casinos, and hotels in the south of France. When he died in Juan-les-Pins, France, in 1954, "his estate quite possibly rivalled that of his father," according to Edwin P.

Hoyt, *The Goulds: A Social History* (New York: Weybright and Talley, 1969), 170, 311–15. The firm's association with the Goulds seems to have ended with their sale of their Virginia utilities in 1925 to Stone & Webster.

The International & Great Northern Railway was the firm's first major client in the Northwest. By 1912 its route had been extended from St. Paul, Minnesota, through North Dakota and northern Montana to Seattle, Washington, with shorter lines crossing the Canadian border to Winnipeg, Manitoba, and Vancouver, British Columbia.

26 Anderson, at this point, had not yet turned officially Republican, but he would certainly have qualified for the sobriquet "wobbly Democrat," used by the newspapers of the day. In the Richmond *Times-Dispatch* of October 26, 1908, a reader in Crewe, Virginia, offered the following answer to the question "What is a Taft Democrat?":

> When a tadpole is turning to a frog there is a space of time when he is neither tadpole nor frog but is undergoing the change. He is not a tadpole, because he is sloughing the tail, and he is not a frog, because he cannot sit down in comfort [in the] holler as a full-fledged frog usually does, he is rather tender at certain points. So I would say that a Taft Democrat would be best described as a tadpole turning to a frog. Give him a little time and you will know where to place him. Wait until after the election.

27 Richmond *Times-Dispatch*, October 18, 1908.

28 Anderson's friendship with President Taft strengthened his ties with the national Republican party. Correspondence between the two from 1909 to 1910 at the Virginia Historical Society shows that Taft sought his advice in appointing federal judges.

In the 1912 election, which sent Woodrow Wilson to the White House, Anderson actively supported the Republican ticket, as well as Taft himself. Four years later, he was the Virginia member of the national committee of the Hughes Alliance, supporting Charles E. Hughes, the Republican presidential candidate who ran unsuccessfully against the incumbent President Wilson. See the undated brochure prepared by the Republican State Executive Committee of Virginia, supporting Anderson for the vice-presidential nomination in 1928, entitled "Henry W. Anderson of Virginia for Vice-President: Foremost Anti-Sectionalist and Advocate of a More Perfect Union," Virginia Historical Society Collection.

29 Henry W. Anderson to Ellen Glasgow, August 31, 1916, Richmond, Virginia. Ellen Glasgow Letters, Alderman Library, University of Virginia.

30 During World War I, President Wilson put Red Cross activities under the direction of the War Council. All of the members of its mission to Rumania, excluding the nursing staff, received military rank. In his letter of July 27, 1916, to Anderson, the chairman of the War Council, H. P. Davison, stressed that "in an undertaking of this kind it is necessary to be not only militarized by commission but to have had an understanding that you, as Chairman of the Commission, are to be recognized as in full authority." Henry W. Anderson, "Organization and Work of the Commission," typescript, Anderson Papers, Virginia Historical Society, 57–60.

31 Anderson to Glasgow, July 18, 1917, Richmond, Virginia, Alderman Library. Henry Anderson and Queen Marie both preferred the English spelling "Roumania," while Ellen Glasgow used "Rumania."

32 Note preserved in Glasgow Papers at the Alderman Library, University of Virginia, quoted by E. Stanly Godbold, Jr., *Ellen Glasgow and the Woman Within* (Baton Rouge: Louisiana State University Press, 1972), 119. Glasgow, *Woman Within*, 231–32.

33 Glasgow, *Woman Within*, 229.

34 Glasgow, *Woman Within*, 233. "Yes, [Anderson] too came to say goodbye. He even came twice, unable to tear himself away from the Queen he had sworn to help. He was a gallant man with a certain old-time courtesy about him . . . the real Virginia, with all Virginia's high traditions and aristocratic point of view. Yes, he too came to say goodbye and I saw how his heart was wrung and how his soul revolted against this going away which was like an abandonment." Marie, Queen of Roumania, *Ordeal: The Story of My Life* (New York: Charles Scribner's Sons, 1935), 320.

35 Glasgow, *Woman Within*, 234–35. Ileana, born in 1909, was nine years old at the time.

36 Glasgow, *Woman Within*, 236–37.

37 Ellen Glasgow, *Barren Ground* (Garden City, N.Y.: Doubleday, Page & Co., 1925), 509, 511.

38 H. I. Borock, "Southern Romance is Dead," review of *Barren Ground*, by Ellen Glasgow, in *New York Times*, Book Review Section (April 12, 1925), 2. Hannah Pakula, *The Last Romantic: A Biography of Queen Marie of Roumania* (New York: Simon & Schuster, 1984), 111. Another American lawyer, William Nelson Cromwell, founder of Sullivan & Cromwell in New York, was so charmed by the queen in Paris that he founded the Society of the Friends of Rumania. Later, when she came to the United States to launch a successful debt issue in October 1926, he sponsored a dinner for one thousand at the Waldorf and accompanied the queen on a cross-country tour in a seven-car private train donated by the railroads. Nancy Lisagor and Frank Lipsius, *A Law unto Itself, The Untold Story of the Law Firm Sullivan & Cromwell* (New York: William Morrow & Co., 1988), 94.

39 Anderson to Glasgow, Sunday Night, n.d., in Glasgow Papers, quoted in Godbold.

40 Henry W. Anderson to E. R. Williams, Easter Sunday, April 20, 1919, Salonika, Greece, Anderson Papers.

41 Ellen Glasgow refers to it in *The Woman Within*, 228, and it is reprinted in Godbold, 111–12.

42 Undated letter written in pencil, quoted by Godbold, 125.

43 Anderson to Glasgow, quoted by Godbold, 125–26.

44 Godbold, 118.

45 Glasgow, *Woman Within*, 229.

46 Godbold, 126.

47 Undated letter, quoted by Godbold, 127.

48 In the interview on June 13, 1985, Mrs. Shield said she felt she had no choice but to burn the letters, because her uncle's instructions were so clear. But she did read them first and found them very touching. Ellen Glasgow had exposed her feelings so completely that Mrs. Shield understood why her uncle did not want the letters read by the public.

Another explanation for his instructions may be that in that generation an attempted suicide and a nervous breakdown were not subjects one could talk about. Anderson was probably trying to keep this part of Ellen Glasgow's life from the public's knowledge. When Marjorie Kinnan Rawlings was doing research in 1953 for a proposed biography of Ellen Glasgow, she pressed Anderson for confirmation of the rumor that they had been secretly engaged. He responded with great emotion and seemed to have difficulty breathing as he said, "I can't possibly answer you. It would violate the ethical principles of a lifetime." Then when she asked again for "a direct statement as to whether or not you were ever engaged," he answered, "If I told you that, I'd have to tell you why it was broken off." David Ribblett, "From Cross Creek to Richmond, Marjorie Kinnan Rawlings Researches Ellen Glasgow," *Virginia Cavalcade* 36 (Summer 1986), 12.

49 Even then, officers at the First & Merchants Bank, which was handling Ellen Glasgow's estate, were worried that there might be grounds for libel in the book. Randolph Williams, who was on the board of First & Merchants, asked Lewis Powell to review the manuscript with that in mind. Though Powell says he found himself "nodding" over some of the longer passages, he saw no grounds for libel. Conversation with Lewis F. Powell, Jr., August 20, 1986.

50 Anderson to Glasgow, undated note quoted in Godbold, 126.

51 Ellen Glasgow's friends, still bitter over Anderson's treatment of her, did not invite him to her private funeral, but he came to her house anyway. Maude Stokes Williams recalled that he "stood in the doorway, tall and proud, half defiant and half crushed." Ribblett, 15.

52 In recognition of his services, Henry Anderson received the following decorations: Grand Officer of the Star of Rumania, Commander of the Order of the Crown and Order of Regina Maria, both classes, from Rumania; Grand Cross of Grand Commander, Order of St. Sava, First and Second classes, and Serbian Red Cross, both from Serbia; Commander of the Royal Order of the Saviour, from Greece; Commander of the Order of Prince Danilo I, from Montenegro; Commander of the Order of St. Anne, with swords, from Russia; the War Cross from Czechoslovakia; and the War Medals of Italy and France.

53 Anderson to E. R. Williams, April 20, 1919.

54 In one political speech Anderson said that the road from Richmond to Washington was so crooked, he could "see the taillight on his own car." Shield, interview, June 13, 1985.

55 Anderson received twenty-eight votes for vice-president. He had had assurances of a much larger vote had his candidate, Lowden, been nominated, but the agreement to put Warren G. Harding forward as the compromise candidate on the tenth ballot was coupled with the agreement to make Calvin Coolidge the candidate for vice-president. What was most "gratifying" to Anderson was the fact that much of the national party's platform was "taken bodily from the platform adopted at Roanoke" by the Virginia Republicans. Richmond *Times-Dispatch*, June 13, 1920, and Richmond *News Leader*, June 14, 1920.

56 Anderson, "Freedom in Virginia," 18.

57 Ibid.

58 L. Stanley Willis, "E. Lee Trinkle: Prelude to Byrd," in *The Governors of Virginia 1860–1978*, ed. Edward Younger and James Tice Moore (Charlottesville: University Press of Virginia, 1982), 227. Anderson, "Freedom in Virginia," 18. There is no indication in the journal that Henry Anderson withdrew from the firm in the fall of 1921 while he conducted his campaign for governor. The only time he appears to have received markedly reduced compensation is dur-

ing the year 1919 when he had returned to the Balkans. Munford, Hunton, Williams & Anderson Journal 3 (1916–25).

59 Godbold, 131.

60 Sixty-seven years would pass before another partner from the firm ran in a statewide campaign for public office. At that time, Charles S. Robb, the Democratic candidate for the U.S. Senate, won the election with 71 percent of the vote.

61 During his service to the three Republican administrations, Anderson was actually living in Washington for months at a time. And George Gibson recalled that in the thirties and forties, Anderson carried three calling cards, one with his Richmond address, one with the address of the Metropolitan Club in Washington, and a third with the address of the Metropolitan Club in New York, and he took great care to give out the appropriate card. George D. Gibson, interview with author, September 26, 1985, Richmond, Virginia.

62 In a special referendum of October 3, 1933, Virginia voted to repeal the Eighteenth Amendment (which had established Prohibition in January 1920) and the state's own Prohibition law (enacted in 1916). After the rejection of Prohibition by Virginia voters in 1933, a revision of Virginia's liquor laws was required. Governor Peery recommended the creation of a three-man board to issue licenses for the sale of beer and wine, to purchase liquors, and to establish state-operated liquor stores. "The object of the law," Peery said, echoing Anderson, "[is] to promote temperance and outlaw the bootlegger and racketeer." Joseph A. Fry, "George C. Peery, Byrd Regular and Depression Governor," *The Governors of Virginia, 1860–1978*, ed. Edward Younger and James Tice Moore, 268.

63 "Henry W. Anderson of Virginia for Vice-President," (1928 campaign brochure), Anderson Papers, 3–4.

64 Walter F. Murphy, "In His Own Image: Mr. Chief Justice Taft and Supreme Court Appointments," in *The Supreme Court and the Constitution, Essays in Constitutional Law from The Supreme Court Review*, ed. Philip B. Kurland (Chicago: University of Chicago Press, 1965), 141, 143. Shield, interview, June 13, 1985. Richmond *News Leader*, March 12, 1930.

In the fall of 1929, Anderson campaigned vigorously for Dr. Brown, the Washington and Lee professor who was the "coalition candidate" for governor supported by "wet," anti-Smith Democrats, as well as by the Republicans. In his speeches Anderson attacked the incumbent governor, Harry Byrd, and his political "machine," claiming that "most of the Governor's alleged reforms have been a part of what I recommended in 1921 but he has always taken the part which strengthened the organization and left out the part [election reform] which increased the liberties of the people." Richmond *Times-Dispatch*, October 31, 1929.

Though John Garland Pollard, the Democratic candidate for governor, and Carter Glass, the junior U.S. senator, had once been "progressives" in the Democratic party who "fought the ever-growing power of the political ring," they had subsequently "accepted office under the patronage of the ring," Anderson pointed out and had "become silent upon its iniquities." Richmond *Times-Dispatch*, October 4, 1929.

65 Richmond *Times-Dispatch*, March 22, 1932, and August 11, 1932. The fact that Anderson consented to give the keynote address to the Third District Republi-

can Convention August 16 raised the hope that he would consent to be drafted as their candidate for Congress, but he declined, and George Cole Scott was nominated.

66 George D. Gibson, interview with author, July 24, 1986, Richmond, Virginia. Gay, 184. Langbourne M. Williams, interview with author, November 11–12, 1986, Rapidan, Virginia.

67 Gibson, interview, July 24, 1986. Lewis F. Powell, Jr., interview with author, August 25, 1986, Richmond, Virginia. The other principal author was Judge R. V. Fletcher, then general counsel of the American Railroads Association. See *Hearings on H.R. 5407 before the Senate Committee on Interstate Commerce*, 67th Congress, 1st Session, May 10, 11, and 12, 1939, at 114, 116. See also Gay, 184–86, and Chapter 9.

68 Stuart Saunders, former president of the Norfolk & Western and Pennsylvania Central Railroad, often talked about Anderson being a legend in the industry, according to Paul Funkhouser, former general counsel of the Norfolk & Western. (Conversation with Paul Funkhouser, February 14, 1987.) DeForest Billiou, a younger partner of Leonard Adkins at Cravath, Swaine & Moore, emphasized the importance of Colonel Anderson's contribution in a class he taught on corporate reorganization at the Yale Law School in 1951. (Conversation with George Clemon Freeman, Jr., February 2, 1987.)

69 Thomas B. Gay, "Henry Watkins Anderson," *Proceedings of the Sixty-fourth Annual Meeting of the Virginia Bar Association* (Richmond: Richmond Press, 1954).

70 Frances Hadfield Richardson lived with her uncle after the death of her mother, his youngest sister (Gertrude Richardson), in 1931 until her marriage to Dr. James Asa Shield in 1934.

71 This anecdote and the ones that follow on Henry Anderson's social life, unless otherwise noted, are from the interview with Frances Richardson Shield, June 13, 1985.

Colonel Jennings C. Wise, former professor-commandant at Virginia Military Institute, colonel with the American Expeditionary Forces in World War I, and then a lawyer in New York, came back to Virginia in the late twenties to get involved in Republican politics. For almost two years, from January 20, 1928, until December 31, 1929, Wise was an associate in the law firm, working for Henry W. Anderson, mainly on Republican matters. He was an assistant attorney general of the United States from 1930 to 1933.

72 Glasgow, *Woman Within*. Shield, interview, June 13, 1985.

73 Shield, interview, June 13, 1985.

74 Conversation with Michael Maupin, who examined the funnel that the finder, an employee at Virginia Electric and Power Company, brought to his office.

75 When Queen Marie's ship, the *Leviathan*, arrived in New York, a Coast Guard cutter went out to greet her carrying an official delegation and "a half dozen Americans who are personally known to the Queen or who have close relations with Rumania and have been invited by the Queen. These include William Nelson Cromwell, Colonel Henry Anderson, Samuel Hill of Seattle and Judge E. H. Gary." *New York Times*, October 18, 1926.

76 King Ferdinand was suffering from inoperable cancer. He died in Pelisor Palace at Sinaia on July 19, 1927. Eleven years later Marie died in the same palace, on July 18, 1938. Pakula, 354, 361.

77 Shield, interview, June 13, 1985.

78 Ibid.

79 James Cremins, former general solicitor of the Seaboard and assistant general counsel of CSX, remembers that there was a strong, almost "cat and dog" rivalry between the two co-receivers of the Seaboard, Henry Anderson and Legh Powell, Jr. In 1946 when the Seaboard came out of receivership, Anderson was made chairman of the board and was given Car Number One. Legh Powell, Jr., who had been made the president, came up with the idea of giving the cars names, rather than numbers, to avoid having to have Car Number Two. Conversation with James Cremins, November 25, 1988.

80 Gibson, interview, May 10, 1984.

81 Powell, interview, July 27, 1984.

82 Powell, interview, August 25, 1986.

83 George D. Gibson, Memo on Conference with Justice Powell, July 30, 1986.

84 Leslie Cheek, Jr., and Mary Tyler Freeman Cheek, interview, October 3, 1988, Richmond, Virginia. Anderson's vision wasn't flawless apparently. The Cheeks remembered that a Winslow Homer watercolor of a Southern scene of workers picking cotton came up for sale for $25,000, and Leslie Cheek urged Anderson to ask the accessions committee to find someone to buy it. But Anderson said, "No. Homer is known for his sea paintings. We want only a sea painting." The watercolor was sold recently for over a million dollars.

85 Adolph D. Williams was a Richmond tobacconist who had helped his wife, Wilkins Coons Williams, build up the collection of art that they subsequently left to the museum along with $2 million in endowment. Arthur Glasgow, brother of Ellen Glasgow, was an engineer who had made a fortune in England by inventing a process of converting waste gas into fuel. During World War I, he had served with Henry Anderson, as vice-chairman of the Red Cross Commission to Rumania. He and his wife, Margaret Branch Glasgow, left a large bequest to the Virginia Museum. Parke Rouse, Jr., *Living by Design: Leslie Cheek and the Arts, a Photobiography* (Williamsburg: The Society of the Alumni of The College of William and Mary, 1985), 103, 107.

86 Conversation with Joseph Carter, February 1, 1986.

87 Paraphrased from Beverley B. Munford, *Random Recollections*, privately printed, 1905, 97–99.

88 Anderson to Williams, April 20, 1919.

89 Shield, interview, June 13, 1985.

90 Ibid. Gladys V. Roberts Thomas, letter to author, January 1, 1986. The sender of the roses was ultimately identified by Frances Shield as Molly McCrea (Mrs. Archibald McCrea), owner of Carter's Grove near Williamsburg, Virginia.

91 Lewis F. Powell, Jr., interview with author, August 1, 1984, Richmond, Virginia. A month before Anderson died, the former Princess Ileana, who had been exiled from Rumania by the Communists in 1948, came to see him. He then gave her the life-sized, half-length portrait of her mother. Sara Bearss, "Marie of Rumania and Henry Anderson of Virginia," *Virginia Country* 10 (April 1987), 28.

6   Thomas Benjamin Gay (1885–1983)

1 In 1879, the year after he came to Richmond, George Ben Johnston, at age twenty-five, performed the first operation in Virginia under Listerism, the foundation of antiseptic surgery, thereby shaking the citadel of "Confederate Medicine and Surgery." There was a fierce rivalry between Dr. Johnston, chief

surgeon at the Medical College of Virginia, and Dr. Hunter McGuire, chief surgeon at the University College of Medicine, and his son, Dr. Stuart McGuire, before the two institutions were merged in 1913. Virginius Dabney, *Virginia Commonwealth University: A Sesquicentennial History* (Charlottesville: University Press of Virginia, 1987), 19–60.

2 The Craigs, who had known him in his boyhood, continued to call him Tom all of his life, though after he was an adult, his other friends called him Ben. T. B. Gay, correspondence with Dr. Stuart L. Craig and Irvin Craig, Hunton & Williams files. Helen Pettway Craig Jefferson, interview with author, May 29, 1987, Richmond, Virginia.

3 Miriam Riggs Gay, interview with author, November 14, 1986, Richmond, Virginia. Miss Ellett's School, or the Virginia Randolph Ellett School, was founded in 1890 in the dining room of a boarding house at 109 East Grace St. It moved several times. From 1895 to 1906 it was at 112 East Franklin Street in Linden Row; then it was on Laurel Street before it moved out to Westhampton in 1917 and became St. Catherine's School. Margaret Meagher, *Education in Richmond* (Richmond: Works Progress Administration Adult Education Project, 1939), 89. Mary Wingfield Scott, *Houses of Old Richmond* (New York: Bonanza Books, 1941), 255. Virginius Dabney, *Richmond: The Story of a City* (Garden City, N.Y.: Doubleday & Co., 1976), 307–8, and conversations with Louise Fontaine Cadot Catterall.

4 George Merritt Nolley, a teacher at Norwood's University School from 1864 to 1892 at 110 North Eighth Street, continued the school as Nolley's Classical School at 410 West Franklin and later at 107 North Pine, from the time of the death of Thomas Norwood in 1892 until 1909. Meagher, 81, 90.

5 According to Thomas B. Gay, Jr., he lived with his maiden aunt for a while after his mother died and supported her. He is listed in the 1902 city directory at 2811 East Grace Street, the home of Stuart D. Craig, and lived with the Craigs until 1904, when he went to the University of Virginia.

6 Pat was Dr. Stuart Lessley Craig, known to his friends in Richmond as Lessley, to friends in New York as Stuart, and to Gay as Pat. Jefferson, interview, May 29, 1987. He became a throat specialist in New York. See Thomas Benjamin Gay to Dr. Stuart Craig, Jr., January 22, 1943, Gay Correspondence, Hunton & Williams files.

7 M. R. Gay, interview, November 14, 1986. Irvin Craig was born September 4, 1896. His parents were Stuart Dunning Craig and Julia Bott Craig.

8 ". . . I first came on the Street [w]ay back in [1899]," said Thomas B. Gay in an interview with the author on June 17, 1982, in Richmond, speaking as if East Main Street were the Wall Street of Virginia. In the same interview, when he was ninety-seven years old, as he talked about the Williams brothers and their business activities, he slipped once and referred to Langbourne as "Mr. Langbourne," the term he had used as a boy, to distinguish him from his brothers. And Margaret Williams McElroy remembered that he often called her father "Mr. Randolph" long after his own name, Gay, had been elevated to the style of the law firm. Margaret Williams McElroy, interview with author, November 14, 1986, Richmond, Virginia.

9 M. R. Gay, interview, November 14, 1986. Langbourne M. Williams, Jr., interviews with author, November 11–12, 1986, Rapidan, Virginia.

10 According to Archibald Robertson in an interview with the author, October 7, 1983, in Richmond, Virginia, William Lile, the dean of the Law School, let Gay

live in a room next to his pavilion. See also M. R. Gay, interview, November 14, 1986.

11 "Seaboard Air Line Railway first became financially embarrassed in 1908 . . . [o]ccasioned, it is believed, by the carrying charges on its large funded debt and that of its constituent companies and the underestimated cost of the extension of its lines from Atlanta, Georgia, to Birmingham, Alabama." Thomas B. Gay, *The Hunton Williams Firm and Its Predecessors, 1877–1954* (Richmond: The Lewis Printing Co., 1971), 151.

12 Unless otherwise noted, all of the information on his life at law school, in Atlanta, Tucson, and Norfolk, is from M. R. Gay, interview, November 14, 1986.

13 After Anderson had struggled first to merge, then to disentangle in 1903, the Norfolk, Portsmouth & Newport News Railway Company (of Portsmouth) from the street railways in Newport News, Hampton, and Old Point Comfort controlled by W. J. Payne, he filed an agreement in 1906 with the State Corporation Commission merging the Berkley Street Railway and Old Dominion Railway Company with Norfolk, Portsmouth & Newport News Company. He changed the company's name to the Norfolk & Portsmouth Traction Company. Anderson became the new company's director and general counsel and served in that capacity until it merged in 1911 with the new Gould-controlled Virginia Railway and Power Company, of which he was also general counsel. T. B. Gay, 119–23.

14 M. R. Gay said that she believed he was actually on the payroll of the Norfolk & Portsmouth Traction Company for the year he was in Norfolk. M. R. Gay, interview, November 14, 1986.

15 T. B. Gay, 49 and 377.

16 In the early 1980s, at the firm's Christmas dinner, a later partner, E. Milton Farley III, told some well-paid young associates that he had come to work for a mere $3,000 a year, and Gay retorted, "And I came to work for no pay at *all!*" M. R. Gay, interview, November 14, 1986.

17 T. B. Gay to John Wingo, February 1, 1972, Richmond, Virginia, replying to Wingo's letter. Correspondence of Thomas B. Gay, Hunton & Williams files.

18 In a letter to M. J. Knoud Saddlery on June 3, 1946, Thomas B. Gay wrote: "I am 5 foot 6 inches tall, and wear a 36 (Short) coat." Correspondence of T. B. Gay, Hunton & Williams files.

19 Leith S. Bremner of Bremner, Parker, Neil, Harris & Williams (a predecessor of McGuire, Woods, Battle & Boothe) was a preeminent trial lawyer in the Virginia bar.

20 Robert Pegram Buford, interview with author, December 18, 1986, Richmond, Virginia.

21 Lewis Powell, Merrill Pasco, and Robert Buford all did trial work with Gay, and all of them remember being uneasy because he used the broad "a" inconsistently. As Lewis Powell put it: "He would shift from broad a to just plain garden variety English in the middle of an argument. That worried me a lot." Lewis F. Powell, Jr., interview with author, July 27, 1984, Richmond, Virginia.

22 The South Atlantic Life Insurance Co. had dropped the "South" by 1913.

23 T. B. Gay, 57–59. Munford, Hunton, Williams & Anderson Journals 1904–15, 362.

24 In 1917 the company's name changed to Old Dominion Iron & Steel Corp. T. B. Gay, 68.

25 The Federal Reserve Bank's first offices were at 1109 East Main Street, next
   door to the State Bank Building. In 1915 it moved to the newly constructed
   Federal Reserve Bank building at Ninth and Franklin and stayed there for
   sixty years. In the late 1970s it moved to the present Federal Reserve Bank,
   on the riverfront between Eighth and Ninth streets. A. Caperton Braxton, a
   senior member of the firm Braxton & Eggleston in Richmond, died March 22,
   1914, at his home in Staunton after a long illness. He had maintained law
   offices and residences in both Richmond and Staunton. In the Constitutional
   Convention of 1901–2, as chairman of the Committee on Corporations, Braxton had fought successfully for a State Corporation Commission with strong
   powers to regulate railroads and utilities. He was considered the author of the
   chapter on corporations in the Constitution. Later he became general counsel
   to the Richmond, Fredericksburg and Potomac Railroad. Obituary, Richmond
   Times-Dispatch, March 23, 1914.

26 T. B. Gay, 139.

27 Thomas B. Gay, Jr., interview with author, March 8, 1987, Richmond, Virginia,
   and M. R. Gay, interview, November 14, 1986.

28 In December 1915 the firm's net profits for the year were divided equally
   among Eppa Hunton, Jr., E. Randolph Williams, and Henry W. Anderson, each
   receiving one-third or $15,542.73. (Munford, Hunton, Williams & Anderson
   Journal 2, 485). When Gay was taken into the partnership on January 1, 1916,
   Hunton's participation was cut back by 6 percentage points from 33 percent
   to 28 percent while Williams and Anderson were cut back only 1 point from
   33 percent to 32 percent to give Gay 8 percent of the 1916 profits. The dis-
   tributions become more complicated when Anderson was in the Balkans from
   the summer of 1917 through 1919, cutting back on his participation in 1917
   and 1918 and receiving no distribution for 1919, when the profits were divided
   among the other three with 36.11 percent for Hunton, 38.89 percent for Williams and 25 percent for Gay. After Hunton retired to be president of the RF
   & P railroad in September 1920, the three remaining partners returned to the
   simpler method of dividing the profits equally. Journal 3, 253.

29 Margaret Williams McElroy, interview with author, November 7, 1984, Richmond, Virginia, and conversation with Thomas B. Gay, Jr., April 7, 1987.

30 McElroy, interview, November 7, 1984, and M. R. Gay, interview, November 14,
   1986. Grace Hospital, a predecessor of Metropolitan Hospital at 701 West
   Grace Street, was only three blocks from the Williamses' house.

31 McElroy, interview, November 7, 1984.

32 M. R. Gay, interview, November 14, 1986.

33 Ibid.

34 On July 31, 1918, Anderson paid 2 percent of the net profits of the firm for
   1917, or $1,043.82, out of his own proportion of those profits for 1917 to Gay
   "in consideration of additional work being imposed upon Mr. Gay by reason of
   Mr. Anderson's absence in Europe." Journal 3, (1916–1925) 125.

35 T. B. Gay, 250. Floridus Stott Crosby was born January 15, 1893, in Staunton
   and received an LL.B. from the University of Virginia Law School in 1917.
   In *Who's Who in the Law*, 1937, he is listed as a member of the firm of Kerr &
   Crosby in Staunton from January 15, 1919 to September 1927, so the date for
   his withdrawal listed on page 49 of Gay, *The Hunton Williams Firm*, "11/15/19"
   is probably a misprint for "1/15/19." In 1927–28 he was commonwealth's attorney for the City of Staunton, and on January 18, 1937, he was appointed judge

for the Staunton Corporation Court by Governor Peery. In 1942 he became judge of the 18th Virginia circuit and resigned in 1955. He died June 19, 1957.

36 Whiting Faulkner, whose nickname was "Screech," came to the firm on January 1, 1920, was made partner on January 1, 1928, and worked on Seaboard Railway matters. He left December 31, 1931, for Wheeling, West Virginia, where he received an appointment as postmaster.

37 January 1, 1928, is the date given for the admission of Faulkner, Preston, and Craig into partnership, by Gay on page 49 of his firm history. The year 1928 is also the date Randolph Williams uses for his memorial to Preston for the Virginia Bar Association, and finally, it is the date used by Irvin Craig in an autobiographical sketch initialed "IGC" and dated "10/30/71." From the firm journals, it appears that the three men were receiving a small portion of the profits as early as 1925. On page 499, Journal 3 (1916–1925), December 31, 1925, Marks is paid $5,634.51; and Faulkner, Preston, and Craig each are paid $1,112.26 "for their shares of net income of the partnership during 1925, as per statement on file." Similar wording is used in 1926, 1927, and 1928. In 1928 Faulkner is paid $8,304.45; Preston and Craig are paid $8,012.40; Marks is paid $13,072.75; and Williams, Anderson, and Gay each are paid $27,632.48.

38 Eppa Hunton IV died in an automobile accident November 23, 1976, just eight months short of his fiftieth anniversary at the firm.

39 Eppa Hunton IV's margin notes on page 49 of a copy of Gay's *The Hunton Williams Firm*. The trading of insults between the Huntons and the Wises had become a tradition by this time. In a footnote to his father's *Autobiography*, Eppa Hunton, Jr., the founder of the firm, recounts an incident he had heard about from General Mat Ransom. It took place during the week after the fall of Petersburg, in April 1865, as the Confederate troops were retreating toward Appomattox:

> General Wise began to criticize General Lee for not ending the war, the result of which he said was inevitable. . . . He finally said that General Lee would be guilty of the murder of every soldier who, after that time, was killed. General Ransom said my father rose in his stirrups and said, "General Wise, you are a damned traitor." General Ransom said he expected pistols to be drawn at once and firing to begin, but that to his infinite surprise and pleasure General Wise turned to him with a smile and said, "Ransom, all the damned fools have not been killed yet." The jesting manner in which General Wise dealt with the matter ended pleasantly what at one time promised to be serious.

Eppa Hunton, *Autobiography of Eppa Hunton* (Richmond: William Byrd Press, 1933), 121.

40 Jennings C. Wise was the son of John S. Wise, a Mahoneite Republican-Readjuster candidate for governor in 1885 and grandson of Henry Wise, governor of Virginia (1856–60) and the Confederate general referred to in the previous note. J. C. Wise's brother, Henry A. Wise, was the Republican candidate who ran unsuccessfully against Harry Byrd for the U.S. Senate in 1932. J. C. Wise worked at the firm as Anderson's assistant from January 30, 1928 to December 31, 1929.

41 After Gay began his retirement in the mid-1950s, he was succeeded by his assistant, Merrill Pasco, who in turn was succeeded by Joseph Carter in 1972.

Taylor Reveley, the current managing partner, took over in 1982. When Cabell Lawton, a former officer of the American Bank, came into the firm in the 1930s as business manager, he took on many of the responsibilities later assigned to the managing partner. Lawton's status in the firm was very nearly equal to that of the senior partners.

42 Many people thought that Gay had grown up on Church Hill, a neighborhood which did not have the social status conferred by West Franklin Street or even Grace Street at that time. Though he lived on Church Hill as a teenager a few years after his mother's death, he spent his infancy on Dodson Street, south of West Main Street, near Hollywood Cemetery, and spent his childhood on Laurel Street, opposite Monroe Park.

To be elected to the Richmond German, a dance group founded in 1867 that for many years introduced the debutantes each year, was a sign of full acceptance into Richmond Society.

43 Robertson, interview, October 7, 1983. James Howard Corbitt (1867–1945) was a lawyer who practiced in Suffolk, and a close friend who frequently accompanied Thomas B. Gay on vacations.

44 Virginius Randolph Shackelford (1885–1949), a lawyer from Orange County, who was a partner with A. Stuart Robertson.

45 Robertson, interview, October 7, 1983.

46 Oliver Jackson Sands, Jr., *A Story of Sport and the Deep Run Hunt Club: What It Is and How It Came to Be* (Richmond: Whittet & Shepperson, 1977), 206–13, and Richmond *Times-Dispatch*, October 14, 1983. "Lauvain" was owned by Mr. Gay and ridden by William Mahoney.

47 Though Anderson took over when the time came to intervene before the Interstate Commerce Commission, the original suit was brought by Gay, and he regarded it as a highlight of his career. T. B. Gay, 158–81, and T. B. Gay, interview, June 17, 1982.

48 Edmund Randolph Williams, Henry Anderson, Thomas B. Gay, Wirt P. Marks, Jr., Whiting C. Faulkner, Edmund M. Preston, Irvin G. Craig, and James R. V. Daniel (October 31, 1925 to June 30, 1927). The ratio of nine partners to two associates persisted until Wise left December 31, 1929, leaving Eppa Hunton IV as the only associate and the ratio at nine to one for the next two years. When George Gibson arrived on January 1, 1931, the day after Whiting Faulkner officially withdrew, the ratio then became eight partners to two associates.

49 The associates were Norman L. Flippen (from April 1, 1932 to July 1, 1943, when he became a partner); H. Merrill Pasco (June 15, 1940, though he was called into the reserves in February of 1941, he was scheduled to come back at the end of the year and was actually making plans to do so on the weekend of Pearl Harbor); Richard W. Emory (July 1, 1940, went to war February 15, 1942, and settled in Baltimore after he got back); B. Warwick Davenport (June 16, 1941); R. Franklin Harward, Jr., (who came September 29, 1941, and left July 14, 1942) and John W. Riely (who came August 1, 1941).

50 "The Securities Exchange Act became law in June of 1934 and required all stock exchanges to be registered with the Securities and Exchange Commission as national security exchanges by October 15th of that year, or cease the conduct of their business." T. B. Gay, 363.

51 According to clippings from the Richmond newspapers, March 5 and 7, 1934.

The *Wall Street Journal*, February 24, 1934, carried a front-page article about Thomas B. Gay and the New York Stock Exchange's challenge to the constitutionality of federal regulations. On the same day the *New York Times* had a less extensive article on page 7.

Though he was a Democrat by tradition, as were all of the firm's partners except Henry Anderson, Gay did not support Roosevelt for election for the third and fourth terms. Thomas B. Gay to Benjamin J. Pitts, October 2, 1944, Hunton & Williams files.

52 T. B. Gay, 363.

53 He was one of the two chairmen in the history of the House of Delegates to serve two terms. Both served during the Second World War.

54 Lewis F. Powell, Jr., interview with author, August 15, 1984, Richmond, Virginia, and T. B. Gay, 287–304. More than six thousand pages of testimony was taken and some three hundred exhibits were filed.

55 In 1941 the city annexed 8.29 square miles of Henrico and 7.27 square miles of Chesterfield. Louis H. Manarin and Clifford Dowdey, *The History of Henrico County* (Charlottesville: University Press of Virginia, 1984), 424–31. Francis Earle Lutz, *Chesterfield: An Old Virginia County* (Richmond: William Byrd Press, 1954).

56 "I know he went back to the office just as regularly after dinner every night as he did after lunch. Also on Saturdays and Sundays, and it was just too much for him." Jefferson, interview, May 29, 1987.

"I think that really broke Irvin's health because the litigation . . . was very prolonged and tiresome, and Irvin . . . was a very slow worker and he was at Hunton, Williams almost every night." Powell, interview, August 15, 1984.

"And then they had the Richmond annexation case, the one where they straightened out the James River and all that sort of stuff. . . . And Benny had charge of that and . . . I don't reckon Benny knew that he was doing it, but anyway he worked that boy . . . to the extent that the boy broke down." Robertson, interview, October 7, 1983.

57 Jefferson, interview, May 29, 1987.

58 In a brief autobiographical sketch, Craig explained that by the end of the war his "health became such that his personal physician and a distinguished New York neurologist advised him that he should not continue with the firm, that he should take at least a year free of any legal activity and that if and when he was able to resume practice it should be on a limited basis. In this situation he withdrew from the firm on April 1, 1945, and resigned from it on April 1, 1946, ending an association of twenty-five years." In October 1947 Craig resumed a limited practice on his own, specializing in corporate law and estate planning until his death on October 19, 1973. He had continued to represent the A. T. Massey Coal Company. He was called their "general counsel" though he would not accept the title officially, since he wanted to be free to regulate his hours. Manuscript in pencil, signed "IGC, 10/30/71" in Hunton & Williams files, and Jefferson, interview, May 29, 1987.

59 Norman Flippen was the only associate at the firm in December 1941 who remained through the next year, and on July 1, 1943, he was elevated to the partnership.

Meanwhile the firm became almost a revolving door for male lawyers who would be hired by the firm, work for a number of months—in the case of Ralph Ferrell and Frank Lowden almost two years—and then they, too, would go off to war. Of the seven associates hired during the war, only two—Ferrell and Lowden—were eventually taken into the partnership with the other returning veterans, Davenport, Pasco, and Riely, on January 1, 1949. (This group of five was nicknamed the "Rinky-Dinks.") The figure of seven associates hired during the war does not include Pat Gibson, who was hired in the last weeks of the war as a replacement for Edmund Preston in the labor practice, though it does include the two women lawyers, Nan Ross McConnell and Sarah Geer Dale.

Those who did not come back from the service or remain with the firm to become partner included:

—Richard W. Emory, who had come July 1, 1940, and worked for George Gibson until February 15, 1942, and went into the navy. Gibson thought he was potentially an exceptionally good lawyer and was disappointed when he decided to go to Baltimore after he was discharged from the navy. Emory was deputy attorney general of Maryland, 1947–48. Then he joined the firm of Venable, Baetjer & Howard, where he is now counsel. Conversation with George Gibson, June 23, 1986, and H. Merrill Pasco to Thomas B. Gay, October 12, 1945. *The American Bar*, 1958, *The Bar Register*, Annual, 1983 (Summit, N.J.: Bar Register Co., 1983).

—R. Franklin Harward, Jr., who came September 29, 1941, and left July 14, 1942.

—William Gibson Harris, later a senior partner in the McGuire firm in Richmond, who came April 1, 1942, and left July 15, 1942, to position himself in Washington (at Covington & Burling) to work on getting a commission despite his health problems.

—William D. Cabell, who came October 21, 1942, but left three years later on September 30, 1945, at the end of the war. He subsequently worked for his uncle, Forrest Hyde, an attorney with offices on Fifth Avenue in New York City, and in February 1946 wrote Gay asking his support for his application to practice before the Washington, D.C., Tax Court. William D. Cabell to Thomas B. Gay, February 1 and February 18, 1946, New York, N.Y., Hunton & Williams files. He is a partner in the firm Cabell, Kennedy and French in New York, and he now lives in Chappaqua, N.Y., and Goochland County, Va.

—Alfred B. McEwen, who came March 22, 1943, and left May 31, 1943.

60 The two partners who went into the service were Eppa Hunton IV and Lewis F. Powell, Jr., leaving seven: Williams, Anderson, Gay, Marks, Preston, Craig, Moore, and Robertson. The number increased to eight when Norman Flippen was elevated to partnership on July 1, 1943. Then it decreased suddenly to six in the spring of 1945 when Edmund Preston died and Irvin Craig left because of ill health.

61 George D. Gibson, interview with author, July 3, 1987, Richmond, Virginia.

62 John Riely, in his talk to the new associates on January 26, 1985, said that World War II was "a very great drain" on the firm and that "Mr. Randolph Williams was going to Police Court, which was not really his style."

63 Virginius Dabney, interview with author, February 14, 1986, Richmond, Virginia. Dabney was a reporter for the Richmond *News Leader* 1922–28, then joined the editorial staff of the *Times-Dispatch* and served as that newspaper's editor 1936–69. Before World War II, he had already written two influential books about the contemporary South, *Liberalism in the South*, 1932, and *Below the Potomac*, 1942, and was awarded a Pulitzer Prize for editorial writing in 1947.

64 Dabney, interview, February 14, 1986. In an interview with author November 11, 1985, in Richmond, Virginia, Oliver Hill said, "Now I'd say my first

association with anybody over at Hunton, Williams was with Edmund Preston . . . a marvelous person." In 1942 Hill and Preston worked together on the Odell Waller case, preparing papers in Hunton, Williams's offices. But by the time Hill came out of the service, Preston had died. Oliver Hill, interview, November 11, 1985.

Odell Waller, a black sharecropper, was convicted of murdering his white landlord. His lawyers petitioned Governor Colgate Darden (1942–46) to commute his death sentence. Though Darden granted a stay of execution and hearings, he did not finally commute the sentence. Waller was executed on July 2, 1942.

65 Richmond *Times-Dispatch*, March 22, 1945.

66 The Wagner-Connery Act, or National Labor Relations Act of July 5, 1935, established the National Labor Relations Board.

67 Robertson, interview with author, October 7, 1983, Richmond, Virginia. In 1944 and 1945, as part of its divestiture under the Public Utilities Holding Company Act, Engineers Public Service sold its transportation properties to Virginia Transit Company. Moore became its general counsel and Robertson, its trial counsel.

68 On July 7, 1942, Gay wrote in a letter recommending Preston to the War Department, Hampton Roads Port of Embarkation, Newport News, Virginia: "During the last four and one-half years, [Preston] has specialized in labor relations work, bringing him into intimate contact with a number of large industrial plants throughout the South, some of which are now engaged in war production. His work has included hearings before the National Labor Relations Board in both complaint and representation cases, appeals from the Board, bargaining with unions on behalf of employers, handling strike cases involving violence, and National War Labor Board matters." Hunton & Williams files.

69 But she was never a full-fledged associate, as Dale and McConnell were. Gay's list of partners and associates, T. B. Gay, 49, gives Elizabeth Tompkins's dates at the firm as May 15, 1923, to September 15, 1923, but Miss Tompkins herself wrote to him in 1971, correcting those dates, saying that she had worked at the firm during the summers of 1921 and 1922, when she was still in law school. She was the first female graduate of the University of Virginia Law School in 1923. Obituary, June 26, 1981, Richmond *Times-Dispatch*; *Who's Who in the Law*, 1937, 944; Elizabeth Tompkins to Thomas B. Gay, March 31, 1971, Richmond, Virginia, Hunton & Williams files.

"Miss T.," as she was known to her friends, was not overly fond of Hunton, Williams's senior partners. She found them just a little bit "snobbish" for her taste. Conversation with Jane Ketron, July 10, 1987.

Elizabeth Tompkins was a partner of Carter Lee Refo from 1954 until she retired in 1979. For a time, she had served as commissioner of accounts for Hanover County and as commissioner in chancery for circuit courts in Richmond and Hanover. She died June 25, 1981, at age eighty-three, after she was struck by an automobile.

70 M. R. Gay, interview, November 14, 1986.

71 Women were admitted as undergraduates in the fall of 1970. See Thomas B. Gay, "Statement to a study committee of the Faculty on the co-education of male and female students in the College of Arts and Sciences at the University of Virginia," November 9, 1967, 44. Hunton & Williams files.

72 Norman Flippen was made a partner at the age of forty-eight. There had been

considerable resistance to making him a partner, since he lacked the social polish and the old Virginia background possessed—or assumed—by the rest of the partners, with the exception of Justin Moore, who blazed his way with sheer ability and a power to attract clients. In a way, Flippen's elevation to the partnership marks the beginning of the democratization and broadening of the partnership, which would accelerate after World War II.

73 Patrick Gibson came to the firm on August 1, 1945, and was made partner on January 1, 1948.

74 The partners had been subsidized by the firm, which made up the difference between their service paycheck and the amount they would have earned had they stayed at home. See Eppa Hunton IV to T. B. Gay, June 25, 1942, Camp Lee, Virginia, and several letters from T. B. Gay to Lewis F. Powell, Jr., and Powell to Gay, 1942–45, in Hunton & Williams files. For example, from one letter (Gay to Powell, July 25, 1942):

> . . . we are of the opinion that all sums paid you by virtue of your commission, either as salary, subsistence allowance, or uniform allowance, is income for which you should fairly account in determining the amount of your participation in the profits of the firm.
>
> I agree with you that these funds should not pass through our books, otherwise we would be subject to Federal income taxation thereon, and I therefore suggest that you advise us of the exact amounts which you have received and contemplate receiving monthly, so that in determining the net amount which you will receive as your participation in the profits, an appropriate charge may be made against you in that connection.

And from another (Gay to Powell, April 17, 1945):

> We have all considered your desire to discontinue your participation in the firm's income as of January 1, 1945, and feel that you should not do so. According to the statement which I have before me, your share of the 1944 profits was $9,575, against which you had withdrawals of $9,475. After crediting your salary checks against this amount, aggregating $5,475, the firm actually paid you $4,000. We all feel we would prefer to continue the matter throughout the current year if that is agreeable to you.

75 The 45th General Hospital was a successor to the Medical College of Virginia Base Hospital, No. 45, the McGuire Unit, in World War I, with which Irvin Craig, Walter Russell Bowie (Mary Munford's nephew, then rector of St. Paul's Church), and many prominent Richmond and Virginia doctors had served. But it soon expanded dramatically, admitting an average of 1,000 patients a month, with as many as 300 in a single day in Rabat, Morocco. Later in Naples, Italy, in one day it had 2,646 patients, more than the total beds available in Richmond hospitals.

Despite a heavy load of work as adjutant, Eppa Hunton IV took to army life with the gusto of his father and his grandfather. A photograph in the *University of Virginia Alumni News* shows him leading an Eli Banana Parade, beating an Ethiopian drum, at a UVA alumni reunion in Italy. His eternally unreconstructed sense of priorities was further evidenced in Naples, when he flung out a giant Confederate flag from his apartment window on the birthday of every Confederate general whose birthday he could remember. Richmond *Times-Dispatch*, June 17, 1960.

76 Lewis Powell's activities with ULTRA are described in the chapter on Powell later in this book.

77 Carl Spaatz (b. 1891) was commander-in-chief of the U.S. Strategic Air Force against Japan after the war in Europe ended. Before that, he was chief of Army Air Force Combat Command in 1942, then chief air adviser to General Eisenhower in North Africa. He commanded the North West African Air Forces in Sicily in 1943, and was commander-in-chief of the U.S. Strategic Air Force in Europe in January 1944. In 1946, he became the Commanding General of the Army Air Force and in 1948 he retired. See also Powell chapter.

78 H. Merrill Pasco, interview with author, June 12, 1985, Richmond, Virginia.

79 Warwick Davenport was "relieved from active service on February 27, 1946 with the rank of lieutenant colonel, which he had held since July 1, 1944," according to T. B. Gay, 385.

80 *Who's Who in America, 1982–83* (Chicago: A. N. Marquis, 1982–83), 2776.

81 John W. Riely, interview with author, May 8, 1984, Richmond, Virginia.

82 Between Ralph Ferrell's graduation from Harvard Law School in 1936 and his coming to the firm in January 1942, he had been special assistant to the attorney general of Virginia, September 1936 to January 1938, and counsel for Southern States Cooperative from January 1938 until January 1942. He was Justin Moore's nephew by marriage. See Gay, 381, 385.

83 Gay, 386. In the brief biography at the back of Gay's history, Lowden is listed as president of the Taft Club of Richmond in 1952. By the end of the 1940s, in addition to Henry Anderson, there were three other full-fledged Republicans in the firm: B. Warwick Davenport, Frank Lowden, and Brice Graves. In the 1952 presidential election, Lewis Powell helped organize "Eisenhower Democrats."

84 Powell, Conversation with author.

85 Brice Graves, who had earned four degrees from the University of Virginia (a B.S. in commerce, an M.S. and a Ph.D. in economics, and an LL.B.) was associated with Cravath, Swaine and Moore in New York from September 6, 1938 to March 16, 1942, and from October 15, 1945 to November 12, 1948. In a 1986 interview Graves said that Williams had persuaded the Supreme Court of Virginia to waive their six months' residency requirement and make him a member of the Virginia bar right away, so that he could become a partner on January 1, 1949. Brice Graves, interview with author, June 19, 1986, Richmond, Virginia.

86 According to Gay's list, James Archibald Weems was an associate from March 1, 1948, to February 28, 1950, and Lawrence E. Blanchard, Jr., was an associate from July 1, 1948, to March 1, 1953. Blanchard was made partner after only five years, the day that Wirt Marks left, in an effort to help retain some of Marks's clients. Since Justin Moore, Jr., arrived July 1, 1950, Blanchard was the lone associate for only a few months although his name was still alone, below the line, on a letterhead used September 1950. It was customary to wait one year before adding an associate's name to the printed letterhead, so Jim Weems's name was never added. Joseph Carter, interview with author, May 14, 1987, Richmond, Virginia; and Lawrence E. Blanchard, interview with author, July 28, 1987, Richmond, Virginia.

87 At that time the chairman of the Executive Committee was appointed on the basis of his seniority as a partner at the firm, according to George Gibson, in a conversation June 23, 1987. During the three years of his transition into re-

tirement, Gay served on the Executive Committee and continued to serve as managing partner until December 31, 1958. Eppa Hunton IV, the most senior member of the Executive Committee, replaced Gay as chairman, and Merrill Pasco replaced Gay as managing partner on January 1, 1959.

88 Richmond *News Leader*, December 21, 1964.

89 After serving as counsel for the Norfolk & Western Railway, then vice president of the Pennsylvania Railroad and Penn Central Transport Company, Paul Funkhouser became president of the Seaboard Coast Line Railroad. When the Seaboard Coast Line merged with the Chessie System in 1982, he became president of the CSX Corporation. Robert Buford had applied for a job at the same time as had Funkhouser and Justin Moore. Pasco, interview, June 12, 1985; and Buford, interview, December 18, 1986.

90 Buford, interview, December 18, 1986.

91 Ibid.

92 Powell, interview, July 27, 1984.

93 Meaning that he organized the corporation under Virginia law, a process "which was fairly simple at that time." Lewis F. Powell, Jr., interview with author, August 1, 1984, Richmond, Virginia.

Philip Morris, now one of the firm's largest and most diversified clients, was established in London in 1847. It was taken over by American stockholders and incorporated in Virginia February 21, 1919. In 1929 the company bought a factory in Richmond and began manufacturing cigarettes in America. *Moody's Industrial Manual*, 1980, vol. 2, 3808; 1986, vol. 2, 3351.

94 Lewis F. Powell, Jr., interview with author, August 25, 1986, Richmond, Virginia.

95 The firm, in turn, celebrated Thomas B. Gay's ninety-fifth birthday with a reception at the annual Judicial Conference for the Fourth Circuit at the Homestead Hotel in Hot Springs. When Gay heard about the firm's arrangements to have hors d'oeuvres and drinks served in a capacious five-room suite reserved for the occasion, he insisted that the party be moved to a conference room downstairs. "Hunton & Williams," he announced, "does not entertain in bedrooms." Conversations with Joan Farley and Nancy Booker, June 26, 1987.

96 Miriam Riggs Gay, who was a social worker from Roanoke at the time, had grown up in Richmond and actually worked at Hunton, Williams during the summer of 1942, the year she finished high school, and the summer of 1943, after her first year of college; so she was no stranger to the world into which she was marrying. M. R. Gay, interview, November 14, 1986.

97 At the firm's Christmas dinner-dance in 1977, Mr. Gay was asked if he would mind answering a question about the romance between Colonel Anderson and Ellen Glasgow. Standing stiffly in white tie and tailcoat, he replied with a bow, "Not at all. I'm always happy to talk about romance. Have you met my bride of five months?"

In the skit the associates gave after that same dinner, a disc jockey, played by Guy Tower, announced "Mr. Thomas B. Gay's recent smash hit single, 'They Tried to Tell Us We're Too Young.'"

98 The cause of his death was probably heart failure, though his son, Thomas B. Gay, Jr., prefers the explanation of a hospital orderly who said, "He was tired and he just punied out." Thomas B. Gay, Jr., interview with author, April 7, 1987, Richmond, Virginia.

7 Thomas Justin Moore (1890–1958)

1 Thomas Justin Moore, Jr., interview with author, January 4, 1985, Richmond, Virginia; and Carolyn Moore McCue, interview with author, December 8, 1987, Richmond, Virginia.

2 T. Justin Moore was the first graduate of Louisiana College, on June 27, 1907, with a B.A. in classics. The private liberal arts college in Pineville, Louisiana, is owned by the Southern Baptist Convention. It was founded in 1906 as the successor to two separate Baptist schools, Mount Lebanon University and Keatchie Female College, just in time to grant Moore a Louisiana College, rather than a Mount Lebanon, degree. Telephone conversation with Dr. Landrom Sallie of Louisiana College, December 12, 1988.

3 McCue, interview, December 8, 1987.

4 A. Willis Robertson was a congressman from 1933 until November 5, 1946, when he was named to fill the unexpired term of Carter Glass in the Senate. He served there until 1965. His son Marion Gordon "Pat" Robertson became a television evangelist and in 1988 was a candidate for the Republican nomination for president.

5 McCue, interview, December 8, 1987. Richmond *City Directories,* 1909 and 1910. The Richmond Academy, a preparatory school, opened in 1903 at Lombardy Street and Park Avenue, and was run by Richmond College (which later became a part of the University of Richmond). The Women's College, Richmond, had been called Richmond Female Institute before the Civil War. In 1916 it closed down, and Westhampton College, which had been established two years earlier as part of Richmond College, took over its land and records. Margaret Meagher, *Education in Richmond* (Richmond: Works Progress Administration Adult Education Project, 1939), 93; and conversation with Jane Thorpe, alumnae director at Westhampton College, November 1988.

6 The house, which is also known as the Barret House, was still standing in 1989. The architectural historian Mary Wingfield Scott described it as "in a way . . . the most perfect of the mansions built in the forties . . . truly Greek in spirit." Mary Wingfield Scott, *Houses of Old Richmond* (New York: Bonanza Books, 1941), 221–23.

7 Moore Jr., interview, January 4, 1985.

8 W. Hamilton Bryson, *Legal Education in Virginia, 1779–1979: A Biographical Approach* (Charlottesville: University Press of Virginia, 1982), 457–62. Also McCue, interview, December 8, 1987.

9 McCue, interview, December 8, 1987.

10 John Williams, telephone conversation, May 22, 1989.

11 Archibald G. Robertson, interview with author, May 25, 1985, Richmond, Virginia.

12 Alexander Barclay Guigon, 1858–1923, had been associated with the Virginia Railway and Power Company and its predecessors since 1896, the same year that Randolph Williams was made president of the Richmond Traction Company. In October 1901 Guigon, representing the Fisher interests, fought Randolph Williams, counsel for the Williams interests, in the bitter battle before city council between the rival streetcar companies for access to the Main Street Line.

After the rival companies merged into what became in 1909 the Virginia

Railway and Power Company, Guigon's position as "general attorney" was similar, though not identical, to that of house counsel, since he still kept up a private practice on the side, as did his assistant Justin Moore.

13 See Richmond *City Directory*, 1914, 963.

14 The steaming cauldrons were removed from the parapets of the Electric Building during the 1920s. The windows of the tenth floor, where the law firm had its offices until 1966, are surmounted with animal heads, while urns and garlands made of colored tile form arches over the twelfth floor. Carlton Norris McKenney, *Rails in Richmond* (Glendale, Calif.: Interurban Press, 1986), 39. Virginia Electric and Power Company occupied the building for sixty years, until its new building at Seventh and Cary streets was finished in 1978.

15 Frances Shield recalled that:

> when Uncle Henry died, . . . Mr. Moore came to call on me—there at the house . . . sat down in the drawing room and said, "You know, when I first applied to the firm to become a member, a young lawyer here, Colonel Anderson was so arrogant . . . [he] let me know that I wasn't the type of lawyer they wanted." . . . sitting there right in the room with the casket. . . . "The next time," he said, "I had a big client or something, and the next time I went to call on them, they accepted me as a lawyer in the firm."
>
> I don't think there was ever any real connection between them, [she went on to say]. And you know, back then, your church affiliation had something to do with how people felt about you, a little. . . . And he was a great Baptist and a Prohibitionist and didn't drink. He was a very rigid Baptist. So all that made a difference.
> (Frances Shield, interview with author, June 13, 1985, Manakin-Sabot, Virginia.)

As late as 1956, Lewis Booker still felt that being a Baptist and a Harvard man in a firm composed mainly of Episcopalians with a University of Virginia connection was a disadvantage, and he felt very close to Justin Moore because they shared that Baptist and Harvard background. Lewis Booker, interview with author, August 2, 1987, Richmond, Virginia.

16 Robertson, interview, May 25, 1985.

17 Even as late as the 1930s, according to George Gibson, "the practice of law in Richmond in that period was an avocation of gentlemen who had no particular proficiency. They thought it was seemly, in some cases, necessary, to go downtown, you see. And there they had shelter and company and something to seem to be doing. And it was not important that they know anything particular about what they were doing. I was a little unimpressed by the Richmond bar, as you can see. But the organization was a very impromptu, amateur effort." George D. Gibson, interview with author, July 24, 1986, Richmond, Virginia.

18 Robertson, interview, May 25, 1985.

19 When they were negotiating Robertson's salary, Moore expressed concern that it be kept within the range of what the young associates at Randolph Williams's firm (Preston, Craig and Faulkner) were then getting. They settled on $3,500 a year, $500 less than Robertson was making as city attorney, with Robertson free to keep whatever fees he made from his own business, but for the rest of his life Robertson felt that Moore had not dealt with him fairly. "My

work was almost exclusively trial work," Robertson explained. "Vepco cases. At
that time they were self insured and defended all their own cases. What had
almost broken Moore down—the volume of those cases—was just incredible.
And I handled them from the Police Court up through the Virginia Supreme
Court. . . . But Moore saw to it that . . . I was never at anytime on the Vepco
payroll." Archibald G. Robertson, interview with author, December 14, 1983,
Richmond, Virginia.

20 "But," he added, "I've met some more people that are just as much that way
since then. . . . I expect Lewis Powell would be one, and another one would be
John Riely." Robertson, interview, May 25, 1985.

21 Robertson, interview, May 25, 1985.

22 When Stone & Webster purchased control of Virginia Railway and Power Company from Frank and Helen Gould in June 1925, it formed Engineers Public
Service Company, a holding company to manage the properties of Virginia
Railway and Power Company, which was soon merged with Spotsylvania Power
Company of Fredericksburg. The power company's name was then changed
to Virginia Electric and Power Company (Vepco) until 1985, when it was reorganized in a holding company, Dominion Resources, which had separate
subsidiaries, Virginia Power, North Carolina Power and West Virginia Power.

23 Robertson, interview, May 25, 1985; and William W. Archer, interview with
author, July 9, 1985, Richmond, Virginia. Archer, who worked as an engineer
for the power company from 1922 until 1950, recalled that Stone & Webster
told Randolph Williams that they would like him to stay on as general counsel if
he would leave his law firm and work exclusively for them, and that Randolph
Williams had refused the offer.

24 In the early 1950s, Justin Moore, Jr. observed the bond that had developed
between them when he used to stop by his father's office to give him a ride
home. "He'd be sitting in Randolph Williams's office, late in the afternoon, just
the two of 'em sitting there talking. . . . And I think [back in 1925] Mr Randolph Williams was so Old Richmond and into so many things that [he] was
probably *glad* to have somebody come and do the boiler-room work with this
fast-growing client that was then starting to get quite complicated." Moore Jr.,
interview, January 4, 1985.

25 George Modlin, president of the University of Richmond from 1946 to 1971
and friend of both father and son, put it this way: "Justin Jr. was the flowering
of those two families. He combined the brilliance of the Moores with the charm
of the Willinghams." George Modlin, interview with author, April 20, 1989,
Richmond, Virginia.

26 Even so, Archibald Robertson said that Justin Moore, Sr., "had more power
than any one person has ever had in Vepco before or since. He damn near ran
the company." Archibald G. Robertson, interview with author, November 21,
1983, Richmond, Virginia. Moore Sr. finally consented to serve as chairman of
the Executive Committee of the Virginia Electric and Power Company's board
of directors in 1956.

27 Moore Jr., interview, January 4, 1985.

28 Ibid.

29 McCue, interview, December 8, 1987. Carolyn (b. 1916) became a full professor of pediatrics at the Medical College of Virginia, the first woman president
of the Richmond Academy of Medicine, and raised two children, while Moore's

other daughter, Cornelia Moore Hall (1921–85), raised four children and lived the more traditional life her mother favored.

In 1945 when Hunton, Williams's first woman associate, Sarah Geer Dale, was assigned to work for Moore after the death of Edmund Preston, she "sort of dreaded working with him," having observed how brusque he could be around the office. But he turned out to be "perfectly *wonderful* to me . . . he praised me and he encouraged me, and I enjoyed working with him," she said. Sarah Geer Dale Gayle, interview with author, August 13, 1985, Richmond, Virginia.

30 "Yes I heard [Colonel Anderson] mention in 1932 that they were inviting Mr. Moore to come upstairs to join our firm. And it was not inviting, it was begging him to come, absolutely. I have no doubt—it is sheer surmise—I have no doubt that Mr. Anderson did say no to begin with. And nobody ever ate his words more completely than he did at that. And the reason was money. In 1932 and '34, in Virginia anyhow, there weren't any clients. There wasn't any business. An occasional old friend would drop in, but not pay anything, you know, for conversation. Mr. Moore, on the other hand, was a very energetic, very practical, thriving person who had the steady payroll account of the Virginia Electric and Power Company. . . . So with his energy and leadership, attributes and monied clients, he was a great stabilizer and a buoyant source of strength for the firm. That's why they wanted him." George D. Gibson, interview with author, September 26, 1985, Richmond, Virginia.

31 John W. Riely, interview with author, April 17, 1986, Richmond, Virginia.

32 Williams, Anderson, Gay, Marks, Preston, Craig, and Moore were the seven partners on April 1, 1932, and Hunton IV, Gibson, Simes, Robertson, and Flippen were the five associates.

33 Justin Moore, Jr., who worked for Robertson in the early 1950s put it this way: "Archie [belonged to] a rare breed . . . a wonderful competitive trial lawyer with the personality that goes with that. Those people have a sixth instinct that the rest of the world doesn't have, like astronauts. There is a certain 'right stuff' to being a trial lawyer." Moore Jr., interview, January 4, 1985.

34 Riely, interview, April 17, 1986.

35 "I don't know just what the aroma was, but the aroma was clearly there. And Mr. Moore got more and more work, and I got more and more experience."

Looking back over what he had learned from two very different lawyers, Riely said, "Mr. Moore was not as demanding a boss as George Gibson, because Mr. Moore did not have quite the knowledge of the English language that George Gibson had. But Mr. Moore . . . knew a tremendous amount about business. . . . He was better as a businessman than as a lawyer." Riely, interview, April 17, 1986.

36 Riely, interviews, April 17, 1986, and May 20, 1986.

37 George D. Gibson, interview with author, July 3, 1987.

38 Gibson, interview, September 26, 1985.

39 Ibid.

40 Moore Jr., interview, January 4, 1985.

41 George Gibson became the principal draftsman of The Virginia Corporate Code in 1956. It was based on the Model Business Corporate Act, the product of the American Bar Association's Business Section (formerly called the Corporation, Banking, & Business Law Section). George Gibson was at one time chairman of this section and a longtime member of its Corporate Laws Com-

mittee. In the most recent revision of the Virginia Code, Allen C. Goolsby III, a partner at Hunton & Williams and also a member of the Corporate Laws Committee, was the principal draftsman.

42 In a special legislative session called by Governor Tuck in January 1947, two major labor laws were passed. "The first, the Public Utilities Labor Relations Act, established procedures for dealing with crises like the Vepco episode" [a strike called by the union against Vepco in the spring of 1946, which Tuck had prevented by drafting Vepco workers into the state militia]. If either party refused to submit to arbitration and a work stoppage impended, the governor was authorized to seize the facility and operate it in the name of the state, until the dispute could be settled. The other and more controversial measure was a 'right-to-work' law prohibiting the requirement of union membership as a condition of employment." William B. Crawley, Jr., "William Munford Tuck," *Governors of Virginia 1860–1978*, ed. Edward Younger and James Tice Moore (Charlottesville: University Press of Virginia, 1982), 313.

43 Moore Jr., interview, January 4, 1985.

44 Moore Jr., interview, January 4, 1985. By that time Moore was considered one of the toughest and most effective appellate lawyers in the state. This must have been the reason that the state came to him with a case involving civil rights. It was an area in which no one in the law firm, since Edmund Preston died in 1945, had any significant experience.

45 The first question concerned the history of the Fourteenth Amendment: did the Congress that submitted it to the states and the state legislators that ratified it contemplate that the amendment would outlaw segregation?

It was "a silly question," according to John Riely, who pointed out in the brief he wrote that summer that the Congress that drafted the Fourteenth Amendment and the state legislatures and conventions that ratified it "both contemplated and understood that it would not abolish segregation in the public schools." See *Supreme Court of the United States, October Term, 1953. Dorothy E. Davis, et al v. the County School Board of Prince Edward County, Virginia, et al.* Brief for Appellees on Reargument, November 30, 1953. T. Justin Moore, Archibald G. Robertson, John W. Riely, and T. Justin Moore, Jr., Counsel for the Prince Edward County School Authorities, J. Lindsay Almond, Jr., Attorney General, Henry T. Wickham, Special Assistant to the Attorney General. p. 5; and John Riely, *"Brown v. The Board,* A Very Personal Retrospective Glance," luncheon talk to Hunton & Williams, reprinted in *Virginia Lawyer* (February 1989), 17–19, 42.

46 This, Davis's last appearance in the Supreme Court, brought the total number to 140, according to Richard Kluger, *Simple Justice* (New York: Vintage Books, 1977), 671.

47 Afterwards when John W. Davis, Justin Moore, and Lindsay Almond were having their picture taken in the cloak room of the U.S. Supreme Court, and Henry Wickham, John Riely, and Justin Moore, Jr., were waiting outside, Moore Jr. heard Marshall say, "If we lose that case, the guy on the right [Moore Sr.] is the one who beat us." Thomas Justin Moore, Jr., interview with author, January 6, 1988, Richmond, Virginia.

48 Oliver Hill was a 1933 graduate of Howard Law School where he was second in his class, after classmate Thurgood Marshall. In 1943 he was a founding partner of Hill, Martin & Robinson, which later became Hill, Tucker & Marsh.

From 1948 to '61, he was special NAACP counsel in Virginia, and in 1948 he was the first black since 1895 to serve on the Richmond City Council.

The Waller case is also discussed in this book, in the chapter about Thomas B. Gay.

49 Hill, interview, November 11, 1985.

50 Ibid.

51 Riely, interview, April 17, 1986.

52 "It wasn't a case that you could make a brilliant argument in. . . . [T]he facts were pretty simple. And, as I said in the article that I wrote, [John W. Riely, "*Brown v. The Board*: A Very Personal Retrospective Glance," *State Education Leader* 3 Spring 1984], the Supreme Court was misled by the black people as far as the history was concerned. And they were intentionally misled. And having decided that the history was relevant, which was a mistake to begin with, because the history was *not* relevant, [the Supreme Court justices] were in a trap which they just by brute force and awkwardness got out of. . . . I really don't think the arguments had a hell of a lot to do with it." Riely, interview, April 17, 1986.

53 Thomas Justin Moore, "School Segregation in Virginia," address at the sixty-fourth annual meeting of the Virginia Bar Association, August 12–14, 1954, reprinted in *Virginia Reports* (Richmond: Richmond Press, 1954), 213.

The second part of the *Brown* decision came down in May 1955, requiring implementation of the 1954 decision "with all deliberate speed." That qualification was intended to give the South time to adjust, but it may actually have made the adjustment more difficult since it raised doubts as to the immediate obligation of the local school officials. See J. Harvie Wilkinson III, *From Brown to Bakke: The Supreme Court and Integration, 1954–1978* (New York: Oxford University Press, 1979), 61–77; Elizabeth S. Black, "Hugo Black: A Memorial Portrait," *Yearbook 1982 Supreme Court Historical Society* 72–94; and "Black Feels Warren's Phrase Slowed Integration," *New York Times*, December 4, 1968.

54 John W. Riely, "The Firm's Involvement with *Brown v. Board of Education*," luncheon talk, January 28, 1985. Riely, "*Brown v. the Board: A Retrospective Glance*."

55 George D. Gibson, "Comments on the Firm of Hunton & Williams," talk at partnership retreat, Wintergreen, October 10, 1986. Another version of Moore's statement is: "If an organization is worth belonging to, I believe it is worth running." Conversation with George D. Gibson, June 24, 1987.

56 George Gibson, Resolution, "In Memoriam, T. Justin Moore, 1890–1958," adopted by the Board of Directors of the Virginia Electric and Power Company, April 16, 1958.

57 Moore Jr., interview, January 4, 1985.

58 Ibid.

59 During the "period of adjustment" in the middle fifties, Robert Buford recalled that "Lewis Powell's star was rising, but there was nothing fading about Mr. Moore." Robert Pegram Buford, interview with author, December 18, 1986, Richmond, Virginia.

60 Gibson, "In Memoriam, T. Justin Moore."

61 Lloyd U. Noland, Jr., conversation, April 7, 1989. Lloyd Noland, Jr., who retired as chairman and chief executive officer of the Noland Company in 1987, said that his father, Lloyd Noland, Sr., who was called "Casey" by his friends, served with Moore on the boards of the Virginia Public Service Corporation

and the Central National Bank. He then retained him as counsel for the Noland interests, which included the plumbing supply company called the Noland Company, Basic Construction Company, Tidewater Construction Company, Biggs Antiques, and the Richmond Hotels. After Moore's death, George Gibson became counsel to Lloyd Noland, Jr., and was succeeded by George Freeman. Allen C. Goolsby III is now counsel to Lloyd Noland III.

8   *Lewis Franklin Powell, Jr. (1907–)*

1 Before Lewis's birth, Powell's father had changed the spelling of his own name to "Louis" because there was someone somewhere down the road he didn't like whose name was Lewis. He never changed it back, and it appears that way on his tombstone. Powell's maternal grandfather was Lewis Temple Gwathmey, so he claims that he is named for both sides of his family. Justice Lewis F. Powell, Jr., interviews, August 15, 1984, and August 26, 1987, Richmond, Virginia.

Although his parents were longtime residents of Chesterfield County, they had moved to Suffolk temporarily at the time of Lewis's birth to help his grandfather, who had opened a meatpacking business there. Lewis F. Powell, Jr., "Reflections," *Virginia Magazine of History and Biography* 96 (July 1988): 315–32.

2 The house was still standing at 4103 Forest Hill Avenue, Richmond, in 1989.

3 "I think we were still in the county [Chesterfield] at the time and probably had to pay some tuition, but the streetcar went near Powhatan, and I rode the streetcar to school." Lewis F. Powell, Jr., interview with author, July 27, 1984, Richmond, Virginia.

4 Powell, interview with author, July 27, 1984.

5 J. Harvie Wilkinson, Jr., interview with author, November 14, 1985.

6 Powell, interview, July 27, 1984.

7 *Of Two Virginia Gentlemen and Their McGuire's University School* (Richmond: The McGuire's School Alumni Association), 45.

8 This award, which was named for the founder of the New York law firm Sullivan & Cromwell, was sponsored by the Southern Society in numerous Southern colleges.

9 The Conference Internationale des Etudiants or CIE.

10 A. M. Sperber, *Murrow: His Life and Times* (New York: Bantam, 1987), 34–35. Powell, interview, August 15, 1984. Murrow was born in Greensboro, North Carolina, but the family moved to the state of Washington before he started school.

11 Powell Sr. and his brother had bought out David Lea while Lewis was at the McGuire School. Powell, interview, August 26, 1987.

12 Powell, interview, August 15, 1984.

13 Powell, interview, August 26, 1987, and Lewis F. Powell, Jr., "Unrecorded Biographical Facts about Your Father," December 15, 1981. John W. Davis (1873–1955) was then senior partner in the New York firm commonly called Davis, Polk. It was founded in 1921 as Wardwell, Gardiner & Reed, by 1925 was called Davis, Polk, Wardwell, Sunderland & Keindl, and finally became Davis, Polk & Wardwell. Although Davis was best known as the unsuccessful Democratic candidate for president in 1924, he was probably the nation's leading appellate lawyer.

Twenty-three years after Powell turned down the job in New York, Davis was the lead lawyer in the *Brown v. Board of Education* litigation, which is discussed in the previous chapter on T. Justin Moore.

14 Powell, interview with author, July 27, 1984.

15 The firm by that time had four partners and two associates.

16 Powell, interviews with author, July 27, 1984, and August 8, 1985, Washington, D.C., and "Unrecorded Biographical Facts."

17 "Looking back on it, I was ashamed of the argument. I read . . . too [many] quotations from cases," Powell said fifty years later. "If I had been experienced, I wouldn't have done that." Powell, interview, August 26, 1987.

18 Powell, interview, August 8, 1985. By the fall of 1934, after the elevation of George Gibson and Eppa Hunton IV to junior partnership in June, the firm had nine partners (Williams, Anderson, Gay, Moore, Marks, Preston, Craig, Hunton, and Gibson) and three associates (Robertson, Flippen, and Simes). Virgil Randolph, who came July 1, 1932, in the place Powell had applied for, had left on December 31, 1933. Powell's arrival one year later brought the total number of lawyers back up to thirteen.

19 Powell, interviews, July 27, 1984, and August 8, 1985.

Gay's claim that Moore was "hogging the staff" was a fairly reasonable one, since Justin Moore already had working for him the two associates he had brought with him, Robertson and Flippen, who spent full-time on power and transit company problems, as well as two partners, part-time: George Gibson on utility financings and eventually Edmund Preston on labor matters. Wirt Marks had Stephen Simes. But Gay had no associate, though he did have one partner, Irvin Craig, doing work for him. Moore, of course, may have argued that the two associates he brought with him were spending all of their time on Vepco matters, while he was rapidly developing other business for the firm and needed help with that.

Randolph Williams and Henry Anderson had no associates working directly for them, though undoubtedly they had access to any associate's services. Williams had at least two intermediate partners doing work for him, Wirt Marks and Edmund Preston, while Colonel Anderson had George Gibson helping him on the railroad reorganizations.

20 "Justice Lewis F. Powell, Jr.," interview by Bill Moyers in the series "Moyers: In Search of the Constitution," June 25, 1987, New York: Public Affairs Television, Inc.

21 Powell, interview, August 25, 1986.

22 The twenty-five-cent lunch included "everything from soup to nuts . . . literally. We had a soup, we had meat, two vegetables, dessert, very good desserts, and . . . a little cup of nuts." Wilkinson, interview, November 14, 1985.

23 Wilkinson's bank was known as State-Planters from 1926 until 1971. In 1963 it combined with five other banks to form United Virginia Bankshares, Inc., the first bank holding company in the state. Its name was changed again in 1971 to United Virginia Bank and, in 1987, when it became a multistate institution, to Crestar.

24 In 1940 Thomas B. Gay was elected a director of State-Planters Bank and Trust Co., and in 1945 he was named general counsel. Harvie Wilkinson became executive vice president in 1952 and president in 1953. Powell, interviews, August 15, 1984, and August 8, 1985; and Wilkinson, interview, November 14, 1985.

25 Wilkinson, interview, November 14, 1985.

26 "My parents were Baptists and they were not active in Richmond Society with a capital S. . . . But I don't think if Mother and Father had been Episcopalians they would have been active in Richmond social life. Neither one of them cared terribly about that." Powell, interview, August 8, 1985. But they cared very much about their church, the Second Baptist Church, and were very active in it, according to Lewis Booker, interview with author, August 2, 1987, Richmond, Virginia.

27 Wilkinson, interview, November 14, 1985.

28 Powell, interview, August 26, 1987.

29 There were still relatively few automobiles in 1914. Dr. M. Pierce Rucker arrived in a horse and buggy. Lewis F. Powell, Jr., interview with author, August 25, 1986, Richmond, Virginia.

30 Powell, interview, July 27, 1984. The record that she set for the high jump at Sweet Briar was four feet eleven and three-quarters inches, Josephine Powell recalled in a conversation on July 14, 1988.

31 In February 1986, I happened to be on an elevator in the Supreme Court building. As the doors were closing, Justice and Mrs. Powell strolled by, arm and arm, their long, athletic strides carrying them down the marble corridor toward their car. When the doors had closed, the young woman who was operating the elevator sighed and said, "Don't they make a handsome couple!"

32 Wilkinson, interview, November 14, 1985.

33 Powell, "Unrecorded Biographical Facts," 6.

34 Despite his influence in the ABA, Gay did not help Powell at all, seeming to prefer that he stay home at the firm attending to the clients. Powell took the opposite approach and did everything he could to help younger members of the firm get involved with the ABA, and in the 1960s he persuaded the Executive Committee to reimburse them for their expenses at the annual meetings.

35 Virginia Democrats had been given permission by the Byrd machine to support Republicans in national elections since 1928 when Al Smith ran against Hoover, and Virginia went for Hoover. Powell, interview, August 8, 1985.

"As you know, I have been a Virginia Democrat, and never have voted Republican in any state election," he wrote to his children in 1981. ". . . My track record in [presidential elections] has been more Republican than Democratic, by a rather wide margin. . . . My primary interests have been foreign affairs, national defense, and the free enterprise system. . . . At the national level, I have thought the Republican Party usually had wiser long range policies in these areas." Powell, "Unrecorded Biographical Facts," 8–9.

36 Josephine ("Jody") Powell, Mrs. Richard Smith, born July 1, 1938; and Ann Pendleton ("Penny") Powell, Mrs. Pendleton Carmody, born September 19, 1940.

37 Powell, interviews, July 27, 1984, and August 25, 1986. "Since I survived," said Powell wryly, "I tend to think Colonel Anderson gave me the best advice."

Though Lewis Powell and his senior partner Henry Anderson were in many ways quite different, they had one important trait in common: a willingness to take risks to enlarge their lives and hence their vision. When the world war of his generation came along, each man insisted on participating in it, though he was past the draft age and under no legal obligation to do so. The immense responsibilities assumed during the war, and the sight of what can happen when societies begin to fall apart, so deepened each man's sense of responsibility to his own society that he behaved quite differently when he came home.

In the eyes of their law partners who stayed at home during the wars, both Henry Anderson and Lewis Powell must have seemed a little reckless in their sudden willingness to expend great quantities of otherwise billable hours on politics and public service.

38 Powell, interview, August 25, 1986.

39 When he went in to London on leave, he usually stayed with Edward R. Murrow and his wife, Janet. He recalled watching his friend give broadcasts from the roof of his building, describing the Blitz to the people in America. Powell, interview, July 27, 1984.

40 Powell, interview, August 26, 1987.

41 Later amalgamated with the RAF into the Northwest African Air Forces.

42 Captain Lewis F. Powell, Jr., to Thomas B. Gay, April 24, 1943, Hunton & Williams files. A WAAF was a woman belonging to the Woman's Army Air Force, equivalent to a WAC in the army or a WAVE in the navy. The work Powell, Irvin Craig, and their senior partner Gay did as counsel to Henrico County in the Richmond-Henrico Annexation Suit of 1939–40 is discussed earlier in the chapter on Thomas B. Gay.

43 ULTRA was "the code name for the most important intelligence coup of the war, the breaking and reading of the top German military codes," Powell wrote in "Reflections," 319.

44 Diane T. Putney, ed., *ULTRA and the Army Air Forces in World War II: An Interview with Associate Justice of the Supreme Court Lewis F. Powell, Jr.*, USAF Warrior Studies (Washington, D.C.: U.S. Government Printing Office, 1987), hereafter cited as *ULTRA Interview*.

45 Ronald Lewin, *ULTRA Goes to War: The First Account of World War II's Greatest Secret Based on Official Documents* (New York: McGraw-Hill, 1978), 246.

46 *ULTRA Interview*, 16.

47 "The Germans never guessed that their most secret messages, encoded on their Enigma machines, were being read regularly. We sometimes read messages Hitler sent to his commanders in the field at the same time the German generals received them. That gave us a unique advantage." Powell, "Reflections," 319.

One could not understand "the magnitude of ULTRA, the effectiveness of it" by hearing it described, "one had to see it," Powell said. For that reason, "Bletchley left a profound impression on me." *ULTRA Interview*, 15, 16, 18.

48 *ULTRA Interview*, 19.

49 Carl Spaatz (b. 1891) had been chief of Army Air Force Combat Command in 1942 and then chief air adviser to General Eisenhower in North Africa where Powell first served under his command. He was also commander of the Northwest African Air Forces in Sicily in 1943, and was made commander-in-chief of the U.S. Strategic Air Force in Europe in January 1944. After the war in Europe ended, he was made commander-in-chief of the U.S. Strategic Air Force against Japan. In 1946 he became the Commanding General of the Army Air Force, and in 1948 he retired.

50 The source of the ULTRA information was the breaking of the ciphers produced by the most sophisticated German cryptographic machine, called "Enigma." If

the Germans had suspected that their Enigma messages were being read by the Allies, they would obviously have resorted to other means of communication immediately.

51 He goes on to say, "If anybody doubts the role of the Air Forces, as I have said frequently, the invasion of Europe would have been impossible without Allied control of the air. The public has never recognized this historic truth." ULTRA *Interview*, 36, 42.

52 Lewis F. Powell, Jr., to Thomas B. Gay, March 30, 1945, Headquarters, United States Strategic Air Forces in Europe (Main), Hunton & Williams files. After the Germans surrendered on May 8, 1945, ending the war in Europe, the Pentagon asked Powell to return to Washington and become the chief Japanese Air Force specialist of the Special Branch. General Spaatz also asked him to go with him to the Pacific. But Powell chose the third alternative, to go to the British Air Ministry as the senior representative of Special Branch with the understanding that he could return to his family, and his law firm, within five or six months. At that time he was promoted to full colonel. ULTRA *Interview*, 63.

53 Correspondence between Thomas B. Gay and Lewis F. Powell, Jr., April–July 1945, Hunton & Williams files.

54 Powell to T. B. Gay, November 24, 1945. In this letter, which is written from The Cloister, Sea Island, Georgia, he anticipates returning to the office on Monday, December 10.

55 Conversation with George D. Gibson, June 23, 1987.

56 Lowell Palmer Weicker, the president and director of E. R. Squibb & Sons, Ltd., was the father of U.S. Senator Lowell P. Weicker.

57 Powell, "Unrecorded Biographical Facts," 7–8, interview August 26, 1987, and television interview with Moyers, June 25, 1987.

58 Powell, "Unrecorded Biographical Facts," 8.

59 Conversation with Gibson, June 23, 1987

60 One of them, Frances Shield, put it this way: During the war, "he met people in a bigger world than he was in, and it sort of fired up his ambition to get there, and that's when there was a great change in Lewis." Frances Shield, interview with author, June 13, 1985, Manakin-Sabot, Virginia.

61 Later the city had to return to the old ward system for electing members of its city council in order to avoid diluting the black vote. This was a compromise necessary to permit an annexation that would comply with the Voting Rights Act. Powell referred to the return to the ward system in the 1971 Senate confirmation hearings as a regrettable but economically necessary step backwards.

62 No change beyond the maturing of his character, which would be expected from the war experience. Wilkinson, interview, November 14, 1985, and Virginius Dabney, interview with author, February 14, 1986, Richmond, Virginia. Dabney is the former editor of the Richmond *Times-Dispatch* and was a member of a foursome—Powell, Gibson, Wilkinson, and Dabney—that had lunch together every month at Miller & Rhoads Tea Room for almost three decades.

63 Lawrence E. Blanchard, Jr., interview with author, July 28, 1987, Richmond, Virginia; and H. Merrill Pasco, interview with author, September 27, 1985, Richmond, Virginia.

One of the lingering regrets of Justice Powell's later years was that "I allowed my name to go in without *insisting* that George's go in, too. But your thinking changes as you mature," he said. Powell, interview, August 25, 1986. In any case, after Moore Sr.'s death, the situation was settled by Moore's name being dropped and Gibson's added to the style on January 1, 1960.

64 Blanchard, interview, July 28, 1987. Lawrence E. Blanchard, Jr. (Duke '42, Columbia Law School '48), now retired as vice-chairman of the Ethyl Corporation, came to the firm July 1, 1948. He worked for Wirt Marks for five years, and then for Lewis Powell. He was made partner March 1, 1953, took part in the dramatic acquisition of Ethyl by the much smaller Albemarle Paper Company in 1962 (often compared to Jonah swallowing the whale), and left to become a vice-president of the Ethyl Corporation December 21, 1966.

65 Anderson had been incapacitated by old age and illness since the late 1940s. When Larry Blanchard came to be interviewed at the firm, in the spring of 1948, he perceived that Colonel Anderson was no longer a participant in the decisions of the firm, at least as far as the hiring of associates was concerned. Williams, however, was active to the day of his death, mainly as the moral leader of the firm. Blanchard, interview, July 28, 1987.

66 According to Merrill Pasco, who was then the assistant managing partner. H. Merrill Pasco, interview with author, June 12, 1985, Richmond, Virginia.

67 Blanchard, who was Marks's associate for five years, said that "Marks was a superb lawyer—one of, if not *the* most able lawyer in Virginia. He was an extremely *combative* lawyer, the very kind of person that you'd want to be your lawyer and dread seeing on the other side of a case." Blanchard, interview, July 28, 1987.

68 When he left Hunton, Williams, Gay, Anderson & Moore, Wirt Marks took with him several major clients including the RF & P Railroad, where he had succeeded Randolph Williams as general counsel; the Bank of Virginia, now Signet Bank; and Virginia Tractor Company.

69 Gibson acknowledged his debt to the Davis, Polk firm agreement for the "philosophical introduction." George D. Gibson, interview with author, September 26, 1985, Richmond, Virginia.

70 "Hunton, Williams, Gay, Moore & Powell, Partnership Agreement," December 29, 1955, 1.

71 "'Two-thirds in interest' or 'majority in interest' of the partners shall mean Partners who in the aggregate are at the time entitled to a percentage in the net income of the Partnership equal to two-thirds or a majority, as the case may be, of the aggregate percentage then distributable to all Partners." Partnership Agreement, 1955, 3.

72 Partnership Agreement, 1955, 4, 13.

73 That first year the rotating members were Archibald G. Robertson and H. Merrill Pasco, who moved up from assistant managing partner to managing partner on December 31, 1958, when Gay retired.

74 Eppa Hunton IV reached his seventieth birthday on July 31, 1974, and died in an automobile accident November 24, 1976.

75 Since the interest that Powell and Gibson had was almost twice as much as that of any other partner, their insistence on the "majority in interest of the Partners" doubled the value of their vote. The 1958 amendment provided that "the permanent members shall serve until resignation, complete attainment of Counsel Status, . . . Disability or Death," and that after Powell and Gibson there were to be no permanent members.

Blanchard recalled his surprise and pleasure at a partners' meeting, probably in 1959, when he, a junior partner, was given a piece of paper and told to write down the names that he would like to see in the firm's style. "I believe [this] *must* have been after Mr. Moore died. . . . Because if Mr. Moore was still living [we wouldn't have had] any durn democratic vote on what the name of the firm ought to be. I'll tell you that." Blanchard, interview, July 28, 1987.

76 As a Supreme Court justice, Powell showed this same skill in delegating tasks to his law clerks, according to John Jeffries, one of his former clerks, now a professor at the University of Virginia Law School. John C. Jeffries, Jr., interview with author, November 2, 1987, Charlottesville, Virginia.

77 Powell, interview, August 26, 1987. This policy was an extension of the belief expressed in the firm's partnership agreement that clients are better served by the teams within the firm than by any single lawyer.

78 Under the doctrine of interposition, the state was supposed to be able to "interpose" its sovereign authority between itself and the federal government. James Jackson Kilpatrick was not a lawyer, and none of the lawyers in the firm supported his conclusions. As John Riely put it, it had come to a choice between the rule of law or revolution, and the lawyers chose the rule of law.

Powell debated Kilpatrick in Richmond at a meeting of the Forum Club that was off the record because the five school board members had agreed not to make any public speeches on "such an inflammatory issue" but instead "to keep a low profile," so that they could keep the schools open. State senator Fitz-Gerald Bemiss was among the legislators who attended that debate and were persuaded by Powell to vote against the interposition resolution in the General Assembly. Powell, interview, August 8, 1985.

79 Lewis F. Powell, Jr., to Edward R. Murrow, January 9, 1959, quoted in Sperber, 545–46.

80 Oliver Hill was a founding partner of the leading black law firm Hill, Tucker & Marsh in Richmond. As counsel for the NAACP's Legal Defense Fund, he argued against T. Justin Moore, Sr., in the Prince Edward case that became a part of *Brown v. Board of Education*, which is discussed in the chapter on Moore. Hill had worked with Powell in the late 1940s on the commission that wrote a new charter for the city of Richmond transforming its governmental structure from a bicameral council (elected by wards) with an elected mayor as the chief executive to a unicameral council (elected citywide), which then appointed a city manager as the chief executive. After the charter was approved, Hill ran for one of the nine seats and became the first black elected to the Richmond City Council in 1948.

81 Oliver W. Hill, article in the series entitled "A Tribute to Justice Lewis F. Powell, Jr.," *Harvard Law Review* 101 (December 1987): 415–16.

82 Powell, interview, August 8, 1985. See also Powell, "Reflections," 322.

83 According to Lawrence Walsh, the year of Powell's presidency will be "remembered as a year of significant achievement. . . . The uniform and undeviating comment of those who worked with him and knew him in this position emphasizes his courtesy, temperance and effectiveness." Walsh, Testimony as Chairman of the ABA Standing Committee on the Federal Judiciary, Hearings, November 2, 1971, 5.

84 George Clemon Freeman, Jr., "A Tribute to Justice Lewis F. Powell, Jr.," *Harvard Law Review* 101 (December 1987): 406–7.

85 Hearings, 115.

86 Mary Lewis Gwathmey Powell (Mrs. Christopher J. Sumner) was born July 1,

1947, and Lewis F. Powell III, on September 14, 1952, creating three pairs of identical birthdates that earned the Powell family a place in Ripley's *Believe It or Not*. July 1 is the birthday of the Powells' oldest daughter, Josephine (Jody), as well as the youngest, Mary (Molly). September 14 is Mrs. Powell's birthday as well as Lewis III's, and September 19 is Justice Powell's as well as that of Ann Pendleton.(Penny), so the six members of the Powell family have only three birthdays among them.

87 But when he was appointed to the Supreme Court, Powell set to work to become a thorough legal scholar. As George Gibson put it, "Lewis Powell never failed to grow up to any job he took on." Conversation with Gibson, June 23, 1987.

88 In this day and age when the word "lawyer" has taken on so many pejorative connotations, it is heartening to remember the pride that Powell and his contemporary Gibson associated with the word. It was the same kind of pride a man who builds ships would associate with "shipwright," a master craftsman's pride in doing a job as well as it can possibly be done, with the hope that he was making the society run a little bit more smoothly.

89 Powell, "Unrecorded Biographical Facts," 13. Powell, "Reflections," 326–27.

90 This was the phrase that Thomas B. Gay would use every time he tried to persuade Powell not to take on yet another activity that would cut into the hours he devoted to the firm.

91 Lewis F. Powell, Jr., interview with author, August 1, 1984, Richmond, Virginia.

92 Both nominees were federal circuit court judges: Clement F. Haynsworth from the U.S. Court of Appeals for the Fourth Circuit (Virginia, West Virginia, Maryland, North and South Carolina) and George H. Carswell from the U.S. Court of Appeals for the Fifth Circuit (which at the time of his nomination included Florida, Georgia, Alabama, Louisiana, Mississippi, and Texas).

93 Powell, television interview with Moyers, June 25, 1987.

94 "And in substance what [Haynsworth] said was, 'You prepare for the hearing before the judiciary committee the same way you would prepare for the most major litigation that you ever had.'" Powell, interview, August 8, 1985.

95 George Clemon Freeman, Jr., "Lewis Powell the Lawyer," unabridged draft of September 1987 submitted to the *Harvard Law Review* for their series "A Tribute to Justice Lewis F. Powell, Jr." A shorter version without this statement was published in December 1987. Thurmond was the senior Republican and Eastland, the senior Democrat on the Senate Judiciary Committee.

96 Powell, interview, August 8, 1985.

97 There were two vacancies to be filled since Hugo Black and John Marshall Harlan had both resigned and then died within a few weeks of one another in the fall of 1971. The cartoon was in the November 24, 1971, Richmond *News Leader*.

98 Powell had intended to withdraw on December 31, 1971, but had to work over New Year's weekend clearing his desk, according to his letter to Chief Justice Burger, January 1, 1972, a copy of which is in the firm files.

9 George Dandridge Gibson (1904–1988)

1 Under the partnership agreement of 1955, Gibson and Lewis Powell were the only remaining "permanent" members of the firm's Executive Committee,

serving until their retirements. Gibson's reign was fairly brief, since he was already sixty-seven in January 1972 and would become counsel four years later, on January 1, 1976. Yet he remained a commanding and highly articulate presence in the Richmond office for a decade longer.

2 Philip Dormer Stanhope, Fourth Earl of Chesterfield (1694–1773), is famous for *Letters to His Son*, filled with advice on manners, etiquette, and deportment. Gibson's models, in his boyhood, were two Richmond men whose deportment was impeccable: Randolph Williams, his cousin and future senior partner; and John Stewart Bryan, owner of the Richmond newspapers and father of his lifelong friends Amanda Bryan Kane (Mrs. Keith Kane) and David Tennant Bryan. Later in his life, Gibson looked up to Ellery Sedgwick, editor of the *Atlantic Monthly*, and Supreme Court Justice Oliver Wendell Holmes, Jr. Pearson Gibson, interview with author, February 21, 1989, Richmond, Virginia, and George D. Gibson, interview, November 24, 1984.

3 Conversations with George Gibson's relatives and childhood friends. Also Virginius Dabney, *Richmond: The Story of a City* (Garden City, N.Y.: Doubleday & Co., 1976), 370.

4 The Episcopal High School yearbook's account of the Dual Contest between the Blackford and Fairfax literary societies states that "Mr. Gibson entertained us for a dozen all-too-brief minutes which he packed with words of such appalling and fascinating length that they completely hypnotized the Honourable Judges, and decisively clinched the Fairfax' claim to the cup." At commencement exercises June 7, 1921, Gibson was awarded first prize for declamation and shared with his close friend and cousin, Langbourne Meade Williams, Jr., the Meade Prize for excellence in scholarship. *Whispers*, vol. 19 (Alexandria: Episcopal High School, 1921), 153. Program for Episcopal High School of Virginia Commencement Exercises, June 7, 1921.

5 That year was at the University of Richmond 1882–83, according to the University of Richmond registrar and conversation with Pearson Gibson, December 16, 1987.

6 George Gibson received a B.A. University of Virginia, 1924; M.A. Harvard, 1925; LL.B. Harvard, 1928. Elizabeth McClung Gibson (Mrs. J. Delafield DuBois) received a B.A. Bryn Mawr, 1927, and Patrick Armistead Gibson, a B.A. University of Virginia, 1928; LL.B. Harvard, 1930; and B.A. Christ Church, Oxford (as a Rhodes scholar), 1933. Stuart Gibson, though he attended the University of Virginia, did not stay long enough to get a degree.

7 George D. Gibson, interview with author, May 10, 1984, Richmond, Virginia.

8 Ibid.

9 The story is told in the chapter on Henry Anderson.

10 Before Gibson came, it had been a secretary's office. Henry Anderson's office was on the southeast corner of the building, and Randolph Williams's was on the southwest corner. The quarters on the tenth floor of the Electric Building were cramped, to say the least, as the firm grew. Pamela Gibson, who was born in 1936, remembers going down to her father's office as a little girl, then being taken into Randolph Williams's office and asking bluntly, "Cousin Randolph, why is it that your office is so *large* and my father's so *small*?" George Gibson was probably mortified at the question, but Randolph Williams, with his neverfailing sense of humor, smiled and said in a conspiratorial whisper, "Because I got here *first*!" Conversation with Pamela Gibson Farrar, October 31, 1987. George D. Gibson, interview with author, July 3, 1987, Richmond, Virginia.

11 George D. Gibson, interview with author, September 26, 1985, Richmond, Virginia. See note 30 in the chapter on Anderson for an explanation of the title's origin and the militarization of the Red Cross Commission during World War I.

12 George D. Gibson, interview with author, July 24, 1986, Richmond, Virginia.

13 At that time, the Seaboard's headquarters were in Norfolk, Virginia.

14 G. D. Gibson, interview, July 3, 1987.

15 George D. Gibson. "Comments on the Firm of Hunton & Williams," at partnership retreat, Wintergreen, Virginia, October 10, 1986, 5.

16 The American Liberty League was a national organization formed in 1934 in opposition to Franklin Delano Roosevelt and his New Deal policies.

17 G. D. Gibson, interview, July 24, 1986.

18 And other lawyers argued for the Fort Scott and the Consolidated Bondholders committees.

19 Leonard Adkins, born May 10, 1893, graduated from Trinity College, Hartford, in 1913 and from the Harvard Law School in 1916. He was hired as an associate by the Cravath firm in 1916 and was made a partner July 1, 1923.

20 G. D. Gibson, interview, July 24, 1986.

21 328 U.S. 495 (1946); 329 U.S. 708 (1947).

22 An idea that "in fact, worked out because of the immense political popularity of the Baltimore & Ohio Railroad and especially its president, Daniel Willard." G. D. Gibson, interview, July 24, 1986.

23 Thomas B. Gay, *The Hunton Williams Firm and Its Predecessors, 1877–1954* (Richmond: The Lewis Printing Co., 1971), 184. "Mr. Anderson's most notable service in this undertaking was the development of a new provision of the Bankruptcy Act entitled Chapter XV, which authorized a statutory court of three judges to make effective financial modifications approved by the Interstate Commerce Commission under the regulatory provisions of Section 20a of the Interstate Commerce Act without requiring thoroughgoing reorganization for the long-range future." See note 67, Chapter 5.

24 G. D. Gibson, interview, September 26, 1985.

25 Ibid.

26 Looking back over his long career, George Gibson thought that what he had enjoyed most about the practice of law was "the intellectual stimulus of seeing bright, good minds at work and the exciting vistas of the world bigger than Franklin Street where I was brought up." G. D. Gibson, interview, September 26, 1985.

27 G. D. Gibson, interview, September 26, 1985.

28 George D. Gibson, interview with author, November 12, 1984, Richmond, Virginia.

29 Ibid.

30 G. D. Gibson, interview, July 24, 1986.

31 Ibid.

32 G. D. Gibson, interview, September 26, 1985.

33 "Pirated" was the verb used by G. D. Gibson, interview, July 3, 1987.

34 Evelyn Brown, interview with author, September 16, 1985, Richmond, Virginia.

35 By today's standards a $10-million financing sounds minor, but it seemed frighteningly large to Gibson then. G. D. Gibson, interviews, May 10, 1984; November 12, 1984; and July 3, 1987.

36 He also argued numerous rate cases for Vepco, and even one labor case, *Vepco v.*

National Labor Relations Board, 312 U.S. 677 (1941), when it reached the Supreme Court.

37 Langbourne Williams was a groomsman at that wedding and found it rather austere by Virginia standards. He claims that the following story, now considered apocryphal, originated when George's father returned from Stockbridge and one of his friends asked if he had enjoyed the wedding. After a long silence, Gibson, senior, replied, "I'll tell you this. I wouldn't trade five of those Yankee weddings for one good Virginia funeral." Langbourne Williams, interviews with author, November 11–12, 1986, Rapidan, Virginia.

38 Pamela Sedgwick Gibson (Mrs. John Farrar) was born on May 10, 1936, and Alice Armistead Gibson (Mrs. Malcolm W. Stothers) on March 18, 1938. After living at 1613 and 1702 Park Avenue, the Gibsons rented a house at 212 River Road from 1943 to 1946, then bought 9 River Road, where George Gibson continued to live until he died on April 3, 1988.

39 "As close as we were," Lewis Powell recalled that Gibson never discussed with him this physical problem. In a conversation March 23, 1988, his daughter Pamela said that the doctors thought he may have had polio as a child.

40 G. D. Gibson, interview, May 10, 1984.

41 Gibson described the war years as a "chaotic time" in the firm, with "an undiminished number of things to do and with a greatly diminished number of people to do them." G. D. Gibson, interview, July 3, 1987.

42 Richard Emory (LL.B. Harvard, 1938) had been born in Baltimore, and at the end of the war, much to Gibson's regret, he returned to Baltimore and eventually became a partner in the firm of Venable, Baetjer & Howard.

Nan Ross McConnell (J.D. University of Richmond, 1943) came to Hunton, Williams October 15, 1943, and left March 15, 1948, to marry Charles Appel. Eventually she became a tax consultant in Marietta, Georgia.

43 G. D. Gibson, interview, July 3, 1987. Harold John Gallagher was a partner in the firm Willkie, Owen, Farr, Gallagher & Walton. Since he was a director and general counsel of the Seaboard Air Line Railway, Anderson, and therefore his assistant Gibson, consulted with Gallagher frequently and knew him very well. Gallagher had been chairman of the Public Utility Section 1934–35.

44 The rift in their relationship in the mid-1940s is referred to by Lewis F. Powell, Jr., interview with author, August 8, 1985, Washington, D.C.; Frances Shield, interview with author, June 13, 1985, Manakin-Sabot, Virginia; and Gibson himself, interview, September 26, 1985.

45 Both Anderson and Moore "had the habit, which I thought illogical, of having me argue first," Gibson recalled. And then the senior lawyer would "come in and give the death blow."

In hearings before the Interstate Commerce Commission on the terms of railroad reorganization plans, Gibson remembered that the argument might be as long as an hour and a half. "And I had to memorize all of it. . . . Of course in those days," he explained, "when the Commission took plenty of time to listen to argument, the argument would cover a lot of questions. And it was naturally a great relief to senior counsel to be spared all that preparation." G. D. Gibson, interview, July 3, 1987.

46 T. Justin Moore, Jr., interview with author, January 6, 1988, Richmond, Virginia.

47 When he was asked about this, George Gibson said that the three justices who had complimented him on his performance in oral argument were John Har-

lan, Jr., Felix Frankfurter, and Stanley Reed. G. D. Gibson, interview, May 10, 1984. Mrs. Walter Robertson, whose husband was assistant secretary of state during the late fifties, recalled that Justice Reed had asked her, at a luncheon at her house, "Who is that young man over there?" When she said George Gibson, he said, "That's right. Well, he made one of the most brilliant arguments in my Court that I have ever heard." Conversation with Mrs. Walter Robertson at Alderman Library Associates dinner, October 9, 1984, Charlottesville, Virginia.

48 Seven cases altogether was the number of Supreme Court cases argued by George Gibson: *Vepco v. National Labor Relations Board*, 312 U.S. 677 with T. Justin Moore, in 1941, and on a different point in 1943, 318 U.S. 752; *Reconstruction Finance Corporation v. Denver & Rio Grande Western Railway Company*, in 1946, 328 U.S. 495; *Insurance Group Committee v. Denver & Rio Grande Western Railway*, with Henry Anderson and John Riely on brief, in 1947, 329 U.S. 708; *Schwabacher v. U.S.*, in 1948, 334 U.S. 182; *Harper v. Virginia Board of Elections*, with Joseph Carter on brief in 1966, 383 U.S. 664; and *Butts v. Harrison*, in 1969, 382 U.S. 806, 383 U.S. 663.

49 At this point George Gibson quipped, "The ratio is getting better!" Notes on George Gibson's Eightieth Birthday Party, May 12, 1987.

50 John W. Riely, interview with author, May 8, 1984, Richmond, Virginia.

51 Ibid.

52 And later Gibson refused, despite Powell's request, to have the name Gibson inserted into the style in front of Powell, where it should have been chronologically, although he did consent to having the firm's name changed, on January 1, 1960, to Hunton, Williams, Gay, Powell & Gibson. As Gibson approached his eightieth birthday, Powell wrote him a letter expressing his regret that he had consented to the 1954 name change in view of Gibson's intellectual prowess and his national stature. Lewis F. Powell, Jr., interview with author, August 25, 1986, Richmond, Virginia. Conversation with George D. Gibson, June 23, 1987.

53 The railroad work included reorganization of the Baltimore & Ohio Railroad under Chapter XV of the Bankruptcy Act in 1938–40; The St. Louis–San Francisco Railroad Company reorganization, 1943–47; the C & O–Pere Marquette merger, 1945–46; the Denver & Rio Grande Western Railroad Company, 1937–47; The Missouri Pacific Railroad Company reorganization, which was completed in 1956; the B & O–C & O exchange offer, 1960–63, which was bitterly opposed by the New York Central and the Pennsylvania Railroad; the C & O acquisition of Western Maryland Railroad; the never-consummated Norfolk & Western merger with C & O, and the formation of the Chessie System in 1973.

54 The name of the Corporation, Banking, and Business Law Section was changed to the Business Law Section in 1987.

55 In an interview on February 21, 1989, his second wife, Pearson Gibson, explained that in his boyhood Gibson had carefully trained himself to pronounce the English language properly. The legend in the office is that when outsiders would ask him, "Where did you get that British accent?" he would answer that his brother Pat had been a Rhodes scholar at Oxford, and he had acquired his accent "by correspondence."

56 "But he blossomed eagerly when facing ability and distinction," Gibson added

in his talk to the partners at the firm's retreat at Wintergreen, October 10, 1986.

57 In Riely's first year at Harvard Law School he got all A's. His second year, he had one B, but still was third in his class of about four hundred, according to the report cards he produced in an interview May 8, 1984. Riely was also on the Board of Editors of the *Harvard Law Review* (1939–41).

58 John S. Shannon (J.D. University of Virginia, 1955) came in the fall of 1955 but stayed only six weeks, and R. Allan Wimbish (LL.B., Virginia, 1955) stayed a year, from June 1956 to June 1957. Shannon went to work with the Norfolk & Western Railroad, and Wimbish went with the Southern Railway. Both are now in the law department of the Norfolk-Southern Corporation: Shannon became executive vice president/law and Wimbish, senior general solicitor.

59 Moore, interview, January 6, 1988.

60 Ibid.

61 Riely, interview, May 8, 1984.

62 His cousins Margaret Williams McElroy and Doreen Bemiss, who were taking the course, persuaded him to come with them.

63 Powell, interviews, August 8, 1985, Washington, D.C., and December 31, 1987, Richmond, Virginia. According to Margaret Williams McElroy, who was in the class with Gibson, his election was a tribute to his popularity with his classmates as well as to his prowess as a speaker. She was amazed to see how sympathetically and effectively Gibson worked with people he would never have come into contact with in the fairly restricted social and legal circles he generally moved in. She remembered that a clerk from Thalhimers department store "with low self-esteem" was particularly grateful to Gibson for his help. Margaret Williams McElroy, interview with author, November 7, 1984, Richmond, Virginia.

64 Conversation with George Clemon Freeman, Jr., June 23, 1988, Richmond, Virginia.

65 Gibson expected his associates to dress appropriately for the life that he would introduce them to. George Freeman discovered this fact soon after his arrival, when he wore a new brown suit to the office. Gibson looked him over carefully, then said, "In the future, George, when you're planning to go on holiday, I hope you will let me know in advance." "But Mr. Gibson," Freeman said, "I'm not going anywhere." "Then why are you dressed for the country?" Gibson asked. Needless to say, the brown suit did not come back to the office. George Clemon Freeman, Jr., conversation with the author, April 10, 1989, Lexington, Virginia.

66 George Clemon Freeman, Jr., interview with author, March 4, 1988, Richmond, Virginia.

67 George D. Gibson. "Elements of Legal Style," *The Business Lawyer* 22 (April 1967), 547. John Subak, general counsel of Rohm & Hass, and Richard Dusenberg, general counsel of Monsanto Chemical Corporation, are two who were still giving Gibson's article to their younger lawyers in 1986. Gibson wrote a later version, entitled "Effective Legal Writing and Speaking," for *The Business Lawyer* 36 (December 1987), 1–9, but they prefer the earlier one.

68 George D. Gibson, "Asian Pot-Pourri," address to the Woman's Club of Richmond, December 1, 1965.

69 Gibson, "Effective Legal Writing and Speaking," remarks to the firm of Hunton & Williams, May 24, 1980, Hunton & Williams Files, 1–2.

70 In representing the railroads and in the power and telephone company rate cases, Riely continued to work under George Gibson's aegis. Otherwise, Riely took charge of Moore Sr.'s non-Vepco clients including Central National Bank, which he represented until 1961, when he was named general counsel to the Bank of Virginia (now Signet).

71 George Gibson, John Riely, and George Freeman were the Hunton & Williams team that worked closely with Joseph Kaufman, general counsel of the C & O, and then with Doyle Morris, its general solicitor, in Cyrus Eaton's effort to build that railroad into one of the nation's largest systems. This effort started with C & O's acquisition of the B & O after a bitter fight with the New York Central, which was led by Alfred E. Perlman and supported by Governor Rockefeller of New York. Subsequently, the expanded C & O absorbed the Western Maryland. Then, to Gibson's amazement, Cyrus Eaton and Jack Fishwick, senior vice-president of the Norfolk & Western, signed an agreement that would have merged their two expanding empires into one that would have dominated the Midwest and the Northeast. The merger was never consummated, however. It was strongly opposed by a number of states and other carriers on antitrust grounds and became hung up in lengthy proceedings before the Interstate Commerce Commission. In addition, Eaton changed his mind and searched for reasons to back out of the deal. Eaton's change of mind came about after his luncheon with George Gibson one day in the C & O Executive Dining Room in Cleveland. Eaton expounded to Gibson his plan for extensive changes in the merged system after the deal went through. Gibson, who had carefully analyzed the post-merger control consequences but had not yet had an opportunity to express his misgivings to Eaton, said, "But are you sure Jack Fishwick will approve?"

"What has that got to do with it?" Eaton responded.

"Well, Mr. Eaton," said Gibson, "because of the way the stock will be held in the new system, it is clear that he, not you, will control the new board."

Subsequently the Penn Central bankruptcy made Commission approval unlikely and the C & O and N & W canceled the agreement. George Clemon Freeman, Jr., conversation with author, April 10, 1989.

72 The firms' Antitrust team in turn evolved from the Environmental and Energy team through the efforts of John Shenefield in business for the utility industry which Gibson and Freeman originated. Shenefield (Harvard A.B. 1960, LL.B. 1965) was an associate, then partner, at Hunton, Williams from 1965 until 1977 when he left to serve in the antitrust division of the Justice Department, as assistant, then associate attorney general 1977–81. He is now a partner in the Washington office of Morgan, Lewis & Bockius.

73 Eppa Hunton IV to Justice Lewis F. Powell, Jr., March 16, 1976, Hunton & Williams Files.

74 Gay and Robertson had gone into semiretirement or, in the language of the partnership agreement, "completely achieved Counsel Status," many years earlier, but their names were still put on the announcement.

75 In November 1988, four partners from the Atlanta firm of Hansell & Post joined Hunton & Williams to create an additional office, the eighth one, in Atlanta, Georgia.

Epilogue

1 Riely's chairmanship began in 1974, when Eppa Hunton IV reached age seventy, and continued until 1986 when illness prevented his seeking reelection. Hugh V. White, Jr., then succeeded Riely as chairman on April 1, 1986.

2 George Gibson, "The Practice of Law in 1998," *The Business Lawyer*, 33 (July 1978), 2125.

3 Powell's contributions as a justice, writing more than 500 opinions, 254 of them opinions of the Court, during his fifteen-and-a-half-year tenure, have been assessed in a number of articles since his retirement on June 29, 1987. Those articles include Frederic L. Kirgis, Jr., "Lewis F. Powell, Jr.," *Washington and Lee Law Review* 42 (Spring 1988) 409–10; George Clemon Freeman, Jr., "Justice Powell's Constitutional Opinions," *Washington and Lee Law Review* 15 (Spring 1988) 411–65; "A Tribute to Justice Lewis F. Powell, Jr.," *Harvard Law Review* 101 (December 1987) 395–420 (with articles by Justice O'Connor, Richard H. Fallon, Jr., George Clemon Freeman, Jr., Gerald Gunther, Oliver W. Hill, and J. Harvie Wilkinson III); "Dedication, Justice Lewis F. Powell, Jr.," *Baylor Law Review* 39 (1988) (with tributes by Justices White and Stevens, Judges Wright and Brown, Charles Allen Wright, George Clemon Freeman, Jr., and F. William McAlpin); Paul W. Kahn, "The Court, the Community and the Judicial Balance: The Jurisprudence of Justice Powell," *Yale Law Journal* 97 (1987). For earlier articles on Justice Powell, see "The Symposium in Honor of Justice Lewis F. Powell, Jr.," *Virginia Law Review* 68 (1982): 161 (with articles by Lillian R. BeVier, Samuel Estreicher, Paul A. Freund, David A. Martin, Richard A. Merrill, Dallin H. Oaks, Paul B. Stephan III, and Christina B. Whitman); Gerald Gunther, "In Search of Judicial Quality on a Changing Court: The Case of Justice Powell," *Stanford Law Review* 24 (1972): 1001; A. E. Dick Howard, "Mr. Justice Powell and the Emerging Nixon Majority," *Michigan Law Review* 70 (1972): 445; Earl M. Maltz, "Portrait of a Man in the Middle—Mr. Justice Powell, Equal Protection and the Pure Classification Problem," *Ohio State Law Journal* 40 (1979): 941; Melvin I. Urofsky, "Mr. Justice Powell and Education: The Balancing of Competing Values," *Journal of Law & Education* 13 (1984): 581; Larry W. Yackle, "Thoughts on *Rodriguez*: Mr. Justice Powell and the Demise of Equal Protection Analysis in the Supreme Court," *University of Richmond Law Review* 9 (1975): 181. See also Lewis F. Powell, Jr., "Reflections," *Virginia Magazine of History and Biography* 96 (July 1988): 315–32.

4 John C. Jeffries, Jr., interview with author, November 2, 1987, Charlottesville, Virginia.

5 J. Harvie Wilkinson III, "A Tribute to Justice Lewis F. Powell, Jr.," *Harvard Law Review* 101 (December 1987) 420.

6 Gerald Gunther, "A Tribute to Justice Lewis F. Powell, Jr.," *Harvard Law Review* 101 (December 1987) 395, 409–14.

7 Lewis F. Powell, Jr., interview with Bill Moyers for "Justice Lewis F. Powell, Jr.," transcript of interview May 1987 for the television series "In Search of the Constitution," Public Broadcasting Service, 36.

8 William J. Brennan, Jr., to George C. Freeman, Jr., February 9, 1989, Washington, D.C., in response to Freeman's article "Justice Powell's Constitutional Opinions," *Washington and Lee Law Review*, 45, 2 (Spring 1988).

9 A younger partner, Robert Dean Pope, expressed the affection the whole law

firm felt for Riely when he wrote (in *The Hunton & Williams Reporter*, vol. 2, no. 7):

> John Riely's brilliance as a lawyer made all the more refreshing his firm and unbending aversion to the pomposity found in many powerful and talented members of the bar. He steadfastly avoided all pretentiousness in his own behavior and was delightfully effective in suppressing it in others. . . . If lawyers and clients marvelled at his legal skills, everyone in this firm cherished the good humor and affection that he only thinly disguised with his feigned grumpiness.

10 The following June it was discovered that George Gibson had an inoperable brain tumor. For the next eight months, he bore his illness with unusual courage, dignity, and wit, honoring his ideal of the civilized life until he drew his last breath on April 3, 1988, at 9 River Road.

Index